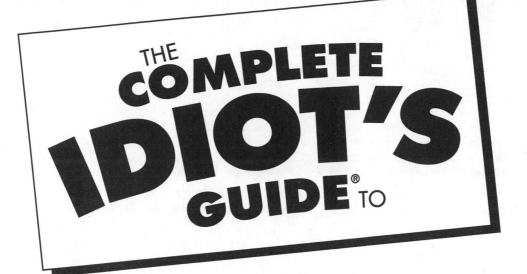

THE **COMPLETE IDIOT'S GUIDE**® TO

Computer Basics

Second Edition

by Joe Kraynak

ALPHA

A Pearson Education Company

To my kids, Nick and Ali, who constantly inspire me to keep up with the latest technology.

Copyright © 2002 by Joe Kraynak

THE COMPLETE IDIOT'S GUIDE TO and Design are registered trademarks of Pearson Education, Inc.

International Standard Book Number: 0-02-864230-9
Library of Congress Catalog Card Number: 2001092313

04 03 02   8 7 6 5 4 3 2 1

Interpretation of the printing code: The rightmost number of the first series of numbers is the year of the book's printing; the rightmost number of the second series of numbers is the number of the book's printing. For example, a printing code of 02-1 shows that the first printing occurred in 2002.

Printed in the United States of America

The Complete Idiot's Reference Card

Windows and the Web Quick Visual Guide

Navigating Windows

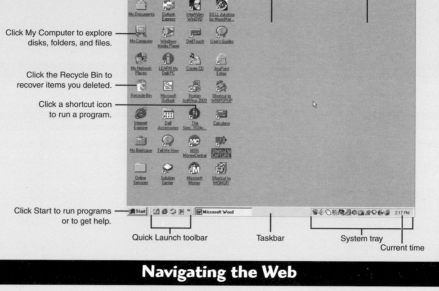

Shortcut icons

Windows desktop

Right-click the desktop for customization options.

Click My Computer to explore disks, folders, and files.

Click the Recycle Bin to recover items you deleted.

Click a shortcut icon to run a program.

Click Start to run programs or to get help.

Quick Launch toolbar

Taskbar

System tray

Current time

Navigating the Web

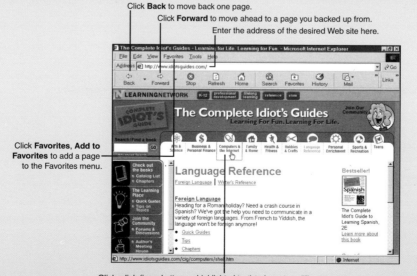

Click **Back** to move back one page.

Click **Forward** to move ahead to a page you backed up from.

Enter the address of the desired Web site here.

Click **Favorites**, **Add to Favorites** to add a page to the Favorites menu.

Click a link (icon, button, or highlighted text) to jump to a different page.

ALPHA

tear here

Savvy Software Shopper's Form

Copy this form and take it with you whenever you go shopping for software. Read the minimum requirements printed on the software package and complete this form to ensure that your computer can run the software.

Software Shopping Form

Program name: _____

Price: _____

Operating system:	Windows Me	Windows 98	DOS
	Windows 95	Windows NT	OS/2
	Windows 3.1		

Processor type: Pentium IV or comparable
Pentium III or comparable
Pentium II or comparable
Pentium MMX or comparable
Pentium Pro or comparable

Processor speed: _____ MHz

Minimum memory (RAM): _____ MB

Desired memory (RAM): _____ MB

Hard drive space: _____ MB/GB

CD-ROM speed: _____

DVD required?   Yes   No

Display/graphics: SVGA   VGA
Colors: _____
Resolution: _____
Video memory: _____ MB

Audio output: 32-bit   16-bit   Other: _____

Modem: 56 Kbps   33.6 Kbps
28.8 Kbps   14.4 Kbps

Special printer?   No   Yes. Type: _____

Additional equipment: Scanner   MIDI input   Joystick
Digital   Microphone   Speakers
camera

_____
_____
_____

Publisher
Marie Butler-Knight

Product Manager
Phil Kitchel

Managing Editor
Jennifer Chisholm

Acquisitions Editor
Eric Heagy

Development Editors
Gayle Johnson
Deborah S. Romaine

Senior Production Editor
Christy Wagner

Illustrator
Jody Schaeffer

Cover Designers
Mike Freeland
Kevin Spear

Book Designers
Scott Cook and Amy Adams of DesignLab

Indexer
Tonya Heard

Layout/Proofreading
Rachel Haynes
Mary Hunt
Lizbeth Patterson
Kimberly Tucker

Contents at a Glance

Part 1: Firing Up Your Computer: Bare-Bones Basics   **1**

1 Setting It Up and Turning It On   3
Plug it in, turn it on, and tune it in.

2 Meeting Windows: Up Close and Personal   13
Navigate your new onscreen desktop with a mouse and keyboard.

3 Launching Your First Program   27
Use your mouse to kick programs into gear.

4 Warming Up with Some Computer Games   35
Have fun while you learn the basics and master some free games.

Part 2: Personalizing Your Work Space   **45**

5 Using a Cool Desktop Background   47
Pick a theme for your desktop and decorate it to suit your tastes.

6 Making Your Computer Play Cool Sounds   59
Replace the beeps with burps, giggles, and other cool sounds.

7 Taking Control of Your Menus and Programs   67
Rebuild Windows to make it work the way you do.

8 Giving Yourself More Room to Work   73
Stretch your desktop for a little more elbow room.

9 Installing and Removing Programs   79
Buy and install a new program and get rid of programs you no longer use.

Part 3: Creating Letters, Greeting Cards, and Other Documents   **89**

10 I Just Want to Type a Letter!   91
Typing 101.

11 Editing and Printing Your Letter   103
Overhaul your text and get it on paper.

12 Designing Personalized Greeting Cards, Banners, and Other Publications   115
First encounters with a desktop publishing program.

13 Creating an Address Book and Other Listy Stuff   125
Make lists and manage your personal records.

14 Form Letters, Mailing Labels, and Envelopes   137
Merge lists with documents to automate mass mailings.

Part 4: Getting Wired to the Internet   **147**

15 Connecting to the Outside World with a Modem   149
Get your computer its own phone.

16 Finding an Information FREEway   161
Get your feet wet with some free trial offers from America Online, CompuServe, and Prodigy.

17 Sending E-Mail: Postage-Free, Same-Day Delivery   177
Send your first e-mail message in less than five minutes.

18 Chatting with Friends, Relatives, and Complete Strangers   193
Find friends, relatives, and strangers online, and type messages back and forth.

19 Poking Around on the Web   205
Use your computer and modem to connect to the Web and experience multimedia sites online.

20 Shopping, Investing, Traveling, and Other Cool Web Stuff   215
Invest, plan your vacation, shop, and research topics on the Web.

21 Publishing Your Own Web Page in Ten Minutes or Less   229
Establish your presence on the Web by building your own Web page online!

Part 5: Kids and Other Homey Stuff   **239**

22 Managing Your Finances   241
Computerize your checking account, manage your budget, and track your investments.

23 Finding and Playing Cool Games   259
Equip your system to play the coolest games, get free games online, and find the best tips and cheats on the Web.

24 Tapping the Power of Educational Software   269
Use your computer as a library, information kiosk, and interactive teaching tool.

25 Safely Introducing Your Child to the Internet   279
Savvy parent's guide to protecting your child on the Internet and exposing your child to the good stuff.

26 Making a Family Photo Album   293
Transform boxes of disorganized photos into a full-color, digitized photo album.

27 Drawing Your Family Tree   307
Use Family Tree Maker to research your lineage and
sketch your family tree, and find the best genealogy
sites on the Web.

Part 6: Tinkering with Computer Gadgets and Gizmos   319

28 Playing Digitized Music Clips   321
Transform your computer into a jukebox, burn your own
CDs, and download MP3 audio clips off the Web.

29 Managing Your Life with a Palm Computer   335
Put your calendar, address book, calculator, e-mail, and
other personal information on a computer that fits in your
pocket.

30 Watching TV and DVD on Your Computer   343
Tune in to your favorite TV shows, play along with game
show contestants, and watch DVD videos on your com-
puter.

31 Playing Film Editor with Digital Video   351
Edit your home videos, enhance your recordings with
background music, and copy your production to a CD.

32 Upgrading for Voice Commands and Dictation   363
Look, Mom, no hands—entering commands and text
without touching the keyboard!

Part 7: Maintaining Your Investment   371

33 Keeping Your Computer Clean   373
Prolong the life of your computer with some good house-
keeping tips.

34 Giving Your Computer a Tune-Up   379
Inexpensive maintenance utilities that can keep your com-
puter running like new.

Appendixes

A Glossary: Speak Like a Geek   389

B More Computer Resources for the Computer Enthusiast   405

Index   409

Contents

Part 1: Firing Up Your Computer: Bare-Bones Basics   **1**

1 Setting It Up and Turning It On   **3**

Finding a Comfortable Home for Your Computer 3
Unpacking Your New Toys 5
Making the Right Connections 6
Bringing the Beast to Life 8
Installing the Software That Runs Your Hardware 9
Now What? 10
Shut It Down or Leave It On? 11

2 Meeting Windows: Up Close and Personal   **13**

The Windows Nickel Tour 13
The Land Where Mouse Is King 15
The Keyboard Is Special, Too 17
   A Special Key Just for Windows 17
   Turbo-Surfing the Web with an Internet Keyboard 18
Ordering from Menus and Dialog Boxes 19
   Clicking Menu Options 19
   Talking with a Dialog Box 20
Bypassing Menus by Using Toolbar Buttons 21
Rearranging the Windows Inside Windows 21
What's on Your Computer? 23
Trashing Files in the Recycle Bin 24
Help Is on Its Way 25

3 Launching Your First Program   **27**

Picking a Program from the Start Menu 27
More Creative Ways to Run Programs 28
   Make Your Own Program Shortcut 28
   Run Programs from Your Keyboard 29
   Make Your Own Programs Folder 30
   Run Programs When Windows Starts 30
Moving a Program to a More Convenient Location 30
Running Programs with a Single Click 31
Opening Documents with a Single Click 32

4 Warming Up with Some Computer Games   35

Installing and Running the Windows Games 35
Using Your $1,000 Computer as a $1 Deck of Cards 37
Becoming a FreeCell Junkie 38
Playing Hearts with Virtual Players 40
Taking a Virtual Risk with Minesweeper 41
Pinball and Internet Games in Windows Me 42

Part 2: Personalizing Your Work Space   45

5 Using a Cool Desktop Background   47

Animating Your Desktop with Themes 47
  Installing Desktop Themes *48*
  Picking Your Favorite Desktop Theme *48*
Messing with the Screen Color 49
Hanging Wallpaper in the Background 51
Controlling the Desktop Icons and Visual Effects 51
What's This Web Tab For? 53
Locking Your Desktop Settings 55
Securing Some Privacy with a Screen Saver 56
  Checking Out the Windows Screen Savers *56*
  Turning a Screen Saver On and Off *57*
  Using a Password for Weak Security *57*

6 Making Your Computer Play Cool Sounds   59

Checking Your Audio Equipment 60
  Adjusting the Volume *60*
  Troubleshooting Audio Problems *62*
Choosing a Different Sound Scheme 63
Assigning Specific Sounds to Events 63
Listening to CDs While You Work 64
Recording Your Own Audio Clips 65

7 Taking Control of Your Menus and Programs   67

Rearranging the Start Menu with Explorer 67
Making Your Own Toolbars 69
  Turning on the Desktop Toolbar *69*
  Transforming a Folder into a Toolbar *69*
Automating Your Programs 71

8 Giving Yourself More Room to Work   **73**

Clearing Desk Space by Making Everything Smaller 73
What About the Color Settings? 74
Rearranging Your Desktop Icons 75
Getting Rid of Icons You Don't Use 76
Hiding the Taskbar 76
Tucking Stuff in Folders 77

9 Installing and Removing Programs   **79**

Buying Software That Your Hardware Can Run 80
Do You Have Enough Disk Space? 82
Installing Your New Program 84
  No Install or Setup File? *84*
  Selectively Installing Components *85*
Does Anyone Use Floppy Disks Anymore? 86
Removing a Program That You Never Use 86

Part 3: Creating Letters, Greeting Cards, and
**   Other Documents**   **89**

10 I Just Want to Type a Letter!   **91**

Making the Transition to the Electronic Page 92
What's with the Squiggly Red and Green Lines?! 94
Inserting Today's Date 94
Making the Text Bigger or Smaller 95
Shoving Text Left, Right, or Center 96
Changing the Line Spacing 97
Inserting Space Between Paragraphs 98
Save It or Lose It 98
Printing Addresses on Envelopes 100

11 Editing and Printing Your Letter   **103**

Selecting Text 103
Cutting and Pasting Without Scissors 104
Oops! Undoing Changes 105
Checking Your Spelling and Grammar 105
Setting Your Margins and Page Layout 106
  Setting the Page Margins *107*
  Picking a Paper Size and Print Direction *108*

Where's Your Paper Coming From? 109
Laying Out Your Pages 109
Saving Paper: Previewing Before Printing 109
Sending Your Letter off to the Printer 110
Hey, It's Not Printing! 110
Project Time! Making Your Own Letterhead 111

**12 Designing Personalized Greeting Cards,
Banners, and Other Publications   115**

What You Need to Get Started 116
Starting with a Prefab Greeting Card 116
Microsoft Publisher Survival Guide 117
Playing with Pictures 119
Text in a Box 120
Layering Pictures and Text Boxes 121
Do-It-Yourself Banners 121
Other Cool Desktop Publishing Stuff 123

**13 Creating an Address Book and Other
Listy Stuff   125**

Tables, Spreadsheets, Databases, and Address Books 126
Making a Simple Address Book with a Word Table 127
Using an Electronic Day Planner 127
Automating Calculations with Spreadsheets 127
Managing Records in a Database 129
Setting Your Own Table 130
Typing in the Little Boxes 130
Rearranging and Resizing Columns and Rows 131
Adjusting the Row Height and Column Width 131
Inserting and Deleting Columns and Rows 131
Sorting Your List 132
Automating Calculations with Formulas 132
Decorating Your Table with Lines and Shading 133
What About Pictures? 134

14 Form Letters, Mailing Labels, and Envelopes   137

The Incredible Power of the Mail Merge Feature 137
The Making of a Form Letter 139
Inserting the Secret Codes 139

Initiating the Merge Operation 143
Printing Addresses on Mailing Labels 144
Printing a Stack of Envelopes for Mass Mailing 145

Part 4: Getting Wired to the Internet   147

15 Connecting to the Outside World with a Modem   149

What Can I Do with My Modem? 149
How This Modem Thing Works 150
Modem Types: Standard, ISDN, DSL, and Cable 151
  Chugging Along with Standard Modems *151*
  Speeding Up Your Connections with ISDN *152*
  The New Kid on the Block: DSL Modems *153*
  The Pros and Cons of Cable Modems *154*
Connecting Your Modem to an Outside Line 154
  Plugging in a Standard, ISDN, or DSL Modem *155*
  Connecting a Cable Modem *156*
Dialing Out: Does It Work? 156
Troubleshooting Your Modem Connection 157

16 Finding an Information FREEway   161

Getting a Free Trial Offer to an Online Service 162
Signing Up for Your Membership 163
Getting Help Online 165
Canceling Your Membership 166
Finding Cheaper, Better Ways to Connect to the Internet 167
  Locating a Local Internet Service Provider *167*
  Gathering the Information You Need to Connect *168*
Setting Up Your Internet Connection 169
Testing Your Internet Connection 172
What Went Wrong: Internet Connection Troubleshooting 173

17 Sending E-Mail: Postage-Free Same-Day Delivery   177

Running Your E-Mail Program for the First Time 177
  Entering E-Mail Settings in Outlook Express *178*
  Entering E-Mail Settings in Netscape Messenger *179*

Addressing an Outgoing Message 180
Checking Your E-Mail Box 182
Sending Replies 182
Adding Photos and Other Cool Stuff 183
Attaching Documents to Your Messages 185
What About Hotmail and Other Free
  E-Mail Services? 186
E-Mail Shorthand and Emoticons 187
E-Mail No-No's 189
E-Mail Security 190

**18 Chatting with Friends, Relatives, and
   Complete Strangers   193**

Hanging Out in Chat Rooms 194
Checking Out the People Who Are Checking You Out ..195
Sending Private Messages 196
Making Your Own Public Chat Room 196
Chatting It Up on the Internet 197
  Chatting It Up at Yahoo! *197*
  Keeping in Touch with Friends and Family *199*
Chatting Privately with Friends and Relatives on
  the Internet 200
What About Audio and Video? 201

19 Poking Around on the Web   205

First, You Need a Web Browser 206
Steering Your Browser in the Right Direction 206
A Word About Web Page Addresses 207
Finding Stuff with Popular Search Tools 208
Opening Multiple Browser Windows 210
Going Back in Time with History Lists 210
Marking Your Favorite Web Pages for Quick
  Return Trips 211
Changing the Starting Web Page 212
Can Cookies Hurt Me? 212

20 Shopping, Investing, Traveling, and Other Cool Web Stuff   215

Keeping Up on News, Weather, and Current Events 216
   Checking Out Web Newsstands *216*
   Getting the Latest Weather Reports *217*
   For Sports Fans Only *218*
Mail-Order Paradise: Shopping on the Web 219
Becoming Your Own Stockbroker 221
Planning Your Next Vacation 222
For Movie Buffs Only 223
Creating Your Own Music Library 224
Getting Technical Support for Your Computer 225

21 Publishing Your Own Web Page in Ten Minutes or Less   229

What Makes a Web Page So Special? 230
Forget About HTML 230
Making a Personal Web Page Right on the Web 231
Placing Your Business on the Web 234
Finding Cool Stuff to Put on Your Page 235

Part 5: Kids and Other Homey Stuff   239

22 Managing Your Finances   241

Choosing a Personal Finance Program 242
Mastering the Basics 242
   Entering Account Information *243*
   Recording Transactions *245*
   Printing Checks *245*
   Reconciling Your Account and Bank Statement *247*
Budgeting 101 248
   Starting with a Budget Template *248*
   Tweaking Your Budget *249*
   Entering Income and Expenses *249*
   Making Adjustments *250*
   Using Your Budget to Stay on Track *250*
Planning Ahead with Financial Calculators 250

Electronic Banking 101 251
  How Much Will This Cost? *251*
  Signing Up for Electronic Transactions *252*
  Paying Your Bills Electronically *253*
  Setting Up Automatic Recurring Payments *254*
  Transferring Cash Between Accounts *255*
  Downloading Transaction Records and Balances *255*
Tracking Your Investments Online 255

23 Finding and Playing Cool Games   259

Shopping for the Right Games 260
Additional Equipment You Might Need 261
Running Stubborn DOS Games in Windows 262
  Running DOS Games and Other Programs *262*
  Running a DOS Game That Won't Budge *263*
Getting Free Games from the Web 264
Buying Games Online 266
Finding Game Reviews and Tips 267

24 Tapping the Power of Educational Software   269

Researching Topics with Multimedia Encyclopedias 269
More Books for Your Reference Library 271
Learning to Read with Your Computer 272
Reinforcing Math Skills 273
Encouraging Your Child to Play with Language 274
Learning to Play the Piano 275
Learning a Foreign Language 276
Bringing Out the Artist in Your Child 277

25 Safely Introducing Your Child to the Internet   279

Explaining the Rules of the Road 280
A Little Personal Supervision Goes a Long Way 281
Censoring the Internet 281
  Using America Online's Parental Controls *282*
  Censoring the Web with Internet Explorer *284*
  Using Censoring Software *285*
Playing Games Online 286
Visiting the White House 288
Visiting Museums and Libraries 289
Helping Your Child Find a Pen Pal 290

26 Making a Family Photo Album   293

Getting a Kodak Picture CD 294
Adding Photos from Another Kodak Picture CD 295
Enhancing and Editing Photos 296
Typing Your Own Captions 297
Printing Your Photos on Photo-Quality Paper 297
Sharing Photos Via E-Mail and Disk 299
Avoiding the Middleman with a Digital Camera 300
  Taking Pictures 301
  Copying Pictures to Your Computer 301
  Ordering High-Quality Photo Prints Online 302
Scanning Photos 303
Creating Your Own Digital Photo Album 304
Changing Yourself and Others with Morphing 305

27 Drawing Your Family Tree   307

Picking a Good Genealogy Program 308
Plugging in Names, Dates, and Relationships 309
Digging Up Your Roots with CD-ROM Databases 309
Researching Your Family Tree Online 311
  Searching Online with Family Tree Maker 311
  Visiting Genealogy Web Sites 312
  Getting Advice Via Newsgroups and E-Mail 313
  Tracking Down Lost Relatives 314
Growing Your Family Tree 315
Printing Your Family Tree 316

Part 6: Tinkering with Computer Gadgets
             and Gizmos   319

28 Playing Digitized Music Clips   321

Understanding CD and MP3 Audio Basics 321
Using Your Computer as a Jukebox 323
  Creating a Custom Playlist with Windows Media Player 324
  Changing Media Player's Skin 326

I Want My MP3: Downloading Music Clips from
the Web 327
Finding and Downloading Music Clips *328*
Playing Your Clips *329*
Copying MP3 Clips to a Portable MP3 Player *330*
Burning Your Own Audio CDs 331
Duplicating CDs *332*
Recording a Custom Mix to a CD *333*

29 Managing Your Life with a Palm Computer   335

Understanding Subcompact Computers 335
Palm Data Entry 101 337
Connecting Your Palm Computer to Your Desktop
Computer 337
Getting Additional Software and Games 340
Installing Add-On Programs *340*
*Beaming Programs and Data over an Infrared
Connection* *341*
Accessorizing Your Portable Device 342

30 Watching TV and DVD on Your Computer   343

The Convergence of TV and Computers 343
Making Your TV Act Like a Computer *344*
Making Your Computer Act Like a TV *345*
Tuning in with Windows 346
Can I Play Interactive Games? 347
Playing DVD Videos on Your Computer 348

31 Playing Film Editor with Digital Video   351

What You Need to Get Started 351
Setting Up Your Audio-Video Equipment 352
Capturing and Saving Your Clips 354
Splicing Your Clips into a Full-Length Movie 356
Adding an Audio Background 357
Smoothing Out Your Transitions 358
Saving Your Movie 359
Sharing Your Movies with Friends and Relatives 359

32 Upgrading for Voice Commands and Dictation 363

What You Need to Get Started 364
"Testing, One, Two, Three": Checking Your
Sound System 364
Installing Your Speech Recognition Software 365
Training the Software to Recognize Your Voice 365
No-Hands Typing with Dictation 367
Entering Voice Commands 369

Part 7: Maintaining Your Investment 371

33 Keeping Your Computer Clean 373

Tools of the Trade 373
Vacuuming and Dusting Your Computer 374
WASH ME: Cleaning Your Monitor 375
Shaking the Crumbs Out of Your Keyboard 376
Thrills and Spills 376
Making Your Mouse Cough Up Hairballs 376
Cleaning Your Printer (When It Needs It) 377
What About the Disk Drives? 378

34 Giving Your Computer a Tune-Up 379

One-Stop Optimization with the Maintenance Wizard 380
Clearing Useless Files from Your Hard Disk 381
Checking for and Repairing Damaged Files and Folders 382
Defragmenting Files on Your Hard Disk 383
Making Windows Start Faster 385
Boosting Performance with Shareware Utilities 386

Appendixes

A Glossary: Speak Like a Geek 389

B More Computer Resources for the Computer Enthusiast 405

Index 409

Introduction

A funny thing happened on the way to the twenty-first century. Computers became more human. By "human," I don't mean "humanoid." I only mean that the computer has evolved from being a stodgy office tool to a revolutionary home appliance, a device designed to help us manage and enjoy our lives more fully.

Sure, you can still use a computer to type and print a letter, but the latest computer technology can completely revolutionize your professional and personal life. Here's just a glimpse of what you can do with a computer, an Internet connection, and some additional equipment:

- ➤ Design and print your own greeting cards, invitations, brochures, and other publications.
- ➤ Shop at mega-malls and specialty shops without leaving your home, and save money, too!
- ➤ Send and receive mail electronically—no postage, and same-day delivery.
- ➤ Carry on video phone conversations with friends, relatives, and complete strangers anywhere in the world—without paying long-distance charges.
- ➤ Plan your vacation, get medical advice, and copy music clips.
- ➤ Reconcile your checkbook, manage your finances, and track your investments.
- ➤ Learn a foreign language or take piano lessons.
- ➤ Play the coolest strategy and action games.
- ➤ Research your lineage and print your family tree.
- ➤ Create and print custom photo albums.
- ➤ Edit your home videos and copy your video clips to CDs or VHS tapes.
- ➤ Find a mate. (I do recommend meeting in person before you make any commitments.)

Sounds pretty cool, huh? Well, it is—assuming, of course, that you know what you're doing. In order to master the high-tech world of computers and electronic gadgets, you must first master the basics. You need to know your way around a computer, how to point and click with a mouse, how to run programs in Windows, and how to enter commands. Once you've mastered a few basics, as explained in the first few chapters of this book, you will be well-prepared to explore and exploit the full power of your computer and the Internet as you proceed through later chapters.

Welcome to *The Complete Idiot's Guide to Computer Basics, Second Edition*

Most computer documentation is based on the assumption that you, the user, are the computer's servant. The documentation lists the parts of the computer and explains how each part works, as if you purchased a computer to impress your friends and neighbors rather than to perform a particular job.

The Complete Idiot's Guide to Computer Basics, Second Edition, is different. Instead of posing the computer as your master, this book places *you* in charge of the computer. This book assumes that you want to do something practical with your computer, and it shows you how to use your computer as you would use any tool to perform practical, hands-on tasks. You'll learn how to do everything from typing and printing letters to editing videotapes.

How Do You Use This Book?

You don't have to read this book from cover to cover (although you might miss some savvy tidbits if you skip around). If you just purchased a computer, start with Chap-ter 1, "Setting It Up and Turning It On," to learn how to get your computer up and run-ning. If you need a quick lesson on using Windows, skip ahead to Chapter 2, "Meet-ing Windows: Up Close and Personal." If you need to get wired to the Internet, check out Chapter 15, "Connecting to the Outside World with a Modem." To provide some structure for this hodgepodge of computer skills and techniques, I've divided this book into the following seven parts:

➤ **Part 1, "Firing Up Your Computer: Bare-Bones Basics,"** covers the bare mini-mum: setting up and turning on your computer, dealing with Microsoft Win-dows, running programs, and warming up with a few games.

➤ **Part 2, "Personalizing Your Work Space,"** shows you how to take control of the Windows desktop (a virtual desktop on which you create documents and play games). Here, you learn how to pick a theme for your desktop, change the background, turn on a screensaver, configure the audio clips, install programs, and give yourself more room to work.

➤ **Part 3, "Creating Letters, Greeting Cards, and Other Documents,"** teaches you everything you need to know to type a letter, change the type size and style, center text, and print your letter. Here, you also learn how to use a desktop pub-lishing program to design and print custom greeting cards, flyers, and banners.

➤ **Part 4, "Getting Wired to the Internet,"** launches you into the world of telecommunications. In this part, you find out how to select and install a modem, connect to an online service, surf the Internet, send and receive elec-tronic mail, surf the World Wide Web, and much more.

➤ **Part 5, "Kids and Other Homey Stuff,"** helps you successfully and safely intro-duce your family to your computer. Here, you learn where to find the best games and educational software, how to manage your finances and investments, safely introduce kids to the Internet, make your own digital photo album, and trace your family's roots.

➤ **Part 6, "Tinkering with Computer Gadgets and Gizmos,"** introduces you to the exciting world of consumer electronics. Here, you learn how to copy MP3 audio clips from the Internet and play them on a portable MP3 player, manage your life with a pocket-size Palm computer, watch TV and DVD movies on your computer, digitize your camcorder video clips, and use dictation software to enter commands and "type" text without touching the keyboard.

➤ **Part 7, "Maintaining Your Investment,"** acts as your computer maintenance guide. Here, you learn how and when to clean your computer and how to give it regular tune-ups to keep it running like new.

Conventions Used in This Book

I use several conventions in this book to make it easier to understand. For example, when you need to type something, here's how it appears:

```
type this
```

Just type what it says. It's as simple as that.

Likewise, if I tell you to select or click a command, the command appears in **bold**. This allows you to quickly scan a series of steps without having to reread all the text.

A plethora of margin notes and sidebars offer additional information about what you've just read. These boxes are distinguished by special icons that appear next to them:

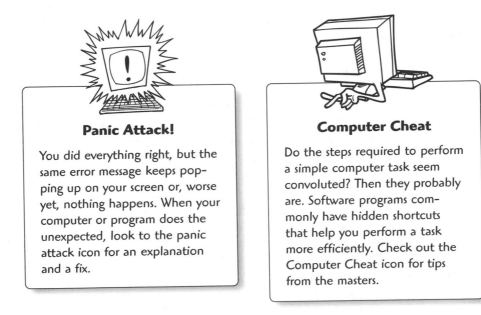

Panic Attack!

You did everything right, but the same error message keeps popping up on your screen or, worse yet, nothing happens. When your computer or program does the unexpected, look to the panic attack icon for an explanation and a fix.

Computer Cheat

Do the steps required to perform a simple computer task seem convoluted? Then they probably are. Software programs commonly have hidden shortcuts that help you perform a task more efficiently. Check out the Computer Cheat icon for tips from the masters.

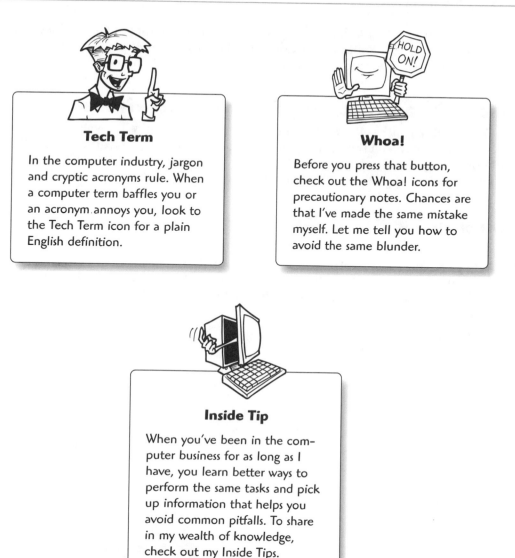

Tech Term

In the computer industry, jargon and cryptic acronyms rule. When a computer term baffles you or an acronym annoys you, look to the Tech Term icon for a plain English definition.

Whoa!

Before you press that button, check out the Whoa! icons for precautionary notes. Chances are that I've made the same mistake myself. Let me tell you how to avoid the same blunder.

Inside Tip

When you've been in the computer business for as long as I have, you learn better ways to perform the same tasks and pick up information that helps you avoid common pitfalls. To share in my wealth of knowledge, check out my Inside Tips.

Acknowledgments

Several people had to don hard hats and get their hands dirty to build a better book. I owe special thanks to Angelina Ward and Eric Heagy for choosing me to author this book and for handling the assorted details to get this book in gear. Thanks to Gayle Johnson for guiding the content of this book, keeping it focused on new users, ferreting out all my typos, and fine-tuning my sentences. And thanks to Robert Patrick for making sure the information in this book is accurate and timely. Christy Wagner deserves a free trip to Aruba for shepherding the manuscript (and art) through production. The Alpha Books production team merits a round of applause for transforming a collection of electronic files into such an attractive book.

Special Thanks to the Technical Reviewer

The Complete Idiot's Guide to Computer Basics, Second Edition, was reviewed by an expert who double-checked the accuracy of what you'll learn here, to help us ensure that this book gives you everything you need to know about computers. Special thanks are extended to that expert, Robert Patrick.

Trademarks

All terms mentioned in this book that are known to be or are suspected of being trademarks or service marks have been appropriately capitalized. Alpha Books and Pearson Education cannot attest to the accuracy of this information. Use of a term in this book should not be regarded as affecting the validity of any trademark or service mark.

Part 1

Firing Up Your Computer: Bare-Bones Basics

Right after you purchase a car, the salesperson sits you down behind the wheel and shows you how to work the controls. You learn the essentials, such as how to tune the radio, activate cruise control, adjust the seat, and work the headlights and windshield wipers.

When you purchase a computer—a much more complicated piece of machinery— you're on your own. You get several boxes containing various gadgets and cables, and it's up to you to figure out how to connect everything, turn it on, and start using it.

To make up for this lack of guidance, this part acts as your personal tutor, leading you step-by-step through the process of setting up and starting your computer and using the controls (the keyboard and mouse) to run programs and enter commands.

Chapter 1

Setting It Up and Turning It On

In This Chapter

➤ Preparing a home for your computer

➤ Unpacking your computer's fragile components

➤ Plugging stuff in

➤ Turning everything on in the correct sequence

➤ Following the startup instructions (if there are any)

Bringing home your first computer is nearly as exhilarating and worrisome as adopting a puppy. You're excited, but you really don't know what to expect or how to get started. Where should you set up your computer? How do you connect everything? What's the proper sequence for turning on the parts? How do you respond to your computer the first time you start it?

This chapter shows you what to expect. Here, you learn how to prepare a space for your computer, set it up, and turn on everything in the correct sequence. This chapter also provides plenty of tips and tricks to help you be sure that you received everything you ordered, to test your computer, and to deal with the unexpected the first time you start your computer.

Finding a Comfortable Home for Your Computer

Your home seems spacious until you take delivery of a new sofa or entertainment center. Then you just can't figure out how you'll wedge that new piece into your existing collection. Likewise, few people spend much time considering where they're going to place their computer until they bring it into their home or office. In their haste to get the computer up and running, they might place the computer on a rickety card table in a dank room, where it teeters precariously until they get the time and money to set it up properly.

This is a risky strategy. Perching your computer on unstable furniture in a damp or dusty room can significantly reduce its life expectancy—not to mention your enjoyment of your computer. Think ahead and prepare your computer area *before* you start connecting components:

➤ Think about how you'll use your computer. If you intend to use it as a tool for the family, don't stick it in the basement next to that treadmill you never use. Place it in a room that's convenient for everyone and where you can supervise your kids.

➤ House the computer next to a grounded outlet that's *not* on the same circuit as a clothes dryer, air conditioner, or other power-hungry appliance. Power fluctuations can damage your computer and destroy files.

➤ Keep the computer away from magnetic fields created by fans, radios, large speakers, air conditioners, microwave ovens, and other appliances. Magnetic fields can mess up the display and erase data from your disks.

➤ Choose an area near a phone jack, or install an additional jack for your modem. (If you purchased the computer mainly for working on the Internet, consider installing a separate phone line for your modem.) If you plan on connecting to the Internet through your cable company, contact the cable company to install a cable connection near the computer.

➤ Place your computer in an environment that is clean, dry, cool, and out of direct sunlight. If you have no choice, cover the computer after turning it off to keep it clean. (Don't cover it when the power's on; it needs to breathe.)

➤ To reduce glare on the monitor, be sure it doesn't directly face a window or other source of bright light. Otherwise, the glare will make it difficult for you to see the screen.

➤ Give the computer room to breathe. The computer has fans and vents to keep it cool. If you block the vents, the computer might overheat.

Panic Attack!

To prevent lightning damage to your computer (which is usually excluded from manufacturer warranties), plug all your computer components into a high-quality surge suppressor. The surge suppressor should have a UL rating of 400 or less, an energy-absorption rating of 400 or more, and a warranty that covers damage to the surge suppressor *and* to your computer. If possible, use an outlet located on an inside wall to further reduce the likelihood that lightning will strike your computer.

Unpacking Your New Toys

When you bring your computer home (or when it's delivered), you will be tempted to tear into the boxes and unpack everything. Before you do, read the following list of precautions for unpacking and connecting your equipment:

➤ Take your time. It's easy to get flustered and make mistakes when you're in a hurry.

➤ Clear all drinks from the work area. You don't want to spill anything on your new computer.

➤ When unpacking your equipment, keep the boxes on the floor to avoid dropping any equipment.

➤ If your computer arrives on a cold day, give the components time (two to three hours) to adjust to the temperature and humidity in the room. Any condensation needs to dissipate before you turn on the power.

➤ Don't cut the boxes. Carefully peel off the packing tape. This serves two purposes: It reduces the risk of your hacking through a cable or scratching a device, and it keeps the boxes in good condition in case you need to return a device to the manufacturer.

➤ If you have trouble pulling a device, such as a monitor, out of the box, turn the box on its side and slide the device out onto the floor. Don't flip the box over and try to pull the box off the device.

➤ Save all the packing material, including the Styrofoam and bubble wrap. Many manufacturers accept returns only if you return the device as it was originally packed. The packing material is also useful if you need to move your computer to a different home or office later.

➤ Read the packing list(s) thoroughly to be sure you received everything you ordered. If something is missing, contact the manufacturer or dealer *immediately*.

➤ Find all the cables. The cables are often stored in a separate compartment at the bottom of the box. They're easy to overlook. (Some cables, including the all-important printer cable, might not be included.)

➤ Inspect the cables. Look for cuts in the cables, and check for bent pins on the connectors. Although you can straighten the pins using tweezers or needle-nose pliers, you can easily snap off a pin, voiding the warranty. If you find a bent or damaged pin, call the manufacturer.

➤ Remove any spacers or packing materials from the disk drives and printer. Cardboard or plastic spacers are commonly used to keep parts from shifting during shipping. To avoid damaging your new equipment, remove these spacers before you turn on your computer.

➤ Unlock any devices that might have been locked for shipping. Some scanners, for instance, have a switch that locks the scanner's carriage in place. That switch might be at the back or bottom of the scanner.

➤ Don't force anything. Plugs should slide easily into outlets. If you have to force something, the prongs are probably not aligned with the holes they're supposed to go in. Forcing the plug will break the prongs.

➤ Don't turn on *anything* until *everything* is connected. On some computers, you can safely plug in devices when the power is on, but check the manual to be sure.

Inside Tip

As you dig through the boxes, find the warranty forms, fill them out, and mail them in. This ensures that if a device goes belly-up within the warranty period, the company will fix or replace the device. Taking time now to complete the forms could save you hundreds of dollars down the road.

Making the Right Connections

When everything is unpacked, arrange all the devices on your desk. If you connect the devices before arranging them, you'll tangle the cables. If you have a standard desktop unit (rare these days), you can place the monitor on top of it. If you have a mini-tower or full tower system unit, you can set it on the floor. (If the floor is carpeted, set the unit on an anti-static pad to prevent static build-up that could damage the sensitive components inside the system unit.)

After everything is properly positioned, you can connect the devices. This is where life gets a bit complicated. Connections differ depending on the computer's design and the types of components you're connecting. For example, although most computers include a central system unit into which you plug the monitor, keyboard, mouse, and printer, some newer computers combine the system unit, monitor, and speakers as a single device into which you plug other devices. In addition, newer computers make greater use of USB (Universal Serial Bus) ports, special receptacles that allow you to connect a string of up to 127 devices to a single receptacle. If your computer comes with a USB mouse and keyboard, you need to plug them into the USB ports instead of into the standard PS/2 mouse or keyboard ports.

To figure out where to plug things in, look for words or pictures on the back (and front) of the central unit (the system unit or combination system unit/monitor). Most receptacles (ports) are marked, and some newer systems even have color-coded cables. If you don't see any pictures next to the receptacles, try to match the plugs with their outlets, as shown in the following figure. Look at the overall shape of the outlet to see if it has pins or holes. Count the pins and holes and be sure there are at least as many holes as there are pins. As a last resort, look for the documentation that came with your computer.

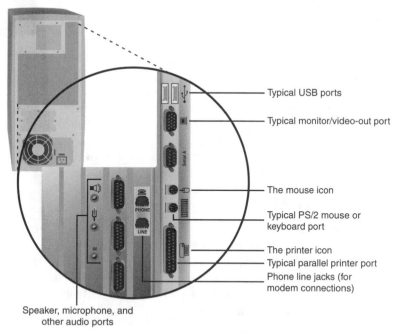

Look for clues on the system unit to figure out where to plug in devices.

Typical USB ports

Typical monitor/video-out port

The mouse icon

Typical PS/2 mouse or keyboard port

The printer icon
Typical parallel printer port
Phone line jacks (for modem connections)

Speaker, microphone, and other audio ports

Bringing the Beast to Life

Dr. Frankenstein must have gotten a real rush just before he flipped the switch and sent that mega-volts jolt through his monster's patchworked body. You get a similar thrill just before you turn on your new computer. What will the screen look like? What sounds will it make? How fast will things pop up on the monitor?

Well, you're about to have all your questions answered as you perform the following steps to start your computer:

1. Press the button on the monitor or flip its switch to turn it on. Computer manufacturers recommend that you turn on the monitor *first*. This allows you to see the startup messages, and it prevents the monitor's power surge from passing through the system unit's components. (On many newer computers, the monitor turns on automatically when you turn on the system unit.)

2. Turn on the printer if it has a power button or switch (many new printers have no power switch). Be sure the online light is lit (not blinking). If the light is blinking, be sure the printer has paper, and then press the online button (if the printer has an online button).

3. If you have speakers or other devices connected to your computer, turn them on.

4. Be sure the floppy disk drive is empty. If it has a floppy disk in it, press the eject button on the drive and then gently remove the disk. (Don't worry about removing any CDs from the CD-ROM drive.)

5. Press the power button or flip the switch on the system unit. (On notebooks and some newer desktop models, you must hold the button for one or two seconds before releasing it.)

Panic Attack!

If this is the first time you're turning on your printer, you must install the ink or toner cartridge. Check the printer manual for instructions.

What happens next varies from one computer to another. Most computers perform a series of startup tests, load a set of basic instructions, and display text messages (white text on a black background) on the monitor. These messages typically disappear before you have time to read them, so don't worry if things seem to rush by too quickly.

Your monitor should then display a colorful screen with a message indicating that the computer is starting Windows. You should then see the Windows desktop, which is shown in the following figure. However, some computers come with their own software that runs a tutorial or displays a special menu on startup.

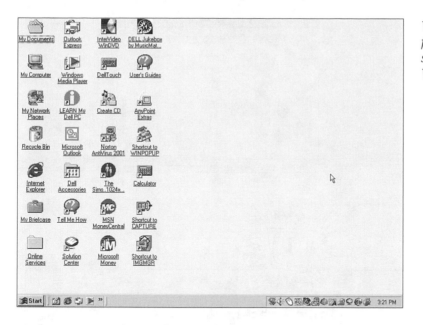

When your computer finally settles down, it should display the Windows desktop.

Installing the Software That Runs Your Hardware

You're not the first person to have turned on your computer. The manufacturer or dealer turned it on right after it came off the assembly line to test the computer before shipping it. However, the manufacturer typically tests the computer without the printer and other accessories connected, so the first time you run your computer with everything connected, Windows runs the Add New Hardware Wizard. (A *wizard* is a series of screens that lead you step by step through the process of performing a task.)

The Add New Hardware Wizard steps you through the process of installing the software (called a *device driver*) that tells Windows how to communicate with a particular device. If a device came with its own device driver (on a floppy disk or CD), use that driver instead of the driver included with Windows. The Add New Hardware dialog box displays a **Have Disk** button, which you can click to install a driver from a disk or CD. Otherwise, you must install the driver from the Windows CD, which should be included with your system. Follow the onscreen instructions, as shown in the following figure, and use your mouse as described here:

➤ To point to an option or button, slide your mouse across the desktop until the tip of the arrow is over the desired button or option.

➤ To select an option or "press" a button, point to the option or button and then press and release the left mouse button without moving the mouse. (This is called a *click*.)

The Add New Hardware Wizard or Add Printer Wizard leads you through the process of installing a device driver.

Panic Attack!

If you have trouble installing a device, read through the installation and troubleshooting sections in the device's manual. If all else fails, look for a technical support telephone number in the manual. The manufacturer's technical support department might be able to help. However, be prepared to pay long-distance charges and to be placed on hold for several minutes.

Now What?

You've arranged everything to your liking, turned everything on, and responded to any startup messages. Now what?

At this point, you're ready to start working (or playing). If the Windows desktop is displayed, as shown in the preceding figure, you can click the **Start** button in the lower-left corner and point to **Programs** to check out which games and programs are installed on your computer. When you're ready to start running programs and performing basic tasks in Windows, move on to Chapter 2, "Meeting Windows: Up Close and Personal."

Shut It Down or Leave It On?

You might be wondering if it's better to leave your computer on or turn it off when you're not using it. In most cases, leaving the computer on is a good idea. Newer system units and monitors have built-in power-saving features that automatically shut down the devices that use the most power (disk drives and monitors) or place them in standby mode.

Turning your computer on and off places additional strain on the power switches and sensitive electrical components. Each time you turn the computer off and back on, the components cool down and heat up, which, over a long period of time, can cause components or solder joints to crack.

When your computer goes into power-saving mode, the screen might go blank. Don't panic. Your computer is just taking a snooze. The best way to wake it up is to press and release the **Shift** key. Sometimes, you can wake your computer by rolling the mouse around, but the **Shift** key is more reliable—and because the **Shift** key doesn't type any characters or enter any commands, it's a safe way to snap your computer out of hibernation.

If you decide to leave your computer on, be sure you save any documents you're working on before you step away from your computer. (You'll learn how to save documents in Chapter 10, "I Just Want to Type a Letter!") Saving a document records the document to the hard drive so that if the power goes out, you don't lose your work.

Inside Tip

Get an uninterruptible power supply (UPS). If you decide to leave your computer on all the time, consider purchasing an un-interruptible power supply to keep a steady flow of current running to your computer during short power outages or brown-outs (those fluctuations that cause your lights to flicker and that might force your computer to restart).

The Least You Need to Know

➤ Place your computer in an environment that is clean, dry, and cool.

➤ Plug all your computer components into a high-quality surge suppressor or un-interruptible power supply to prevent damage from lightning and power fluc-tuations.

➤ When inserting a connector into a port, be sure the pins align with the holes, and never force the connection.

➤ Turn on all the components that are connected to the central unit before you turn on the central unit so that your computer can identify the components during startup and you can view the startup messages.

➤ The first time you run your computer, you might need to install hardware driv-ers (software that tells Windows how to use specific devices).

➤ It's okay to leave your computer on when you're not using it, but be sure you save your work before you step away from the computer.

Chapter 2

Meeting Windows: Up Close and Personal

In This Chapter

➤ First encounters with your new electronic desktop

➤ Mastering your mouse and keyboard

➤ Conversing with menus and dialog boxes

➤ Moving, resizing, and hiding windows on your desktop

➤ Deleting files and folders (and getting them back)

When you start your computer, it automatically runs some version of Windows: Windows Me (Millennium Edition), Windows 98, Windows 95, or Windows 2000 (or Windows NT for networked computers). But what is Windows?

If you pry off the top of your desk and hang it on the wall, you have Windows … well, sort of. Although its initial appearance might be deceiving, Windows is little more than an electronic desktop that's displayed on a two-dimensional vertical surface—your computer's monitor. It even comes complete with its own *desktop utilities*, including a calculator, a notepad, and a blank canvas that you can doodle on during your breaks. This chapter teaches you the basics of how to work on your new computerized desktop.

The Windows Nickel Tour

When you first start your computer, your new desktop appears, very neat and tidy. Several *icons* (small pictures) dot the surface of the Windows desktop, and a gray strip called the *taskbar* appears at the bottom of the screen, as shown in the following figure. On the left end of the taskbar is the all-important **Start** button, which opens a menu containing the names of all the programs installed on your computer.

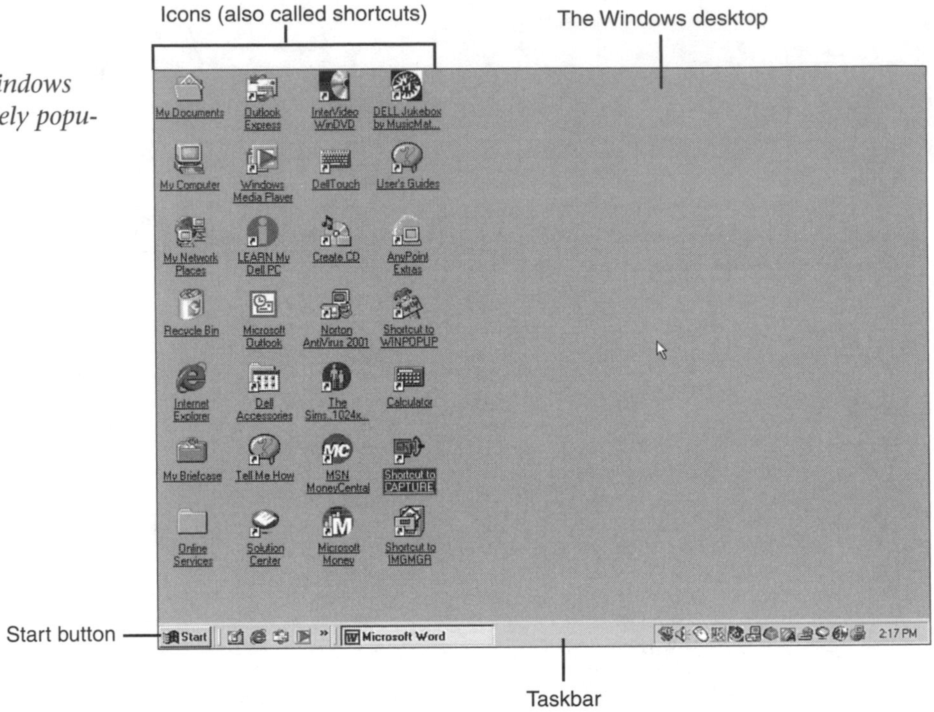

Initially, the Windows desktop is sparsely populated.

Icons (also called shortcuts)

The Windows desktop

Start button ——— Start

Taskbar

Before we start exploring the Windows desktop, find out which version of Windows you have. This book assumes you are using a relatively new computer that is running Windows 95, 98, NT, 2000, or ME. For performing basic tasks, these versions of Windows are nearly identical. To find out which version of Windows you're running, hold down the **Alt** key and *double-click* (click the left mouse button twice quickly) the **My Computer** icon. If **My Computer** is underlined, you don't need to double-click—hold down the **Alt** key while single-clicking the **My Computer** icon.

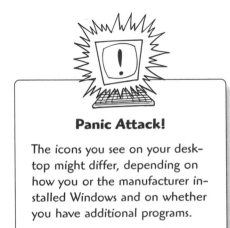

Panic Attack!

The icons you see on your desktop might differ, depending on how you or the manufacturer installed Windows and on whether you have additional programs.

If the icon names are underlined, you have a version of Windows that's more recent than the original Windows 95, and Web Style is turned on; you click an icon once to run its corresponding program. If the icon names are not underlined, you must double-click the icon to run the program. To turn Web Style on, take the following steps:

14

1. Double-click the **My Computer** icon.

2. Click **View** in the menu bar near the top of the window and click **Folder Options.** (If **Folder Options** is not on your **View** menu, open the **Tools** menu by clicking it, and then click **Folder Options.**)

3. If you have Windows 98, click **Web Style,** and then click the **OK** button. For later versions of Windows, including Windows Me, be sure **Enable Web content on my desktop** and **Enable Web content in folders** are selected, and click **OK.**

4. Click **File** in the menu bar, and click **Close.**

With Web Style on, you simply point to icons to select them and single-click icons to activate them. With Web Style off, you click to select and double-click to activate.

Inside Tip

Web Style makes your Windows desktop look and act like an Internet Web page. On a Web page, you click icons, buttons, or underlined text (called links) to jump from one page to another. See Chapter 19, "Poking Around on the Web," for more information. Web Style is a key feature of the post–Windows 95's "Active Desktop," a design that integrates Windows with the Web.

The Land Where Mouse Is King

Windows was designed to make it possible for managers and politicians alike to be able to use computers. Instead of having to press special key combinations to enter commands, the person can point to what he or she wants and then click a button to select or activate it. Fortunately, smart people can also take advantage of the mouse by mastering the following basic mouse moves:

➤ **Point.** Roll the mouse around till the tip of the onscreen arrow (the *pointer*) is over the item you want.

➤ **Click.** Point to something (usually an icon or menu command), and then press and release the left mouse button. Be careful not to move the mouse when you click, or you might click the wrong thing or move an object unintentionally.

➤ **Right-click.** This is the same as clicking, but you use the right mouse button. A couple years ago, the right mouse button was pretty useless. Now it is mainly used to display *context menus,* which contain commands that apply only to the currently selected object.

➤ **Double-click.** This is also the same as clicking, but you press and release the mouse button twice quickly without moving the mouse.

➤ **Drag.** Point to an object, and then hold down the left mouse button while you move the mouse. You typically drag to move an object, to draw (in a drawing or paint program), or to select text (in a word-processing program). In some cases, you can drag with the right mouse button; when you release the mouse button, a context menu typically appears, asking what you want to do.

➤ **Key+click or Key+drag.** In some to cases, you can perform additional tricks with your mouse by holding down a key while clicking and dragging. For example, you can Alt+click the **My Computer** icon to view its properties or Ctrl+drag an icon to copy it instead of moving it.

Similar in shape to the standard two-button mouse, Microsoft's IntelliMouse has a small gray wheel between the left and right buttons, as shown in the following figure. In applications that support the IntelliMouse (including most new Microsoft applications), you can do two things with the wheel: Spin it and click it. What spinning and clicking do depends on the application. For example, in Microsoft Word, you can use the wheel to scroll more accurately, as outlined here:

➤ Rotate the wheel forward to scroll text up; rotate backward (toward yourself) to scroll down.

➤ To pan up or down, click and hold the wheel while moving the mouse pointer in the direction of the text you want to bring into view. (Panning is sort of like scrolling but smoother.)

➤ To autoscroll up or down, click the wheel, and then move the mouse pointer up (to scroll up) or down (to scroll down). Autoscrolling remains turned on until you click the wheel again.

➤ To zoom in or out, hold down the **Ctrl** key and rotate the wheel. Rotate forward to zoom in or backward to zoom out.

The IntelliMouse sports a wheel to simplify scrolling.

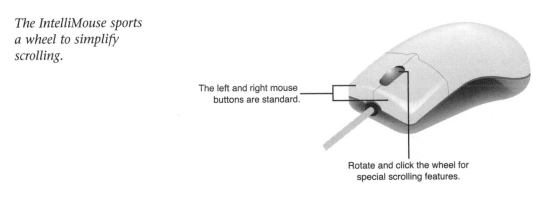

The left and right mouse buttons are standard.

Rotate and click the wheel for special scrolling features.

The Keyboard Is Special, Too

Although the keyboard has lost some of its glory to the mouse, it still retains its importance as the primary tool for inserting text and bypassing clunky menu systems. To master the computer keyboard, you must be familiar with not only the typing keys, but also some of the more unique keys described here:

➤ **Function keys.** The 10 and 12 F keys at the top or left side of the keyboard (**F1**, **F2**, **F3**, and so on) were frequently used in older programs to quickly enter commands. **F1** is still used to display help in Windows and most Windows programs, and you can assign function keys to perform specialized tasks in most programs.

➤ **Arrow keys, Page Up, Page Down, Home, and End.** Also known as *cursor-movement* keys, these keys move the *cursor* (the blinking line or box) around on the screen.

➤ **Numeric keypad.** This is a group of number keys positioned like the keys on an adding machine. You use these keys to type numbers or to move around on-screen. Press the **NumLock** key to use the keys to enter numbers. When **NumLock** is turned off, the keys act as arrow or cursor-movement keys. Most computers automatically turn on **NumLock** on startup.

➤ **Ctrl and Alt keys.** The **Ctrl** (control) and **Alt** (alternate) keys give the other keys magical powers. For example, in Windows, you can press **Ctrl+S** (hold down the **Ctrl** key and press **S**) to quickly save a document.

➤ **Esc key.** You can use the **Esc** (escape) key in most programs to back out of or quit what you are currently doing.

➤ **Print Screen/SysRq.** This key sends a copy of your screen to your printer or to the Windows Clipboard, which is pretty useless unless you're a nerd who writes computer books and is hard up for some illustrations.

➤ **Scroll Lock.** Another fairly useless key, **Scroll Lock** (in some programs) makes the arrow keys push text up and down on the screen one line at a time instead of moving the cursor up and down.

➤ **Pause/Break.** The king of all useless keys, **Pause/Break** is used to stop your computer from performing the same task repeatedly, something that older programs occasionally enjoyed doing.

A Special Key Just for Windows

Many newer keyboards have an extra key that has the Windows logo on it. You can use this Windows key to quickly enter certain commands, as outlined in the following table.

Windows Key Shortcuts

Press	To
▦	Open the Start menu.
▦+Tab	Cycle through running programs.
▦+F	Find a file.
Ctrl+▦+F	Find a computer on a network.
▦+F1	Display the Windows Help window.
▦+R	Display the Run dialog box (for running programs).
▦+Break	Display the System Properties dialog box.
▦+E	Run Windows Explorer to manage folders and files.
▦+D	Minimize or restore all program windows.

Turbo-Surfing the Web with an Internet Keyboard

The latest craze in the keyboard market is the *Internet keyboard,* a keyboard that contains additional, programmable keys that you can assign to specific Web pages or to your favorite programs (see the following figure). Instead of typing the address of the Web page you want or poking around on menus to find the desired Web page, program, or document, you simply press one of the programmable keys.

An Internet keyboard contains keys you can assign to your favorite Web pages and programs.

(Photo courtesy of Logitech, Inc.)

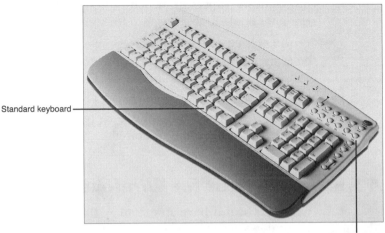

Standard keyboard

Programmable keys

Ordering from Menus and Dialog Boxes

Computer technology hasn't quite reached the point of *2001: A Space Odyssey* (you know, that 1968 Stanley Kubrick flick in which the astronauts actually converse with Hal, the computer that runs the spaceship). However, Windows provides several ways for you to "talk" to your computer by clicking buttons, selecting menu commands, and responding to *dialog boxes* (onscreen fill-in-the-blank forms).

Clicking Menu Options

The Windows interactive tool of preference is the *menu*. You'll find menus everywhere: on the left end of the taskbar (the Windows **Start** menu), in menu bars near the top of most program windows, in toolbars, and even hidden inside objects. To open a menu, you simply click its name, and it drops down or pops up on the screen. Then you click the desired menu option. (To display a hidden—*context*—menu, right-click the desired object or the selected text or image.)

As you flip through any menu system, you might notice that some of the menu options look a little strange. One option might appear pale. Another might be followed by a series of dots. And still others have arrows next to them. Their appearances tell all:

Computer Cheat

To quickly open a menu without lifting your fingers from the keyboard, hold down the **Alt** key and press the key that corresponds to the underlined letter in the menu's name. For example, press **Alt+F** to open the **File** menu. Press **Shift+F10** to display a context menu for the currently selected text or object.

➤ Light gray options are unavailable for what you are currently doing. For example, if you want to copy a chunk of text but you have not yet selected the text, the **Copy** command is not available; it appears light gray.

➤ An option with an arrow next to it opens a submenu that requires you to select another option. Point to the option to open the submenu.

➤ An option with a check mark indicates that an option is currently active. To turn the option off, click it. This removes the check mark; however, you won't know it, because selecting the option also closes the menu.

➤ An option followed by a series of dots (...) opens a dialog box that requests additional information. You learn how to talk to dialog boxes in the next section.

Whoa!

To further confuse new users, Microsoft has come up with something called the "smart" menu, which lists only the most commonly selected options. To view additional options, you must point to a double-headed arrow at the bottom of the menu. In addition, the menu is designed to customize itself, so options automatically move up on the menu the more often you use them. In other words, you never know where they'll be. In case you can't tell, I think smart menus are pretty dumb.

Talking with a Dialog Box

If you choose a menu command that's followed by a series of dots (...), the program displays a *dialog box* requesting additional information. You must then navigate the dialog box, select the desired options, type any required text entries, and give your okay—all using the following controls:

Tabs. If a dialog box has two or more "pages" of options, tabs appear near the top of the pages. Click the tab for the desired options.

Text boxes. A text box is a "fill in the blank"; it allows you to type text, such as the name of a file.

Option buttons. Option buttons (also known as *radio buttons*) allow you to select only one option in a group. Click the desired option to turn it on and turn any other selected option in the group off.

Check boxes. Check boxes allow you to turn an option on or off. Click in a check box to turn it on if it's off or off if it's on. You can select more than one check box in a group.

List box. A list box presents two or more options. Click the desired option. If the list is long, you'll see a *scrollbar*. Click the scrollbar arrows to move up or down in the list.

Drop-down list box. You see only one item when you first view this kind of list box. The rest of the items are hidden initially. Click the arrow to the right of the box to display the rest of the list, and then click the desired item.

Spin box. A spin box is a text box with controls. You can usually type a setting in the text box or click the up or down arrow to change the setting in predetermined increments. For example, you might click the up arrow to increase a margin setting by .1 inch.

Slider. A slider is a control you can drag up, down, or from side to side to increase or decrease a setting. Sliders are commonly used to adjust speaker volume, hardware performance, and similar settings.

Command buttons. Most dialog boxes have at least three buttons: **OK** to confirm your selections, **Cancel** to quit, and **Help** to get help.

Bypassing Menus by Using Toolbar Buttons

Although menus contain a comprehensive list of available options, they are a bit clunky. To perform a task using a menu, you must click the menu name, hunt for the desired command, and then select it. To help you bypass the menu system, most programs include *toolbars* that contain buttons for the most frequently used commands. To perform a task, you simply click the desired button.

Rearranging the Windows Inside Windows

Each time you run a program or open a document in Windows, a new window opens on your desktop. After several hours of work, your desktop can become as cluttered as a real desktop, making it difficult to locate your desktop utilities and documents. To switch to a window or reorganize the windows on the desktop, use any of the following tricks:

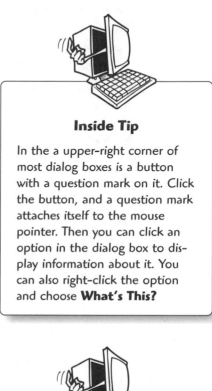

Inside Tip

In the a upper-right corner of most dialog boxes is a button with a question mark on it. Click the button, and a question mark attaches itself to the mouse pointer. Then you can click an option in the dialog box to display information about it. You can also right-click the option and choose **What's This?**

Inside Tip

Some of the pictures used to identify buttons are no more helpful than Egyptian hieroglyphics. To view the name of a button, rest the mouse pointer on it. A little yellow box, called a ScreenTip, pops up, showing the button's name.

➤ To quickly change to a window, click its button in the taskbar. (To hide the window later, click its taskbar button again, or click the Minimize button in the upper-right corner of the window.)

➤ If you can see any part of a window, click it to move it to the front of the stack.

➤ To quickly arrange the windows, right-click a blank area of the taskbar and, from the shortcut menu that appears, choose one of the following options: **Tile Horizontally**, **Tile Vertically**, or **Cascade.**

➤ To close a window (and exit the program), click the **Close** button (the one with the X on it) that's located in the upper-right corner of the window.

➤ To increase the size of a window so that it takes up the whole screen, click the **Maximize** button (just to the left of the **Close** button). The **Maximize** button then turns into a **Restore** button, which you can click to return the window to its previous size.

➤ To shrink a window, click the **Minimize** button (two buttons to the left of the **Close** button). The minimized window appears as a button on the taskbar. Click the button on the taskbar to reopen the window.

➤ To resize or reshape a window that is not at its maximum size, place your mouse pointer in the lower-right corner of the window, and when the pointer turns to a double-headed arrow, drag the corner of the window.

➤ To move a window, drag its title bar. (You can't move a maximized window because it takes up the whole screen.)

You can also control your windows from the taskbar. Whenever you run a program, a button for it appears in the taskbar. The button acts like a toggle switch; click the program's button to open the program's window, and click again to hide the program's window. Right-click a program's button to display options for minimizing, maximizing, restoring, moving, resizing, or closing the program's window.

Try this trick: Click a program's button in the taskbar, and then **Ctrl+click** all other program buttons. Right-click one of the buttons and click **Minimize.** All program windows are minimized, returning you to the Windows desktop. Pretty cool, huh? Well, there's actually an easier way in Windows 98 and later. To the right of the **Start** button is a tiny toolbar called the Quick Launch toolbar, which contains buttons for Internet Explorer (Microsoft's Web browser), Outlook Express (an e-mail program), Web Channels, and the desktop. Click the **Show Desktop** button to quickly return to the Windows desktop. Click the button again to return to your programs.

Inside Tip

If a window cannot display everything it contains, a scrollbar appears along the right side or bottom of the window. Click the arrow at either end of the scrollbar to scroll in the direction the arrow is pointing. To scroll faster, drag the scroll box inside the scrollbar in the desired direction. To scroll one screenful up or down, click inside the scrollbar above or below the scroll box.

What's on Your Computer?

Windows gives you two ways to poke around on your computer and find out what's on your disks. You can double-click the **My Computer** icon (located on the desktop), or you can choose **Start, Programs, Windows Explorer** (in Windows Me, choose **Start, Programs, Accessories, Windows Explorer**).

If you double-click **My Computer** in Windows 95 or 98, Windows displays icons for all the disk drives on your computer, plus three folder icons: **Control Panel** (which allows you to change system settings), **Printers** (for setting up a printer), and **Dial-Up Networking** (for Internet access). To find out what's on a disk or in a folder, double-click its icon. (Remember, if your icons are underlined, click once; double-clicking these icons might perform the action twice.) In Windows Me, My Computer displays icons for all disks plus an icon for the Control Panel. The **Dial-Up Networking** and **Printers** icons are in the Control Panel.

Windows Explorer is My Computer's older, more capable sibling. It allows you to perform the same basic tasks you can perform in My Computer, but it provides a two-pane window that displays a folder list on the left and a file list on the right. This two-paned layout lets you easily copy and move files and folders from one disk or folder to another by dragging them from one pane to the other, as shown in the following figure. (A *folder*, also called a *directory*, is a receptacle for storing related files. Folders help you keep your files organized.)

Drag a file from its current location to the desired folder.

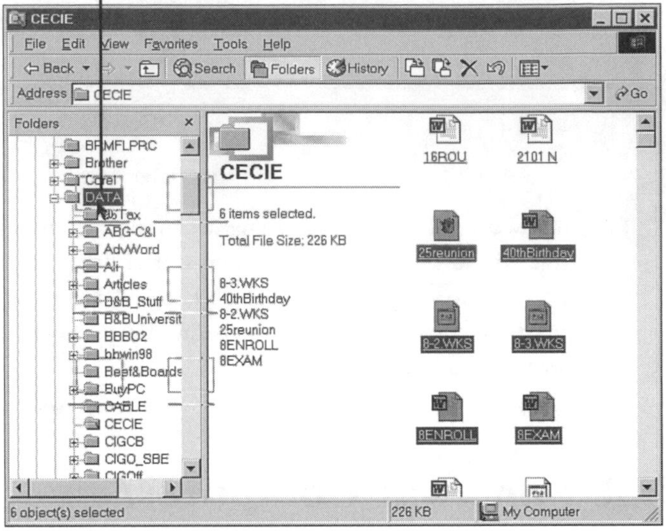

Windows Explorer is a useful tool for copying and moving files.

CECIE

File   Edit   View   Favorites   Tools   Help

Back   Search   Folders   History

Address   CECIE   Go

Folders

BRMFLPRC
Brother
Corel
DATA
　BbTax
ABG-C&I
AdvWord
Ali
Articles
B&B_Stuff
B&BUniversit
BBBO2
bbwin98
Beef&Boards
BuyPC
CABLE
CECIE
CIGCB
CIGO_SBE
CIGOff

CECIE

6 items selected.

Total File Size: 226 KB

8-3.WKS
40thBirthday
8-2.WKS
25reunion
8ENROLL
8EXAM

16ROU   2101 N

25reunion   40thBirthday

8-2.WKS   8-3.WKS

8ENROLL   8EXAM

6 object(s) selected   226 KB   My Computer

Computer Cheat

Make Windows Explorer more accessible. Minimize all program windows so that you can see the Windows desktop. Open the **Start** menu and display the icon for Windows Explorer. Using the right mouse button, drag Windows Explorer from the menu to a blank area on the desktop. Release the mouse button and click **Create Shortcut(s) Here.**

Trashing Files in the Recycle Bin

Windows comes complete with its own trash compactor. Whenever a file or icon has outlived its usefulness, either drag it over the trash can icon (the **Recycle Bin**) and release the mouse button or click the file in My Computer or Windows Explorer to select it and then click the **Delete** button (the button with the X on it just below the menu bar). This moves the file to the **Recycle Bin** without permanently deleting it, so you can recover it later if the need should arise.

Pulling things out of the **Recycle Bin** is as easy as dragging them into it. Double-click the **Recycle Bin** icon to display its contents. If the icon names are underlined, rest the mouse pointer on the icon you want to restore to highlight it. If the icon names are not underlined, click the item you want to restore to select it. **Ctrl+point** or **Ctrl+click** to select additional items. Open the **File** menu and click **Restore.**

Help Is on Its Way

If you plan to thrive in the world of computers, learn how to use the help system in Windows and your Windows programs. These online help systems might not provide the detailed hand-holding instructions you find in books, but they usually provide the basic information you need to get started.

Inside Tip

To change the properties of the **Recycle Bin,** including the maximum amount of disk space it can use, right–click the **Recycle Bin** icon and click **Properties.**

If you get stuck in Windows, click the **Start** button, and then click **Help.** The Help window appears, offering a table of contents and an index. Click the **Contents** tab or **Home** button if you're searching for general information about how to perform a task or use Windows. If you get a list of topics with little book icons next to them, double-click a book icon to view additional subtopics, and then double-click the desired topic.

For specific help, click the **Index** tab or button. Click inside the text box at the top, and then start typing the name of the feature, command, or procedure for which you need help. As you type, the list scrolls to show the name of the topic that matches your entry. Double-click the desired topic. For a more thorough search, click the **Search** tab, if available, and perform your search. In Windows Me, a **Search** text box is located in the upper-right corner of the Help window; type your search phrase and press **Enter** or click **Go.**

The Least You Need to Know

➤ When you start your computer, Windows presents you with an electronic desktop on which you do all your work.

➤ With the mouse, you click an object or command by resting the tip of the mouse pointer on the item and then pressing and releasing the left mouse button.

➤ A keyboard is used mainly for typing text, but it can also be used to quickly enter commands.

➤ When you choose an option that's followed by three dots, Windows displays a dialog box asking for additional information.

➤ Three buttons appear in the upper-right corner of every window. Use these buttons to open, close, or quickly hide or restore the window.

➤ To manually resize a window, drag its lower-right corner.

➤ To see what's on your computer, click or double-click the **My Computer** icon.

➤ To delete a file or icon, drag it over the **Recycle Bin** icon and release the mouse button.

➤ For more information about Windows, click the **Start** button and then click **Help.**

Chapter 3

Launching Your First Program

In This Chapter

➤ Picking a program from the **Start, Programs** menu

➤ Running programs right from the Windows desktop

➤ Quickly launching programs from the taskbar

➤ Rearranging programs on the **Start** menu

An empty desktop might be a rare and beautiful sight, but it's useless. To get something done, have some fun, or at least make your boss think you're productive, you need a little clutter. You need to run a program or two.

The standard (albeit slow) method of running a program is to open the **Start** menu and click the name of the desired program. (The next section shows you just what to do.) However, Windows provides several more creative and much faster ways to run programs with a single click of the mouse. In this chapter, you get to try various techniques for running programs so that you can settle on the method you like best.

Picking a Program from the Start Menu

Whenever you install a program, the installation utility places the program's name on the **Start, Programs** menu or one of its submenus. To run the program, you simply click the **Start** button, point to **Programs**, point to the desired program group (the name of the program's submenu), and click the program's name, as shown in the following figure.

*You can find all installed programs on the **Start**, **Programs** menu.*

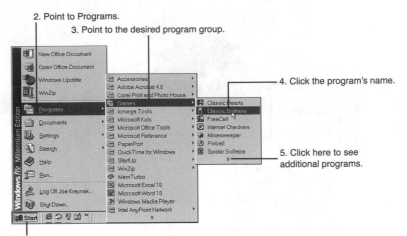

2. Point to Programs.

3. Point to the desired program group.

4. Click the program's name.

5. Click here to see additional programs.

1. Click the Start button.

Inside Tip

For some programs, the installation utility places a shortcut icon on the Windows desktop or at the top of the **Start** menu so you don't have to poke around on the **Start** menu to find the program.

More Creative Ways to Run Programs

Think of the **Start** menu as a storage cabinet in your basement. If you need something, you can always find it in the storage cabinet, but it's not the most convenient location. You might store your heavy-duty party-size cookware in the cellar, but you store the pots and pans you use daily right next to your stove.

The same is true in Windows. It's fine to run the programs you rarely use from the **Start** menu or one of its submenus, but if you use a program frequently, you need to place it in a more convenient location and use the techniques described in the following sections to run the program.

Make Your Own Program Shortcut

As you saw in the previous chapter, the Windows desktop displays a few icons, called *shortcuts,* that let you run commonly used programs. Unlike bona fide icons that represent files, these "dummy" icons merely point to the original file. Windows displays a small arrow in the lower-left corner of each shortcut icon to indicate that it is not an actual file icon.

If you frequently run a program, you can create your own shortcut for that program and place it on the Windows desktop by performing the following steps:

1. Open the **Start** menu, point to **Programs**, and open the submenu that contains the desired program.

2. Point to the program you want to add to the desktop.

3. Hold down the **Ctrl** and **Shift** keys, and drag the program to a blank area on the desktop.

4. Release the mouse button and the **Ctrl** and **Shift** keys. Windows places a shortcut icon for the program on the desktop.

You can create desktop shortcuts for just about any object in Windows: a disk, folder, file, or program. Simply right-click the icon and choose **Create Shortcut.** This places the shortcut inside the same window or on the same menu as the original. You must then drag the icon to a blank area of the desktop.

Inside Tip

Deleting a shortcut does not delete the original file it points to. However, deleting an actual file or program icon does delete the corresponding document or program file. Be careful whenever you choose to delete any icon.

To quickly arrange icons on the desktop, right-click a blank area of the desktop, point to **Arrange Icons**, and click **Auto Arrange.** (If you turn off the **Auto Arrange** feature, you can drag icons anywhere on the desktop.)

Run Programs from Your Keyboard

You don't need a fancy programmable keyboard to have quick keyboard access to your programs. Windows lets you program any standard keyboard to run programs with a single key press. But first, you must assign a keystroke to the desired program. To do so, follow these steps:

1. Right-click the program's icon and choose **Properties.** (The icon might be on the **Start**, **Programs** menu, on the Windows desktop, or in My Computer or Windows Explorer.)

2. Click in the **Shortcut Key** text box.

3. Press the key that you want to use to run this program. You can use any key except **Esc, Enter, Tab, Spacebar, Backspace, Print Screen,** or any function key or key combination used by Windows. If you press a number or character key, Windows automatically adds **Ctrl+Alt+** to create a *key combination*. For example, if you press A, Windows will create the **Ctrl+Alt+A** key combination, and you will press **Ctrl+Alt+A** (hold down **Ctrl** and **Alt,** and then press A) to run the program.

4. Click **OK.**

29

Make Your Own Programs Folder

Did you get a little carried away making your own program shortcuts? If you did, consider storing your shortcuts in a separate folder so that they won't clutter your desktop. It's easy. Just right-click a blank area on the desktop, point to **New**, and click **Folder**. Windows places a new folder on the desktop. Type a name for the folder and press **Enter**. Drag the desired program icons from the desktop over your new folder icon and release the mouse button; this moves the shortcuts to the folder, removing them from the desktop. You can click or double-click your folder icon to view its contents. Drag the folder to any edge of the Windows desktop to transform it into a toolbar; this gives you one-click access to the programs you use most frequently.

Run Programs When Windows Starts

Here's one last trick. If you always run a particular program right after starting your computer, you can make Windows run the program for you on startup. Here's how:

1. Right-click a blank area of the taskbar and click **Properties**.

2. Click the **Start Menu Programs** tab.

3. Click the **Advanced** button. This displays the entire **Start** menu and its submenus in Windows Explorer.

4. Click the plus sign next to **Programs**.

5. Change to the folder that contains the program you want Windows to run on startup, and then select the program icon by pointing to it (if its name is underlined) or clicking it (if the name is not underlined).

6. Scroll down the folder list on the left until you can see the StartUp folder.

7. Drag the highlighted program icon from the file list on the right over the StartUp folder on the left, and release the mouse button.

The next time you start your computer, Windows will start and then automatically run the program you just placed in the StartUp folder.

Inside Tip

Here's a quicker way to copy programs to the StartUp folder: Open the **Start** menu, point to **Programs,** and point to the program you want Windows to run on startup. Hold down the **Ctrl** key while dragging the icon over the StartUp program group and then over the **Startup** submenu. Release the mouse button.

Moving a Program to a More Convenient Location

If Windows buries your favorite program five levels down on the **Start** menu, you don't have to live with it. You can move your programs to place them right at your fingertips. Simply open the menu on which the program appears, and then drag the program to the desired location—to the **Programs** submenu, the top of the **Start** menu, another submenu, a blank area on the desktop, or the programs folder you created a moment ago. If you drag the program to a different location on the **Start** menu, a horizontal bar appears as you drag the program, showing where it will be placed (see the following figure). When the bar shows the desired location, release the mouse button.

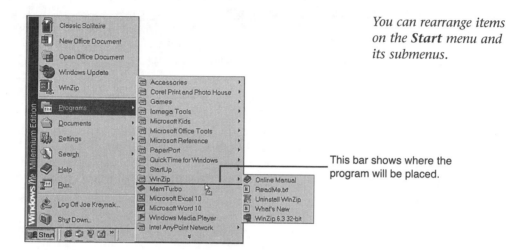

You can rearrange items on the Start menu and its submenus.

This bar shows where the program will be placed.

Running Programs with a Single Click

In late versions of Windows 95, Microsoft introduced a nifty little program launch pad called the Quick Launch toolbar. This toolbar roosts just to the right of the **Start** button and provides single-click access to commonly used programs. Initially, the Quick Launch toolbar contains the following four buttons:

Launch Internet Explorer Browser runs Microsoft's Internet Explorer, a program for navigating the World Wide Web.

Launch Outlook Express runs Microsoft's e-mail program to allow you to send and receive electronic mail over an Internet connection.

Inside Tip

Tip 1: Drag the top edge of the taskbar up to make the taskbar taller. Tip 2: Drag the taskbar to the top, left, or right side of the desktop and see what happens. Tip 3: Right-click a blank area of the taskbar and click **Properties** to view additional options.

Show Desktop minimizes all open program windows to take you imme-diately to the Windows desktop.

View Channels displays a list of Web sites you can click to immediately "tune in to" the most commercialized sites on the Web.

To add your own buttons to the Quick Launch toolbar, simply drag the desired pro-gram icon to a blank spot on the toolbar and release the mouse button. If the new button does not immediately appear, drag the vertical bar just to the right of the Quick Launch toolbar to the right to make the toolbar bigger. You can also turn on other similar toolbars or create your own toolbar; right-click a blank area of the taskbar and point to **Toolbars** to check out your options.

Opening Documents with a Single Click

When you install a program, Windows associates that program with certain docu-ment types. For example, if you install Microsoft Word, Windows associates Word with all document files whose names end in .doc. Whenever you click or double-click a document icon that's associated with Word, Windows automatically runs Word and opens the document in Word.

Tech Term

Filenames consist of two parts: the main filename and its extension (the last one to three characters that follow the period). Windows typically hides the filename extensions in My Computer and Windows Explorer. To view extensions, open My Computer, open the **View** or **Tools** menu, and click **Folder Options.** Click the **View** tab and click **Hide File Extensions for Known File Types** to remove the check mark. Click **OK.**

If you frequently open a particular document to edit it or refer to it, consider placing a shortcut icon for that document on the Windows desktop or in the Quick Launch toolbar. Use My Computer or Windows Explorer to change to the folder in which the document is stored, and then, using the right mouse button, drag the document's icon to the desired location. Release the mouse button and click **Create Shortcut(s) Here.**

The Least You Need to Know

➤ You can right-drag a program icon to a blank area on the desktop to create your own program shortcut.

➤ You can right-click an icon and click **Properties** to assign a key combination to a program.

➤ You can drag a program icon from a submenu to a more convenient location on the **Start** menu.

➤ For one-click access to a program or document, drag its icon to the Quick Launch toolbar.

➤ You can reconfigure the taskbar by dragging its top edge up to make it taller or by dragging it to a different location on the desktop.

Chapter 4

Warming Up with Some Computer Games

In This Chapter

➤ Honing your mouse skills with Solitaire

➤ Feeding your addiction for FreeCell

➤ Playing Hearts against some virtual friends

➤ Finding mines without blowing yourself up

Before you drive your first golf ball or try to ace your first serve in tennis, you take a few practice swings to warm up. This prevents you from completely missing the ball or throwing out your back.

Similarly, before you get into the thick of the battle with your computer, you should warm up with a few games. Windows comes with several games (Solitaire, FreeCell, Hearts, and Minesweeper) that are very helpful for honing your mouse skills and having a little fun in the process. This chapter teaches you the basics of playing these games and throws in a few tips to help you win.

Installing and Running the Windows Games

The first step in playing the Windows games is to find the games. When you or the computer manufacturer installed Windows, the installation utility might not have installed the games. To determine if the games are installed, click the **Start** button, and point to **Programs**. If you don't see the **Games** menu, point to **Accessories** and look for **Games**. If you have a **Games** menu, you're in luck. Point to it, and then click the name of the game you want to play.

If the **Games** menu is nowhere to be found, the games are not installed. To install the games, take the following steps:

1. Insert the Windows CD into your computer's CD-ROM drive.

2. Click the **Start** button, point to **Settings**, and click **Control Panel.** The Windows Control Panel appears.

3. Click or double-click the **Add/Remove Programs** icon. The Add/Remove Programs Properties dialog box appears.

4. Click the **Windows Setup** tab, as shown in the following figure. Windows Setup checks to determine which components are installed on your computer. The **Components** list displays groups of related components; for example, **Accessories** includes the Calculator and Paint programs. The check boxes indicate the following:

> **A clear box** (no gray, no check mark) indicates that none of the components in this group are installed.

> **A clear box with a check** (a check mark but no gray) indicates that all the components in this group are installed.

> **A gray box with a check** (gray and a check mark) indicates that some of the components in this group are installed.

Some components are installed.

You can easily determine which Windows components are installed.

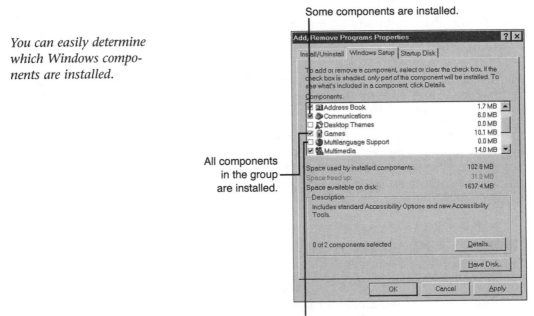

All components in the group are installed.

No components are installed.

5. If **Games** is not in the list, double-click **Accessories** or click **Accessories** and click the **Details** button. (In Windows Me, **Games** is its own group. In earlier versions of Windows, the games are part of the Accessories group.)

6. Click the check box next to **Games** to place a check mark in the box.

7. Click **OK**. In Windows Me, this closes the Windows Setup dialog box, and Windows Setup copies the necessary files from the Windows CD. In earlier versions of Windows, clicking **OK** returns you to the original list of components, and you must click **OK** again.

If Windows displays a message telling you to restart your computer, save all open documents, exit all open programs, and click the option to restart your computer. When your computer starts, the Windows **Start, Programs** or **Start, Programs, Accessories** menu will have a **Games** submenu listing the Windows games. Windows 95 and later versions all come with four standard games: Solitaire, FreeCell, Hearts, and Minesweeper. Windows Me features additional games, including Spider Solitaire, Pinball, and Internet versions of Backgammon, Checkers, Hearts, Reversi, and Spades.

Using Your $1,000 Computer as a $1 Deck of Cards

Whenever I walk into a school or business, I invariably see three or four computers with Solitaire up and running. Workers and managers alike seem to love honing their mouse skills on a daily basis, and Solitaire and FreeCell are definitely the games of choice.

Because the rules of Solitaire are common knowledge, I won't go into boring detail about how to play the game. However, dealing and moving the cards around on-screen requires knowledge of the basic moves:

➤ When you start the game, Windows automatically deals the cards. To start a new game, open the **Game** menu and click **Deal.**

➤ To move a card, drag it to the desired stack. To move a string of cards from one stack to another, drag the topmost card in the stack to the desired stack, as shown in the following figure.

➤ To flip through the cards in the deck, click the deck.

➤ To move an ace or other card up to a suit stack (in the upper-right corner of the window), double-click the card.

➤ To undo a move, open the **Game** menu and click **Undo.**

➤ To set scoring options, open the **Game** menu, click **Options**, enter your preferences, and click **OK.**

Use the Game menu to re-deal
and to set scoring options.

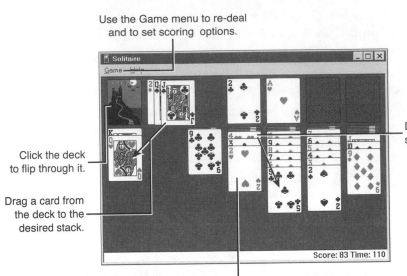

Click the deck
to flip through it.

Drag a card from
the deck to the
desired stack.

Drag the topmost card in the
stack to the desired stack.

Double-click a card to it up to its suit stack.

*Solitaire can help you hone your click, double-click,
and dragging skills.*

Becoming a FreeCell Junkie

FreeCell is reverse Solitaire. You start with eight stacks of cards, all face up, four free cells, and four home cells. To win, you must create a stack of cards for each suit in the home cells, and the cards of each stack must be arranged from lowest to highest, starting with the ace. The free cells act as temporary storage areas for the cards, so you can move cards around from stack to stack. If you fill the free cells and have no other move available, you lose.

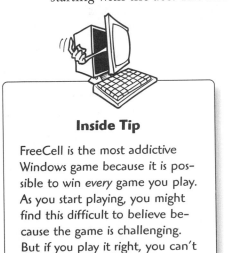

Inside Tip

FreeCell is the most addictive Windows game because it is possible to win *every* game you play. As you start playing, you might find this difficult to believe because the game is challenging. But if you play it right, you can't lose.

To play FreeCell, follow these steps:

1. Click the **Start** button, point to **Programs**, **Games** (or **Programs**, **Accessories**, **Games**), and click **FreeCell**. A blank FreeCell window appears.

2. Open the **Game** menu and click **New Game**. FreeCell deals eight stacks of cards, all face up.

3. Look at the bottom of each stack to determine if you can move a black or red card onto a card of the opposite color that is one level higher (for example, a red 5 onto a black 6). Click the card you want to move.

4. Move the mouse pointer over the card onto which you want to move the selected card, and click. When you move the mouse pointer over the card, a down
arrow appears, indicating that the move is legal, as shown in the following figure. If no arrow appears, you can't move the card.

Use the free cells
to move cards.

FreeCell places exposed
aces in the home cells.

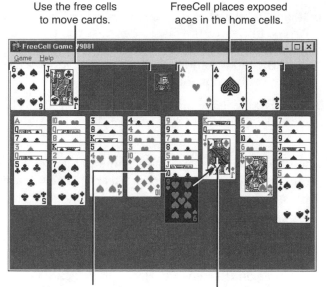

*With FreeCell, every
game is winnable.*

You can move one or
more cards from one
stack to another.

The down arrow
indicates that this
move is legal.

5. If the card on which you want to play is
buried under a stack, you can uncover the
card by dragging cards off it and onto the
free cells, but be careful not to use up all your
free cells.

6. If you have a blank stack, you can start a new
stack in its place by dragging one or more
cards to the empty stack.

7. When you uncover an ace, FreeCell automatically adds it to one of the four home spaces
in the upper-right corner. FreeCell also moves
any exposed cards that can be placed on the
aces (2, 3, 4, and so on) up to their corresponding aces.

8. If you complete all four home stacks (from
ace up to king), FreeCell displays a dialog box

Inside Tip

You can move a stack of cards to
another card. For example, you
can move a stack consisting of a
red jack, black 10, and red 9 onto
a black queen. However, there
must be enough open free cells to
make the move. To move a stack,
click the stack you want to move,
and then click the card to which
you want the stack moved.

congratulating you and asking if you want to play again. If you're a true addict or addict wannabe, click **Yes** and keep playing!

Playing Hearts with Virtual Players

Hearts is a multiplayer game designed to be played on a network; however, you can play against three computer players. In Hearts, the low score wins. You try to give your hearts (each worth one point) and the queen of spades (worth 13 points) to the other players, or you try to "shoot the moon" and win all the hearts and the queen of spades to score zero and penalize your opponents 26 points each.

I've found this to be the most aggravating game of the bunch; the computer players are ruthless! However, in case you like the thrill of stiff competition, here's how you play:

1. Click the **Start** button, point to **Programs,** and then **Games,** and click **Classic Hearts** (or click **Start, Programs, Accessories, Games, Hearts**). The Microsoft Hearts Network dialog box asks for your name.

2. Type your name in the **What's your name?** text box.

3. To play against the computer players, click **I want to be dealer** and click **OK.** (If you're connected to a network, you can click **I want to connect to another game** to play against real people on the network. Hearts then asks you to enter the name of the dealer's computer.)

4. Click the three cards you want to pass to the player to your left, as shown in the following figure. In most cases, you want to get rid of the queen of spades and any high hearts you're holding, but if you're trying to shoot the moon, those are the very cards you want to keep. (For every fourth deal, no cards are passed.)

5. Click the **Pass** button (labeled **Pass Left, Pass Right,** or **Pass Across,** depending on the hand). Each player passes three cards to the left, so you end up with three new cards.

6. Click **OK** to accept the new cards (you have no choice).

7. If one of the other players has the 2 of clubs, he or she plays it. If you have the 2 of clubs, click it to play the card. (The 2 of clubs always starts the game.)

8. Moving clockwise, each player plays a card of the same suit (a club in the first round). If you don't have a club, you can play any card except

Computer Cheat

If you're obsessed with winning every game, and you get in a jam, you can still win. Press **Ctrl+Shift+F10,** click **Abort,** and play any card. FreeCell automatically moves all cards to the home stacks and chalks up another win.

the queen of spades or a heart. The player who plays the highest card of the same suit as the first card played takes the cards and leads the next round. (You cannot lead with a heart unless someone played a heart in a previous round.)

9. Continue playing until you and the other players have played all your cards. When you're done, Hearts displays the score. Click **OK** to start a new hand. (The first person to reach 100 loses.)

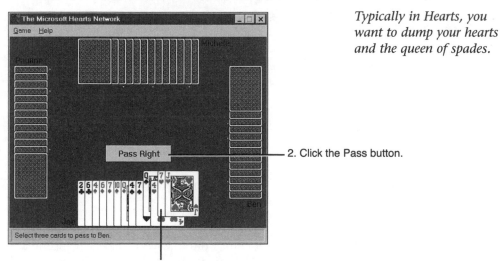

Typically in Hearts, you want to dump your hearts and the queen of spades.

2. Click the Pass button.

1. Select three cards to pass to another player.

Taking a Virtual Risk with Minesweeper

Minesweeper is a game of strategy in which several mines are hidden under a grid of tiles. Your job is to turn over the tiles in an attempt to find out where the mines are located—without getting blown up. Turn over the wrong tile, and you're history!

This might sound a little confusing at first. After all, you're supposed to uncover the mines, right? Well, not exactly. Your goal is to flip over all the tiles *surrounding* the tile that hides the bomb. When you flip a tile (by clicking it), a number appears in the square to indicate how many surrounding squares contain bombs. These numbers help you determine which tiles are hiding bombs and reduce the risk of blowing yourself up.

Let's start a game, and you'll see how this works:

1. Click the **Start** button, point to **Programs** and then **Games,** and click **Minesweeper** (or click **Start, Programs, Accessories, Games, Minesweeper**). The Minesweeper grid appears, displaying 64 tiles hiding 10 mines.

2. The first move is the most risky. Cross your fingers and click a tile. May the force be with you. If you're lucky, the tile and any neighboring tiles that are not hiding mines flip over, and numbers appear next to some tiles. For example, a 3 means that three bombs are hidden under the eight tiles that surround the 3.

3. Analyze the numbers to predict where a mine is hidden. For example, in the following figure, you know there's a mine under the second tile in the sixth row because of the 1 in the third square of row 5. The only unflipped tile that borders this 1 is the second tile in row 6.

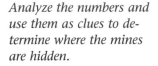

Analyze the numbers and use them as clues to determine where the mines are hidden.

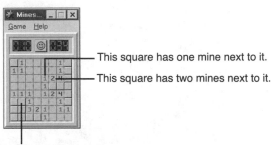

This square has one mine next to it.

This square has two mines next to it.

You know that this tile is hiding a mine because it is the only tile that's next to a square containing the number 1.

4. As you flip tiles, you can right-click a tile that you suspect is hiding a mine. Right-click once to flag the tile, right-click again to place a question mark, or right-click a third time to remove the question mark.

5. Continue flipping and flagging tiles until you blow yourself up or find all 10 mines. When you successfully locate all the mines, the little smiley face at the top of the window dons a pair of sunglasses to help you celebrate. If you mess up, the smiley face turns into a sad face; click the sad face to start over.

Minesweeper offers several options for making the game more interesting and challenging. You can even create your own custom games by specifying the number of tiles and mines to use. (For more challenging games, choose more mines and fewer tiles. For easier games, choose more tiles and fewer mines.) You can find these options on the **Game** menu.

Pinball and Internet Games in Windows Me

If you shelled out a grand for a new computer or plopped down fifty bucks for the Windows Me upgrade, you have a virtual game room on your computer. Not only do you have the classics—Solitaire, FreeCell, Hearts, and Minesweeper—but also you can now play Spider Solitaire, Pinball, and a host of Internet games. Just click the **Start** button, point to **Programs** and then **Games**, and click the desired game. Read through the following list to get up and running in a hurry:

➤ In Pinball, shown in the following figure, hold down the **Spacebar** to pull back the plunger that sends the ball into play, and then release the **Spacebar** to send the ball on its way. The **Z** key works the left flipper, and / works the right flipper. The period key (.) nudges the table to the left, **X** nudges the table to the right, and the up arrow nudges the table up. **F4** toggles between full-screen and window mode. **F2** starts a new game.

➤ To win Spider Solitaire, you drag cards from one stack to another (10 stacks total) to create matching suits in order from king down to ace. When you arrange a stack from king to ace, the stack is removed from the screen. The object is to remove all cards from the screen using the fewest possible moves. After the computer deals the cards, it leaves you with five stacks of cards in the lower-right corner of the screen. When you have no moves, click one of these stacks to deal more cards. (Tip: Avoid using the extra stacks until you absolutely need them.)

➤ If you choose to play any of the Internet games (Backgammon, Checkers, Hearts, Reversi, and Spades) and you have an Internet connection, Windows connects you to Microsoft's game center, Zone.com, and pits you against another player somewhere in the world.

Press Z for this flipper.

Press / for this flipper.

Spacebar pulls the plunger back to serve the ball.

Windows Me comes with a cool arcade game—Pinball.

The Least You Need to Know

➤ The Windows games might not be installed on your computer. Display the Windows Control Panel (**Start, Settings, Control Panel**), double-click the **Add/Remove Programs** icon, and click the **Windows Setup** tab to install missing components.

➤ To run a game, select the desired game from the **Start, Programs, Accessories, Games** menu.

➤ Each game has its own **Help** menu to bring you up to speed.

➤ You play Solitaire in Windows just as you play the game with a real deck of cards, except that you need to know how to click and drag.

➤ When playing FreeCell, don't stick a card in a free cell unless you know that you'll be able to play it in the near future.

➤ When playing Hearts, dump your hearts and the queen of spades on unsuspecting players unless you're pretty sure you can win all hearts and the queen of spades.

➤ To win at Minesweeper, analyze those numbers carefully. Those who guess lose.

➤ To become more productive in Windows, uninstall the computer games and get to work!

Part 2
Personalizing Your Work Space

If you're like most people, you enjoy decorating your home or office to add your own personal touch. You might paint the walls a different color, hang a few photos of friends or family members, or populate your shelves with knickknacks or Beanie Babies.

In similar ways, you can decorate your computer desktop. Windows provides the tools you need to change the color of your desktop, pick a theme for icons and mouse pointers, turn on an animated screen saver, create your own icons and menus, and install additional games and other programs. This part shows you how to completely renovate your computerized desktop.

Chapter 5

Using a Cool Desktop Background

In This Chapter

➤ Jazzing up the appearance of your desktop with themes

➤ Picking your own color scheme

➤ Hanging some self-adhesive wallpaper

➤ Making your desktop look like a Web page

➤ Transforming your desktop into a custom newsroom

➤ Turning on a screen saver included with Windows

Are you tired of your Windows desktop? Do your shortcut icons look dumpy next to those of your friends and colleagues? Do you want to jazz up your work area? Put it in motion with some animated graphics? Make your Windows desktop the envy of your department? Of course you do.

In this chapter, you make your personal computer more personal. Here you learn how to take control of the Windows desktop to make it look and act the way you want it to.

Animating Your Desktop with Themes

Spreading your work out on the standard Windows desktop is about as exciting as spending an eight-hour day in a gray cubicle—the surroundings are anything but inspiring. Fortunately, Windows provides a selection of *desktop themes* to revitalize your working environment. Each desktop theme contains a graphical desktop background and specialized icons, mouse pointers, and sounds. For example, the Jungle theme places a jungle scene on the Windows background and plays animal sounds when certain events occur, such as Windows startup.

Installing Desktop Themes

To use a desktop theme, first be sure that the desktop themes are installed on your computer. Open the **Start** menu, point to **Settings**, and click **Control Panel.** Double-click the **Add/Remove Programs** icon, and then click the **Windows Setup** tab. If the **Desktop Themes** check box is blank, click the box to place a check mark in it. Then insert the Windows CD into your computer's CD-ROM drive, click **OK**, and follow the onscreen instructions. When the installation is complete, you're ready to pick a theme that suits your tastes.

Whoa!

The desktop themes consume about 30 megabytes of disk space. If you're running low on disk space, install only one or two themes. To install selected themes, double-click **Desktop Themes** instead of clicking the check box next to it. Then click the check box next to each theme you want to install.

Whoa!

If your computer seems a bit sluggish after you turn on a desktop theme, you might want to disable it. Desktop themes require disk space and memory that some computers just can't spare.

Picking Your Favorite Desktop Theme

Let the fun begin! Take the following steps to check out the available desktop themes and pick your favorite theme:

1. lick the **Start** button, point to **Settings**, and click **Control Panel.**

2. In the Control Panel, double-click the **Desktop Themes** icon. If you're working in Windows Me, you have a simplified Control Panel that might not show all the Control Panel icons. Click **View all Control Panel options** on the left side of the Control Panel window, then click the **Desktop Themes** icon. The Desktop Themes dialog box appears, as shown in the following figure.

3. Open the **Theme** drop-down list, and choose the desired desktop theme.

4. The selected theme appears in the preview area. To preview the screen saver, click the **Screen Saver** button. (You'll learn more about screen savers near the end of this chapter in the section "Securing Some Privacy with a Screen Saver.")

Select a theme.

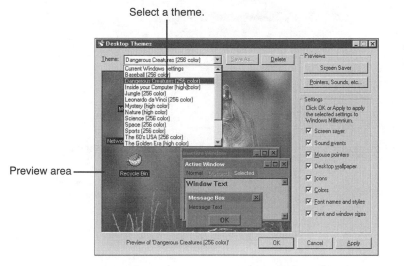

Select the desired desktop theme.

Preview area

5. Windows plays the screen saver. Move the mouse pointer or press the **Shift** key to turn it off.

6. To preview mouse pointers, sounds, and icons, click the **Pointers, Sounds, etc.** button.

7. The Preview window appears. Click the tab for the type of object you want to preview: **Pointers, Sounds,** or **Visuals.** Double-click an item in the list to display it in the preview area or play a sound. When you're done, click the **Close** button.

8. You can disable individual components of the desktop theme by clicking the name of each component to remove the check mark from its box. Click **OK** to save your settings.

Messing with the Screen Colors

A desktop theme makes a nice novelty item, but the color combinations and fonts used in some of the themes can make it almost impossible to decipher the text and get any work done. If you're looking for a more subtle change in the desktop appearance, try tweaking the color scheme yourself.

To try out various color combinations, right-click a blank area of the desktop and click **Properties.** The Display Properties dialog box appears. Click the **Appearance** tab to access the color schemes and options shown in the following figure.

Pick a prefab color scheme or create your own.

Select a scheme from this list.

Select the desired color and/or font.

Select the object whose appearance you want to change.

To change the colors and/or fonts used for the desktop, for windows, and for dialog boxes, here's what you do:

1. Open the **Scheme** drop-down list and click the name of a theme that piques your interest. (You might have to try several themes to find one that's close to your ideal.)

Panic Attack!

I've seen many a desktop with icons that overlap. If your desktop seems overly cluttered, try respacing the icons. In the **Item** list, choose **Icon Spacing (Horizontal)** or **Icon Spacing (Vertical)** and increase the **Size** setting.

2. To change the properties of an object (the desktop, a window's title bar, a button, or some other item), click the object in the preview area in the top part of the dialog box, or open the **Item** drop-down list and click the object's name.

3. Set the desired size and color for the selected object using the **Size** spin box and **Color** drop-down list. (Size is specified in points; there are 72 points per inch.)

4. If the object contains text, use the **Font**, **Size**, and **Color** controls to specify your preferences for the text style, size, and color.

5. Repeat steps 2 through 4 for any other objects whose properties you want to change.

6. Click **OK.**

Hanging Wallpaper in the Background

Have you ever decorated your desk with wallpaper? Of course not! Maybe a new coat of varnish, some paint, or even contact paper, but never wallpaper. Well that's about to change. In Windows, you can use wallpaper to add a more graphic background to your desktop.

To hang wallpaper in Windows, first right-click a blank area of the desktop and click **Properties.** Click the **Background** tab, if necessary, to bring it to the front. In the list of backgrounds, near the bottom of the window, click the name of the desired wallpaper. If the preview area shows a dinky icon in the middle of the screen, open the **Display** drop-down list and click **Tile** (to use the image as a pattern to fill the screen) or **Stretch** (to make the image as big as the desktop). Click **OK.**

You can use a favorite Web page or your own digitized photos or computer graphics as wallpaper. Windows can use any Web page (whose filename ends in .html) and any common image file types (.bmp, .gif, and .jpg) as backgrounds. You can draw an image using the Paint program (included with Windows), scan an image (if you have a scanner), use a digitized photo, or even copy a picture from the Internet. Just be sure you save the image in the proper format—.bmp, .gif, .jpg, .dip, or .png.

The list of backgrounds displays the names of all Web pages and bitmapped (.bmp) files stored in the Windows folder. To use a file stored in a different folder or to use a .gif or .jpg file as the background, click the **Browse** button, change to the disk and folder that contain the Web page or image, and double-click its name. To learn how to change to a disk and folder, see "Save It or Lose It" in Chapter 10, "I Just Want to Type a Letter!"

Inside Tip

To copy an image from the Web, right-click the image, and choose the command for saving the picture. Use the Save As dialog box to save the file to the Windows folder on drive C. To save a Web page, open the page in Internet Explorer, and then open the **File** menu and click **Save As.** For details on how to navigate the Web, skip ahead to Part 4, "Getting Wired to the Internet."

Controlling the Desktop Icons and Visual Effects

A quick glance at the desktop icons might give you the impression that they're immutable. However, Windows does provide a set of options for controlling the appearance and behavior of these icons and other visual elements that make up the desktop.

51

To change the appearance of the icons, right-click a blank area of the Windows desktop and click **Properties**. In the Display Properties dialog box, click the **Effects** tab (see the following figure), and take any of the following steps:

➤ To change the appearance of one of the desktop icons, click the icon, and then click the **Change Icon** button. Click the desired icon and click **OK**.

➤ To display only the icons' names when you choose to view the desktop as a Web page, turn on **Hide icons when the desktop is viewed as a web page.** (This option is unavailable in Windows Me.)

➤ To display larger icons, turn on **Use large icons.**

➤ To make the icons look a little fancier, turn on **Show icons using all possible colors.** (This consumes slightly more memory.)

➤ To make windows, menus, and lists appear to spread out onto the desktop (instead of just popping up onscreen), turn on **Animate windows, menus, and lists** (in Windows 95 or 98) or **Use transition effects for menus and tooltips** (in Windows Me).

➤ To make the onscreen type appear less blocky, turn on **Smooth edges of screen fonts.**

➤ To display the contents of a window while you're dragging it across the screen, turn on **Show window contents while dragging.** (By default, Windows displays only an outline of the window you're dragging.)

When you're done entering your preferences, click **OK** to save your settings and return to the desktop.

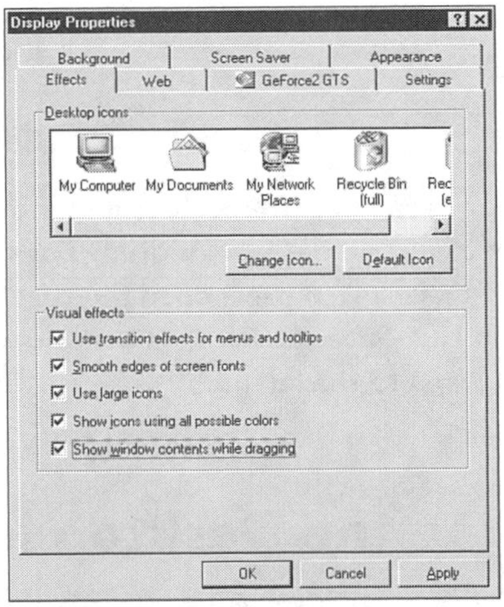

*The **Effects** tab lets you change the appearance of icons and other desktop effects.*

What's This Web Tab For?

Microsoft was a little subtle about unveiling its plot for global domination. There were no great speeches, no press releases, not even the standard printed manifesto. Instead, Microsoft released a new version of Windows 95 that included a deceptively revamped Windows desktop, called the "active desktop," which it then included in Windows 98 and Windows Me.

Although it's nearly identical in appearance to the old desktop, this new desktop includes several features designed to make it more customizable and to integrate it with the Internet (specifically, the Web) and with any of your network connections. Here's a list of what the active desktop has to offer:

➤ **Web Style.** You met Web Style in Chapter 2, "Meeting Windows: Up Close and Personal." With Web Style on, Windows gives you one-click access to your files, folders, and programs.

➤ **Quick Launch toolbar.** You met the Quick Launch toolbar in Chapter 3, "Launching Your First Program." This toolbar and the whole taskbar-toolbar approach give you easy access to the programs you run most often.

➤ **Channel bar.** When you choose to view the desktop as a Web page, the channel bar pops up on the right side of the screen. This bar contains buttons for sites that supposedly have the best content on the Web in Microsoft's judgment. If you're connected to the Internet, you can click one of the channel bar buttons to quickly access a site.

➤ **Active desktop components.** Active desktop components are windows to the Internet. These objects can pull data from the Internet and display it on your desktop to provide you with up-to-the-minute news, stock prices, sports scores, weather reports, and much more. As you will see in this section, you can snatch active desktop components right off the Web.

The **Web** tab (in the Display Properties dialog box) is your key to mastering the active desktop and turning on active desktop components. If you don't have an Internet connection, or if you're not sure whether you do, work through Part 4 first. You can then add active components to your desktop by taking the following steps:

1. Right-click a blank area of the Windows desktop, point to **Active Desktop,** and click **Customize My Desktop.** The Display Properties dialog box appears.

Panic Attack!

If your **New** button is ghosted (appears light gray) and doesn't do anything, Web Style is not on. Click the check mark next to **View my Active Desktop as a web page** or **Show web content on my Active Desktop** to activate the **New** button.

2. Click the **Web** tab. The Web options allow you to view the desktop as a Web page and add components.

3. Click **New.** The New Active Desktop Item dialog box appears, asking if you want to go to the Active Desktop Gallery.

4. Click **Visit Gallery** (in Windows Me) or **Yes** (in Windows 95 or 98). This runs Internet Explorer and connects you to the Internet if you are not already connected. Internet Explorer loads the Active Desktop Gallery Web page.

5. Follow the trail of links to the desktop component you want. A page appears, as shown in the following figure, describing the component and displaying a link or button for downloading it. (A *link* is an icon, graphic, or highlighted text that points to another Web page or file.)

Active desktop components are readily available on the Web.

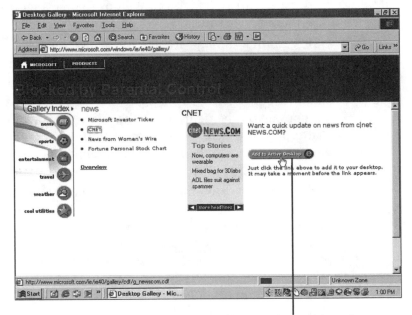

Click the link to add the active component to your desktop.

6. Click the link or button to download (copy) the component and place it on your desktop. Internet Explorer displays a dialog box, asking for your confirmation.

7. Click **Yes.**

8. A second dialog box appears, indicating that Windows will set up a subscription for this component. (A subscription simply tells Windows to download updated information automatically at a scheduled time.) Click **OK.** Internet Explorer downloads the component and places it on the desktop.

Locking Your Desktop Settings

If you share your computer with a colleague at work or with other family members at home, you don't want the other people reconfiguring Windows after you have painstakingly entered your preferences. To prevent others from messing up your desktop, you can set up Windows for multiple users. To do so, take the following steps:

1. Click the **Start** button, point to **Settings**, and click **Control Panel**.

2. Double-click the **Passwords** icon. If you're working in Windows Me, the Control Panel might not display the **Passwords** icon. Click **View all Control Panel options**, on the left side of the Control Panel window; then click the **Passwords** icon.

3. Click the **User Profiles** tab.

4. Make sure the option **Users can customize their preferences and desktop settings** is selected.

5. Make sure both options under **User Profile Settings** are checked.

6. Click **OK.**

When you start Windows, a dialog box prompts you to enter your name and password. Instruct each person who uses your computer to enter a unique name and (optional) password when prompted to log on. Any preferences or desktop settings the user enters are then stored under that person's name. They do not affect settings that the other users enter.

Panic Attack!

If you forget your password, you can still use Windows, but you'll lose your customized settings. Write down your password and keep it in a safe place. If you do lose your password, just press the **Esc** key when Windows prompts you to enter your name. Now, go to the Windows folder on drive C, and find the file that has your username. The file has a .pwl extension, but you might not see the extension. Delete this file and restart Windows. When Windows prompts you to type your name, type your name, type a new password, and click **OK.**

When a user is done using the computer, he or she should log off. To log off, click the **Start** button and choose **Log Off** *yourname* (*yourname* varies, depending on who's logged on). When the confirmation dialog box appears, click **Yes.** (In earlier versions of Windows, you must choose **Start, Shut Down** to display the option for logging off.) Windows restarts without restarting your computer and displays a dialog box prompting the next user for his or her name and password.

Securing Some Privacy with a Screen Saver

Have you ever seen a school of fish swimming across a computer screen? How 'bout a flock of flying toasters? A shower of meteors? A pack of creepy crawling cockroaches? If you've seen any of these animated patterns scurrying about a monitor, you have already witnessed screen savers in action.

In addition to functioning as an interesting conversation piece, screen savers serve a useful purpose: They deter passersby from snooping at your screen while you're away from your desk. For example, if you play Solitaire all day at work and you don't want your boss to know about it, you can activate a screen saver whenever you step away from your desk. You can even set up the screen saver with password protection so that nobody can turn it off without knowing the password.

Inside Tip

The best screen savers that are included with Windows are part of the desktop themes. If you selected a theme earlier in this chapter, you have already selected a screen saver. The following sections show you how to change the screen saver's properties.

Checking Out the Windows Screen Savers

Windows comes with several of its own screen savers. To check out the selection, right-click a blank area of the Windows desktop, click **Properties,** and click the **Screen Saver** tab. Open the **Screen Saver** drop-down list and click the name of a screen saver that appeals to you, as shown in the following figure. To view the screen saver in action, click the **Preview** button. To deactivate the screen saver (and return to the Display Properties dialog box), roll the mouse or press the **Shift** key.

Even if you installed the desktop themes, your list of screen savers might come up a little short. Some Windows screen savers, including the popular Scrolling Marquee, are not installed during a typical Windows installation. Run Windows Setup again (**Start, Control Panel, Add/Remove Programs, Windows Setup** tab), double-click **Accessories,** and be sure the **Screen Savers** check box is clear (not gray) and is checked. Click **OK,** and then click **OK** again to save your changes and exit Windows Setup.

The Scrolling Marquee is great for keeping family members and co-workers informed when you're away from your desk. Open the **Screen Saver** list and click **Scrolling Marquee.** Click the **Settings** button. Drag over the text in the **Text** box, type the desired message, and click **OK.** Click **OK** to save your changes and close the Display Properties dialog box. When the Scrolling Marquee screen saver kicks in, it displays your message, scrolling across the screen.

Check out the screen savers included with Windows.

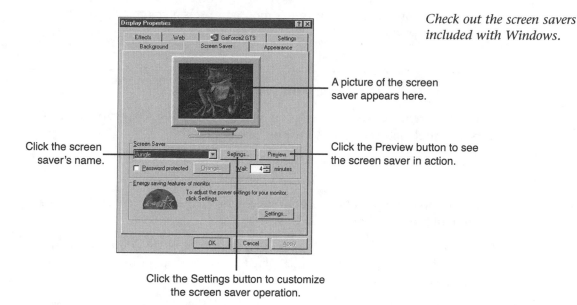

A picture of the screen saver appears here.

Click the screen saver's name.

Click the Preview button to see the screen saver in action.

Click the Settings button to customize the screen saver operation.

Turning a Screen Saver On and Off

To turn on a screen saver, first select the desired screen saver, as explained in the preceding section. Click the arrows to the right of the **Wait ___ Minutes** spin box to specify how long your system must remain inactive (no typing and no mouse movement) before the screen saver kicks in. To specify how the screen saver operates (for example, the number of flying windows), click the **Settings** button, enter your preferences, and click **OK** to return to the Display Properties dialog box. To save your settings, click **OK.**

When your computer has been inactive for the specified period of time, the screen saver kicks in. To turn off the screen saver, simply move the mouse or press the **Shift** key.

Using a Password for Weak Security

Don't let that **Password protected** option next to the screen saver lull you into a false sense of security. The screen saver password is designed only to prevent someone from taking a quick peak at your screen. As a deterrent against computer hackers, it's about as effective as locking your bike with a paper-clip chain. If someone wants to use your computer, all the person has to do is turn it off, turn it back on, and then disable the screen saver before it kicks in.

However, if you're looking for some free security, the screen saver password is better than nothing. To make the screen saver require a password, click the **Password protected** check box, and then click the **Change** button. Type the desired password in the **New password** and **Confirm new password** text boxes, and click **OK.** Whenever you return to your computer and move the mouse or press a key to turn off the screen saver, it will prompt you to enter your password.

The Least You Need to Know

➤ To install or remove Windows features, run **Add/Remove Programs** from the Control Panel, and click the **Windows Setup** tab.

➤ To preview and select from available desktop themes, click the **Desktop Themes** icon in the Windows Control Panel.

➤ To access most customization options for the desktop, right-click a blank area of the desktop and click **Properties.**

➤ To change the size, color, and font used for a feature of the Windows desktop, click the **Appearance** tab in the Display Properties dialog box and use the settings available there.

➤ To give your desktop a graphic background, select the desired wallpaper on the **Background** tab in the Display Properties dialog box.

➤ To prevent other users from changing your desktop settings, use the **Passwords** icon in the Control Panel to set up your computer for multiple users.

➤ To turn on a screen saver, right-click the Windows desktop, click **Properties,** click the **Screen Saver** tab, open the **Screen Saver** drop-down list, and click the desired screen saver.

Chapter 6

Making Your Computer Play Cool Sounds

In This Chapter

➤ Testing your sound card and speakers

➤ Adjusting the volume and balance

➤ Making Windows play some different tunes

➤ Playing audio CDs while you work

➤ Turning your computer into a recording studio

In addition to the beeps and grunts your computer emits at startup, it's capable of producing more refined tones. When you start Windows, for instance, it ushers itself in with heavenly harp music or some other short audio clip. When you open a menu, close a window, or exit a program, Windows plays a unique audio clip for each of these actions or *events*. If you listen closely as you work in Windows, you'll be able to link each sound with its event.

If you keep listening closely (over several weeks), these sounds might start to annoy you and inspire an overwhelming desire to smash your speakers. Before you take such drastic action, read through this chapter. Here you'll learn how to pick a different sound scheme, assign different sounds to various Windows events, and even mute your system altogether. As an added bonus, this chapter shows you how to play audio CDs in your computer's CD-ROM drive.

Checking Your Audio Equipment

If you've ever prepared for a speech or presentation, you know how important it is to test your equipment before show time. After setting up and turning on the microphone, you hold it a few inches from your mouth and do the standard "Testing ... one ... two ... testing ..." thing. Well, before you start messing with audio clips in Windows, you should test your sound card and speakers to be sure they are operating properly. Here's what you do:

1. Open the **Start** menu, point to **Settings**, and click **Control Panel**.

2. Double-click the **Sounds** icon. The Sounds and Multimedia Properties dialog box appears, as shown in the following figure. If you're working in Windows Me and you don't see the **Sounds** icon, click **View all Control Panel options** on the left side of the Control Panel window.

Use the Sounds and Multimedia Properties dialog box to test your computer's audio output.

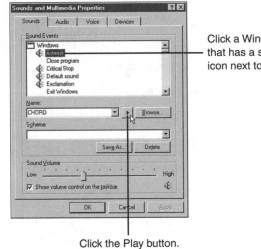

Click a Windows event that has a speaker icon next to it.

Click the Play button.

3. Click the name of a Windows event that has a speaker icon next to it, and then click the **Play** button (next to the **Browse** button).

At this point, Windows should play the audio clip that's assigned to the selected event. If you can't hear the clip, try adjusting the volume (as explained in the next section), or skip ahead to the troubleshooting section to track down less-obvious causes.

Adjusting the Volume

The big problem with computer audio is that there are too many volume controls. You might find a volume control on the sound card (where the speakers plug in), on the speakers, and in Windows. In addition, if you're playing a computer game that has audio clips (most do), it might have its own volume control!

The trick to adjusting the volume is to start with the obvious controls first: the volume dials on the sound card and speakers. Set these controls to the desired level. If you're not sure which way to turn them, set them at the halfway point.

Next, check the volume control in Windows. Right-click the speaker icon in the lower-right corner of your screen, and click **Open Volume Controls** to display the Volume Control (or Play Control) window. (The Volume Control window's name varies, depending on your system's audio hardware, but the basic controls should be similar.) Open the **Options** menu and click **Properties**. In the **Show the following volume controls** list, be sure each check box (except **PC Speaker**) is marked, and then click **OK**. This gives you access to all the available volume controls, as shown in the following figure.

Drag a Balance slider to the left or
right to change the balance.

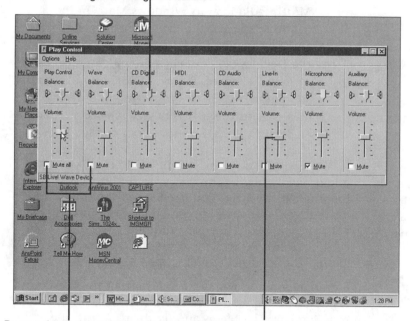

The Play Control (or Volume Control) window lets you set the volume and balance.

Be sure the Mute and Mute
All options are not checked.

Drag a Volume or Play Control slider up to
increase volume or down to decrease it.

Be sure the **Mute** option below each control is *not* checked (**Mute** disables a device). The **Mute all** option, below the leftmost control, can mute all the controls; make absolutely sure **Mute all** is *not* checked. Drag the slider for each volume control to the desired position. Repeat the steps from the preceding section to test the volume settings and readjust the settings as desired.

Tech Term

On the right end of the taskbar is a reserved area that displays the current time, the speaker icon, and icons for other programs that Windows is running in the background. (When Windows is printing a document, a little printer icon appears.) This area is known as the **system tray.**

Panic Attack!

If the **Scheme** list provides only the **Windows Default** and **No Sounds** options, the schemes are not installed. Run **Add/Remove Programs** from the Control Panel, click the **Windows Setup** tab, double-click **Multimedia,** and be sure **Multimedia Sound Schemes** is selected. Pop in the Windows CD, click **OK** to close the Multimedia dialog box, and click **OK** again to start the installation.

Troubleshooting Audio Problems

So you've adjusted all the volume controls, and you still can't get a peep out of your computer. What's the problem? Read through the following list to check for the most common causes of computer audio problems:

➤ Are the speakers plugged into the right jack on the sound card? (It's easy to plug the speakers into the microphone or input jack by mistake.)

➤ If you have amplified speakers, are they plugged into a power source? If the speakers have a power switch or button, are the speakers turned on?

➤ Are the audio features enabled for the sound card? In the Windows Control Panel, double-click the **Multimedia** icon (or the **Sounds and Multimedia** icon in Windows Me). On the **Audio** tab, under **Playback**, open the **Preferred Device** list and choose your sound card. Click the **Devices** tab, and click the plus sign (+) next to **Audio Devices**. Right-click the name of your sound card and click **Properties**. Be sure **Use audio features on this device** is selected, and click **OK**. Click **OK** to save your changes.

If Windows still doesn't play the audio clips, you might need to dig a little deeper to find the cause of the problem. Perhaps, you need to reinstall the sound card's driver, or maybe the sound card is conflicting with another device on your computer. (A conflict occurs when two devices try to use the same settings and/or resources at the same time.)

Fortunately, Windows has a collection of troubleshooters that can help you track down the causes of common hardware problems and fix them. To run the Sound troubleshooter, display the Windows Help screen (choose **Start, Help**), and then take one of the following steps:

➤ In Windows Me, click the **Troubleshooting** link, click **Audio-visual problems**, click **Sound troubleshooter,** and follow the onscreen instructions; the troubleshooter displays a series of questions to lead you through the process of fixing the problem.

➤ In Windows 95 or 98, click the **Contents** tab, click **Troubleshooting** (at the bottom of the list), and click **Windows 98 Troubleshooters.** Click **Sound,** and follow the onscreen instructions.

Choosing a Different Sound Scheme

When you're certain that your audio system is working properly, you can try out various sound schemes included with Windows. A sound scheme is a collection of audio clips assigned to various Windows events (such as opening or exiting a program).

To check out different sound schemes, double-click the **Sounds** icon in the Windows Control Panel (or **Sounds and Multimedia** in Windows Me), as explained previously in "Checking Your Audio Equipment." Open the **Scheme** list, and click the name of the sound scheme you want to try (refer to the following figure). Click the **OK** button.

Assigning Specific Sounds to Events

Picking a sound scheme is like choosing a vacation package. Each scheme provides all the settings you need for a consistent, thematic sound. If you want more control over which sounds Windows plays for the various events, you can assign a specific audio clip to each event.

To assign audio clips to events, display the Sounds and Multimedia Properties dialog box as explained earlier in this chapter. In the **Sound Events** list, click the event whose sound you want to change. Open the **Name** list and click the name of the desired audio clip, as shown in the following figure. To preview the sound, click the **Play** button (to the left of **Browse**). To save your settings, click **OK**.

Inside Tip

In Part 4, "Getting Wired to the Internet," when you start poking around on the Internet, you might stumble upon some cool audio files. If the filename ends in .wav, you can assign the audio file to a Windows event. Save the file to the Windows/Media folder on your hard drive, and it will appear in the Sound list.

Windows lets you assign specific sounds to individual Windows events.

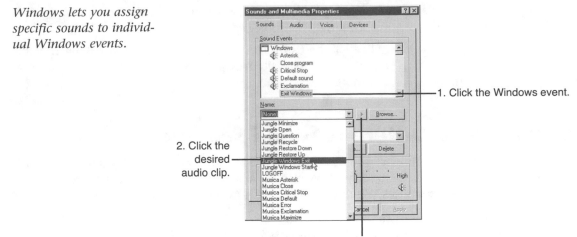

1. Click the Windows event.

2. Click the desired audio clip.

3. Click the Play button to play the clip.

Listening to CDs While You Work

Do you like to listen to some relaxing background music while you work? Well, just pop your favorite CD into the CD-ROM drive and start jammin'! If your computer has a sound card, the audio will play through the speakers. If not, plug a set of headphones into the headphone jack on the CD-ROM drive. (If you plug in headphones, control the volume by using the volume control on the CD-ROM drive.)

Windows should start to play the audio CD as soon as you insert it. If Windows does not start to play the CD, Alt+click **My Computer**, and then click the **Device Manager** tab. Click the plus sign (+) next to **CDROM**, and then double-click the name of your CD-ROM. Click the **Settings** tab, and be sure there is a check mark in the **Auto Insert Notification** box. Click **OK** to save your changes, and then click **OK** again to close the System Properties dialog box. With **Auto Insert Notification** turned on, Windows should start playing your audio CD as soon as you insert it.

Panic Attack!

If your CD-ROM drive has no headphone jack or volume control, don't worry. Manufacturers are finally beginning to realize that the additional jack and volume control are superfluous. Just plug your headphones into the speaker jack on your sound card.

Windows Me uses a utility called Media Player to play the CD (see the following figure). Earlier versions of Windows (Windows 95 and 98) use a utility called CD Player, which isn't quite as snazzy but plays audio CDs just as well. If the Media Player or CD Player window does not appear immediately, it might start as a minimized window; click its button in the taskbar. If the player didn't start, click the Windows **Start** button, point to **Programs** and then to **Entertainment**, and click the option for running the player. You can use the player's buttons just as you would the buttons on any standard audio CD player.

To learn more about playing CDs, copying tracks from CDs to your hard drive, creating your own custom play lists, and downloading and playing audio clips on the Internet, see Chapter 28, "Playing Digitized Music Clips." Chapter 28 even shows you how to copy audio clips to a portable MP3 player to take your show on the road.

Click CD Audio.

Click Play to start playing the CD.

Click Stop to turn it off.

Go back to the previous track.

Fast-forward to the next track.

Media Player lets you use your computer as a standard audio CD player.

Recording Your Own Audio Clips

Now that you know how to assign sounds to Windows events and play audio CDs, you're ready to completely customize the Windows sound machine. Using the Windows Sound Recorder, you can record your own voice (if you have a microphone) or snippets from audio CDs, save your recordings as files, and then attach them to specific Windows events! Sounds pretty cool, eh? But first, you need to run Sound Recorder and use it to "tape" audio clips.

To run Sound Recorder in Windows 98 or Windows Me, open the **Start** menu, point to **Programs**, **Accessories**, **Entertainment**, and then click **Sound**

Panic Attack!

Many musical groups now put out CDs that include music videos, digitized photos, and other multimedia offerings. Don't be surprised if a menu or program pops up on your screen when you insert an apparently ordinary audio CD.

Recorder. (In Windows 95, select **Start, Programs, Accessories, Multimedia, Sound Recorder.**) The Sound Recorder appears, as shown in the following figure. Recording your voice is easy: Click the **Record** button, speak into the microphone, and then click the **Stop** button. Recording bits of music from CDs is a little tougher, because you must flip back and forth between Sound Recorder and CD Player—you have to be pretty fast with the mouse.

When you're done recording, open Sound Recorder's **File** menu and select **Save.** Type a name for the file. Unless you specify otherwise, Sound Recorder saves the recording as a .wav file and tacks on the .wav extension to the filename. If you plan to attach the sound to a Windows event, change to the Windows/Media folder before you click the **Save** button. To attach your new recording to a Windows event, follow the instructions given in the earlier section "Assigning Specific Sounds to Events."

You can use Sound Recorder to record your voice or audio CD clips.

3. Open the File menu and click Save to save the recording as a file.

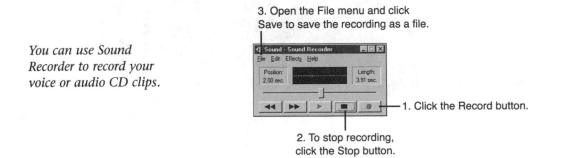

1. Click the Record button.

2. To stop recording, click the Stop button.

The Least You Need to Know

➤ To access the volume controls, double-click the speaker icon on the right end of the taskbar.

➤ To check out the Windows sound schemes, double-click the **Sounds** or **Sounds and Multimedia** icon in the Windows Control Panel.

➤ To pick a different sound scheme, open the **Scheme** list in the Sounds and Multimedia Properties dialog box and click the desired sound scheme.

➤ To assign a different sound to a Windows event, click the event in the Sounds and Multimedia Properties dialog box, and then choose the desired sound from the **Name** list.

➤ To play an audio CD, just pop it into your computer's CD-ROM drive.

➤ You can use Sound Recorder to record your voice, sound effects, or clips from audio CDs, and then you can attach those sounds to Windows events.

Mmmph....

Chapter 7

Taking Control of Your Menus and Programs

In This Chapter

➤ Rearranging your **Start** menu with Windows Explorer

➤ Transforming the Windows desktop into a toolbar

➤ Transforming a folder into a toolbar

➤ Scheduling programs to run automatically

If you've ever spent a few hours cleaning and reorganizing your office, you know that, with a little effort, you can transform your office from a disorganized mess into a model of neatness and efficiency. The same is true of the Windows desktop.

By putting in a little time up front, you can redesign your desktop to conform to the way you work. You can place commands in more convenient locations on the **Start** menu, make your own desktop icons, transform folders into toolbars, and use Task Scheduler to automatically run programs for you. By the end of this chapter, you'll have the Windows desktop of your dreams!

Rearranging the Start Menu with Explorer

In Chapter 3, "Launching Your First Program," you learned how to drag program groups and individual programs to different locations on the **Start** menu. In the process, you probably noticed that dragging and dropping items on the **Start** menu is not the smoothest operation around. As you drag an object, menus open and close, making it difficult for you to drop the object in a precise location.

An easier way to rearrange items is to display the **Start** menu as a folder in Windows Explorer and then drag icons from one of the **Start** menu's folders to another. Try it yourself:

1. Right-click the **Start** button and click **Explore.** This starts Windows Explorer, which opens the **Start** folder.

2. Click the plus sign next to **Programs**, and then click the plus sign next to any subfolders that appear below the Programs folder.

3. To move a submenu, drag its icon to the desired location in the folder list. For example, to move the **Accessories** menu to the top of the **Start** menu, drag the Accessories folder over the Start folder. (To move it back to its original location, drag the Accessories folder over the Programs folder.)

4. To move a program, first change to the folder that currently contains the program (in the folder list on the left).

5. In the folder list, be sure you can see the destination folder (the folder to which you want to move the program).

6. Drag the program's icon from the file list (on the right) over the destination folder, and release the mouse button (see the following figure).

*Windows Explorer is a great tool for restructuring your **Start** menu.*

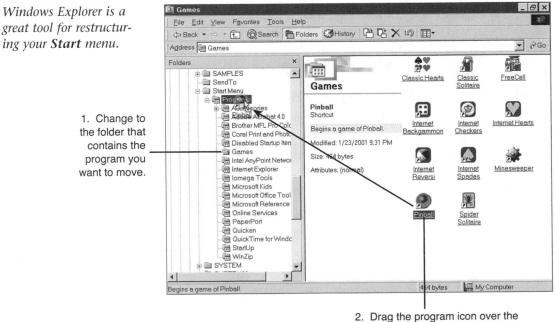

1. Change to the folder that contains the program you want to move.

2. Drag the program icon over the desired destination folder.

68

To turn off any of the toolbars, right-click a blank area of the taskbar, point to **Toolbars**, and click the name of the toolbar you want to turn off.

Automating Your Programs

I have one of those fancy coffee pots that brews a fresh pot of coffee every morning just before I roll out of bed—assuming I remember to feed it coffee and water before I hit the sack. Wouldn't it be great if Windows could run your favorite programs for you?

Well, you'll be happy to hear that Windows can do just that. With the Windows Task Scheduler, you simply tell Windows the days of the week and time of day you want it to run the program, and Windows runs the program at the scheduled time(s). Not only is Task Scheduler useful for running the programs you use most often, but it's great for running disk cleanup and maintenance utilities on a regular basis.

To schedule a program to run, take the following steps:

1. Open the **Start** menu, point to **Programs**, **Accessories**, **System Tools**, and then click the **Scheduled Tasks** icon. The Scheduled Tasks window appears.

2. Click or double-click the **Add Scheduled Task** icon. This runs the Scheduled Task Wizard.

3. Read the Task Scheduler overview, and then click **Next**.

4. Click the program you want Task Scheduler to run, as shown in the following figure, and click **Next**.

Computer Cheat

Instead of taking the standard steps for creating a toolbar, you can simply drag any folder from My Computer or Windows Explorer over a blank area of the taskbar and release the mouse button. Windows automatically converts the folder into a toolbar.

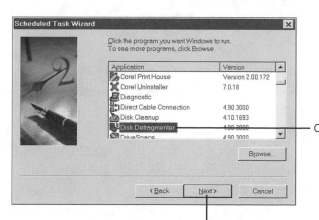

Click Next.

Pick the program you want Task Scheduler to run for you.

Click the program's name.

5. Choose how often you want Task Scheduler to run the program, and then click **Next.** (For example, you can have Task Scheduler run the program daily, weekly, one time only, or whenever you start your computer.)

6. Specify the time of day and the days of the week on which you want Task Scheduler to run the program.

7. (Optional) Click **Open Advanced Properties** and enter additional preferences for running the program. (The available options vary from one program to another, so you'll have to improvise here.)

8. Click **Finish.**

Computer Cheat

To have a program automatically run at startup, make a shortcut icon for the program, and move it to the **Start, Programs, StartUp** folder.

When Task Scheduler is running, its icon appears in the system tray (at the right end of the taskbar). To disable Task Scheduler (prevent it from running programs), double-click its icon, open the **Advanced** menu, and click **Stop Using Task Scheduler.**

The Least You Need to Know

➤ To display the contents of the **Start** menu in Windows Explorer, right-click the **Start** button and click **Explore.**

➤ To turn on the Desktop toolbar, right-click a blank area on the taskbar, point to **Toolbars,** and click **Desktop.**

➤ To transform any folder into a toolbar, drag the folder icon over a blank area of the taskbar and release the mouse button.

➤ Use the Task Scheduler to automatically run a favorite program on specified days and times.

➤ When Task Scheduler is running, an icon for it appears in the taskbar.

Chapter 8

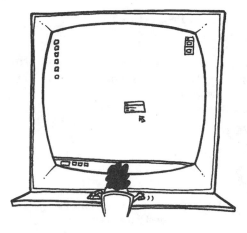

Giving Yourself More Room to Work

In This Chapter

➤ Shrinking your desktop icons down to size

➤ Messing with your display's color settings

➤ Trashing icons you don't use

➤ Hiding the taskbar when you don't need it

➤ Reorganizing your desktop with folders

Your Windows desktop can become every bit as cluttered and unmanageable as a real-life desktop. Fortunately, your Windows desktop is much easier to tidy up. You can shrink everything on your desktop to give yourself more room, rearrange the icons, dump icons that you don't use, hide the taskbar, and even tuck icons in separate folders to keep them out of the way.

Sound like fun? Heck no, but by learning to organize your desktop, you can work more efficiently and give yourself more time to do the fun stuff. This chapter shows you just what to do.

Clearing Desk Space by Making Everything Smaller

Wouldn't it be great if you could grab the edges of your monitor and stretch it? Maybe turn your 15-inch monitor into a big-screen, 21-inch version? Well, you can't, but you can do the next best thing—shrink everything on the desktop to give yourself a little more real estate. Here's what you do:

1. Right-click a blank area of the desktop and click **Properties.**

2. Click the **Settings** tab.

3. Drag the **Screen area** slider to the right one or more notches, as shown in the following figure. As you drag, watch the preview area to see how the new setting affects the display.

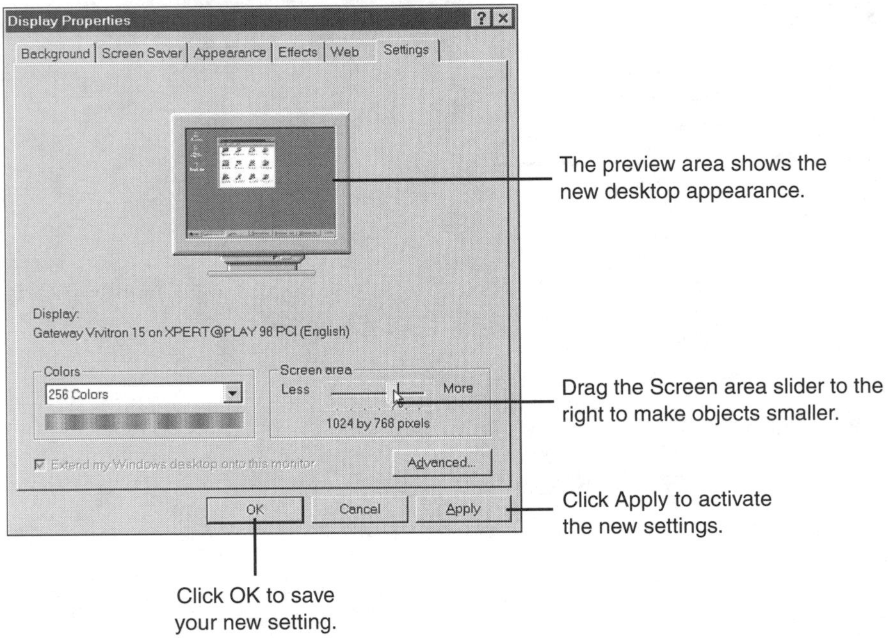

The preview area shows the new desktop appearance.

Drag the Screen area slider to the right to make objects smaller.

Click Apply to activate the new settings.

Click OK to save your new setting.

You can't make your display bigger, but you can make everything on it smaller.

4. When the preview area shows the desired desktop appearance (or the slider won't budge), click **Apply.**

5. Click **OK** to save your settings.

What About the Color Settings?

As you were fiddling around with the screen area setting, you might have noticed the **Colors** drop-down list off to the left (refer to the preceding figure). This list provides options for increasing or decreasing the number of colors used to display everything from icons to digitized photos. With more colors at its disposal, the monitor can display high-quality images more realistically.

So you want the highest setting possible, right? Well, not exactly. To display additional colors, your computer's display card and processor must work a little harder. Additional colors also consume more memory. The basic approach here is to choose the lowest setting that provides satisfactory quality. I set my display to 256 colors, which does a fairly good job of displaying photos and other detailed graphics. If you do any photo or video editing, you might want to bump up the setting.

Rearranging Your Desktop Icons

Although the icons on the desktop provide convenient access to all your programs and files, you can get a little carried away with them. In about 15 minutes, you can completely cover the surface of the desktop with shortcuts, making it nearly impossible to find anything. Fortunately, Windows has several tools to help you reorganize the icons on your desktop. Try the following techniques:

➤ To move an icon, drag it to the desired location.

➤ To have Windows rearrange the icons for you, right-click the desktop, point to **Arrange Icons,** and click **By Name, By Size, By Type,** or **By Date.**

➤ To have Windows line up the icons without rearranging them by name, size, type, or date, right-click the desktop and click **Line Up Icons.**

➤ To have Windows automatically line up icons when you move them, right-click the desktop, point to **Arrange Icons,** and click **Auto Arrange.**

Panic Attack!

Can't read the icon names? Don't worry. You can make some adjustments. Open the Display Properties dialog box again. To make the text bigger, click the **Settings** tab, click the **Advanced** button, and choose **Large fonts.** If icons overlap, click the **Appearance** tab, choose one of the **Icon spacing** options (**Vertical** or **Horizontal**) from the **Item** list, and increase the spacing.

Inside Tip

A fancy desktop packed with animated shortcuts and fancy wallpaper is cool, but all that fancy stuff consumes precious resources. To keep your computer running at top speed, opt for a clean, simple desktop.

Getting Rid of Icons You Don't Use

The best way to clear space on your desktop is to delete the icons you never use. First, select the icon you want to delete. If Web Style is on, point to the icon; if Web Style is off, click the icon. Ctrl+point or Ctrl+click to select additional icons. Then drag any one of the selected icons over the **Recycle Bin** icon and release the mouse button. Windows displays a dialog box asking for your confirmation. Click **Yes.**

Remember, if you delete an icon or other object by mistake, you can get it back. Double-click the **Recycle Bin** icon, click the icon that you accidentally deleted, and then open the **File** menu and click **Restore.**

Inside Tip

If you try to move an icon and it jumps to a different location, Auto Arrange is on. To turn it off, right–click the desktop, point to **Arrange Icons,** and click **Auto Arrange.**

Computer Cheat

To quickly delete icons, files, or folders, right–click any one of the selected items and click **Delete.**

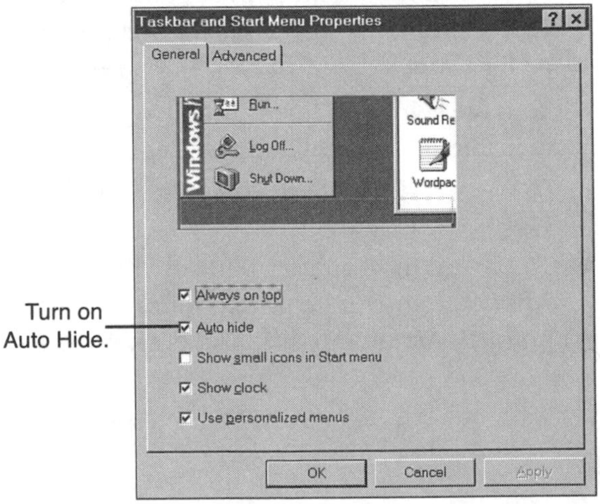

Give yourself some elbow-room.

Hiding the Taskbar

The taskbar is a great tool to have around, but when you're working on a document, playing a game, or viewing a Web page, you need that extra half-inch of screen space where the taskbar resides. To reclaim the space, make the taskbar hide itself when you're doing other stuff:

1. Right-click a blank area of the taskbar and click **Properties.**

2. Click **Auto hide,** as shown in the following figure.

3. Click **OK.**

Turn on Auto Hide.

Inside Tip

To make your taskbar larger, move the mouse pointer over the taskbar's top edge, so that the pointer appears as a two-headed arrow, and then drag up. With Auto hide on, you don't have to worry about the taskbar taking up too much screen space.

As you work, the taskbar hides below the bottom of the screen (unless you moved the taskbar to a different edge of the screen). To bring the taskbar back into view, simply move the mouse pointer to the edge of the screen where the taskbar normally appears.

Tucking Stuff in Folders

Another trick for cleaning up your desktop is to stuff icons into folders. For example, you might have one folder for all your business programs, another for games, and a separate folder for documents you commonly work on. To make a new folder, right-click the desktop, point to **New**, and click **Folder.** Type a name for the folder, and then click outside the icon to save the name.

After you have a folder in place, you can move icons from the desktop by simply dragging and dropping the icons onto the new folder icon.

Inside Tip

After moving the shortcut icons to your new folder, drag and drop the folder icon to the top, left, or right edge of the screen or over the taskbar to create a toolbar containing buttons for all the shortcuts in the folder.

The Least You Need to Know

➤ Use the Display Properties dialog box to shrink everything on the desktop and increase your work area.

➤ If you mess with your display's **Colors** setting, choose a setting of 256 colors or more.

➤ To have Windows automatically arrange the icons on the desktop, right-click the desktop, point to **Arrange,** and click **Auto Arrange.**

➤ If you don't use a particular shortcut icon, drag it to the Recycle Bin.

➤ To hide the taskbar, right-click it, choose **Properties,** and turn on **Auto hide.**

➤ To create a folder, right-click the desktop, point to **New,** and click **Folder.**

Chapter 9

Installing and Removing Programs

In This Chapter

➤ Picking programs your computer can run

➤ Finding out if your computer has room for a new program

➤ Installing a program in 10 minutes or less

➤ Running CD-ROM programs

➤ Getting rid of the programs you don't use

For me, the term "install" triggers flashbacks to the weekend I spent installing our new water heater. I envision misplaced tools, lost parts, leaking pipes, and a badly bruised ego.

Although installing a program is typically less traumatic, the process can have similar, unforeseen problems. For instance, you might pick up the wrong version of the program—the Macintosh version rather than the Windows version. Or the program might have a quirky installation routine that doesn't install all the components you need.

This chapter is designed to help you avoid the most common pitfalls, deal with unexpected problems, and successfully install your new programs.

Buying Software That Your Hardware Can Run

Even the most experienced computer user occasionally slips up and buys a program that his or her computer can't run. The person might own a PC running Windows and pick up the Macintosh version of the program by mistake. Or maybe the program requires special audio or video equipment that the person doesn't have.

Before you purchase any program, read the minimum hardware requirements that are printed on the outside of the package to determine if your computer has what it takes to run the program:

Computer type. Typically, you can't run a Macintosh program on an IBM-compatible computer (a *PC* or *personal computer* that runs *Windows*). If you have a PC, be sure the program is for an IBM PC or compatible computer. (Some programs include both the Macintosh and PC versions.)

Operating system. Try to find programs that are designed specifically for the operating system you use. If your computer is running Windows 98, don't buy a program developed for Windows Me. (Although Windows Me can run most applications designed for Windows 98, Windows 98 might have problems running some Windows Me programs.)

Free hard disk space. When you install a program, the installation routine copies files from the installation disks or CDs to the hard disk. Be sure your hard disk has enough free disk space, as explained in the next section.

CPU requirements. CPU stands for *central processing unit*. This is the brain of the computer. If the program requires at least a Pentium III processor, and you have a Pentium II, your computer won't be able to run the application effectively.

Tech Term

Throughout this book, I use the terms "program," "application," and "software" interchangeably. These terms all refer to the instructions that tell a computer how to perform specific tasks.

Type of monitor. All newer monitors are SVGA (Super Video Graphics Array) or better, and most programs don't require anything better than SVGA. Some games and graphics programs require a specific type of display card, such as a 3D card or an advanced video card.

Mouse. If you use Windows, you need a mouse (or some other pointing device). A standard two-button Microsoft mouse is sufficient. Some programs have special features you can use only with an IntelliMouse.

Joystick. Although most computer games allow you to use your keyboard, games are usually more fun if you have a joystick.

CD-ROM or DVD-ROM drive. If you have a CD-ROM or DVD-ROM drive, it usually pays to get the CD-ROM or DVD-ROM version of the application instead of using a floppy-disk version. This simplifies the program installation, and the CD or DVD version might come with a few extras. Check for the required speed of the drive as well.

Sound card. Most new applications require sound cards. If you plan on running any cool games, using a multimedia encyclopedia, or even exploring the Internet, you'll need a sound card. Some applications can use an old 8-bit sound card, but newer applications require a 16-bit or better sound card, which enables stereo output.

Amount of memory (RAM). If your computer does not have the required memory (also known as *RAM*, short for *Random Access Memory*), it might not be able to run the program, or the program might cause the computer to crash (freeze).

Tech Term

Many people confuse memory with disk space. Your computer uses **memory** to store data and software instructions temporarily while your computer is actively processing the data and instructions. Memory provides the computer with fast access to data and instructions, but when you turn off your computer, whatever is stored in memory is erased. **Disk storage,** on the other hand, stores data and instructions permanently. When your computer needs data or instructions, it reads from the disk and stores the information in memory, where it can process it.

You can find out most of what you need to know from the System Properties dialog box. Hold down **Alt** and double-click **My Computer** to display the System Properties dialog box, as shown in the following figure. The **General** tab displays the operating system type and version number, the type of processor, and the amount of RAM. Click the **Device Manager** tab and click the plus sign next to a device type to view the make and model number. For instance, click the plus sign next to **Display Adapters** to determine the type of video card that's installed.

The System Properties dialog box can tell you a lot about your computer.

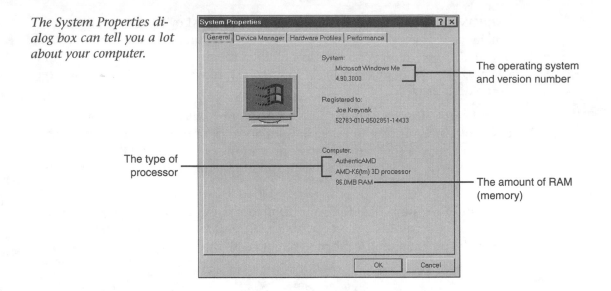

The operating system and version number

The type of processor

The amount of RAM (memory)

For more detailed system information, check out the Windows System Information tool. Open the **Start** menu, point to **Programs, Accessories, System Tools**, and click **System Information.** (If **System Information** is not on the menu, you must install it from the Windows CD. Open the Windows Control Panel, click **Add/Remove Programs**, click the **Windows Setup** tab, and be sure **System Tools** is checked.)

Inside Tip

Before you go shopping for programs, tear out the Savvy Software Shopper's Form at the front of this book and make some copies of it. Use the forms to record each program's minimum hardware requirements.

Do You Have Enough Disk Space?

Most new computers sport a multi-gigabyte hard drive that has enough free space to last you well into the twenty-first century. However, you should be sure that your new program will fit on the disk before you start the installation. If you try to stuff a program on a hard disk that's nearly full, you'll have some serious warning messages to deal with, and you can count on your system's locking up sometime during the procedures.

Checking the available disk space is easy. Right-click the icon for your hard disk drive in My Computer or Windows Explorer, and click **Properties**. The Properties dialog box displays the total disk space, the amount in use, and the amount that's free, as shown in the following figure.

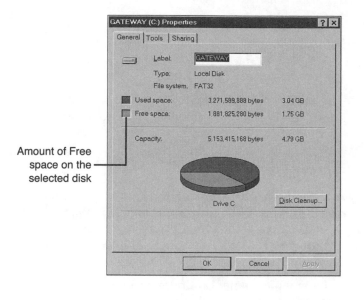

Windows displays the available space remaining on the disk.

Amount of Free space on the selected disk

Inside Tip

Many programs create temporary files and then forget to delete them. Click **Start, Find, Files or Folders** (or **Start, Search, For Files or Folders** in Windows Me). In the **Named** text box, type *.tmp. In the **Look in** text box, select the disk you want to search, or type c:\ to search drive C. Be sure **Include subfolders** is selected (in Windows Me, click **Search Options** and then click **Advanced Options**). Click **Find Now** or **Search Now.** Open the **Edit** menu, choose **Select All,** and then press the **Delete** key.

If your hard disk does not have sufficient free space for installing the program, you can free up some disk space by taking the following steps:

➤ Display the disk's Properties dialog box. On the **General** tab, click the **Disk Cleanup** button (refer to the preceding figure), and follow the onscreen instructions to clear unnecessary files from the disk. If you have an older version of Windows (Windows 3.1 or Windows 95 without the Internet Explorer upgrade), the **Disk Cleanup** button is unavailable.

➤ Uninstall any programs you no longer use, as explained later in this chapter.

➤ Be sure the Recycle Bin does not contain any files you might need by double-clicking the **Recycle Bin** icon. To empty the Recycle Bin, open the **File** menu and click **Empty Recycle Bin.**

➤ Run Windows Setup again, as explained in Chapter 4, "Warming Up with Some Computer Games," and remove any Windows components you no longer use.

Installing Your New Program

Nearly every program on the market comes with an installation component (called Setup or Install) that does everything for you. If the program is on CD-ROM, you can usually pop the disc into your CD-ROM drive, click a few options to tell the program that it can install the program according to the default settings, and then kick back and watch the installation routine do its thing.

Panic Attack!

If you cannot find the Setup or Install file, Windows can help you locate the file that *initiates* the installation routine. Open the **Start** menu, point to **Settings,** and click **Control Panel.** Double-click the **Add/ Remove Programs** icon. Click the **Install** button, and follow the onscreen instructions.

If the program comes on floppy disks, or if the setup component on the CD doesn't start automatically when you insert the disc, take the following steps to kick-start the setup routine:

1. If you haven't inserted the program CD or the first floppy disk into the drive, insert the CD or disk now.

2. Double-click **My Computer** on the Windows desktop.

3. Double-click the icon for your CD-ROM or floppy drive. This displays a list of files and folders on the disk or CD.

4. Double-click the file named **Setup, Install** or its equivalent (refer to the program's installation instructions if necessary). This starts the installation utility.

5. Follow the onscreen instructions to complete the installation.

No Install or Setup File?

Ninety-nine-point-nine percent of the programs you encounter have an Install or Setup file, so you shouldn't have any problem. However, if the program does not have its own setup utility, take the following steps to copy the program files to a folder on your computer's hard disk:

1. In My Computer, double-click the icon for drive C.

2. Right-click a blank area in the window, point to **New**, and click **Folder.**

3. Type a unique name for the folder, and then double-click the folder icon to open it.

4. Open another My Computer window, and change to the drive that contains the program disk or CD.

5. Press **Ctrl+A** to select all the files on the disk or CD, and then press **Ctrl+C** to copy them.

6. Change to the folder you just created, and press **Ctrl+V** to paste the files into the folder.

The file for running the program is typically marked with an icon that looks like the program's logo. Using the right mouse button, drag and drop this icon onto the Windows desktop, and then click **Create Shortcut(s) Here.** You can now use this icon to run the program.

Computer Cheat

To quickly copy a file from your hard disk to a floppy disk in drive A, right-click the file, point to **Send To,** and click **Floppy A.**

Selectively Installing Components

Many newer programs can consume several hundred megabytes of disk space, making it unwise to install the entire program on your hard disk. These large programs typically offer the option to run the program from the CD or install only the most commonly used components.

If the setup routine gives you the option of running the program from the CD or hard disk and your hard disk has plenty of free space, choose to run the program from the hard disk. You'll find that the program runs much faster, and you won't have to insert the CD every time you want to use the program. Choose to run the program from the CD only if your hard disk is running out of space.

Many setup routines provide an option for running the standard (typical), minimal, or custom installation, as shown in the following figure. Again, unless your hard disk is running out of storage space, choose the standard installation. This installs the most common components. If you'd like to see what's available and order *a la carte,* perform a custom installation.

When in doubt, choose the standard or typical installation.

Setup Type

Click the type of Setup you prefer, then click Next.

⦿ Typical — Program will be installed with the most common options. Recommended for most users.

○ Compact — Program will be installed with minimum required options.

○ Custom — You may choose the options you want to install. Recommended for advanced users.

Destination Directory

C:\...\Chronicle Encyclopedia of History — Browse...

< Back   Next >   Cancel

Does Anyone Use Floppy Disks Anymore?

Floppy disks are fast becoming extinct, but you might still receive small programs on floppy disks. Before installing a program from floppy disks, it's a good idea to write-protect the disks (if they are not already write-protected). Write protection locks the disk, preventing the disk drive from making any changes to it. If you hold the disk with the label facing up and away from you, the write-protect tab is in the upper-left corner of the disk. Slide the tab up so that you can see through the hole in the disk.

Panic Attack!

Some programs allow only a certain number of installations or require you to enter a password or registration number during installation. The installation utility then records this information on the floppy disk. In such cases, you might need to remove write protection in order to proceed.

Removing a Program That You Never Use

Your hard disk isn't an ever-expanding universe on which you can install an unlimited number of programs. As you install programs, create documents, send and receive e-mail messages, and view Web pages, your disk can quickly become overpopulated.

One of the best ways to reclaim a hefty chunk of disk space is to remove (uninstall) programs that you don't use. Unfortunately, you cannot just nuke the program's main folder to purge it from your system. When you install a Windows program, it commonly installs files not only to the program's folder but also to the \Windows, Windows\System, and other folders. It also edits a complicated system file called the Windows Registry. If you remove files without removing the lines in the Registry that refer to those files, you might encounter some serious problems. In short, you can't remove a program from your computer simply by deleting the program's files.

To remove the program safely and completely, you should use the Windows Add/Remove Programs utility:

1. Click the **Start** button, point to **Settings**, and click **Control Panel.**

2. Click the **Add/Remove Programs** icon. The Add/Remove Programs Properties dialog box appears.

3. Click the **Install/Uninstall** tab if it is not already selected. At the bottom of the window is a list of installed programs.

4. Click the name of the program you want to remove, as shown in the following figure.

Inside Tip

If the name of the program you want to remove does not appear in the Add/Remove Programs list, use the program's own setup utility to remove the program. Search the program's submenu on the **Start, Programs** menu or in the program's folder for a Setup or Install option.

Let Windows remove the program for you.

Click the program you want to remove.

Click the Add/Remove button.

5. Click the **Add/Remove** button.

6. One or more dialog boxes lead you through the uninstall process, asking for your confirmation. Follow the onscreen instructions to complete the process.

7. If the program you removed has a shortcut icon on the desktop, you might have to delete this manually. Right-click the icon, and click **Delete.**

The Least You Need to Know

➤ Software provides the instructions your computer needs in order to perform a task.

➤ Not all programs run on all computers. Before buying a program, be sure your computer meets the requirements that are printed on the program's box.

➤ Alt+double-click **My Computer** to view important information about your computer.

➤ In most cases, you can simply pop a CD-ROM program into your computer's CD-ROM drive to start the installation routine.

➤ To install a program, use My Computer to change to the CD-ROM or floppy drive in which the program diskette or CD is loaded, and double-click the **Setup** or **Install** icon.

➤ To remove a program that you no longer use, open the Windows Control Panel and double-click the **Add/Remove Programs** icon.

Part 3

Creating Letters, Greeting Cards, and Other Documents

Playing Solitaire and fiddling with the Windows desktop can keep you entertained for hours, but you didn't lay down a thousand bucks for a computer only to use it as a 99-cent deck of playing cards. You want to make something, print something, poke around on the Internet … you want to use the computer to get more out of life!

In this part, you begin to become productive with your computer as you learn how to type and format letters and greeting cards, add images, and print your letter or custom publication. Along the way, you'll even learn how to perform some basic tasks, such as saving, naming, opening, and printing your documents.

Chapter 10

I Just Want to Type a Letter!

In This Chapter

➤ Typing on an electronic page

➤ Inserting the date and time from your computer

➤ Making your text big and pretty

➤ Shoving your paragraphs around on a page

➤ Saving the document you created

When my wife and I purchased a new computer for our home, I was dazzled by the hardware: the state-of-the-art processor, the all-in-one fax-copier-scanner-printer, the big-screen monitor, the surround sound audio system, and the super-speed cable modem. With this bad boy, we'd be cruising, rather than surfing, the Internet; building our own Web sites; scanning family photos; and editing videos!

As I ran down the list of all the cool things we could do with our new computer, my wife just stared at the screen. When I finished, she looked at me and said, "I just want to type a letter."

With the popularity of the Internet and other computer technologies, it's easy to forget that many people still use a computer primarily to type and print documents. In this chapter, you learn how to type, format (style), and save a document using the most popular word processor on the planet—Microsoft Word.

Panic Attack!

Although this chapter uses Microsoft Word to show you basic word processing features, don't worry if you're using a different word processor. The basic features and commands covered in this chapter differ only slightly between word processing programs. If you don't have Word or WordPerfect installed on your computer, run WordPad, which is included with Windows. Open the **Start** menu, point to **Programs** and then **Accessories,** and then click **WordPad.**

Making the Transition to the Electronic Page

When you run Word (or whatever word processor is installed on your computer), it displays a blank "sheet of paper." The program also displays a vertical line called the *cursor* or *insertion point* to show you where the characters will appear when you start typing. Just below the insertion point is a horizontal line that marks the end of the document, as shown in the following figure. As you type, this line moves down automatically to make room for your text.

The best way to learn how to type in a word processor is to start typing. As you type, keep the following information in mind:

➤ If the text is too small to read, open the **Zoom** list, as shown in the preceding figure, and pick 100%. If the text is still too small, make it bigger, as explained in the "Making the Text Bigger or Smaller" section later in this chapter.

➤ Press the **Enter** key only to end a paragraph and start a new paragraph. Within a paragraph, the program automatically *wraps* the text from one line to the next as you type.

➤ Don't press the **Enter** key to insert a blank line between paragraphs. Later in this chapter, I'll show you a better way to add space between paragraphs.

➤ Use the mouse or the arrow keys to move the insertion point around in the document. If you're working on a long document, use the scroll bar to move more quickly.

➤ Delete to the right; Backspace to the left. To delete a character that's to the right of the insertion point, press the **Delete** key. To delete characters to the left of the insertion point, press the **Backspace** key.

Insertion point

Choose 100% to view the
text as it will appear in print.

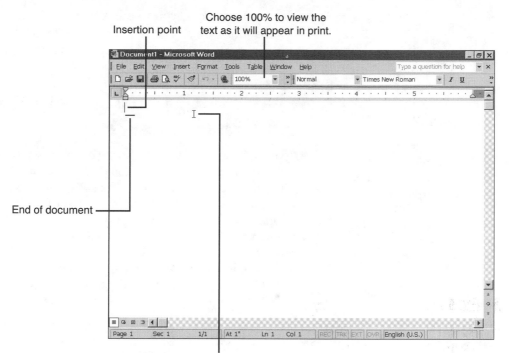

End of document

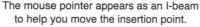

The mouse pointer appears as an I-beam
to help you move the insertion point.

Start typing!

In addition to allowing you to zoom in and out on a page, most word processing programs offer various views of a page. To change to a view, you typically open the **View**
menu and click one of the following view options (in Word, you can quickly switch
to a view by clicking a button for the desired view in the lower-left corner of the document window):

➤ **Normal** shows your document as one continuous document. In Normal view,
the word processor hides complex page formatting, headers, footers, objects
with wrapped text, floating graphics, and backgrounds. Scrolling is smooth because this view uses the least amount of memory.

➤ **Print Layout** provides a more realistic view of how your pages will appear in
print. Print Layout displays graphics, wrapping text, headers, footers, margins,
and drawn objects. This uses a lot of memory, however, and might make scrolling a little jerky.

➤ **Web Layout** displays a document as it will appear when displayed in a Web
browser. In Web Layout view, a word processor displays Web page backgrounds,
wraps the text to fit inside a standard browser window, and positions the graphics as they will appear when viewed online.

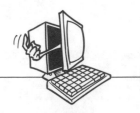

➤ **Outline** allows you to quickly organize and reorganize your document by dragging headings from one location to another in the document.

Inside Tip

If you really just want to type a letter and you're using Microsoft Word, you can run Word's Letter Wizard to have Word format your letter for you. See "The Making of a Form Letter" in Chapter 14, "Form Letters, Mailing Labels, and Envelopes," for details.

What's with the Squiggly Red and Green Lines?!

As you type, you might get a strange feeling that your sixth-grade English teacher is inside your computer, underlining your spelling mistakes. Whenever you type a string of characters that Word can't find in its dictionary, Word draws a squiggly red line under the word to flag it for you so that you can immediately correct it. If the word is misspelled, right-click the word and choose the correct spelling from the context menu. (A squiggly green line marks a questionable grammatical construction.)

If the squiggly lines annoy you, you can turn off automatic spell checking. Open the **Tools** menu and click **Options.** Click the **Spelling & Grammar** tab, and turn off both **Check spelling as you type** and **Check grammar as you type.** Click **OK.**

Inserting Today's Date

When you're typing a letter, you should include the date as part of the heading, just below your address. Of course, you could type the date, but that's too much like work. Have Word insert the date for you. Open the **Insert** menu and click **Date and Time**. Click the desired format and click **OK,** as shown in the following figure.

You can have your word processor insert the date or time for you.

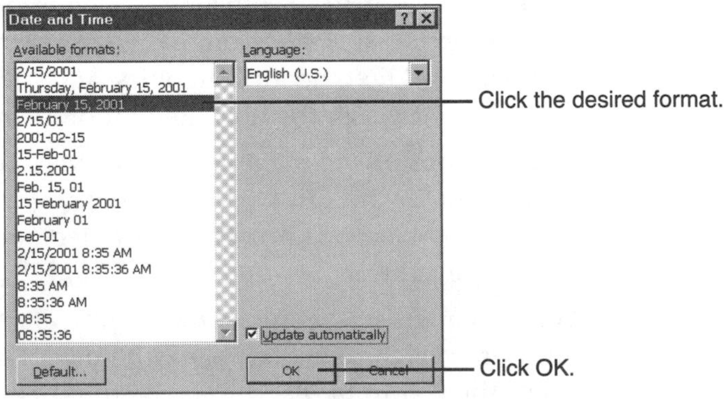

Date and Time
Available formats:
2/15/2001
Thursday, February 15, 2001
February 15, 2001
2/15/01
2001-02-15
15-Feb-01
2.15.2001
Feb. 15, 01
15 February 2001
February 01
Feb-01
2/15/2001 8:35 AM
2/15/2001 8:35:36 AM
8:35 AM
8:35:36 AM
08:35
08:35:36
Language:
English (U.S.)
Update automatically
Default...
OK
Cancel
Click the desired format.
Click OK.

Panic Attack!

If the date or time is not current, your computer has the wrong information. Double-click the time display on the right end of the Windows taskbar, and use the resulting dialog box to reset the date or time.

Making the Text Bigger or Smaller

When you first start typing, you might notice that there's nothing fancy about the text. Word processors choose the dullest, dreariest-looking typestyle available. To give your text a facelift, try choosing a different typestyle (or *font*) and varying the size and attributes of the text.

To change the appearance of existing text, drag over the text to *highlight* it. Highlighting displays white text on a black background to indicate that the text is selected. Then choose the desired formatting options from the Formatting toolbar, as shown in the following figure. (By the way, you also can change the properties of the text before you start typing.)

Tech Term

Technically, a **font** is a collection of characters that share the same typestyle and size. (Type size is measured in points; a point is approximately $1/72$ of an inch.) Most programs use the terms "font" and "typestyle" interchangeably.

Inside Tip

Where do you get fonts? Windows comes with dozens of fonts. Most word processors and desktop publishing programs come with additional font sets. You can purchase font collections on CD or download (copy) fonts from the Internet, but you probably already have more fonts than you will ever use.

Use the Formatting tool-bar to quickly change the text's appearance.

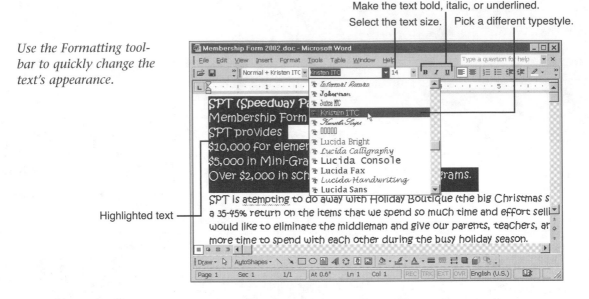

Make the text bold, italic, or underlined.

Select the text size. | Pick a different typestyle.

Highlighted text

Shoving Text Left, Right, or Center

As you type a document, you might want to center a heading or push a date or address to the right side of the page to set it apart from surrounding text. To quickly change the text alignment, click anywhere inside the paragraph and then click one of the following buttons on the Formatting toolbar:

 Align Left pushes all lines of the paragraph against the left margin.

 Center positions each line of the paragraph at an equal distance from both the left and right margins.

 Align Right pushes all lines of the paragraph against the right margin. This is a useful option for placing a date in the upper-right corner of a page.

 Justify inserts spaces between the words as needed to make every line of the paragraph the same length, as in newspaper columns.

 The Formatting toolbar also contains buttons for creating numbered and bulleted lists. Simply highlight the paragraphs that you want to transform into a list and then click the desired button: **Numbering** or **Bullets.**

To indent the first line of a paragraph, you can press the **Tab** key at the beginning of the paragraph or enter a setting for the first line indent. Most word processors display a ruler, as shown in the following figure, that lets you quickly indent paragraphs and set *tab stops*. (Tab stops determine where the insertion point stops when you press the **Tab** key.) To indent text and change margins and tab stop settings, here's what you do:

➤ To place a tab stop, click the button on the far-left end of the ruler to select the desired tab stop type (left, right, center, or decimal). Then click in the lower half of the ruler where you want the tab stop positioned.

➤ To move a tab stop, drag it left or right. To delete it, drag it off the ruler.

➤ To indent the right side of a paragraph, drag the right indent marker to the left.

➤ To indent the left side of a paragraph, drag the left indent marker to the right. (The left indent marker is the rectangle below the upward-pointing triangle.)

➤ To indent only the first line of a paragraph, drag the first line indent marker to the right. (This is the downward-pointing triangle on the left.)

➤ To create a hanging indent, drag the hanging indent marker to the right. (This is the upward-pointing triangle on the left.)

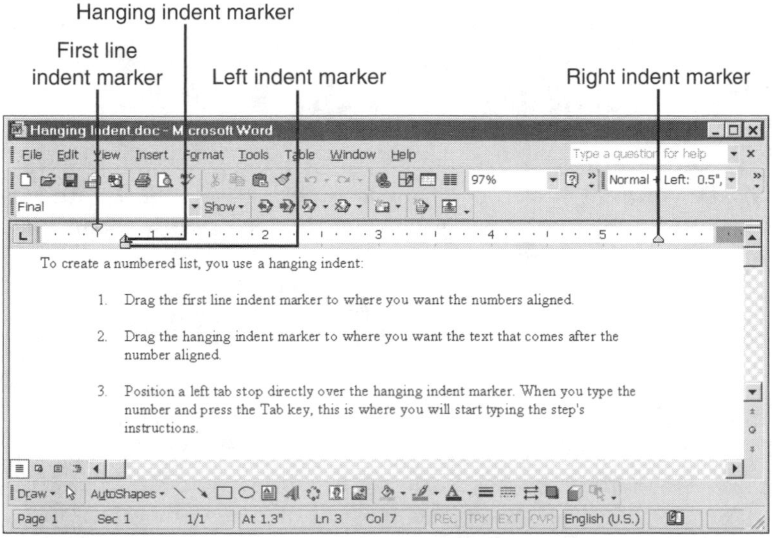

Use the ruler to quickly indent paragraphs and set tabs.

Changing the Line Spacing

Here's a section just for kids. If you're working on a five-page paper for school, and you have only two-and-a-half pages of material, you can stretch this out by double-spacing:

1. Press **Ctrl+A** to select all the text.

2. Open the **Format** menu and click **Paragraph.** The Paragraph dialog box pops up on your screen.

3. Open the **Line spacing** list and click **Double.**

4. Click **OK.**

Computer Cheat

If your teacher wises up and issues formatting restrictions on your next assignment, bump up the text size by one point (this is barely noticeable), use the **File, Page Setup** command to increase the margins, and increase the line spacing by only a few points instead of double-spacing. An even more subtle technique is to use a larger font. Some fonts, such as Arial and Times New Roman, take up more space at the same point size than other fonts.

Inserting Space Between Paragraphs

Leaving space between paragraphs helps the reader easily see where one paragraph ends and another begins. Of course, you can insert blank lines between paragraphs by pressing the **Enter** key twice at the end of a paragraph, but that's a sloppy technique that limits your control over paragraph spacing later.

By specifying the exact amount of space you want inserted between paragraphs, you ensure that the amount of space between paragraphs is consistent throughout your document.

To change the space between paragraphs, drag over the paragraphs to highlight at least a portion of each paragraph. (You don't need to highlight all of the first and last paragraphs.) Open the **Format** menu and click **Paragraph.** Under **Spacing,** click the arrows to the right of **Before** or **After** to specify the amount of space (measured in points) you want to insert before or after each paragraph. In most cases, 6 points of extra spacing does the trick. Click **OK.**

Save It or Lose It

Unless you're the type of person who loves the thrill of risking everything for no potential gain, you should save your document soon after you type a paragraph or two. Why? Because right now, your computer is storing everything you type in RAM (Random Access Memory). A little dip in your local electric company's power grid can send your document off to never-never land. To prevent losing your work, save it to a permanent storage area—your computer's hard disk.

The first time you save a document, your program asks for two things: a name for the document and the name of the drive and folder where you want the document stored. Here's the standard operating procedure for saving documents in most Windows programs:

1. Click the **Save** button on the toolbar, or open the **File** menu and click **Save.** The Save As dialog box appears, asking you to name the file.

2. Click in the **File name** text box and type a name for the file, as shown in the following figure. The name can be up to 255 characters long, and you can use spaces, but you cannot use any of the following taboo characters: \ / : * ? " < > |

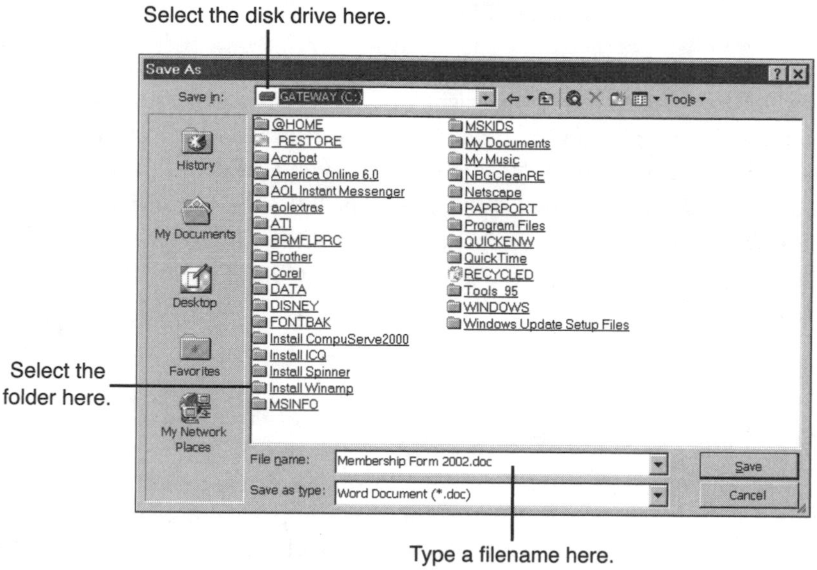

Select the disk drive here.

Use the Save As dialog box to save your document to your computer's hard disk.

Select the folder here.

Type a filename here.

3. Open the **Save in** list and click the letter of the disk on which you want to save the document (typically drive C).

4. In the file/folder area, double-click the folder in which you want the document saved. (To save the document in a folder that's inside another folder, repeat this step.)

5. Click the **OK** or **Save** button. The file is saved to the disk.

From now on, saving this document is easy; you don't have to name it or tell the program where to store it ever again. The program saves your changes in the document you already created and named. You should save your document every 5 to

Inside Tip

If you pass up the folder you wanted to select, you can back up. Click the **Up One Level** button.

10 minutes to avoid losing any work. In most programs, you can quickly save a document by pressing **Ctrl+S** or by clicking the **Save** button on the program's toolbar.

Inside Tip

Most new word processors are set up to save files in the My Documents folder. If you create your own folders for storing documents, you might want to set up one of these folders as the one your word processor looks to first. In Word, open the **Tools** menu and click **Options.** Click the **File Locations** tab, click **Documents** (under **File types**), and click the **Modify** button. Use the Modify Location dialog box to pick the desired drive and folder, and then click **OK** to return to the Options dialog box. Click **OK** to save your changes. Now, whenever you choose to open or save a document, Word will display the contents of the folder you selected.

Printing Addresses on Envelopes

Are you one of those people who carefully types and formats a letter and then addresses the envelope by hand? You're not the only one. Many people become frustrated trying to figure out how to print an address on an envelope. Fortunately, Word can help.

To print one envelope, open the **Tools** menu, click **Envelopes and Labels**, and be sure that the **Envelopes** tab is up front (see the following figure). Type the recipient's name and address in the **Delivery address** text box. Click in the **Return address** text box and type your address. You can format selected text in the **Delivery address** or **Return address** text boxes by highlighting the text and pressing the key combination for the desired formatting—for example, **Ctrl+B** for bold. You can also right-click the text to choose additional formatting options.

Inside Tip

Chapter 14 shows you how to merge an address book with a Word document to generate a stack of personally addressed letters, mailing labels, or envelopes.

Before you print, click the **Options** button. This displays the Envelope Options dialog box, which lets you specify the envelope size and the fonts for the delivery and return addresses. The **Printing Options** tab lets you specify how the envelope feeds into your printer. Enter your preferences and click the **OK** button.

Enter the recipient's address.

Envelopes and Labels

Make your envelope look as professional as your letter.

Envelopes | Labels

Delivery address:

Phil Donahue
2108 West 58th Place
Chicago, Illinois 60629

Print

Add to Document

Cancel

Options...

E-postage Properties...

☐ Add electronic postage

Return address: ☐ Omit

Oprah Winfrey
834 North Clark Street
Chicago, Illinois 60608

Preview

Feed

When prompted by the printer, insert an envelope in your printer's manual feeder.

Type your address.

If you need to manually load the envelope into your printer, load away. All printers are different; check your printer's documentation to determine the proper loading technique. When the envelope is in position, click the **Print** button to print it.

Whoa!

Before printing on a relatively expensive envelope, print on a normal sheet of paper to check the position of the print. You can then make adjustments without wasting costly supplies.

The Least You Need to Know

➤ Use the **Zoom** list to zoom in if the text is too small.

➤ Use the arrow keys or the mouse to move the insertion point.

➤ Use the **Insert, Date and Time** command to insert the current date.

➤ Drag the mouse pointer over text to highlight it.

➤ Use the buttons in the Formatting toolbar to quickly style and align your text.

➤ To display additional formatting options for selected text, right-click the text.

➤ To avoid losing your document, press **Ctrl+S** to save it to your computer's hard disk.

➤ Save early, and save often.

Chapter 11

Editing and Printing Your Letter

In This Chapter

➤ Ten quick ways to highlight text

➤ Cutting, copying, moving, and dragging text

➤ Saving your neck with the **Undo** button

➤ Tweaking the page margins

➤ Printing your masterpiece

➤ Designing your own letterhead

Is your letter perfect? Are you sure? Take a 10-minute break, come back, and read it again with fresh eyes. Chances are your letter has at least a couple of minor flaws and possibly even some major organizational problems. To perform the required fixes and purge common errors from your letter, you need to master the tools of the trade. This chapter shows you how to use your word processor's editing tools to copy, move, and delete text, and how to check for and correct spelling errors and typos.

After your letter is perfect, this chapter shows you how to transform the document displayed onscreen into a printed product. If you stick with me to the end of the chapter, I'll even show you how to combine text and graphics to create your own custom letterhead.

Selecting Text

Before you can do anything with the text you just typed, you must select it. You can always just drag over text to select it (as explained in the preceding chapter), but Word offers several quicker ways to select text. The following table shows these techniques.

Quick Text Selection Techniques

To Select This	Do This
Single word	Double-click the word.
Sentence	**Ctrl+click** anywhere in the sentence.
Paragraph	Triple-click anywhere in the paragraph. Alternatively, position the pointer to the left of the paragraph until it changes to a right-pointing arrow, and then double-click.
Several paragraphs	Position the pointer to the left of the paragraphs until it changes to a right-pointing arrow. Then double-click and drag up or down.
One line of text	Position the pointer to the left of the line until it changes to a right-pointing arrow, and then click. (Click and drag to select additional lines.)
Large block of text	Click at the beginning of the text, scroll down to the end of the text, and **Shift+click.**
Entire document	Press **Ctrl+A.** Alternatively, position the pointer to the left of any text until it changes to a right-pointing arrow, and then triple-click.
Extend the selection	Hold down the **Shift** key while using the arrow keys, **Page Up**, **Page Down**, **Home**, or **End**.

Cutting and Pasting Without Scissors

Every word processor features the electronic equivalent of scissors and glue. With the cut, copy, and paste commands, you can cut or copy selected text and then insert it in a different location in your document. You can even copy or cut text from one document and paste it in another document!

To cut or copy text, select it, and then click either the **Cut** or the **Copy** button on the toolbar. Move the insertion point to where you want the text inserted, and then click the **Paste** button. Note that cutting a selection deletes it (until you paste it somewhere), whereas copying it leaves the selection in place and creates a duplicate.

Whenever you cut or copy data in any Windows program, Windows places the data in a temporary storage area called the *Clipboard*. In the old days, the Clipboard could store only one chunk of data. If you cut one selection and then cut another selection, the second selection would bump the first selection off the Clipboard. Office 2000 (which includes Word 2000) upgrades the Clipboard, enabling it to store 12 selections (24 in Office XP). When you cut or copy two or more selections, the Clipboard toolbar appears, displaying an icon for each copied or cut selection. To paste the selection, click its icon. To paste all of the cut or copied selections, click the **Paste All** button. If the Clipboard toolbar does not appear in Word 2000, right-click any toolbar and click **Clipboard.** In Word 2002 (part of the Office XP suite), open the **Edit** menu and click **Office Clipboard.** This displays a Clipboard task pane on the right, providing a list of the 24 most recently cut or copied selections. Double-click the desired selection to paste it.

Oops! Undoing Changes

What if you highlight your entire document, intending to change the font size, and then press the **Delete** key by mistake? Is your entire document gone for good?

Nope.

As you cut, paste, delete, and perform similar acts of destruction, your word processor keeps track of each command and lets you recover from the occasional blunder. To undo the most recent action, open the **Edit** menu and choose **Undo,** or click the **Undo** button (the button with the counterclockwise arrow on it) in the Standard toolbar. You can continue to click the **Undo** button to undo additional actions. Click the **Redo** button (the clockwise arrow) to undo the Undo action or to again perform the action you just performed.

Computer Cheat

To quickly move selected text, just drag it to the desired location in the document and release the mouse button. To copy the text, hold down the **Ctrl** key while you drag.

Whoa!

After you save your document and close it, you cannot reopen it and undo actions you performed during a previous work session.

Checking Your Spelling and Grammar

In the preceding chapter, you learned that Word automatically checks for typos and spelling errors as you type. If you turned off that option, you can initiate a spelling check by opening the **Tools** menu and selecting **Spelling and Grammar** or by clicking the **Spelling and Grammar** button on the Standard toolbar.

Word starts checking your document and stops on the first questionable word (a word not stored in the spelling checker's dictionary or a repeated word, such as "the the"). The Spelling and Grammar dialog box displays the word in red and usually displays a list of suggested corrections, as shown in the following figure. (If the word appears in green, the grammar checker is questioning the word's usage, not its spelling.) You have several options:

➤ If the word is misspelled and the **Suggestions** list displays the correct spelling, click the correct spelling and then click **Change** to replace only this occurrence of the word.

➤ Double-click the word in the **Not in Dictionary** text box, type the correction, and click **Change.**

➤ To replace this misspelled word and all other occurrences of the word in this document, click the correct spelling in the **Suggestions** list and then click **Change All.**

➤ Click **Ignore** or **Ignore Once** if the word is spelled correctly and you want to skip it just this once. Word will stop on the next occurrence of the word.

➤ Click **Ignore All** if the word is spelled correctly but is not in the dictionary and you want Word to skip all other occurrences of this word in the document.

➤ Click **Add** or **Add to Dictionary** to add the word to the dictionary so that the spelling checker never questions it again in any of your Office documents (the dictionary is shared by all Office applications).

Don't place too much trust in your spell checker. It merely compares the words in its dictionary to the words in your document and highlights any string of text that's not in the dictionary. If you typed "its" when you should have typed "it's," the spelling checker won't flag the error. Likewise, if you correctly type a scientific term that is not in the spelling checker's dictionary, the spelling checker will flag the word, even if it is correct. Proofread your documents carefully before considering them final.

When Word completes the spelling check, it displays a dialog box telling you so. Click **OK.**

Click the correct spelling if it's listed.

If Word finds a misspelling and displays the correct spelling, your options are easy.

Click Change or Change All.

Setting Your Margins and Page Layout

After typing a document, you might be tempted to just click the **Print** button on the Standard toolbar to crank out a paper copy of the document. Avoid the temptation.

You usually just end up wasting paper and being sorely disappointed with the results. Before you print, you should check the Page Setup options.

To display the Page Setup options, open the **File** menu and select **Page Setup.** The Page Setup dialog box appears, presenting three tabs for changing various page and print settings. In the following sections, you learn how to use this dialog box to set margins and control how Word prints text on the pages.

Setting the Page Margins

The very first time the Page Setup dialog box appears, the **Margins** tab is up front, as shown in the following figure. If it's hiding, click it to bring it to the front. This tab lets you change the top, bottom, left, and right margins. Click the up or down arrow to the right of each margin setting to change the setting in increments of .1 inch, or click in a margin setting text box and type a more precise measurement.

Inside Tip

To check the spelling of a single word or paragraph, double-click the word or triple-click the paragraph to select it before you start the spelling checker. When Word is done checking the selection, it displays a dialog box asking if you want to check the rest of the document.

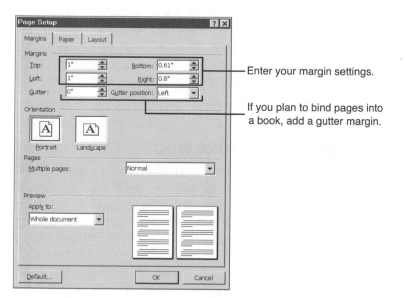

Set the page margins for the entire document.

Enter your margin settings.

If you plan to bind pages into a book, add a gutter margin.

The **Margins** tab offers several additional options for special printing needs:

➤ **Gutter** lets you add margin space to the inside margin of the pages, in case you plan to insert the pages into a book or binder.

107

➤ **From edge** specifies the distance from the top of the page to the top of the *header* and from the bottom of the page to the bottom of the *footer*. (The **From edge** options are on the **Layout** tab in Word 2002.)

➤ **Mirror margins** are useful if you plan to print on both sides of a sheet of paper. When this option is on, Word makes the inside margins of facing pages equal.

➤ **2 pages per sheet** or **Multiple pages** shrinks the pages of your document so that Word can print two pages on a single sheet of paper.

➤ **Apply to** lets you apply the margin settings to the entire document from this point forward in the document or to only selected text. This is useful for long documents that might require different page layouts for some sections.

Tech Term

A **header** is text that appears at the top of every page in a document. A **footer** is the same thing, but it appears at the bottom of every page. To add a header or footer, open the **View** menu and click **Header and Footer.** A word processor typically hides headers and footers in Normal view. To see how your header or footer will look on a page, change to Print Layout (or Page Layout) view, as explained in "Making the Transition to the Electronic Page" in Chapter 10, "I Just Want to Type a Letter!"

Picking a Paper Size and Print Direction

Usually, you print a document right side up on 8½ × 11 inch piece of paper. In some cases, however, you might need to print on legal-size paper or print a wide document, such as an announcement or sign, sideways on the page. If that's the case, check out the **Paper** or **Paper Size** tab. On this tab, you can pick from a list of standard paper sizes or specify a custom size. You can also select a print orientation: **Portrait** (to print normally, as in this book) or **Landscape** (to print with the longer edge of the paper at the bottom). **Landscape** is especially useful if you choose the **2 pages per sheet** option. (In Word 2002, you can find the **Portrait** and **Landscape** options on the **Margins** tab.)

Where's Your Paper Coming From?

If you always print on standard $8^1/_2 \times 11$ inch paper, you don't really need to worry about where the paper is coming from. Your printer is set up to use the default paper tray, which is typically loaded with $8^1/_2 \times 11$ inch paper, and all your programs know that. However, if you need to print envelopes, banners, or any other paper that's not $8^1/_2 \times 11$ inch, check the **Paper** or **Paper Source** tab before you start printing just to be sure that Word is set up to use the right tray.

Laying Out Your Pages

The last tab in the Page Setup dialog box is the **Layout** tab. You can safely ignore most of the options on the **Layout** tab. Just be sure you don't miss the following three options:

➤ **Vertical alignment.** The **Vertical alignment** list is very useful for making one-page documents (such as a short letter) look good on the page. Open the list and select **Center** to center the document on the page. This option is especially useful for printing cover pages and letters. To make the document fill the entire page, select **Justified.**

➤ **Line Numbers.** The **Line Numbers** button is useful for legal and literary pieces. These types of documents often contain line numbers so that people can refer to the line numbers when discussing the documents instead of quoting entire lines and sounding really boring. To insert line numbers, click the button and enter your preferences.

➤ **Borders.** The Borders button opens the Borders and Shading dialog box, which allows you to add a border around your entire page or at the top, bottom, left, or right margin.

Saving Paper: Previewing Before Printing

Before you print the document, click the **Print Preview** button on the Standard toolbar. This gives you a bird's-eye view of the page, lets you quickly flip pages, and provides rulers that you can use to drag the margin settings around. To exit print preview, press the **Esc** key or click the **Close** button just above the preview area (not the **Close** [X] button in the upper-right corner of the application's window, because this will exit the application).

Computer Cheat

If you have a short document with a few lines of text stranded on the last page, click the **Shrink to Fit** button on the Print Preview toolbar. Word automatically decreases the font size of all the text to pull the excess text to the bottom of the previous page.

Sending Your Letter off to the Printer

When you have your printer working successfully with any of your Windows applications, printing is pretty simple. Be sure your printer has plenty of paper and ink or toner, turn on the printer, open your document, and click the **Print** button.

To take more control of the printing—to print extra copies, print sideways on the page (in landscape mode), collate copies, select a print quality, or enter other settings—you must display the Print dialog box. To do this, open the **File** menu and select **Print** instead of clicking the **Print** button. You can then use the Print dialog box, shown in the following figure, to enter your preferences.

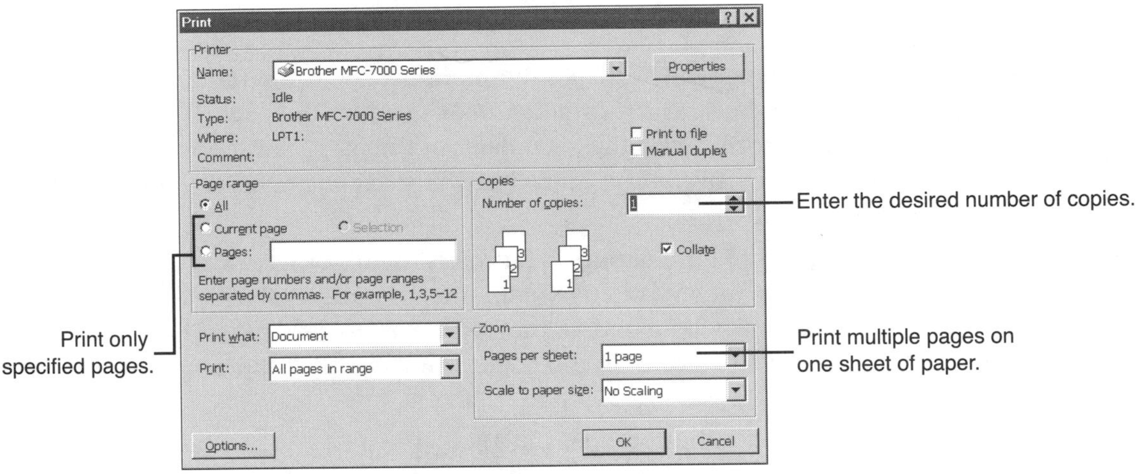

Print only specified pages.

Enter the desired number of copies.

Print multiple pages on one sheet of paper.

Enter your printing preferences.

Hey, It's Not Printing!

If Word refuses to start printing your document, you'll have to do a little troubleshooting. The following questions can help you track down the cause:

➤ Is your printer plugged in and turned on?

➤ Does your printer have paper? Is the paper tray inserted properly?

➤ Is the printer's On Line light on (not blinking)? If the On Line light is off or blinking, press the **On Line** button to turn on the light and make the printer print.

➤ Display the Print dialog box again, and be sure **Print to file** is not selected. This option sends the document to a file on your disk instead of to the printer.

➤ Is your printer marked as the default printer? In My Computer, double-click the **Printers** icon. Right-click the icon for your printer, and be sure that **Set As Default** is checked. If there is no check mark, select **Set As Default.**

➤ Is the printer paused? Double-click the printer icon on the right end of the taskbar, open the **Printer** menu, and be sure that **Pause Printing** is not checked. If there is a check mark, click **Pause Printing.**

➤ Is the correct printer port selected? In My Computer, double-click the **Printers** icon, and then right-click the icon for your printer and choose **Properties.** Click the **Details** tab, and be sure that the correct printer port is selected—LPT1 in most cases.

Project Time! Making Your Own Letterhead

A plain-vanilla, text-only letter is fine if you're writing to your accountant, but if you're trying to impress a prospective employer or add a personal touch to a friendly letter, try creating your own letterhead. All you need to do is add a clip-art graphic, your address, and a code for inserting the date. The following instructions lead you step by step through the process:

1. Click the **New Blank Document** button.

2. Open the **Insert** menu, point to **Picture**, and click **Clip Art.**

3. Use the Insert ClipArt dialog box or task pane to find the picture you want to use for your letterhead.

4. In Word 2000 or earlier, click the desired clip-art image and then click the **Insert Clip** button. In Word 2002, double-click the image. (Close or minimize the Insert ClipArt dialog box when you're done.)

5. Right-click the image you inserted in step 4, and then click **Format Picture.**

6. Click the **Layout** tab, click **In front of text**, and click **OK.** This lets you move the image without affecting the text you will type later.

7. Resize and move the image as desired to place it in the upper-left corner of the page.

8. Drag the **Left Indent** marker to the right to move the insertion point out from under the image, as shown in the following figure.

9. Type your name and address (or your business name and address) on separate lines, as you would type the inside address in any letter.

10. Open the **Insert** menu and click **Date and Time.**

11. Click the desired format for the date, be sure **Update automatically** is checked, and click **OK.** Word inserts the date as a code, so whenever you open this letterhead, Word inserts the current date.

Drag the left indent marker to indent the
inside address to the right of the picture.

*Create your own letter-
head.*

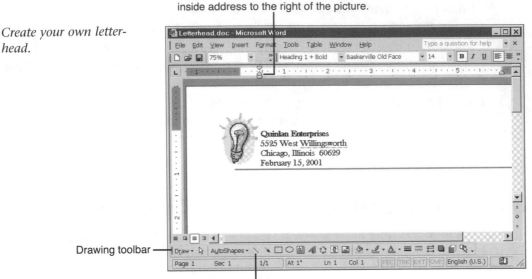

Drawing toolbar

Line button

Computer Cheat

You can use a page border to
create some fancy stationery.
Open the **Format** menu and
click **Borders and Shading.**
Click the **Page Border** tab.
Choose the desired line style or
open the **Art** list and choose a
graphic border. In the **Preview**
area, click the top and right border lines to leave only the left
and bottom border lines in
place.

12. (Optional) Right-click any toolbar and click
    Drawing to turn on the Drawing toolbar.

13. Click the **Line** button on the drawing
    toolbar.

14. Hold down the **Shift** key and drag a line
    from left to right, just below your address,
    as shown in the preceding figure. When you
    release the mouse button, a line appears.

15. Click the **Line Style** button and choose the
    desired line thickness.

16. Click the **Line Color** button and choose the
    desired line color.

When you're finished, press **Ctrl+S**. Open the **Save as
type** list and click **Document Template (*.dot).** Name
the document and save it as you normally would. By
saving your letterhead as a template, you can use the
File, New command to open it and use it to create a
new letter without affecting the original template.

The Least You Need to Know

➤ To select a single word, double-click it; a sentence, **Ctrl+click** it; a paragraph, triple-click it.

➤ To move selected text, drag it to the desired location and release the mouse button. To copy text, hold down the **Ctrl** key while dragging.

➤ Click the **Undo** button to reverse the last action you performed or command you entered.

➤ To initiate a spelling check, click the **Spelling and Grammar** button.

➤ Before you print a document, open the **File** menu, click **Page Setup,** and check the margin settings and page layout options.

➤ Before you print a document, click the **Print Preview** button to see how the document will appear when printed.

➤ To quickly print a document, no questions asked, click the **Print** button. For more control over printing, choose **File, Print.**

➤ If your document doesn't start printing, double-click the printer icon on the right end of the taskbar to determine what's wrong.

Chapter 12

Designing Personalized Greeting Cards, Banners, and Other Publications

---

In This Chapter

➤ Getting started with a desktop publishing program

➤ Picking a greeting card off the rack

➤ Customizing greeting cards and other publications

➤ Combining pictures and text (without losing anything)

➤ Printing a banner for your next party

Word processors make great blue-collar programs. They're excellent for typing and printing memos, letters, and reports, but they fall short when it comes to creating fancy designer publications that dazzle the eye. Unless you're a master of page layout, you'll find it nearly impossible to create a greeting card, banner, or tri-fold brochure using a word processor.

To create these specialized publications, you need a program that provides precise control over pictures and text. You need a desktop publishing program. In this chapter, you learn how to use a desktop publishing program to design and build your own greeting cards, banners, business cards, and other custom publications.

What You Need to Get Started

Before you get too excited over the possibilities, first be sure you have a desktop publishing program installed on your computer. Many new computers include Microsoft Publisher or Broderbund's Print Shop Deluxe. If you have Microsoft Publisher, you've

hit pay dirt, because this chapter uses Publisher to illustrate the cool publications you can create. If you don't have Publisher, don't worry. Most desktop publishing programs offer similar tools and commands for creating publications and for inserting and manipulating text and graphics.

Inside Tip

If your computer didn't come with a desktop publishing program, check the CD or disks that came with your printer. Many printer manufacturers include a copy of a basic desktop publishing program to show off the printer's capabilities.

Starting with a Prefab Greeting Card

Popular desktop publishing programs pride themselves on never leaving you with a blank screen. On startup, these programs typically display a window or dialog box that lists the available publication types: greeting card, brochure, flyer, business card, banner, and so on. You simply choose the desired type of publication and click the **OK** or **Next** button to initiate a publication wizard or open a ready-made publication.

If Microsoft Publisher is installed on your system, take the following steps to initiate the Publishing Wizard and create your own custom greeting card. If you don't have Publisher, read along anyway to see how it's done:

1. Click the **Start** button, point to **Programs**, and click **Microsoft Publisher.** Publisher displays a list of publication types.

2. Click **Greeting Cards** to view a list of greeting card types.

3. Click the desired greeting card type. The preview area on the right displays the available ready-made cards, as shown in the following figure.

4. Click the card that best suits your tastes. In Publisher 2002, a publication wizard starts as soon as you click a card, providing a task pane on the left with options for customizing the card. If you're using Publisher 2002, use the options in the task pane to complete your publication, and skip steps 5 through 8. If you're using an older version of Publisher, proceed with step 5.

5. Click the **Start Wizard** button.

6. Follow the wizard's instructions to enter your preferences.

7. When you've entered your final preference, click the **Finish** button. The wizard announces that you've done everything you needed to do and offers to create the publication.

8. Click **Create It**, and then sit back and watch as the wizard does its paste-up work.

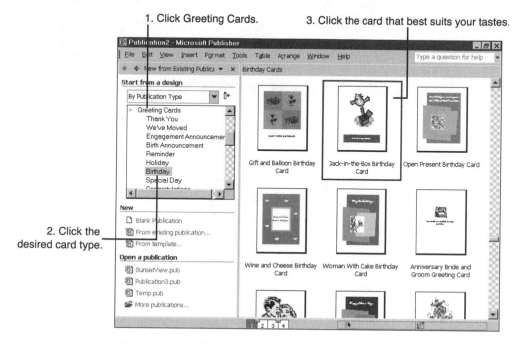

Microsoft Publisher lets you pick a card off the rack.

When Publisher is done slapping together your greeting card, it displays the card in the work area on the right. To the left of the work area is the Wizard pane, where you can change the overall design, layout, color scheme, and other settings that control your publication. To make a change, click the desired category in the Wizard list at the top, and then click the desired setting or enter the requested information at the bottom. You can hide the Wizard pane at any time by clicking the **Hide Wizard** button below the pane or the Close (X) button in the upper-right corner of the pane.

Microsoft Publisher Survival Guide

Your first glance at the publication that the wizard created might just turn you to stone. The page is dinky, the graphics look sloppy, and the text looks as if the wizard is trying to fit it on the head of a pin. Before you can do anything, you need to know how to zoom in and out and flip from one page to the next.

First, zoom in. Open the **Zoom** drop-down list in the Standard toolbar and choose the desired zoom percentage—75 percent is usually sufficient. Just below the work area are the page flippers, as shown in the following figure. Click the icon for the desired page to quickly display it. You already know how to use the scrollbars; you'll get plenty of scrollbar practice in Publisher.

Before you start working, be sure you can see everything.

Choose the desired zoom percentage.

You can hide the wizard for more room to work.

Tools for inserting objects

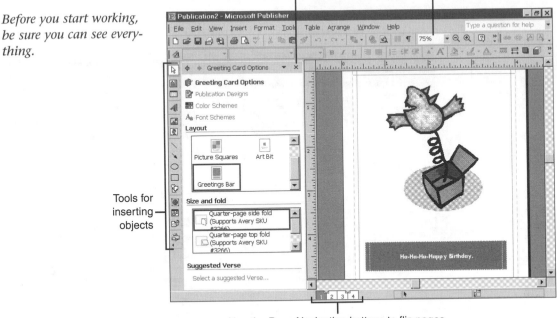

Use the Page Navigation buttons to flip pages.

After you have everything in plain sight, you're ready to fiddle with the publication. However, there are a few additional things that might not seem obvious at first:

➤ In Publisher 2000 and earlier versions, a dialog box pops up on your screen every 15 minutes, reminding you to save your work. Reply the first time and save your file, but if this dialog box becomes too annoying, turn it off. Choose **Tools, Options**, click the **User Assistance** tab, and click **Remind to save publication** to remove the check mark. Publisher 2002 has more-sophisticated tools for preventing data loss, so this option is unavailable.

➤ In Publisher 2000 and earlier versions, the **Undo** button doesn't have a drop-down list as in Word, but you can undo more than one action by clicking the button several times.

➤ You will encounter two types of text boxes, normal and WordArt, which might look the same. To edit text in a normal text box, click in the text box to position the insertion point, and type your changes (just pretend that you're working in Word). For WordArt "text boxes," double-click the box to display a dialog box for editing the text. Edit your text and click **OK**.

➤ The dotted lines are page layout guides. They don't print. They just help you align stuff more precisely.

➤ Some publications have a text frame off to the side that displays information about the publication. This won't print. In fact, nothing placed in the gray area outside the page will print. You can drag objects onto this work area as you lay out your pages.

➤ A greeting card might have a graphic on the first page that looks as though it doesn't fit on the page. Don't worry about it. Publisher does this wrap-around thing with the graphic so that it prints on both the front and back of the card. It's actually pretty cool.

Tech Term

Every object on a Publisher page is a **frame.** Text is contained in a text frame, images hang out in picture frames, and WordArt objects are held in WordArt frames. Frames make it easy to rearrange objects on a page.

Playing with Pictures

Whenever you start with a ready-made greeting card, the desktop publishing program chooses which picture to place on the front and any other graphics for the inside and back of the card. What if you don't like the picture? Are you stuck with it? Should you run the wizard and try a different design? No! Simply replace the picture with a different clip art image.

In most desktop publishing programs, including Microsoft Publisher, you simply double-click the existing image and select a new image from the program's clip art library. If that trick doesn't work, click the image and press the **Delete** key to get rid of it. Choose the **Insert, Picture, Clip Art** command, and use the resulting dialog box or task pane to select and insert the desired image.

If the picture ends up in the wrong location or is too big or too small, move or resize it as needed. First, click the image to select it and display its handles (small black squares or circles that allow you to resize the image). Drag the image to move it or drag a corner handle to resize it. Microsoft Publisher also features a cropping tool that lets you "trim" the edges of the image. Click the **Crop** button, as shown in the following figure, and then drag a handle toward the center of the image to trim an edge off the image. (If you crop too much, drag the handle away from the image to uncrop it.) You can find the **Crop** button on the Picture toolbar in Publisher 2002 or the Formatting toolbar in earlier versions. Remember, to turn on a toolbar, right-click any toolbar and click the name of the desired toolbar.

Crop button

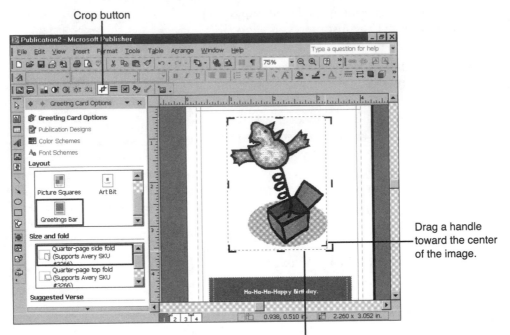

Drag a handle toward the center of the image.

The selection line shows where you'll be snipping.

Trim an image to remove unwanted parts.

Inside Tip

Moving a text frame is kind of tricky. You can't just drag the center of the frame, as you do when you move a picture. First, click the outline of the frame so that handles appear around it. Drag the border that defines the frame.

Text in a Box

Unlike word processors, which let you type right on a page, desktop publishing programs don't let you place anything on a page unless it's in a *frame* or *box*. To place text in your publication, you must first draw a text box and then type something in that box. As you fine-tune your publication, you can drag and stretch the box as needed to position it on the page and accommodate your text.

To create a text frame or text box, click the **Text Frame Tool** or **Text Box** button. The mouse pointer turns into a crosshair pointer. Position the pointer where you want the upper-left corner of the frame to appear, and then drag down and to the right to create a frame of the desired height and width. When you release the mouse button, Word inserts the text frame. Type your text in the frame, and use the Formatting toolbar to style the text.

A ▪▪▪ If you fill the frame, Publisher displays an **Overflow** button at the bottom of the text frame. You have two options: resize the frame to make it larger, or *spill* the text into another frame, first create a new frame. Click the text frame that contains the text, click the **Create Text Box Link** button, and then click inside the new, blank text frame. Publisher automatically moves any text that doesn't fit inside the first text frame to the second text frame.

Layering Pictures and Text Boxes

Working with two or more frames (or *objects*) on a page is like making your own collage. The trouble with frames is that when you place one frame on top of another, the top frame blocks the bottom one and prevents you from selecting it. You have to flip through the stack to find the frame you want.

Publisher and most other desktop publishing programs offer tools to help you rearrange the frames in a stack. You can send an object that's up front back one layer or all the way to the bottom of the stack, or you can bring an object from the back to the front. First, click the object you want to move (if possible). Some objects are buried so deep that you can't get to them. In such a case, you have to move objects from the front to the back to get them out of the way until you find the one you want.

After selecting the object that you want to move, open the **Arrange** menu, point to **Order**, and select the desired movement: **Bring to Front, Send to Back, Bring Forward, Send Backward, Bring in Front of Text,** or **Send Behind Text.**

Do-It-Yourself Banners

You're throwing a birthday party for your friend, and you've already created a custom birthday card and churned out the party invitations. With the big date fast approaching, you realize that a banner would jazz up the party décor, but you have no idea

Inside Tip

Linked frames are great for newsletters. You can start a story on the front page and then print the rest of the story in a frame on the next page or anywhere in the newsletter.

Inside Tip

If you have a half-dozen frames on a page and you want to nudge them all to the right, you don't have to move each frame individually. Click the **Pointer Tool** and **Shift+click** each object you want to move. Drag one of the frames, and all the rest will follow like little sheep. To group the objects and make them act as a single object, right-click one of the objects and click **Group.** (To ungroup the objects, right-click the grouped object and click **Ungroup.**)

where to start. Never fear. Your handy-dandy desktop publishing program has just the thing you need.

If you're using Microsoft Publisher, choose **File, New**, and click **Banners** in the publications list. The steps you use to pick a banner and initiate the Publishing Wizard are nearly identical to those given earlier in this chapter for creating a greeting card. The only difference is that in step 2, you choose **Banners** instead of **Greeting Cards**. After starting the wizard, simply follow the onscreen instructions and enter your preferences.

Although creating a banner is easy, printing it might be fairly complicated, depending on your printer. Many printers require you to flip levers or follow a special procedure for loading banner paper into the printer. In addition, you might need to change the print settings in Windows to indicate that you're printing a banner. Even if you're printing the banner on standard $8^1/_2 \times 11$ inch sheets of paper (to tape together after printing), you might need to specify that you're printing a banner. Failing to do so might cause the printer to chop off the print area where you tape together the sheets that make up the banner.

In most cases, you choose the **File, Print** command and then click the **Properties** button to access the setting for printing a banner. Click the **Paper** tab, and then choose **Banner**. Enter any other settings as desired, and click **OK**. Load your banner paper as specified in your printer documentation, and then click **OK** to start printing.

With some printers, the settings are not so obvious. You might need to create your own custom paper size and/or enter overlap settings to make your printer overlap the pages by a fraction of an inch (see the following figure). Overlapping pages makes the print run off the edge of one sheet onto the next so that you don't end up with white vertical lines on your banner.

Specify an overlap to prevent gaps in the banner.

Some printers require that you enter a special print setting to print banners.

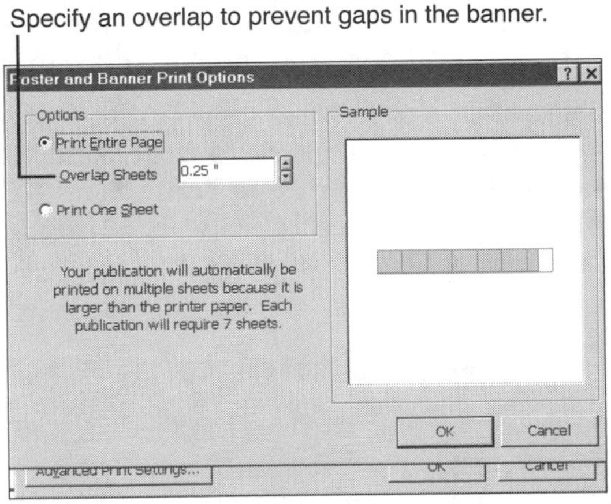

Other Cool Desktop Publishing Stuff

Just a few short years ago, home-based desktop publishing programs focused primarily on greeting cards and banners. However, with more and more people starting their own small businesses, these programs have expanded their offerings to include flyers, business cards, newsletters, catalogs, brochures, and even Web pages! The following figure displays a portion of a tri-fold brochure created with Publisher.

As long as you have the skills required for moving and resizing graphics and text frames, you can create and customize any personal or business publication you need.

Whoa!

If you plan on printing your publication on thicker paper or card stock (for business cards), be sure you adjust the thickness setting on your paper feeder. Otherwise, the paper might become jammed or fail to feed through the printer.

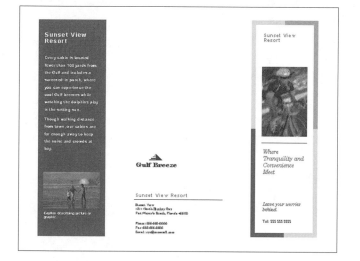

A brochure is a great tool for advertising products.

The Least You Need to Know

➤ To create a new publication, issue the **File, New** command and follow the onscreen instructions.

➤ To add text to a publication, you must first draw a text box or text frame.

➤ To insert a clip art image, open the **Insert** menu, point to **Picture,** and click **Clip Art.**

➤ To move a text frame, first click the frame's outline and then drag the selected frame.

➤ To resize a graphic or text frame, first click the frame or graphic and then drag one of its handles.

➤ To move a text frame, click the outline of the frame and then drag the frame's border.

➤ To send a frame back one layer in a stack, click the frame, open the **Arrange** menu, point to **Order,** and click **Send Backward.**

Chapter 13

Creating an Address Book and Other Listy Stuff

In This Chapter

➤ Becoming a data pack rat

➤ Making your own electronic address book

➤ Sorting entries by last name or first name

➤ Using tables to align text in columns

➤ Adding formulas to automate calculations

➤ Illustrating your table with graphics

Unless you're a hermit, you probably have an address book packed with the names, addresses, and phone numbers of your friends and relatives. You might have a day planner that contains a list of business contacts or a wallet or purse packed with business cards. If you're a parent, team lists, practice schedules, and important school dates dangle from your refrigerator or cabinet doors. You might even have Post-it Notes stuck to the walls and countertops to remind you of important dates.

How would you like to consolidate this loose collection of notes and papers and keep it in one location—on your computer? In this chapter, you learn how to use various programs to organize and manage names, addresses, phone numbers, dates, and other important information.

Tables, Spreadsheets, Databases, and Address Books

Now don't get all excited and start typing a list of names and addresses in your word processor. Doing so will create a mess you'll only have to clean up later. First, pick the right tool for the job:

➤ To create a simple address book, membership directory, or other list without leaving your word processor, use a table, as explained in the following section.

➤ To create a full-featured address book for personal or business use, enter your data in a personal information manager, such as Microsoft Outlook (see the section "Using an Electronic Day Planner"). You can use an address book to store names, mailing addresses, e-mail addresses, phone and fax numbers, and pertinent information about each contact.

Inside Tip

Tables are great for aligning any text in columns. For example, you can create a two–column table for laying out your resumé. Use the left column to list dates and the right column for job descriptions and information about training and education.

➤ If you want more control over the layout of your records, or if you have numerical data, such as membership fees you need to track, enter your data in a *spreadsheet,* as explained in "Automating Calculations with Spreadsheets" later in this chapter.

➤ For more flexibility and control over your data, use a *database,* as explained in "Managing Records in a Database." A database is great for generating reports. A *relational database,* such as Access, can even extract and combine data from two or more databases.

Tech Term

A **database** is a collection of records. A **relational database** is a data management program that can extract data from two or more databases. A relational database can combine the data from one or more databases to create a single report. For instance, with a relational database, you can create an invoice that combines part numbers and prices from one database with customer names and addresses from another database.

Making a Simple Address Book with a Word Table

Are you looking for a no-frills address book that doesn't require you to learn another program? Consider creating your address book using Word's table feature. You simply create a table consisting of several columns and rows and then type in the names and addresses, as shown in the following figure. You can even use the table along with Word's mail merge feature to automate mass mailings, as explained in Chapter 14, "Form Letters, Mailing Labels, and Envelopes." For details on creating a table in Word, see the "Setting Your Own Table" section later in this chapter.

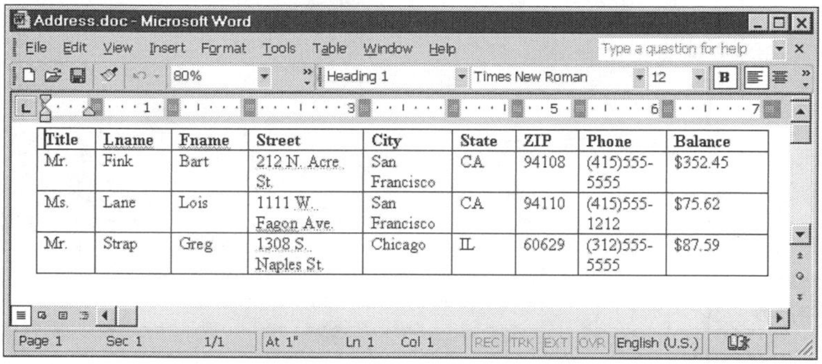

Word's table feature lets you create a basic address book.

Using an Electronic Day Planner

Many computers come with an electronic version of a day planner, commonly called a personal information manager (PIM for short). One of the most popular PIMs is Microsoft Outlook, shown in the following figure. With Outlook, you can send and receive e-mail messages, keep track of appointments and special dates (such as anniversaries and birthdays), create a to-do list, and even manage your documents.

Of course, I can't cover all that nifty stuff in this section, but I *can* tell you how to create your own address book in Outlook. First, click the **Contacts** icon. Then click the **New Contact** button (on the left end of the button bar). The New Contact dialog box appears. Enter the person's name, address, phone number, e-mail address, and other contact information. Click the **Save and New** button to save the address card and display a new blank card, or click **Save and Close** to close the window.

Automating Calculations with Spreadsheets

Generally speaking, PIMs and databases are better tools for entering, locating, and extracting information. However, if your data consists primarily of numerical entries, and you need to analyze that data or perform calculations using those entries, use a spreadsheet.

Send and receive e-mail.　　Log appointments.

Outlook Today - Microsoft Outlook

File　Edit　View　Favorites　Tools　Help

Find　Type a contact to find　　　Back

Local Information Store · Outlook Today · 　　　Address

Outlook Shortcuts

Thursday, February 15, 2001　　　Customize Outlook Today ...

Inbox

Calendar

Contacts

Tasks

Notes

My Shortcuts

Other Shortcuts

Calendar

Today

▸ 11:00 AM - 12:00 PM　Dentist Appointment

12:00 PM - 1:00 PM　Lunch w/Tom

3:00 PM - 4:00 PM　Meet prospective client

Tasks

☐ Tune snow thrower
☐ Call PTA Reps
☐ Get roofing estimates
☐ Write check for band banquet
☐ Shop for anniversary present

Messages

Inbox	0
Drafts	1
Outbox	0

Create and check your to-do list.

Write notes to yourself.

Create an address book.

Outlook can help you manage your life.

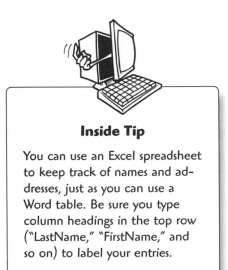

Inside Tip

You can use an Excel spreadsheet to keep track of names and addresses, just as you can use a Word table. Be sure you type column headings in the top row ("LastName," "FirstName," and so on) to label your entries.

A spreadsheet program, such as Microsoft Excel, displays a grid consisting of multiple rows and columns that intersect to form little boxes called *cells*. Each cell has an *address* consisting of its column letter and row number; for example, the cell in the upper-left corner is A1. You type your entries just as you would type them in a table. Press the **Tab** or down arrow key to move from one cell to the next, and then type your entries in each cell.

What makes spreadsheets special is that you can enter a formula in a cell that performs a calculation and displays the results. For example, the formula $=(A1+B1+C1)/3$ totals the values in the cells A1, B1, and C1 and divides the total by 3 to determine the average. Later in this chapter, you learn how to enter basic formulas in a Word table.

Managing Records in a Database

The Cadillac of data management tools is the database program. A database program lets you design your own forms for collecting data, making data entry as easy as filling in the blanks. As shown in the following figure, the form represents a single *record* in the database consisting of several *field* entries.

Each record consists of multiple field entries.

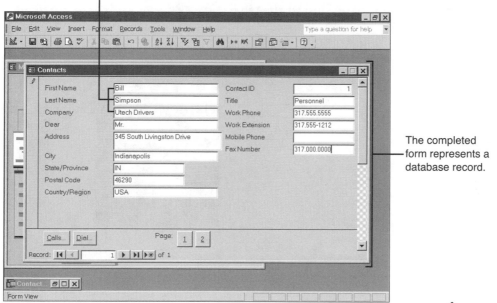

The completed form represents a database record.

With a database program, you complete forms to enter records into the database.

After you have entered the data for several records, you can use the database tools to find, sort, or filter records. *Filtering* consists of restricting the number of records the database displays; for example, you can tell the database to display only records for February 2001. In addition, you can create reports, which pull data from one or more databases and then organize and summarize the data.

Inside Tip

Most database programs have sample databases, wizards, and other tools to help you create forms and reports. Use these tools to create basic forms and reports and then customize them to suit your needs. Don't try to go it alone when you're first learning about databases. This is pretty complicated stuff.

Setting Your Own Table

Early in this chapter, I promised to show you how to create a simple address book using a Word table, so let's get started. First, click the **Insert Table** button. This opens a list showing a graphic representation of the columns and rows that make up a table. Drag down and to the right to highlight the desired number of rows and columns. If you need more columns or rows than first shown, drag beyond the bottom or right side of the grid to expand it (see the following figure). When you release the mouse button, Word inserts the table.

*Use the **Insert Table** button to set the number of rows and columns.*

Click the Insert Table button.

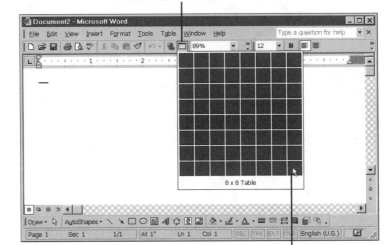

Drag over the desired number of columns and rows.

Typing in the Little Boxes

After the table is in place, start typing your entries. In the top row, type headings for each column; for instance, type LastName, FirstName, and Address. These headings allow Word to find and extract data from the table to create mailing labels and personally addressed letters, as explained in the next chapter.

If an entry is too wide for the column, Word automatically resizes the columns or wraps text inside a cell to accommodate the entry. If you prefer to resize the columns and rows yourself, skip ahead to the next section.

Whoa!

When typing column headings, don't type any spaces. For example, use "LName" or "LastName" instead of "Last Name." Using spaces confuses the mail merge feature, discussed in Chapter 14.

Press the **Tab** key to move from one cell (box) to the next, or click in the cell. When you reach the end of a row, press the **Tab** key to move to the next row. If you're in the last cell of the last row, pressing the **Tab** key creates a new row, so you can continue typing entries.

Rearranging and Resizing Columns and Rows

A table never turns out perfect the first time. Maybe you want more space between the topmost row and the rest of the table, or maybe you just don't like how Word is wrapping entries in the cells. In the following sections, you learn tricks for restructuring your table.

Adjusting the Row Height and Column Width

The easiest way to adjust the row height and column width is to drag the lines that divide the columns and rows. When you move the mouse pointer over a line, the pointer changes into a double-headed arrow; that's when you can start dragging. If you hold down the **Alt** key and drag, the horizontal or vertical ruler shows the exact row height or column width measurement. (You can also drag the column or row markers inside the rulers to change the row height and column width.)

Inserting and Deleting Columns and Rows

When you start typing entries in a table, you might find that you have either too many rows or columns or too few. Either problem is easy to correct:

> ➤ To insert one or more rows, click in the row where you want the new row added (or drag over the desired number of rows) and choose **Table, Insert, Rows Above**, or **Rows Below**.

Computer Cheat

To have Word automatically adjust the row height and column width to accommodate your entries, select the row(s) or column(s) that you want to change, and then open the **Table** menu, point to **AutoFit,** and choose the desired option.

Inside Tip

You can merge two or more cells to create a cell that spans multiple columns or rows. For example, you might want to type a heading at the top of your table. Drag over the cells that you want to transform into a single cell, open the **Table** menu, and select **Merge Cells.** To split a cell, select the cell and choose **Table, Split Cells.**

➤ To insert one or more columns, first select an existing column (to insert two columns, select two columns). Then, choose **Table, Insert, Columns to the Left**, or **Columns to the Right**.

➤ To delete rows or columns, drag over the rows or columns you want to delete and choose **Table, Delete, Rows** or **Columns**. (If you press the **Delete** key instead, Word removes only the contents of the rows or columns.)

Sorting Your List

Tables commonly contain entries that you need to sort alphabetically or numerically. If you create a table of phone numbers for people and places that you frequently call, for example, you might want to sort the list alphabetically to make it easy to find people.

To sort entries in a table, first select the entire table (or the portion that contains the entries you want to sort). If you have a row at the top that contains descriptions of the contents in each column, be sure it is not selected; otherwise, it is sorted along with the other rows.

Open the **Table** menu and select **Sort**. Open the **Sort by** list and select the column that contains the entries to sort by. For example, if you want to sort by last name and the last names are in the second column, select **Column 2.** Open the **Type** drop-down list and select the type of items you want to sort (**Number, Text**, or **Date**). Select the desired sort order: **Ascending** (1, 2, 3 or A, B, C) or **Descending** (Z, Y, X or 10, 9, 8). Click **OK** to sort the entries.

Automating Calculations with Formulas

If your table includes numerical entries, such as membership dues or contributions, you might want to include a basic formula that totals a column of numbers.

Although a Word table is not designed to perform the complicated mathematical operations that an Excel spreadsheet can handle, tables can perform some basic calculations. For example, to total a column of numbers, take the following steps:

1. Click in the cell directly below the column of numbers you want to total.

2. Open the **Table** menu and click **Formula**. By default, the Formula dialog box is set up to total the values directly above the current cell.

3. Click **OK** to total the numbers.

Decorating Your Table with Lines and Shading

Your table might appear bland at first sight, but you can spice it up with some borders and shading. By far, the easiest way to embellish your table is to use the Auto-Format feature. Click anywhere inside the table, open the **Table** menu, and select **Table AutoFormat.** Select the desired design for your table and click **OK.**

If you don't like the prefab table designs that Word has to offer, you can design the table yourself using the Borders and Shading dialog box. To change the borders or add shading to the entire table, be sure the insertion point is somewhere inside the table; you don't have to select the entire table. To add borders or shading to specific cells, select the cells. Then open the **Format** menu and select **Borders and Shading** to display the Borders and Shading dialog box.

To add borders around cells or around the entire table, click the **Borders** tab. Select any of the border arrangements on the left, or create a custom border by inserting lines of a specific thickness, design, and color. Open the **Apply to** drop-down list, and choose **Table** (to apply the lines to the entire table) or **Cell** (to apply lines to only selected cells). You can turn individual border lines on or off by clicking them in the **Preview** area, as shown in the following figure.

To shade cells with color or gray shading, click the **Shading** tab. In the **Fill** grid, click the color that you want to use to shade the table or selected cells. Under **Patterns,** click a color and percentage to add a pattern of a different color to the shading. For example, you might choose green as the fill and use a 50 percent yellow pattern to brighten the green. When you finish entering your border and shading preferences, click **OK** to apply the changes to your table.

Computer Cheat

For quick formatting, use the Tables and Borders toolbar. Right-click any toolbar and click **Tables and Borders.** In addition to buttons for formatting tables, this toolbar contains the **Eraser** button, which lets you quickly erase the lines that define cell boundaries.

Use the Borders and Shading dialog box to jazz up your table.

Click a button or click a line in the Preview area to place or remove a line.

Shading tab

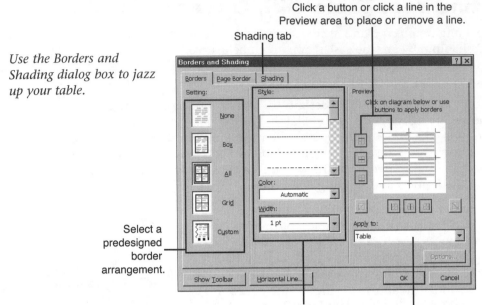

Select a predesigned border arrangement.

Select a line style, thickness, and color.

Choose to apply the style to selected cells or the entire table.

What About Pictures?

Can you add pictures to a table? Of course! In fact, a table is the perfect tool for aligning graphics and text. For example, you can use a table to create your own catalog. Simply insert graphics in the left column, type product descriptions in the center column, and add prices to the right column.

Before you insert a picture, be sure the insertion point is in the cell into which you want to insert the picture. Use the **Insert**, **Picture**, **Clip Art**, or **From File** command to insert the image. If you resize the image, you might need to resize the cell.

Inside Tip

You can use a two-column table to lay out your resumé. In the upper-left cell, insert a clip art image that's appropriate for the job opening.

134

The Least You Need to Know

➤ Use a table to create and print simple lists.

➤ A personal information manager, such as Microsoft Outlook, features superior tools for creating and using an address book.

➤ Use a spreadsheet for any data on which you need to perform calculations.

➤ A database is most useful for heavy-duty data management and for producing forms and reports.

➤ To create a table in Word, click the **Insert Table** button and drag over the desired number of rows and columns.

➤ If you use a table to create your address book, type column headings in the first row.

➤ To adjust the width of a column, drag the line on the right side of the column.

➤ To sort the records (rows) in a table, select all the records and then issue the **Table, Sort** command.

Chapter 14

Form Letters, Mailing Labels, and Envelopes

In This Chapter

➤ Making your very own form letter

➤ Automating mass mailings

➤ Printing mailing labels for your Christmas cards

➤ Printing a stack of envelopes

Whether you run your own small business or just have lots of friends and relatives, mailing announcements, invitations, and greeting cards can become a major ordeal. Fortunately, Microsoft Word and most other popular word processors include a *mail merge* feature that can automate the task for you.

In this chapter, you learn how to create your own form letter and use Word's mail merge feature to merge that form letter with a list of names and addresses to generate a stack of personally addressed letters. You also learn how to use the mail merge feature to print a stack of matching envelopes. By the end of this chapter, all you'll have to do is stuff the envelopes and peel and stick the stamps.

The Incredible Power of the Mail Merge Feature

The mail merge feature is a powerful tool that merges a standard document, such as a form letter or mailing label, with a *data source,* such as an address list, to generate a

Tech Term

A **data source** can be any document that contains a collection of records consisting of data entries. A data source may be a table, spreadsheet, database, or address book.

series of unique documents. For example, the mail merge feature can merge a form letter with an address list to generate a stack of letters personally addressed to each person on the list.

Here's how it works: First, you create a form letter with *field codes* that tell your document which pieces of data to extract from the data source and where to insert them in your document. For instance, the field code <<LastName>> tells mail merge to grab data entries from the LastName column in the data source. When you execute the mail merge operation, mail merge generates a single document for each name in the data source. You can use mail merge to generate your form letters and print matching envelopes or mailing labels, as shown in the following figure.

Mail merge generates a unique document for each record in a table.

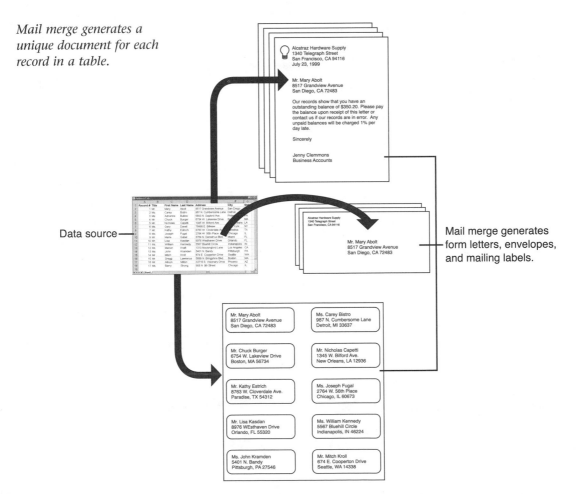

Data source

Mail merge generates form letters, envelopes, and mailing labels.

The Making of a Form Letter

How you compose your form letter is your business. You can type it from scratch, use a template, or seek help from the Letter Wizard. Omit any information that Word obtains from the data source during the merge, such as the person's name and address. After you complete the letter, you will insert field codes into the letter (one for the person's name, one for the address, and so on). These codes tell mail merge which entries to extract from the data source and where to insert those entries.

Computer Cheat

The easiest way to write and format a letter is to use the Letter Wizard. In Word 2002, choose **Tools, Letters and Mailings, Letter Wizard.** In Word 2000, choose **Tools, Letter Wizard.** The Letter Wizard dialog box displays a fill-in-the-blank form that you can use to specify your preferences and enter information such as the inside address, the salutation, and the closing.

Inserting the Secret Codes

Assuming you created an address book in the preceding chapter, you should have everything you need to perform a mail merge: a form letter and a data source. You can now use the mail merge feature to insert field codes in your form letter.

The steps vary, depending on which version of Word you're using. In Word 2002, follow these steps:

1. Create or open your form letter.

2. Crank down the **Tools** menu, point to **Letters and Mailings**, and select **Mail Merge Wizard.** The Mail Merge task pane appears, providing instructions on how to proceed.

3. Under **Select document type**, click **Letters** to tell Word to use your letter as the main document in the merge.

4. Click **Next: Starting document.** The Mail Merge Wizard prompts you to specify the document you want to use.

5. Be sure **Use the current document** is selected, and then click **Next: Select recipients.** The Mail Merge Wizard prompts you to specify your data source.

6. Select one of the following options and perform the necessary steps to select the source of data that you want to use for the merge:

> **Use an existing list** lets you use a data source you have already created. Select this option and then click **Browse** to display a dialog box that lets you pick the data source file.

> **Select from Outlook contacts** lets you use your Outlook contact list as the data source. Select this option and then click **Choose Contacts Folder** to select the contacts file you want to use as the data source.

> **Type a new list** leads you through the process of creating an address book containing the data that you want to merge with your form letter. Select this option and then click **Create** to display a fill-in-the-blank dialog box for adding names and addresses to your address book.

7. Click **Next: Write your letter.** The Mail Merge Wizard instructs you to compose your letter if you have not already done so and provides a list of options for inserting codes into your letter.

8. Position the insertion point where you want to insert a piece of data from the database. For example, you might move the insertion point just below the date to insert the person's name and address.

Panic Attack!

The Mail Merge Wizard in Word 2002 tries its best to match its fields to the fields in your data source, but it's not perfect. Click the **Match Fields** button in the lower-left corner of the Insert Address Block or Insert Greeting Line dialog box to adjust the match-ups.

9. Click the link for inserting the desired information. For example, click **Address block** to insert the recipient's name and address, as shown in the following figure. Click **Greeting line** to insert a greeting, such as "Dear Mr. Spock,." To insert individual merge codes that correspond with fields in your database, click the **More items** link and pick the desired code.

10. Enter your preferences in the resulting dialog box and click **OK.** For example, if you chose to insert a greeting line, you can choose to insert the person's first name, title, and last name, or just the last name, in the greeting. The Mail Merge Wizard inserts a merge code into the document, such as {{{{AddressBlock}}}}, which will extract the corresponding data from the data source.

11. Repeat steps 8 through 10 to insert additional merge field codes.

12. Click **Next: Preview your letters.** The Mail Merge Wizard merges your form letter with your data source, creates a collection of personalized letters, and displays the first letter.

13. Click the >> button to preview the next letter or the << button to preview the previous letter. (You can edit individual letters if desired.)

Click the Address block link to insert the recipient's name and address.

Select the information you want to include.

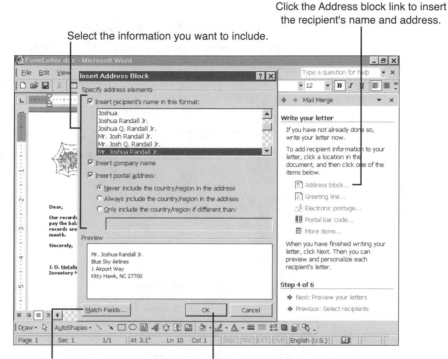

Click Match Fields to make sure Word is looking for the information in the correct data source fields.

Click OK.

Insert field codes to pull entries from the data source into your letter.

In Word 2000, the process is a little more straightforward because you insert a code for each individual data entry. The Mail Merge Helper can lead you through the process. Here's what you do:

1. With your form letter displayed onscreen, crank down the **Tools** menu and select **Mail Merge.** The Mail Merge Helper dialog box appears. It leads you step-by-step through the merge operation.

2. Click **Create** (under **Main Document**), select **Form Letters,** and click **Active Window.** This tells Word to use your letter as the main document in the merge.

3. Under **Data Source,** click **Get Data** and click **Open Data Source.**

4. Select the document that contains the desired records, and click **Open.** (This might be a spreadsheet, a database file, or a Word document containing a table.)

5. The Microsoft Word dialog box appears, telling you that your form letter has no merge fields (as if you didn't know). Click **Edit Main Document.** Word returns you to your form letter and displays the Mail Merge toolbar.

6. Position the insertion point where you want to insert a piece of data from the database. For example, you might move the insertion point a couple lines down from the date to insert the person's name and address.

7. Open the **Insert Merge Field** drop-down list and click the desired field, as shown in the following figure. This inserts a code (such as <<FirstName>>) that will pull specified data (a person's first name, in this case) from the data source and insert it into your letter.

Click Insert Merge field.

*Insert field codes by se-lecting them from the **Insert Merge Field** list.*

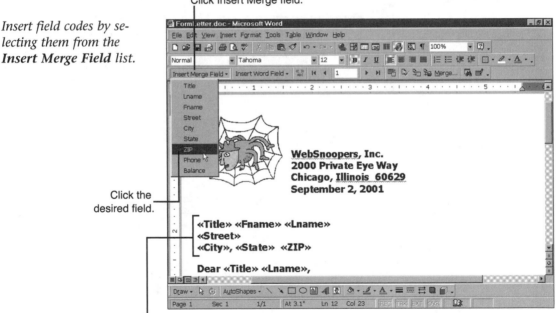

Click the desired field.

Word plugs in the field codes at the insertion point.

8. Repeat step 7 to insert additional merge field codes. Add punctuation and spaces between the codes as necessary. For example, if you are assembling codes to insert the recipient's address, you need to add spaces and commas in the following way:

```
<<Title>> <<FirstName>> <<LastName>>
<<Address>>
<<City>>, <<State>> <<ZIP>>
```

9. If your database contains information that you want to insert in the salutation or body of the letter, insert a field merge code wherever you want that information to appear. You might, for example, use the following salutation:

```
Dear <<Title>> <<LastName>>,
```

Initiating the Merge Operation

Now comes the fun part. After you have inserted the desired field codes, you're ready to initiate the merge operation and generate your personalized letters. Again, the steps vary slightly, depending on whether you're using Word 2002 or an early version.

Whoa!

Don't type your field codes. Typing field codes into your form letter doesn't work. No matter how easy it is, Word just doesn't recognize these codes. You must select the code from the **Insert Field Code** list.

In Word 2002, click **Next: Complete the merge.** You can then click the **Print** link to print the letters or click **Edit Individual Letters** to create a new document consisting of a personally addressed letter for everyone in the data source. (I always choose to edit individual letters so that I can check for errors before printing.) When you're ready to print, just click the **Print** button.

If you're using an earlier version of Word, follow these steps:

1. Click the **Merge** button (on the Merge toolbar). The Merge dialog box appears, as shown in the following figure, offering the following options for controlling how Word merges the form letter and data source:

    Merge to lets you merge to the printer, to a new document, or to your e-mail program. It's a good idea to merge to a new document so that you can check for errors before printing. You can also flip through the merged document and personalize the form letters that Word generates.

    Records to be merged lets you select a range of records so that you can create letters for only selected records in the data source.

    When merging records tells Word whether to insert blank lines when a particular field in a record is blank.

    Query options displays a dialog box that lets you sort the merged letters or create letters for a specific collection of records.

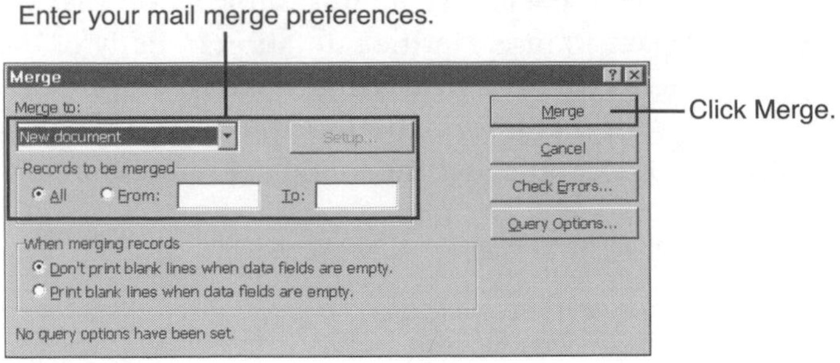

Enter your mail merge preferences.

Use the Merge dialog box to initiate the mail merge operation.

Click Merge.

2. Enter your merge preferences, and then click the **Merge** button. If you choose to merge to the printer, Word starts printing the letters. If you choose to merge to a new file, Word opens a new document window and places the merged letters in this window. You can then print them as you would print any document.

Printing Addresses on Mailing Labels

Now that you have a stack of letters, you need to address them. You can do this by using a mailing label as your main document and merging it with the data source.

In Word 2002, follow the same steps that you followed earlier in this chapter in the section "Inserting the Secret Codes," but when you get to step 3, select **Labels.** There's nothing tricky here; follow the Mail Merge Wizard's instructions in the task pane, and you'll be ready to start stuffing envelopes in no time.

In earlier versions of Word, take the following steps to enlist the aid of the Mail Merge Helper:

1. Open the **Tools** menu and select **Mail Merge.** The Mail Merge Helper dialog box appears.

2. Click **Create** (under **Main Document**) and select **Mailing Labels.** The Microsoft Word dialog box pops up and asks if you want to change the document type or create a new main document.

3. Click **New Main Document.**

4. Under **Data Source,** click **Get Data** and click **Open Data Source.**

5. Select the same data source document you used for your form letter, and click **Open.** The Microsoft Word dialog box appears, telling you that it needs to set up the main document.

6. Click **Set Up Main Document.** The Label Options dialog box appears, asking you to specify the type and size of the mailing labels on which you intend to print.

7. Choose the correct label type and size, enter any additional printing preferences for your mailing labels, and click **OK.** The Mail Merge Helper displays the Create Labels dialog box, which prompts you to insert the merge field codes for creating the label.

8. Click the **Insert Merge Field** button and select the desired field code.

9. Repeat step 8 to insert additional field codes. Type any required punctuation and spaces between codes. (To change the font used for the label, drag over the codes, right-click the selection, and click **Font.**)

10. Click **OK.**

After you have entered the field codes, you're ready to execute the merge operation and print your mailing labels. Follow the same steps you performed earlier in this chapter in the section "Initiating the Merge Operation."

Printing a Stack of Envelopes for Mass Mailing

At the beginning of this chapter, I promised that after you learned how to use mail merge, all you would need to do is stuff envelopes and peel and stick mailing labels. I lied. You can reduce your workload even more by printing the addresses directly on your envelopes.

To use the mail merge feature to print envelopes, follow the same steps you followed to create mailing labels, but when prompted to choose the document type, choose **Envelopes.** After you enter the field codes and give your okay, Mail Merge Helper returns you to the main document, where your field codes are laid out on an "envelope." Type your name and return address in the upper-left corner to have it printed on the envelope. You can then click the option for executing the merge and printing your envelopes.

Inside Tip

Print your mailing labels on inexpensive printer paper, and hold the printed addresses over a sheet of labels to check the alignment. You can move the addresses down by adding blank lines before the first line of field codes or by using the **Format, Paragraph** command to add space before the first line. To move the addresses to the right, add spaces to the left of each line.

Inside Tip

If you're mailing tri-fold newsletters or brochures, you don't need an envelope. Simply create a new main document and position the field codes where you want the addresses printed (typically the center of the page). You can then print the addresses directly on the back of the brochures or newsletters.

The Least You Need to Know

➤ To use the mail merge feature, you need a main document and a data source.

➤ Field codes tell mail merge where to obtain each data entry.

➤ To use the mail merge feature in Word 2002, open the **Tools** menu, point to **Letters and Mailings,** and click **Mail Merge Wizard.** In earlier versions of Word, open the **Tools** menu and click **Mail Merge.**

➤ The first step in performing a mail merge is to specify the type of document you want to create: a form letter, mailing labels, or envelopes.

➤ The second step in performing a mail merge is to specify the location of your data source.

➤ After specifying the location of the data source, you can insert field codes in your main document where you want specific data entries inserted.

➤ To initiate the merge, click **Next: Complete the merge** (in Word 2002) or click the **Merge** button on the Merge toolbar (in earlier versions of Word).

Part 4

Getting Wired to the Internet

Faster than Federal Express. More powerful than the Home Shopping Network. Able to leap wide continents in a single click. Look, up on your desktop. It's a phone! It's a network! No, it's the Internet!

With your computer, a modem, and a standard phone line, you have access to the single most powerful communications and information network in the World—the Internet. The chapters in this part show you how to get wired to the Internet and use its features to exchange electronic mail, chat with friends and strangers, shop for deals, manage your investments, plan your next vacation, research interesting topics, and even publish your own creations via the Web!

Chapter 15

Connecting to the Outside World with a Modem

In This Chapter

➤ Ten good reasons to buy a modem

➤ Grasping the basic principles of modem talk

➤ Understanding ISDN, DSL, and other modem acronyms

➤ Getting your modem up and running

➤ Dialing out with your modem

How would you like to access the latest news, weather, and sports without stepping away from your computer? Track investments without having to call a broker or wait for tomorrow's newspaper? Connect to an online encyclopedia, complete with sounds and pictures? Order items from a computerized catalog? Send a postage-free letter and have it arrive at its destination in a matter of seconds? Mingle with friends and strangers in online chat rooms? Transfer files from your computer to a colleague's computer anywhere in the world?

With your computer, a modem, and a subscription to an online service or Internet service provider, you can do all this and more. This chapter introduces you to the wonderful world of modems and shows you how to connect your computer to the outside world.

What Can I Do with My Modem?

A modem is the single most liberating tool for your computer. With a modem and a computer, you can connect to other computers located down the block, across town, or anywhere in the world—assuming that the remote computer lets you in. Here's a sample of some of the cool stuff you can do with your modem:

➤ Get the latest news, up-to-the-minute stock prices, sports scores, weather reports, and travel information.

➤ Shop anywhere in the world, track down hard-to-find products, and even place an order on the Web.

➤ Research any topic imaginable without leaving your home or office.

➤ Take classes on everything from using your computer to speaking Spanish.

➤ Exchange e-mail (electronic mail) messages with anyone in the world who has an e-mail account.

➤ Chat with friends, relatives, and complete strangers by typing and transmitting messages back and forth.

➤ Save on long-distance service by placing long-distance calls over the Internet. (By connecting a video camera to your computer, you can even talk face to face.)

➤ Play games in two-player mode. If you have a game that lets you play games in two-player mode by using a modem, the program probably contains all the tools you need to play the game over the phone lines. Refer to the user manual that came with the game.

➤ Transfer files between your computer at work and your computer at home.

➤ Publish your own documents electronically on the Web. You can publish a personal page, family page, or business page, including photos, original drawings, and even audio and video clips.

Tech Term

Kbps stands for kilobits per second, which is equivalent to 1,000 bits per second. Faster speeds, such as those achieved over cable and network connections, are commonly expressed in Mbps, or megabits per second, which is equivalent to 1,000,000 bits.

How This Modem Thing Works

A *modem* (short for MOdulator DEModulator) is essentially a phone for computers. A phone converts incoming signals from a phone line into audio output that you can hear. In a similar manner, a standard modem converts the analog signals that travel over phone lines into digital signals that the computer can process. To send a signal, a standard modem converts the digital signal from your computer into an analog signal that can be transmitted over phone lines. A cable modem converts RF (radio frequency) signals into digital signals and acts as a tuner, network card, and modem all rolled into one. Modems transfer data at different speeds, commonly measured in *bits per second* (*bps*). The higher the number, the faster the modem can transfer data. Common rates for standard modems include 28,800bps, 33,600bps, and 56,800bps. Because these modem speed numbers are becoming so long, manufacturers have started to abbreviate them. You'll commonly see speeds listed as 33.6Kbps or 58.8Kbps. When they start dropping the "bps" and list something like 56K, you know it's really fast. Although you pay more for a higher transfer rate, you save time and decrease your phone bill by purchasing a faster modem.

Modem Types: Standard, ISDN, DSL, and Cable

If your computer is not equipped with a modem, you need to do a little shopping. However, before you visit your local computer store, you should do a little homework and check out your modem options. The following sections explain the major differences between modems and introduce special features you might want to consider.

Chugging Along with Standard Modems

Because standard modems are the least expensive of the lot and because they can send and receive signals over standard phone lines, they remain the most popular type of modems. However, not all standard modems are created equal. As you shop for a modem, you should consider the following features:

➤ **Speed.** Don't settle for anything slower than 56Kbps.

➤ **Internal versus external.** Most computers come with an internal modem that's built into the computer. All you see of the modem are jacks for connecting the modem to a phone line and (optionally) plugging in a phone. An external modem sits outside the computer and connects to the computer's serial (COM, or communications) port or a USB (Universal Serial Bus) port using a cable. External modems typically have indicator lights that can help you troubleshoot connection problems. Before you purchase an internal modem, be sure your computer has an open *expansion slot*. Before purchasing an external modem, be sure you have an open serial or USB port.

➤ **Serial port or USB connection.** If you decide to purchase an external modem and your computer is equipped with one or more USB ports, opt for the USB modem. USB allows you to connect up to 127 devices to a single port, giving your computer virtually unlimited expandability. This leaves your sole serial port open for other devices.

➤ **ITU or V.90 support.** ITU or V.90 is the international standard for 56K modems. You might find modems that advertise the x2 standard. In the past, these modems did not conform to the V.90 standard, but newer x2 modems support V.90.

➤ **Fax support.** Like fully equipped fax machines, a fax/modem allows you to exchange faxes with a conventional fax machine or another computer that has a fax/modem.

Tech Term

Your computer has a big circuit board inside it that everything else plugs into. This board is called the **motherboard.** The motherboard typically has five or more **expansion slots** that are about a half-inch wide and four to six inches long, depending on the slot type. On most computers, the expansion slots are located in the back. You can plug smaller circuit boards, called expansion cards, into these slots to upgrade your computer and add capabilities. For example, you can add a network card for connecting your computer to a network or add a modem card to dial into an online service.

➤ **Voice support.** If you plan on having your computer answer the phone and take messages, be sure the modem offers voice support. Without voice support, your modem can answer the phone, but it can only emit annoying screeching noises—which is useful for making telemarketers back off.

➤ **Videoconferencing support.** Some modems are also designed to handle video calls, sort of like on *The Jetsons*. Of course, you'll need a video camera to take advantage of this feature.

Standard modems offer three benefits: the modem itself is inexpensive and easy to install, the modem plugs into a standard phone jack, and online services offer modem connections at bargain rates. However, for speedy Internet connections, consider the options described in the following sections.

Whoa!

56K pushes the limits of phone line communications. The phone company limits connection speeds to 53K, although there is some talk of raising the speed limit. You will rarely see data transfers at 56Kps. Expect a maximum speed of about 40 to 45Kbps, and that's only when your modem is receiving data. A 56K modem still sends data at 28.8 to 33.6Kbps due to other limitations, such as line noise.

Speeding Up Your Connections with ISDN

Unlike standard modems that must perform analog-to-digital conversions, ISDN deals only with digital signals, supporting much higher data transfer rates: 128Kbps, which is more than twice as fast as 56K modems. ISDN modems use two separate 64Kbps channels, called *B channels,* that, when used simultaneously, achieve the 128Kbps transfer rates. This two-channel approach also lets you talk on the phone while surfing the Web; one channel carries your voice while the other carries computer signals at 64Kbps (half speed). When you hang up, the modem can use both channels for computer communications. A third, slower channel (channel D) is used by the phone company to identify callers and do basic line checking, so you don't really need to think about it.

Shop for the ISDN service before you shop for an IDSN modem or adapter, and ask your phone company for recommendations. The performance of your ISDN connection relies on how well your ISDN adapter works with your phone company's connection.

The New Kid on the Block: DSL Modems

Short for *digital subscriber line,* DSL promises to put a big dent in the ISDN market and challenge cable companies. Using standard phone lines, DSL can achieve data transfer rates of up to 1.5Mbps, or even 9Mbps if you're within 2 miles of a DSL connection center. At 1.5Mbps, a DSL modem is about 25 times faster than a standard 56Kbps modem. DSL achieves these rates over standard analog phone lines by using frequencies not used by voice signals. The only drawback is that because DSL is a relatively new product (although the technology has been around awhile); it might not be available in your area or supported by your online service.

Several types of DSL are available, including ADSL and SDSL. In North America, ADSL (Asynchronous DSL) is most common. "Asynchronous" indicates that the system uses different data transfer rates for upstream and downstream communications—typically 32Mbps for downstream traffic and 32Kbps to 1Mbps for upstream traffic. In Europe, SDSL (Symmetric DSL) is most common. SDSL lines use the same data transfer rates for both upstream and downstream traffic.

Because there is no single DSL standard, don't purchase a modem without first checking with your phone company. Most DSL providers market their service as a package deal and include a DSL modem that works with the service.

Whoa!

Although ISDN might sound like the ideal solution for home and small-business use, ISDN setup and service can be expensive. Call your phone company, and add up the costs before you decide.

Whoa!

Before you jump on the DSL bandwagon, do some research and ask your phone company to provide details on the cost, reliability, and performance boost you can expect from your DSL service. DSL is a relatively new technology, and it might fall a little short of the hype.

The Pros and Cons of Cable Modems

Like cable television connections, a cable Internet connection supports high-speed data transfers to your PC, allowing you to cruise the Internet at the same speed you can flip TV channels. In addition to speed, cable modems are relatively inexpensive (starting at about $200) and are easy to install. You can expect to pay about $40 to $60 per month for cable Internet access, which makes it competitive with ISDN service. However, cable modems do have a few drawbacks:

➤ **Availability.** Your cable company might not offer Internet cable service.

➤ **Variable connection speeds.** Cable service is set up to serve a pool of users. The more users connected to one service station, the slower the connection. Although cable companies commonly advertise 8Mbps data transfer rates, the rate you'll experience will likely be around 1 to 2Mbps.

➤ **Upload problems.** Cable was developed to bring signals into homes, not carry them out. However, cable companies are developing two-way systems to eliminate this limitation. Chances are that if your cable company offers Internet access, it also offers upload capabilities.

Inside Tip

Although a satellite service, such as DirecPC, offers speedy connections, it's tough to set up, the satellite connection is iffy at times, the service is relatively expensive, and you need a modem to carry outgoing signals. This isn't the best option for a new user.

When shopping for a cable connection, your primary consideration is how the cable service handles return signals. Most services use either *telephone-return* or *RF-return*. With RF-return, the cable modem transmits signals along the cable. With telephone-return, the modem sends signals along a standard modem connection. Before you purchase a modem, check with the cable service to determine the type of return system it uses.

Connecting Your Modem to an Outside Line

Most computers are equipped with an internal modem. If your computer does not have a modem, you have several options:

➤ Get an external serial modem, and (with the computer turned off) plug the modem into your computer's serial port (commonly labeled COM1 or COM2). When you restart your computer, Windows leads you through the process of installing the modem's software.

➤ Get an external USB modem, plug it into your computer's USB port, and follow the onscreen instructions to install the software. (One of the benefits of USB is that it allows you to safely connect devices to your computer when the power is on.)

➤ Hire a service technician or get help from a knowledgeable friend to install and set up an internal modem. Although installing and setting up an internal modem is usually easy, you need to follow a long list of safety precautions to ensure that you don't damage any equipment. In addition, internal modems occasionally cause conflicts with other devices, and troubleshooting these conflicts can be a very complicated process.

Plugging in a Standard, ISDN, or DSL Modem

After the modem is installed, connect it to the phone line. If you're setting up a standard or DSL modem, use a phone cord (with RJ-11 connectors) to connect the line-in or Telco jack on the modem to the phone jack on the wall. If you're setting up an ISDN adapter, use an ISDN cable (with RJ-45 jacks) to connect the ISDN-U port or NT-1 port with the ISDN wall jack.

To share the phone line with a phone or fax machine, use another phone cord to connect the phone jack on the modem to the phone or fax machine as shown in the following figure.

Side view of modem

You can plug a phone or fax machine into the phone jack.

PHONE

Line-in or telco jack connects to the telephone line.

TELCO

MIC

LINE OUT

Connect a phone to your modem so that you can place calls when you're not using your modem.

Connecting a Cable Modem

Unless you're the resident handyman in your neighborhood, I strongly recommend that you shell out the $50 to your cable company to hire a professional to install your cable modem, or try to talk them into giving you a free installation, because they'll make a ton of money off you in the long run. The installation can be fairly complex:

➤ If your computer does not have a network card, you must install a new network card, typically called an *Ethernet adapter*. This card has an outlet on the back that allows you to plug your cable modem into the computer. (If your computer has a USB port, you can purchase a USB/Ethernet adapter that allows you to connect the cable modem to the USB port.)

➤ If there is no cable connection to your computer, you must add a splitter to an existing cable and run a cable to your modem. Because most cable modems are external, you'll need to plug the cable modem into a power source.

➤ After your cable modem is connected to the cable, to the network card, and to a power source, you must install network protocols that let your computer communicate with the cable company's network. Installing the correct protocols and entering the required settings can be a real headache.

I recommend that you hire a professional installer, because a professional has the equipment needed to test for and repair any cable problems, install the required networking protocols, enter the correct settings, and get your cable connection up and running in a hurry. And, if you have trouble connecting, you have someone to call for help.

Dialing Out: Does It Work?

To be sure that your computer acknowledges having a modem, use your modem to make your next phone call (assuming you have a phone connected to your modem). Click **Start, Programs, Accessories, Communications, Phone Dialer.** Type the phone number you want to dial, and click **Dial.** When someone answers, pick up the receiver on your phone and start talking.

Of course, you can't dial out with your cable modem, so is there any way to test it? Most cable modems are external and have several indicator lights on the front. Typically, one or more lights must be lit, not flashing, to indicate a stable connection. Check the modem manual to determine what these status lights indicate. In general, if the lights are all out, be sure your modem is plugged in and turned on. If two or more lights are flashing, the modem is either trying to establish a connection or telling you there's a problem.

In addition, if you plugged the cable modem into a network card, the network card should have a light that indicates a stable network connection. In most cases, the light should be solid.

Troubleshooting Your Modem Connection

If your computer and Windows do not acknowledge the fact that a modem is installed, you might have to do a little troubleshooting. Fortunately, the Windows Modem Troubleshooter can help. To troubleshoot problems with a standard modem, take the following steps to run the Modem Troubleshooter:

1. Open the **Start** menu and click **Help.**

2. Click the **Contents** tab, if needed, to bring it to the front. (In Windows Me, skip this step.)

3. Click **Troubleshooting** (at the bottom of the **Contents** list).

4. Click **Hardware & System Device Problems** (in Windows Me), or **Windows 98 Troubleshooters** (in Windows 98), or an equivalent command, depending on your version of Windows. The Windows help system displays a list of trouble-shooters.

5. In Windows Me, click **Hardware, memory, & others.** In other versions of Windows, skip to step 6.

6. Click **Modem** to start the Modem Troubleshooter. In the right pane, the trouble-shooter displays a list of questions, as shown in the following figure.

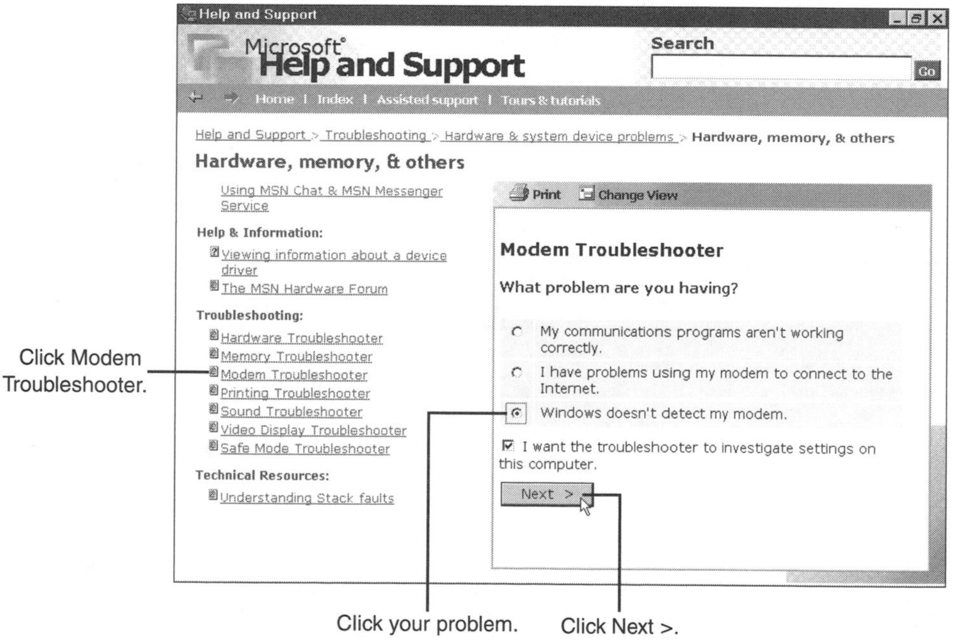

Click Modem Troubleshooter.

Click your problem.   Click Next >.

The Windows Modem Troubleshooter can help you track down and correct problems.

7. Click the answer that best represents the problem.

8. Click **Next** > and follow the Modem Troubleshooter's instructions to complete the troubleshooting process and correct the problem.

A cable modem connection is more like a network connection than a phone connection. If your cable modem is failing to connect, the problem might be with your networking card, the installed network protocols, or other network settings. If you have trouble connecting with a cable modem, run the Networking Troubleshooter.

Inside Tip

Windows features several troubleshooters for tracking down everything from mouse problems to audio system failures. If, in Chapter 16, "Finding an Information FREEway," you have trouble connecting to the Internet even though your modem is functioning, run the Networking Troubleshooter. A wrong network setting can prevent Windows from establishing a connection to an ISP.

The Least You Need to Know

➤ You can use a modem to connect to the Internet or a commercial online service, play multiplayer games over the phone lines or a cable connection, connect to a desktop computer from a remote location, or place free long-distance phone calls over the Internet.

➤ Although you can squeak by with a 28.8Kbps modem, a 56Kbps modem makes cruising the Web much more enjoyable.

➤ ISDN modems are preferable to standard modems because ISDN deals with digital-to-digital signals, which support significantly higher data transfer rates than standard analog-to-digital modems.

➤ DSL modems offer faster connections rates than even ISDN and have the included advantage of being used through regular phone lines.

➤ Call your cable company to find out if the company provides cable modem service for your area.

➤ To use a phone along with a standard modem, plug the phone into the modem's phone jack and connect the line jack on the modem to the incoming phone line jack on the wall.

➤ If Windows doesn't detect your modem, run the Modem Troubleshooter.

costs $21.95 per month. Call 1-800-FREE-MSN (1-800-373-3676) or visit www. msn.com for more information and a free month trial.

➤ **Prodigy Internet.** This gives you unlimited access for $19.95 per month ($198 or $16.50 per month if you make a one-year commitment). Prodigy also offers several other payment plans, including the Low Usage Plan ($9.95 per month for 10 hours plus $1.50 for each additional hour). Prodigy Internet is more like an ISP than a commercial service, offering few members-only perks. Call 1-800-PRODIGY (1-800-776-3449) or visit www.prodigy.com for more information.

The next section shows you how to sign up for a subscription to these services. When you sign up as a new member, the service provides information about its free trial period.

Signing Up for Your Membership

Check your Windows desktop for an **MSN** or **Online Services** icon. The **MSN** icon is for The Microsoft Network. The **Online Services** icon contains additional icons for America Online, Prodigy, EarthLink, and AT&T WorldNet. Click one of these icons and follow the onscreen instructions to install the online service's program from the Windows CD, connect to the service, and sign up.

The installation program uses the modem to dial a toll-free number that lists local numbers. After you select a local number (and usually an alternative number in case the first number is busy), the installation program disconnects from the toll-free connection and then reconnects you locally. Most services then ask you to supply the following information:

➤ Your modem's COM port. To determine the COM port, double-click the **Modems** icon in the Control Panel, click your modem's name, and click **Properties**.

Whoa!

The rates listed here do not include phone charges. If the service does not have a local phone number for where you live, you might end up paying long-distance rates to connect. Some services offer 800 numbers but typically charge a per-minute rate to use that number.

Panic Attack!

If the **Online Services** icon is not on the desktop, it might not be installed. Double-click the **Add/Remove Programs** icon in the Windows Control Panel, click the **Windows Setup** tab, be sure the **Online Services** check box is checked, and click **OK.**

➤ Your modem's maximum speed. (Most services support up to 56K connections. Many services also offer ISDN and DSL support.)

➤ Any special dialing instructions, such as a number you must dial to connect to an outside line.

Whoa!

If you have call waiting, it will disconnect you if anyone calls when you're online. Before typing the phone number, type the code required to disable call waiting (in most cases, *70) followed by a couple of commas. The commas insert delay times so that the code can take effect before the program dials the phone number. (Check with your phone company to determine the code you must enter to disable call waiting, and ask if a service charge is added each time you disable call waiting.)

➤ Your name, address, and telephone number, as shown in the following figure.

➤ A credit card number and expiration date. (Even if the service offers a free trial membership, you must enter a credit card number. If you don't feel safe entering your credit card number online, get the phone number of the service and set up your account over the phone.)

➤ The name (screen name) and password you want to use to log on to the service. Write down your screen name and password in case you forget it. Without this information, you will not be able to connect.

➤ An acceptance of the terms of service (TOS) or rules you must follow to continue using the service. If you break the rules, the service might terminate your account. Read the TOS so that you know what you're getting into.

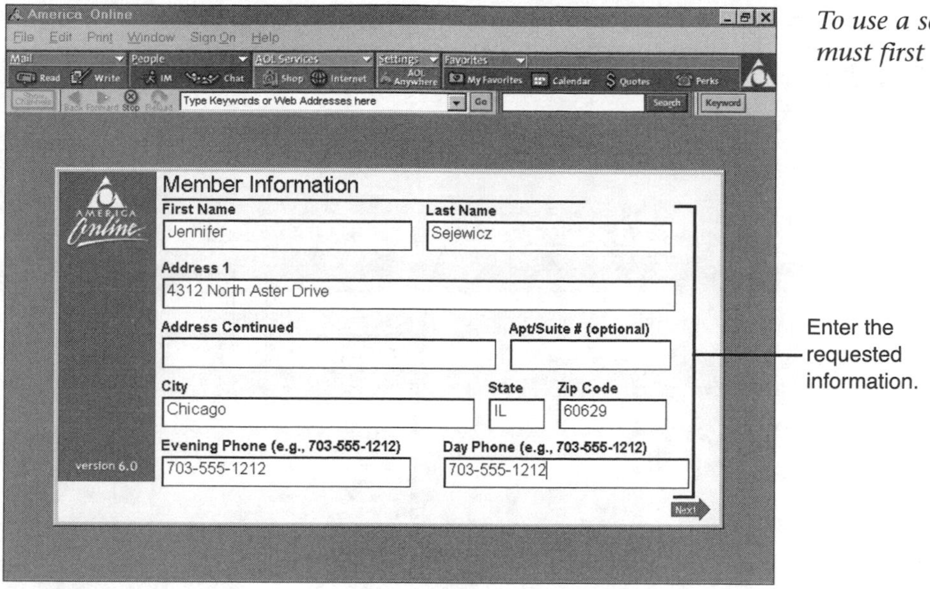

To use a service, you must first register.

Enter the requested information.

Getting Help Online

Because online services differ, I can't give you specific instructions on how to navigate each service, send e-mail messages, post notes on message boards, or chat online. The steps vary from one service to another.

However, all online services display a toolbar or other navigational tool with buttons or links that point to popular features. For example, in America Online, you click the **You've Got Mail** button to access your electronic mailbox. Click the **Internet** button to open a menu for accessing various Internet features, such as the Web, newsgroups (Internet message boards), or the Internet Yellow Pages.

In addition, all commercial services have their own help systems, which typically consist of both online and offline help. Offline help is installed on your hard drive as part of the program and provides general instructions on how to use the service. Online help typically provides assistance for more-specific issues, such as problems you encounter when trying to read e-mail messages. Simply open the **Help** menu and choose the desired type of help. The following figure shows a typical online help screen in America Online.

The best way to learn how to use a service is to explore it on your own and master the help system. If you run into problems and the help system doesn't have the answer, send your question to a technical support representative via e-mail or ask your question in one of the member chat rooms. Most members are friendly and eager to help.

Choose a subject.   Double-click a specific article.

Online help is a great tool for troubleshooting problems.

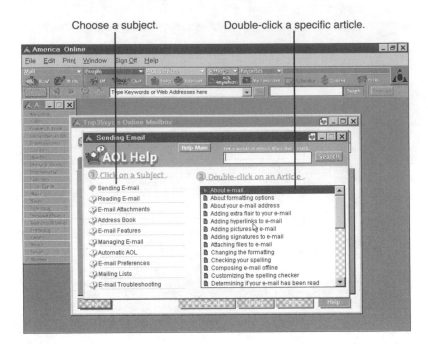

Canceling Your Membership

If you're not satisfied with your online service, don't just stop using the service. Unless you cancel your membership, your online service will dutifully charge the monthly fee to your credit card whether you use the service or not. If you choose to no longer use the service, be sure you cancel your membership before the next month's billing period begins.

Of course, most services don't let you cancel your membership online. You need to call a customer service representative so that the person can grill you on why you want to dump the service. Here's a list of the customer service numbers for the major online services:

Panic Attack!

If the phone number printed here doesn't work, check the online help system or the service's billing area for a customer service phone number.

America Online: 1-888-265-8008

CompuServe: 1-800-848-8990

Prodigy: 1-800-213-0992

Microsoft Network: 1-800-386-5550

Finding Cheaper, Better Ways to Connect to the Internet

Commercial online services are great if you like to be a member of a virtual community or if you're just a little hesitant about exploring the digital world on your own. If you've become addicted to meeting new friends in America Online's chat rooms and you have a well-established e-mail address that all your friends and relatives use to contact you, you probably want to remain a member.

However, online services can be somewhat expensive, and they don't always provide fast, reliable Internet service. In addition, online services often have quirky e-mail systems that make it difficult to exchange e-mails and attached files with nonmembers. If you're looking for a cheap way to establish a pure Internet connection and you're not interested in any members-only perks, consider connecting through an ISP.

Locating a Local Internet Service Provider

To find an ISP, flip through the Yellow Pages and look under Internet Service Providers or Internet Online Service Providers. To find a good ISP, ask your friends, relatives, and colleagues for recommendations. Ask the following questions:

➤ How much does the service charge per month? Do you get unlimited connect time for one price?

➤ Was it easy to set up the connection?

➤ If you had trouble setting up the connection, did the company offer quality assistance?

➤ Do you ever have trouble connecting to the service? (Some ISPs oversell their services, making it difficult to connect during high-traffic hours.)

➤ Does the ISP provide a fast, reliable connection? (Again, ISPs who oversell their services might provide slow Internet connections or be quick to disconnect users during busy hours.)

➤ Has the ISP ever messed up your bill? (I once had an ISP double-charge me for three months running and then threaten to cancel my account.) Be sure the company has its act together. This is good advice even if you're going with a big-name national service.

If you don't have the Yellow Pages or any friends, relatives, or colleagues, skip ahead to the section called "Setting Up Your Internet Connection" later in this chapter. The Windows Internet Connection Wizard can help you track down an ISP.

If you don't mind putting up with a steady stream of onscreen advertisements, try a free Internet service, such as NetZero (at www.netzero.com or call 1-800-333-3633), Juno (at www.juno.com or call 1-800-654-JUNO), or Address.com (at www.address. com). Many of these "free" Internet services started to feel the financial pinch late in

167

the year 2000 and either went out of business or began to limit the number of hours of free connect time. Don't be surprised if one of the companies mentioned here is no longer in business. If the company still is in business and is offering free service, be sure to read the fine print.

Inside Tip

A fast, reliable Internet connection is most important, but tracking down a bottleneck can be difficult. At times, the entire Internet can slow down due to high traffic or multiple system failures. A bad phone connection or outdated telephone company equipment can restrict the data flow to your computer. Even your own computer, if it's bogged down trying to run too many programs, can make a fast connection seem slow.

Gathering the Information You Need to Connect

To set up your account, you need information and settings that tell your computer how to connect to the ISP's computer. Obtain the following information:

➤ **Phone number or network settings.** If you're using a standard, ISDN, or DSL modem to connect, you must have the phone number of the connection site nearest to you. If you have a high-speed cable or satellite connection, your computer connects to the cable company's network, so you must obtain the required network settings, including the computer name and address.

➤ **Username.** This is the name that identifies you to the ISP's computer. It is typically an abbreviation of your first and last names. For example, Jill Eikenhorn might use jeikenhorn as her username. If you have a unique last name and you're concerned that someone might use your name to stalk you, use a cryptic nickname. You can choose any name you like, as long as it is not already being used by another user.

➤ **Password.** The ISP might let you select your own password or might assign you a password. Be sure to write down the password in case you forget it.

➤ **Connection type.** Most ISPs offer PPP (Point-to-Point Protocol), but ask to be sure. PPP is simply a "language" that two computers agree to speak in order to communicate over the Internet. An older protocol called SLIP (Serial Line Internet Protocol) is a little slower and less reliable, but some ISPs still support it.

➤ **Domain name server.** The domain name server (DNS) is a computer that's set up to locate computers on the Internet. Each computer on the Internet has a unique number that identifies it, such as 197.72.34.74. Each computer also has a domain name, such as www.hollywood.com, which makes it easier for people to remember the computer's address. When you enter a domain name, the domain name server looks up the computer's number and locates it.

➤ **Domain name.** This is the domain name of your service provider's computer, such as internet.com. You use the domain name in conjunction with your username as your e-mail address—for example, jeikenhorn@internet.com.

➤ **News server.** The news server lets you connect to any of thousands of newsgroups on the Internet to read and post messages. Newsgroups are electronic bulletin boards for special-interest groups. The news server name typically starts with "news" and is followed by the service provider's domain name—for example, news.internet.com.

➤ **Mail server.** The mail server is in charge of electronic mail. You need to specify two mail servers: POP (Post Office Protocol) for incoming mail, and SMTP (Simplified Mail Transfer Protocol) for mail you send. The POP server's name typically starts with "pop" and is followed by the service provider's domain name, such as pop.internet.com. The SMTP server's name typically starts with "smtp" or "mail" and is followed by the service provider's domain name, such as smtp.internet.com. (See Chapter 17, "Sending E-Mail: Postage-Free Same-Day Delivery," for details.)

➤ **E-mail address.** If you plan to receive e-mail messages, you need an e-mail address. Your address typically begins with your username followed by an "at" sign (@) and the domain name of your service provider—for example, jeikenhorn@internet.com.

Panic Attack!

If you keep getting error messages indicating that the page doesn't exist or can't be found when you try to open several different Web pages, you might have the wrong DNS address. Some ISPs might even change the DNS address they use, although they typically notify you of any changes via e-mail. If you run into problems, call your ISP's tech support line.

Setting Up Your Internet Connection

After you have all the information you need, you can run the Internet Connection Wizard and enter the connection settings (as discussed in a moment). The wizard displays a series of screens prompting you to enter each piece of information. If you're using a standard, ISDN, or DSL modem to connect, the wizard creates a **Dial-Up Networking** icon that you can click to establish your connection. If you're connecting via cable modem or over a network, the wizard enters settings instructing your Web browser and e-mail program to establish a connection via the Local Area Network (LAN).

Whoa!

Before you connect to the Internet, a Windows component called Dial-Up Networking must be installed. Open **My Computer** to see if the **Dial-Up Networking** icon is there. If it's missing, open the Windows Control Panel, double-click **Add/Remove Programs,** click the **Windows Setup** tab, double-click **Communications,** and place a check mark next to **Dial-Up Networking**. Click **OK,** click **OK** again, and follow the onscreen instructions to install Dial-Up Networking.

Although I would really like to give you step-by-step instructions for using the Internet Connection Wizard, the steps vary depending on which Internet Connection Wizard you're using and whether you're dialing direct to connect or connecting over a LAN; Microsoft keeps changing it. However, I can tell you how to start the wizard and tell you what to watch out for:

➤ To start the Internet Connection Wizard, click the **The Internet, Internet Explorer,** or **Connect to the Internet** icon on your Windows desktop.

➤ If the preceding step didn't work, the Connection Wizard might be hiding on your system. Check the **Start, Programs, Accessories, Internet Tools** menu for an option named **Get on the Internet,** or check the **Start, Programs, Internet Explorer** menu for an option called **Connection Wizard.** In Windows Me, check the **Start, Programs, Accessories, Communications** menu for the **Internet Connection Wizard** option.

➤ After the wizard starts, follow the onscreen instructions to set up your Internet account. The first or second screen displays several options for setting up your account. If you already have an ISP, choose the option for using your existing ISP. If you are connecting via cable modem or satellite, or if your computer is on a network, choose the option for connecting via LAN. If you have a modem and you don't have an ISP, choose the option for locating a new ISP and setting up an account. The wizard will dial a toll-free number to obtain a list of available ISPs and local numbers.

➤ If you need to find an ISP, the wizard asks for your area code and the first three digits of your phone number. It then downloads a list of ISPs available in your area, as shown in the following figure. You need to register with the service and provide a credit card number. The wizard downloads the required connection settings for you, so you don't have to enter them manually.

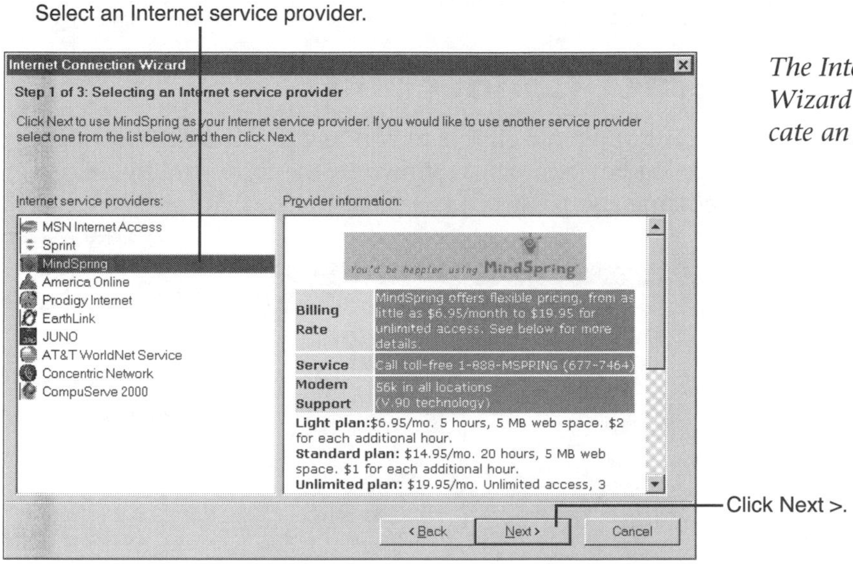

Select an Internet service provider.

The Internet Connection Wizard can help you locate an ISP in your area.

Click Next >.

➤ If you have already set up an account with a service provider in your area, you must manually enter the connection settings. This is no biggie; the wizard steps you through the process. When asked whether you want to view the Advanced settings, however, click **Yes** so that you can check the settings.

➤ If asked to specify a logon procedure, leave **I don't need to type anything when logging on** selected, even though your ISP requires you to enter a name and password. This option is for services that require you to manually log on using a terminal window or logon script. Most ISPs do not require this.

➤ Most ISPs automatically assign you an IP (Internet Protocol) address when you log on, so don't choose to use a specific IP address unless your ISP gave you one.

➤ If your ISP requires you to use a specific DNS server address, choose **Always use the following** and enter the DNS address in the **DNS Server** text box. If your ISP offers a secondary DNS, enter it so that you can still navigate if the first DNS

171

is busy. Many ISPs now use dynamic DNS addressing, which automatically routes you to the best DNS server for your location.

➤ The wizard also asks you to enter settings for connecting to the ISP's news and mail server. You can do this later or enter the settings now.

If you ran the Internet Connection Wizard to set up a standard, ISDN, or DSL modem connection, run My Computer and double-click the **Dial-Up Networking** icon. The Dial-Up Networking folder contains icons for any ISPs that you have set up. Right-drag the icon for your ISP to a blank area of the Windows desktop, release the mouse button, and click **Create Shortcut(s) Here.** If you're connecting via cable or network, you won't be using Dial-Up Networking; you have a permanent connection.

Testing Your Internet Connection

After you have an icon, you can double-click it to connect to the Internet. When you double-click the icon, a dialog box appears, as shown in the following figure, prompting you to type your username and password (supplied by your ISP).

When you double-click the icon you just created, this dialog box appears.

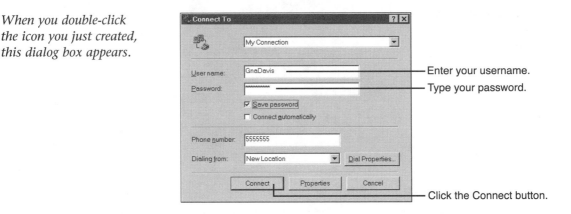

Enter your username.
Type your password.
Click the Connect button.

Type your username and password. If desired, check the **Save password** check box. This saves your username and password, so you won't have to type them the next time you log on. If you share your computer with someone else and you do not want that person using your Internet connection, leave the check box blank. Click the **Connect** button.

After you click the **Connect** button, Dial-Up Networking dials into your service provider's computer and displays messages indicating the progress, such as Dialing ..., Checking username and password ..., and Connecting .... Assuming that Dial-Up Networking could establish a connection, a dialog box appears, indicating that you are now connected. You can now run Internet programs (as explained in later chapters) to navigate the World Wide Web, send and receive e-mail, and so on.

Panic Attack!

If you don't have the **Save password** option, Client for Microsoft Networks is not installed. In the Control Panel, double-click the **Network** icon, click the **Add** button, and double-click **Client.** Click **Microsoft** and then double-click **Client for Microsoft Networks.** Be sure that **Client for Microsoft Networks** is selected as the **Primary Network Logon,** and then click **OK.**

What Went Wrong: Internet Connection Troubleshooting

If your connection proceeds smoothly the first time, lucky you. Most first attempts fail for some reason or another. You might have forgotten to type your password, or your Dial-Up Networking connection might have a wrong setting. If the connection fails, check the following:

➤ Did you type your username and password correctly? (If you mistyped this information or if your ISP entered it incorrectly on the system, Dial-Up Networking typically displays a message indicating that the system did not accept your password.) Retype your username and password, and try connecting again. (Passwords are typically case sensitive, so type the password *exactly* as your service provider specifies.)

➤ Was the line busy? Again, Dial-Up Networking typically displays a message indicating that the line was busy. If several people are connected to the service, you might have to wait until someone signs off. Keep trying.

➤ Check your Dial-Up Adapter settings. Display the Windows Control Panel and double-click the **Network** icon. Click **Dial-Up Adapter,** and click the **Properties** button. Click the **Bindings** tab, and be sure there is a check

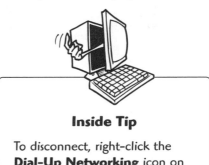

Inside Tip

To disconnect, right-click the **Dial-Up Networking** icon on the right end of the taskbar, and then click **Disconnect.** (The icon looks like two tiny overlapping computers.)

mark next to **TCP/IP->Dial-Up Adapter,** as shown in the following figure. (If NetBEUI or IPX/SPX are listed, be sure they are *not* checked.)

Tech Term

TCP/IP stands for Transmission Control Protocol/Internet Protocol. More simply, TCP/IP is the language that two computers use to communicate over the Internet. NetBEUI and IPX/SPX are two protocols commonly used for networks.

➤ Be sure you have selected the correct server type. In the Control Panel, double-click the **Dial-Up Networking** icon. Right-click the icon for connecting to your ISP, and choose **Properties.** Click the **Server Type** tab. Open the **Type of Dial-Up Server** drop-down list and choose the correct server type (specified by your service provider)—usually **PPP.**

➤ Did your modem even dial? Go to the Windows Control Panel and check your modem setup. Be sure that you've selected the correct modem and COM port.

➤ Do you have reliable phone lines? Unplug your modem from the phone jack and plug a phone into the jack. Do you get a dial tone? Does the line sound fuzzy? If you don't hear a dial tone, the jack is not working. If the line is fuzzy when you make a voice call, it has line noise, which might be enough to disconnect you.

Be sure TCP/IP is linked to your dial-up adapter.

174

The Least You Need to Know

➤ Sign up for a free trial offer with America Online. Try to get 250 hours for free.

➤ Use everything on America Online. Send a couple of e-mail messages, check the Internet features, prowl the chat rooms, click buttons, open menus, and use the help system when you get in a jam.

➤ Keep track of the time you spend online, and be sure you don't exceed the free trial limits. (To check your bill, press **Ctrl+K,** type billing, and click **Display Your Current Bill Summary.**)

➤ Just before the free trial period expires, call 1–888–265–8008 and cancel your membership (unless you have fallen in love with AOL and its online community).

➤ Find a local ISP, and gather the information you need to establish a connection.

➤ Run the Internet Connection Wizard and set up a dial-up connection for the ISP.

Chapter 17

Sending E-Mail: Postage-Free Same-Day Delivery

In This Chapter

➤ Giving your e-mail program directions to the post office

➤ Addressing and sending e-mail messages

➤ Checking your electronic mailbox

➤ Jazzing up your messages with photos and fancy fonts

➤ Attaching files to outgoing messages

➤ Following proper e-mail etiquette

How would you like to send a message to your friend and have it arrive in a matter of seconds instead of days? Send dozens of messages every day without paying a single cent in postage? Never again stare out your window waiting for the mail carrier?!

Well, your dreams are about to come true. When you have a connection to the Internet and an e-mail program, all these benefits are yours. In this chapter, you'll learn how to start taking advantage of them.

Running Your E-Mail Program for the First Time

The hardest part about e-mail is getting your e-mail program to connect to your Internet service provider's e-mail server. If you are using one of the major commercial online services, such as America Online or CompuServe, you can relax; the installation program took care of all the details for you. You simply click the e-mail or mailbox button and start using it.

However, if you connect through an ISP, you must use a separate e-mail program (such as Outlook Express or Netscape Messenger) and enter settings that tell it how to connect to the *mail server*. Before you start your e-mail program, be sure you have the following information from your ISP:

➤ **E-mail address.** Your e-mail address is usually all lowercase and starts with your first initial and last name (for example, jsmith@iway.com). However, if your name is John Smith (or Jill Smith), you might have to use something more unique, such as JohnHubertSmith@iway.com.

➤ **Outgoing mail (SMTP).** The SMTP (Simple Mail Transfer Protocol) server is the mailbox into which you drop your outgoing messages. It's actually your Internet service provider's computer. The address usually starts with "mail" or "smtp," such as mail.iway.com or smtp.iway.com.

Tech Term

Your online service or ISP has a **mail server** that acts as a post office. Whenever you send a message, the "post office" directs it to the specified destination. When someone sends you a message, the "post office" stores it in a special folder that acts as your mailbox. You then use an e-mail program to retrieve and display your messages.

➤ **Incoming mail (POP3).** The POP (Post Office Protocol) server is like your neighborhood post office. It receives incoming messages and places them in your personal mailbox. The address usually starts with "pop," such as pop.iway.com.

➤ **Account.** This one is tricky. It could be your username, the name you use to log on to your service provider (for example, "jsmith"), or something entirely different assigned to your account by your ISP.

➤ **Password.** Typically, you use the same password for logging on and for checking e-mail. I can't help you here; you picked the password or had one assigned to you.

After you have the preceding information, you must enter it into your e-mail program. The following sections show you how to enter e-mail connection settings in Outlook Express and Netscape Messenger.

Entering E-Mail Settings in Outlook Express

Before you can enter connection settings, you must run Outlook Express. Click the **Outlook Express** icon on the Windows desktop or on the Quick Launch toolbar, or run the program from the **Start**, **Programs** or **Start**, **Programs**, **Internet Explorer** menu.

When you first run Outlook Express, the Internet Connection Wizard starts and steps you through the process of entering the required information, as shown in the following figure. Just follow the onscreen instructions. If the Internet Connection

Wizard does not start, or you need to enter information for a different e-mail account, open the **Tools** menu and choose **Accounts.** Click the **Add** button, choose **Mail,** and follow the onscreen instructions to enter the settings.

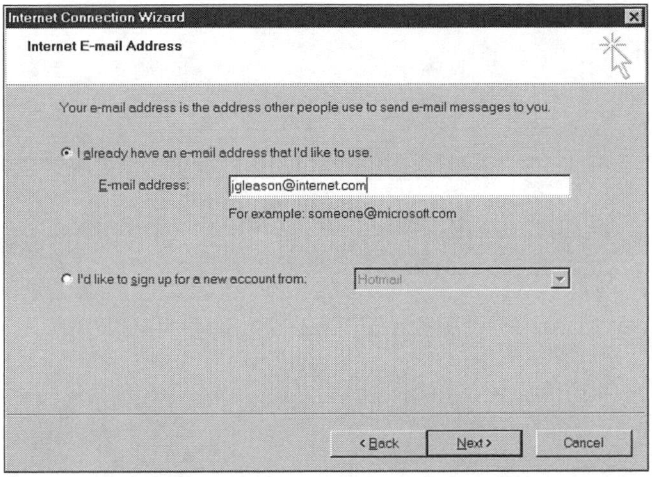

Before you can use Outlook Express, you must enter connection settings.

Entering E-Mail Settings in Netscape Messenger

To enter connection settings in Netscape Messenger, first run the program. Click **Start, Programs, Netscape Communicator, Netscape Messenger.** After it's running, take the following steps to enter settings for your mail server:

1. Open the **Edit** menu and choose **Preferences.**

2. Click on the plus sign next to **Mail & Newsgroups** to display a list of categories.

3. Click **Identity**, and enter the following information in the **Identity** panel, as shown in the following figure:

    Your name. This is your legal name or nickname, such as Nyce&EZ.

    E-mail address. This is the address people will use to write to you or respond to your messages.

    Reply-to address. If you want people to reply to an e-mail address other than the e-mail address you entered above (for instance, if you have two e-mail accounts), enter the preferred e-mail address here.

    Organization. If you work for a company or run your own business, you can enter its name here.

    Signature File. A signature is a file you create (typically in a text editor) that includes additional information about you or a clever quote. You can skip this for now.

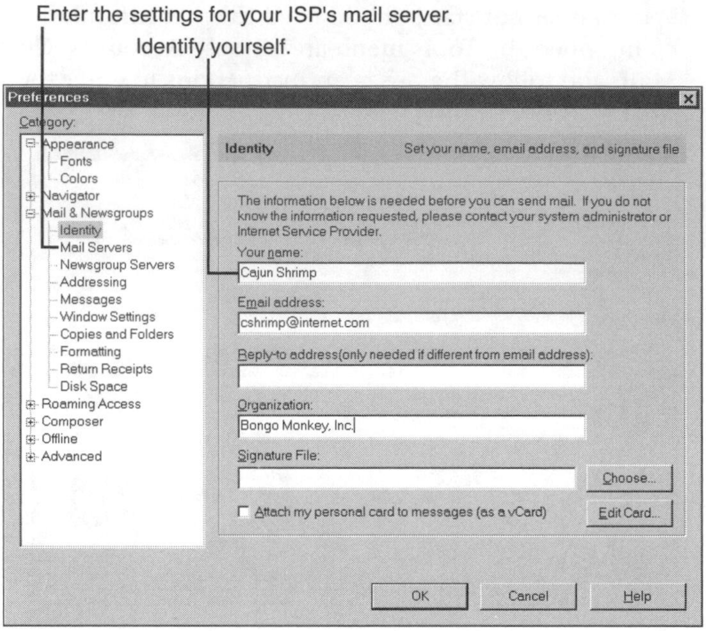

Enter the settings for your ISP's mail server.

Identify yourself.

Netscape Messenger makes it easy to enter the necessary settings.

> **Preferences** ☒
>
> Category:
> - Appearance
>   - Fonts
>   - Colors
> - Navigator
> - Mail & Newsgroups
>   - Identity
>   - Mail Servers
>   - Newsgroup Servers
>   - Addressing
>   - Messages
>   - Window Settings
>   - Copies and Folders
>   - Formatting
>   - Return Receipts
>   - Disk Space
> - Roaming Access
> - Composer
> - Offline
> - Advanced
>
> **Identity**   Set your name, email address, and signature file
>
> The information below is needed before you can send mail. If you do not know the information requested, please contact your system administrator or Internet Service Provider.
>
> Your name:
> `Cajun Shrimp`
>
> Email address:
> `cshrimp@internet.com`
>
> Reply-to address (only needed if different from email address):
>
> Organization:
> `Bongo Monkey, Inc.`
>
> Signature File:
> [Choose...]
>
> ☐ Attach my personal card to messages (as a vCard)   [Edit Card...]
>
> [OK]   [Cancel]   [Help]

4. Click **Mail Server,** and enter the following information in the **Mail Server** panel:

   Mail server user name. This is the username you use to log on to your Internet account, such as "jsmith."

   Outgoing mail (SMTP) server. This is the address of the server in charge of handling outgoing mail.

   Incoming mail server. This is the address of the server that handles incoming e-mail messages.

   Mail server type. Choose the type of server used for incoming mail: POP or IMAP. Obtain this information from your service provider.

5. Click the **OK** button to save your settings and close the dialog box. If you have trouble connecting to your mail server later, perform these same steps to change settings or correct any typos you might have made.

Addressing an Outgoing Message

The procedure for sending messages over the Internet varies, depending on which e-mail program or online service you're using. In most cases, you first click the button for composing a new message. For example, in Outlook Express, you click the **New Message** or **New Mail** button. A window appears, prompting you to compose your message.

Click in the **To** box and type the person's e-mail address (see the following figure). Then click in the **Subject** box and type a brief description of the message. Click in the large box near the bottom of the window and type your message. When you're ready to "mail" your message, click the **Send** button.

4. Click here to
send the message.

1. Type the person's
e-mail address here.

Sending mail with a typical Internet e-mail program (Outlook Express).

```
Congratulations!                                          _ □ ✕
File  Edit  View  Insert  Format  Tools  Message  Help
  ⬛       ✂      ▣     ▣      ↺       ⟳      ᴬᴮᶜ      📎        ↓!
 Send    Cut    Copy   Paste   Undo    Check  Spelling   Attach    Priority
From:    jgleason@internet.com  (mail)
To:      jimmagdilla@internet.com
Cc:
Subject: Congratulations!

Jim--

Congrats on the promotion. Does this mean you'll be installing an
in-ground, heated pool? We're still best friends, aren't we?

Jackie
```

2. Type a brief description
of the message here.

3. Type your message here.

Some e-mail programs send the message immediately. Other programs place the messages you send in a temporary outbox; then, when you're ready to send the messages, you click the button to initiate the send operation. For example, in Outlook Express, you click the **Send and Receive** button. Outlook Express then sends all messages from the Outbox and checks for incoming messages.

Inside Tip

Most e-mail programs, including Outlook Express and Netscape Messenger, include e-mail address books. Instead of typing the person's e-mail address, you simply select it from a list. To quickly display the address book, press **Ctrl+Shift+B** in Outlook Express or **Ctrl+Shift+2** in Messenger. To add someone to your address book, click the button for creating a new contact, and then enter the person's name, e-mail address, and other contact information.

Check your online service's help system to determine if there's anything quirky about entering e-mail addresses.

Checking Your E-Mail Box

When someone sends you an e-mail message, it doesn't just pop up on your screen. The message sits on your service provider's mail server until you connect and retrieve your messages. There's no trick to connecting to the mail server—assuming that you entered the correct connection settings. Most programs check for messages automatically on startup or display a button you can click to fetch your mail. The program retrieves your mail and then displays a list of message descriptions. To display a message, click or double-click its description, as shown in the following figure.

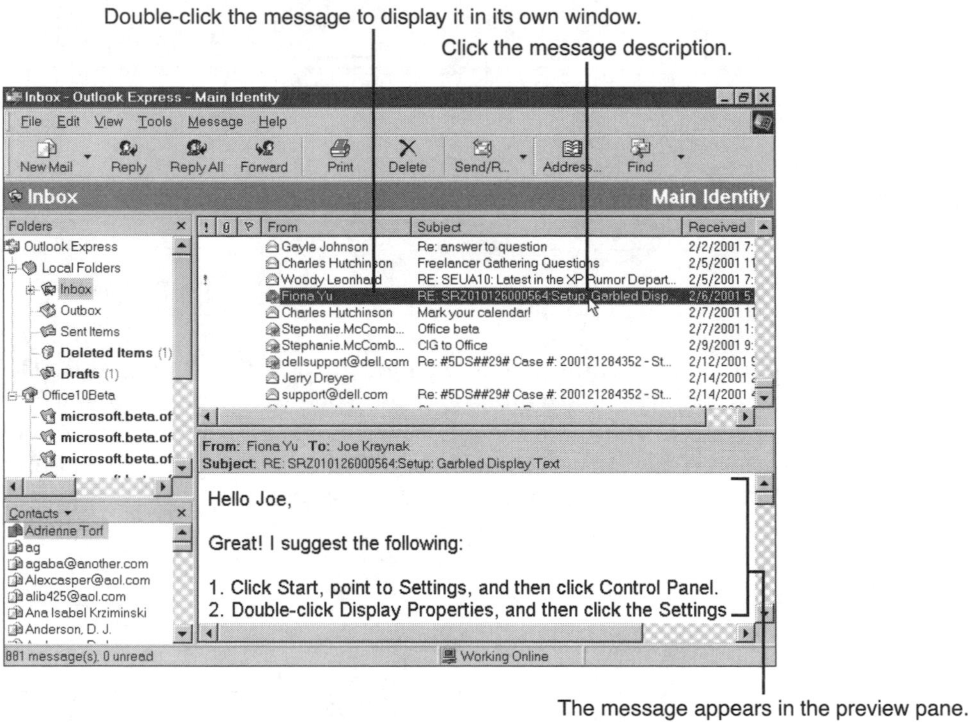

Double-click the message to display it in its own window.

Click the message description.

The message appears in the preview pane.

You can quickly display the contents of messages you receive.

Sending Replies

To reply to a message in most e-mail programs, you select the message and then click the **Reply** or **Respond To** button. This opens a window that automatically inserts the e-mail address of the person who sent the message, along with the sender's description of the message, usually preceded by "Re:" Many e-mail programs also include the contents of the previous message so that the recipient can easily follow the conversation. To differentiate between the sender's original message and your reply, some e-mail programs add a right angle bracket (>) at the beginning of each line of the original message. To respond, type your message in the message area, and then click the **Send** button.

Inside Tip

Most e-mail programs use several folders to help you keep your messages organized. For example, Outlook Express stores the messages you receive in the Inbox folder, messages that are waiting to be sent in the Outbox folder, messages you sent in the Sent Items folder, messages you deleted in the Deleted Items folder, and messages you composed but chose not to send in the Drafts folder. To switch from one folder to another, click the desired folder. To display a message you received, for instance, click the Inbox folder and then click the description of the message.

If you received a message that you would like to pass along to other recipients, you can forward the message. First, click the message you want to forward, and then click the **Forward** button. In the **To** text box, enter the e-mail addresses of the people to whom you want to forward the message. Your e-mail program automatically inserts the original message in the message area. If you would like to add an introduction to or comment about the original message, type this text in the message area. When you're ready to forward the message, click the **Send** button.

Adding Photos and Other Cool Stuff

How would you like to add a photo to your message or jazz it up with some fancy fonts? Most e-mail programs let you use special type styles and sizes, add backgrounds, insert pictures, and embellish your messages with other formatting options.

Both Netscape Messenger and Outlook Express offer a toolbar that contains buttons for the most common enhancements. In Outlook Express, shown in the following figure, you can use the

Inside Tip

When replying to a long message, delete most of the original material from the message you received, leaving only one or two lines to establish the context. This makes the message travel faster and takes up less disk space on the recipient's computer.

Whoa!

When you send a message that has pictures, lines, and fancy fonts, the e-mail program sends it as a Web page. The recipient's e-mail program must support Web page formatting; otherwise, the message will appear to be packed with cryptic codes.

toolbar to make text bold or italic, add bulleted and numbered lists, and insert pictures, horizontal lines, links, and other objects. (If the toolbar does not appear, check the **Format** menu for an **HTML** option. HTML stands for Hypertext Markup Language, the coding system used to format Web pages.)

The buttons for inserting pictures and formatting text work the same way as in your word processing and desktop publishing programs. The only new thing here is the button for inserting *links*. () To insert a link, first you drag over the text you want to appear as the link. You then click the button for inserting the link, type the address of the Web page you want it to point to, and click **OK**. You can also drag links from a Web page into the message area and plop them right down in the message area. (You'll learn more about links in Chapter 19, "Poking Around on the Web.")

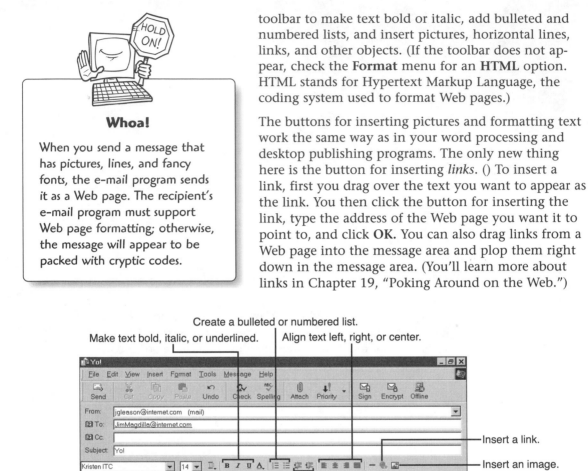

Many e-mail programs let you design fancy messages.

Attaching Documents to Your Messages

You can fit most e-mail messages on a Post-it Note. A person typically rifles off a message or reply in less than a minute. However, there are times when you might want to send something more substantial—perhaps an outline for a book, a photo of yourself, a copy of an article you found on the Web, or a document with its formatting intact.

Tech Term

A **link** is highlighted text that points to another Web page.

Whatever the case, you can send files along with your messages by creating *attachments*. An attachment is a file in its original condition and format that you tack on to the message. For instance, if you have a resumé you created in Word, you can e-mail it as an attachment to a prospective employer. That person could then open the resumé in Word and view or print it. Without attachments, you would need to copy the text of the resumé and paste it into your e-mail message, losing any formatting you applied to the text and any graphics you inserted.

The process for attaching a file is fairly simple, but the steps vary, depending on which e-mail program you use. In most e-mail programs, you follow the same steps as you do for composing and addressing the message. First you click a button (for example, **Attach** or **Insert File**). This displays a dialog box that lets you select the file you want to send. The dialog box looks just like the dialog box you use to open files. Change to the folder that contains the file you want to send, and then double-click the file's name. When you are ready to send the message along with the attachment, simply click the **Send** button.

Many word processing and spreadsheet programs have built-in support for e-mail, allowing you to send a document right from the program. In Word, for instance, you open the document you want to send, and then you open the **File** menu, point to **Send To,** and click **Mail Recipient.** This displays the e-mail program's toolbar with text boxes for typing the recipient's e-mail address and a description of the message.

If you receive a message that contains an attached file, your e-mail program usually displays some indication that a file is attached. For example, Outlook Express displays a paper clip icon. If you double-click the message (to display it in its own window), an icon appears at the bottom of the window or in an attachments text box. You can double-click the icon to open the file, or right-click and choose **Save** to save the file to a separate folder on your hard drive.

In many cases, when someone forwards a message to you, the person's e-mail program sends the forwarded message as an attachment. If the message has been forwarded several times, you might need to meander through a long line of attachments to view the original message.

Panic Attack!

When you receive an attachment, you should use an antivirus program to scan the file before opening it (if it's a document) or running it (if it's a program). Programs are especially notorious for carrying viruses, but documents can contain macro viruses, which can cause as much havoc. (Most antivirus programs have an option to run in the background, and they automatically scan attachments when you choose to open them or save them to disk.)

What About Hotmail and Other Free E-Mail Services?

You probably have heard of "free e-mail" services, such as Hotmail, Yahoo!, and Juno, and wondered why anyone would need free e-mail. Isn't all e-mail free? Does your ISP charge extra for it? Of course, your e-mail account is included with the service that your ISP provides; your ISP does not charge extra for it. But there are several good reasons to explore these free e-mail services:

➤ Free e-mail is typically Web-based, allowing you to send messages and check your mail on the Web. If you travel, you can manage your e-mail from anywhere in the world using any computer that's connected to the Internet. You don't need a computer that has your e-mail account settings on it.

➤ Free e-mail lets everyone in your home or business have his or her own e-mail account. When Junior starts corresponding with his chat room buddies, he'll want his privacy, and he can have it with his own e-mail program.

➤ Free e-mail gives you another e-mail address for registering "anonymously" for free stuff. Whenever you register for contests, shareware, and other freebies on the Internet, you must enter your e-mail address. Use your free e-mail account to register so that companies will send any junk mail to that address, and keep your real e-mail address private.

➤ Free e-mail provides you with a stable e-mail address. In the event that you change ISPs, you don't need to notify all your friends, relatives, and colleagues that you changed your e-mail address.

To get a free e-mail account, connect to any of the following sites, click the link for free e-mail, register, and follow the instructions at the site to start using your free e-mail account:

Hotmail	www.hotmail.com
ZDNet onebox	www.zdnet.com
Yahoo!	mail.yahoo.com
address.com	www.address.com
Excite	mail.excite.com

To find more free e-mail services, use your favorite Web search page to search for the phrase "free e-mail."

E-Mail Shorthand and Emoticons

If you want to look like an e-mail veteran, pepper your messages with any of the following *emoticons* (pronounced *ee-mow-tick-ons*). (You might need to turn your head sideways in order for them to look like tiny faces.) You can use these symbols to show your pleasure or displeasure with a particular comment, to take the edge off a comment you think might be misinterpreted, and to express your moods:

:) or :-)	I'm happy, it's good to see you, or I'm smiling as I'm saying this. You can often use this to show you're joking.
:D or :-D	I'm really happy or laughing.
;) or ;-)	Winking.
:(or :-(	Unhappy. You hurt me, you big brute.
;(or ;-(	Crying.
:| or :-|	I don't really care.
:/ or :-/	Skeptical.
:# or :-#	My lips are sealed. I can keep a secret.
:> or :->	Devilish grin.
;^)	Smirking.
%-)	I've been at this too long.
:p or :-p	Sticking my tongue out.
<g>	Grinning. Usually takes the edge off whatever you just said.

187

<vbg>	Very big grin.
<l>	Laughing.
<lol>	Laughing out loud.
<i>	Ironic.
<s>	Sighing.
<jk>	Just kidding (these are also my initials).
<>	No comment.

In addition to the language of emoticons, Internet chat and e-mail messages are commonly seasoned with a fair share of abbreviations. The following is a sample of some of the abbreviations you'll encounter and be expected to know:

AFAIK	As far as I know
BRB	Be right back
BTW	By the way
CUL8R	See you later
F2F	Face to face (usually in reference to meeting somebody in person)
FAQ	Frequently asked questions (Many sites post a list of questions that many users ask along with the answers. They call this list a FAQ [pronounced like *fact* without the "t"].)
FOTCL	Falling off the chair laughing
FTF	Another version of face to face
FYA	For your amusement
FYI	For your information
HHOK	Ha ha; only kidding
IMHO	In my humble opinion
IMO	In my opinion
IOW	In other words
KISS	Keep it simple, stupid
LOL	Laughing out loud
MOTOS	Member of the opposite sex

OIC	Oh, I see
PONA	Person of no account
ROTFL	Rolling on the floor laughing
SO	Significant other
TIC	Tongue in cheek
TTFN	Ta ta for now

E-Mail No-No's

To avoid getting yourself into trouble by unintentionally sending an insulting e-mail message, you might want to consider the proper protocol for composing e-mail messages. The most important rule is to NEVER EVER TYPE IN ALL UPPERCASE CHARACTERS. This is the equivalent of shouting, and people become edgy when they see this text on their screen. Likewise, take it easy on the exclamation points!!!

Secondly, avoid confrontations in e-mail. When you disagree with somebody, a personal visit or a phone call is usually more tactful than a long e-mail message that painfully describes how stupid and inconsiderate the other person is. Besides, you never know who might see your message; the recipient could decide to forward your message to a few choice recipients as retribution.

If you are in marketing or sales, avoid sending unsolicited ads and other missives. Few people appreciate such advertising. In fact, few people appreciate receiving anything that's unsolicited, cute, "funny," or otherwise inapplicable to their business or personal life. In short, don't forward every little cute or funny e-mail message, "true" story, chain letter, joke, phony virus warning, or free offer you receive.

Whoa!

When you strongly disagree with someone on the Internet, via e-mail or (more commonly) in newsgroups, it's tempting to flame the person with a stinging, sarcastic message. It's even more tempting to respond to a flaming message with your own barb. The resulting flame war is usually a waste of time and makes both people look bad. Also, don't bombard your enemy's e-mail account with a billion messages in an attempt to make the person's e-mail server crash. Even if it works, it's not very nice.

Finally, avoid forwarding warnings about the latest viruses and other threats to human happiness. Most of these warnings are hoaxes, and when you forward a hoax, you're just playing into the hands of the hoaxers. If you think that the warning is serious, check the source to verify the information before you forward the warning to everyone in your address book.

E-Mail Security

E-mail messages are more like postcards than sealed letters. Anyone with the proper software, know-how, and desire can read your missives as they bounce from server to server to their destination.

To keep your messages private, use an e-mail encryption program. An encryption program scrambles your message when you send it and allows the recipient to decode the message upon receipt. Here's a quick overview of how this works:

1. You and your friend install the encryption program.
2. You create a set of encryption keys: a private key and a public key.
3. You keep your private key and send your public key to your friend.
4. Before your friend sends you a message, she uses your public key to encrypt the message.
5. When you receive the message, you use your private key to decrypt it.

You can also use an encryption program to digitally sign a message and verify your identity. You attach a digital signature to the message, and your friend can use your public key to verify that you're really the one who sent the message and that it wasn't tampered with along the way.

Internet Explorer and Netscape Messenger both support S/MIME (Secure/Multipurpose Internet Message Extension). With S/MIME, you obtain a digital ID from a certifying authority, such as VeriSign (www.verisign.com), and install it. You can then send your public key to people from whom you want to receive secure e-mail messages. VeriSign's e-mail security software can even protect e-mail you exchange on the Web.

After installing your digital ID, you must set up your e-mail program to use it:

➤ In Outlook Express, choose **Tools, Accounts.** Click the name of your mail server, and then click **Properties.** Click the **Security** tab and then do one of the following: Turn on **Use digital ID,** click the **Digital ID** button, and choose your certificate; or click **Select Certificate** and choose your certificate. When sending a message, click the **Digitally Sign Message** button before clicking **Send.**

➤ In Netscape Messenger, click the **Security** button, click **Messenger,** and be sure **Encrypt mail messages** and **Sign mail messages** are both checked.

When you send a digitally signed message, your public key is attached to the message, allowing others to send you encrypted messages. When you receive a digitally signed message from someone, you must add the person's public key to your address book so that you can send the person encrypted messages. The procedure varies, depending on the e-mail program you're using. Refer to your e-mail program's help system for details.

For a more comprehensive privacy-protection program, try PGP (Pretty Good Privacy) Corporate Desktop. This software not only encrypts e-mail messages but can also help prevent unauthorized access to your computer. For more information, visit www. pgp.com, or go to the Network Associates home page at www.nai.com and click the link for PGP.

The Least You Need to Know

➤ To set up a new e-mail account in Outlook Express, open the **Tools** menu, choose **Accounts,** click the **Add** button, choose **Mail,** and follow the on-screen instructions.

➤ To access the e-mail settings in Netscape Messenger, open the **Edit** menu, click **Preferences,** and click **Mail & Newsgroups.**

➤ To create a new e-mail message, click the **Compose** or **New Message** button or its equivalent in your e-mail program.

➤ Incoming e-mail messages are often stored in the Inbox. Simply click the Inbox folder and then click the desired message to display its contents.

➤ To reply to a message, select the message and then click the **Reply** button.

➤ To attach a document to an outgoing message, click the button for attaching a file and then select the desired document file.

➤ If you receive a message that has a file attached to it, right-click the file's name and click the **Save** command.

➤ DON'T TYPE A MESSAGE USING ALL UPPERCASE CHARACTERS.

➤ If you're exchanging sensitive information via e-mail, encrypt your messages before sending them.

Chapter 18

Chatting with Friends, Relatives, and Complete Strangers

In This Chapter

➤ Experiencing the lively banter in chat rooms

➤ Sneaking a peek at a chatter's identity

➤ Chatting in private rooms

➤ Contacting friends and relatives with instant messages

➤ Adding other dimensions with audio and video

Every couple of months, I come across a news story about a couple that met in an on-line chat room and decided to get married. The woman usually sounds as dumb as a brick, and the guy typically looks like some shady character who probably has three other wives and a dozen kids waiting for their child support checks. I could be wrong, but the negative speculation is a lot more interesting than the gushy story they put in the news.

Be that as it may, online chat does provide a fun and inexpensive way to meet people and "talk" with friends, relatives, colleagues, and complete strangers. In the right chat room, you can even make new business contacts and find a new job! When you're in a chat room, you simply type and send a message, and it immediately pops up on the screen of every person in the chat room. When anyone else in the chat room sends a message, it pops up on your screen. This makes for a frenetic conversation that can be fun to watch. This chapter introduces you to the wonderful world of chat.

This chapter shows you how to use various chat tools in commercial online programs and on the Internet. You learn how to converse in chat rooms, check out a person's profile (identity), use instant-message programs to chat privately with friends and relatives, and use the audio and video features of your computer to place video "phone calls" on the Internet.

Hanging Out in Chat Rooms

Commercial online services, such as America Online and CompuServe, have their own exclusive chat rooms, where members gather during all hours of the day and night to share interests, argue politics, discuss movies, flirt with one another, and explore various topics. If you subscribe to one of these online services, you can enter any of the standard chat rooms and start conversing, or just sit back and watch the messages scroll by.

To enter a chat room on America Online, first sign on and then cancel the ads that invariably pop up on your screen. (To cancel an ad, don't just click the close button in the upper-right corner of the ad's window. The ad will just pop up later. Click the button near the bottom of the ad, typically labeled **No Thanks.**) This brings you to the Welcome window. Click the **People** button on the America Online toolbar (near the top of the window) and click **Find a Chat.** Double-click the desired chat category in the list on the left, and then double-click the desired chat room on the right. (The number next to each chat room indicates the number of people currently in the room.) America Online displays a chat window, as shown in the following figure.

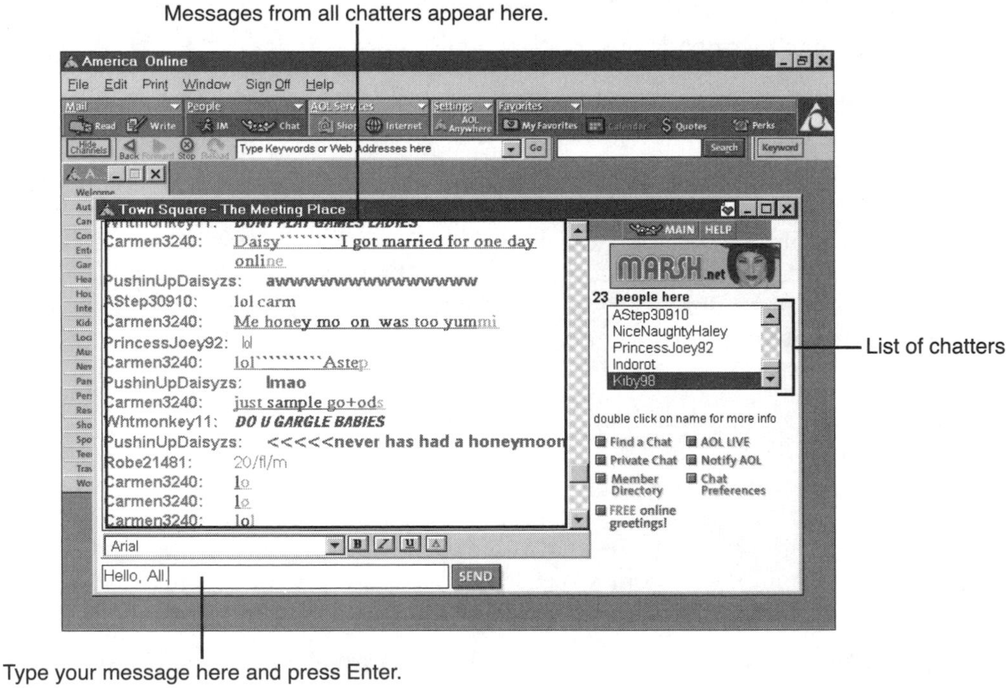

Messages from all chatters appear here.

List of chatters

Type your message here and press Enter.

The chat window contains the controls you need to start chatting.

Before you start chatting, read the messages to get a feel for the content and tone of the room. When you're ready to jump in, type your message and press **Enter** or click the **Send** button. To leave the chat room, simply close its window. You can then select a different room from the Find a Chat window. In the following sections, you learn how to use more cool chat tools in America Online.

Checking Out the People Who Are Checking You Out

Every member of America Online has the opportunity to create a *profile* that lists the person's age, marital status, geographical location, hobbies, and other pertinent information. In most cases, the profile information is either overly cryptic or an outright lie, so you can't rely on it. However, the lies people tell usually reveal something about them, and they provide a key to understanding the individual.

To check out a person's profile, double-click the person's name in the list of chatters displayed on the right side of the window, and then click the **Get Profile** button. This displays the profile information that the person entered, as shown in the following figure.

Panic Attack!

America Online chat rooms are limited to 23 members. If a room is full, America Online automatically bumps you into a room like the one you selected. For instance, if you chose The Flirts Nook and it's full, America Online might bump you into The Flirts Nook 103.

Edit Your Online Profile	_ □ X

To edit your profile, modify the category you would like to change and select "Update." You must be at least 13 years old to fill out a Profile.

Your Name:	Joe
City, State,	Aruba, Carribean
Sex:	⊙ Male ○ Female ○ No Response
Marital Status:	
Hobbies:	Hang gliding, wind surfing, mountain climbing, sky diving
Computers Used:	Pentium IV
Occupation:	Self-made millionaire
Personal Quote:	Trust yourself

Create a Home Page   ☐ Include a link to my AOL Hometown Home Page in my Member Profile

Update   Delete   Cancel   My AOL   Help & Info

As my profile reveals, I'm as exciting as I think I am.

To check and edit your own profile, press **Ctrl+K**, type profile, press **Enter**, and then, when the Member Directory dialog box appears, click the **My Profile** button near the top of the dialog box. Read the warning box that tells you that whatever information you enter is publicly accessible, and click **OK.** Enter your personal information (or whatever you want people to think about you), and click the **Update** button.

Sending Private Messages

If you strike up a conversation with someone who has completely captured your interest, you might want to grab a table for two in the corner and have your own private conversation. How do you do this?

Well, you have two options. The easiest way is to send the person an IM, or instant message. An IM appears only on your screen and the recipient's screen. To send an IM, double-click the person's name in the list of chatters on the right, and then click the **Send Message** button. Type your message and click the **Send** button. The Send Instant Message window remains on your screen, displaying a running dialog between you and your friend, but you both remain in the public chat room.

If you would like to leave the public chat room, or if you want to chat in private with two or more other people, create your own private room. Under the list of chatters, click the **Private Chat** button. Type a name for your chat room, and click **Go Chat.** You must then send an IM to your friend to tell the person the name of your private chat room. (To quickly display the Send Instant Message window, press **Ctrl+I.**) Private rooms are great if you and your pals are trying to have a serious discussion and some moron keeps interrupting and hassling you; simply create a private room and keep the jerk off the invitation list.

Whoa!

Although most America Online members are fairly nice folks, there are plenty of creeps online. Don't give out personal information such as your last name, phone number, address, or passwords. Some people might pose as customer service reps and request this information. Don't believe them.

Inside Tip

If someone invites you to a private chat room, the person must tell you the name of the room. To go to the room, click the **Private Chat** button, type the name of the room, and click **Go Chat.**

Making Your Own Public Chat Room

Are you the consummate host or hostess? Do you love throwing parties and mingling with your guests? Do you live for the thrill of greeting people and making them feel welcome? If you answered "Yes" to these questions, or if you're just plain bored with the chat rooms that AOL offers, consider creating your own public chat room. Here's what you do:

1. Click the **People** button on the America Online toolbar, and click **Start Your Own Chat.** America Online displays a dialog box asking if you want to create a public or private room.

2. Click the **Member Chat** button to create a public room. America Online now asks you to pick a category for the room, as shown in the following figure.

You can host your own chat room.

Type a name for your room.

Double-click the desired chat room category.

3. In the chat category list (on the left), double-click the desired category name.

4. Click in the text box under **3** and type the desired name for your room.

5. Click **Go Chat** and then sit back and twiddle your thumbs until people start arriving.

Chatting It Up on the Internet

There's no doubt about it—chat sells. People flock to online chat rooms where they can be anyone they want to be, travel incognito, and carry on in the relative safety of virtual worlds.

Although America Online first popularized chat rooms, many Internet companies have finally figured out that chat sells and have developed their own chat rooms, where anyone with an Internet connection and a Web browser can converse. The following sections show you where to find these chat services on the Web.

Panic Attack!

When the last person leaves a chat room, America Online automatically closes down the room and deletes it from the service. Talk about cleaning up after the party!

Chatting It Up at Yahoo!

Yahoo! has always been considered a premier Internet search site. Now, Yahoo! has injected its power and simplicity into the Internet chat arena. To access Yahoo!'s chat rooms, first run your Web browser and use it to register for Yahoo! Chat. The following steps show you how to use Internet Explorer (a Web browser installed on most PCs) to connect to Yahoo! and register for its chat rooms:

1. Double-click the **Internet Explorer** icon on the Windows desktop or click the **Launch Internet Explorer Browser** button on the Quick Launch toolbar.

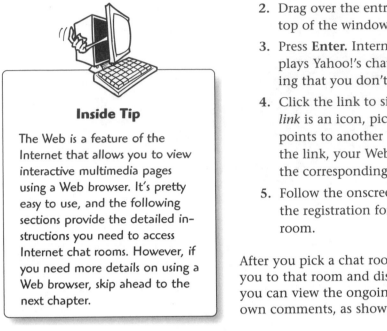

Inside Tip

The Web is a feature of the Internet that allows you to view interactive multimedia pages using a Web browser. It's pretty easy to use, and the following sections provide the detailed instructions you need to access Internet chat rooms. However, if you need more details on using a Web browser, skip ahead to the next chapter.

2. Drag over the entry in the **Address** box near the top of the window and type chat.yahoo.com.

3. Press **Enter.** Internet Explorer opens and displays Yahoo!'s chat page with a message indicating that you don't have a Yahoo! ID.

4. Click the link to sign up for Yahoo! Chat. (A *link* is an icon, picture, or highlighted text that points to another Web page. When you click the link, your Web browser automatically opens the corresponding page.)

5. Follow the onscreen instructions to complete the registration form and enter the desired chat room.

After you pick a chat room, Yahoo! automatically takes you to that room and displays a chat window, where you can view the ongoing conversation and add your own comments, as shown in the following figure.

Messages from all chatters appear here.   A list of people in the chat room

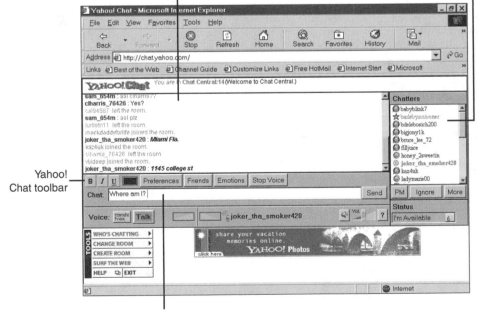

Yahoo! Chat toolbar

Type your message here and press Enter.

Yahoo! brings chat rooms to the Web.

After you are in a chat room, you can start chatting. The ongoing discussion is displayed in the large frame in the upper left. To send a message to the other chatters, click inside the **Chat** text box just below the ongoing discussion, type your message, and press **Enter.** When you tire of this simple banter, try the following:

➤ Click the **Emotions** button, and double-click an emotion (bow, agree, smile, or some other gesture) to send a text description of it.

➤ Right-click the name of someone in the room. This displays a dialog box that lets you find out more about the person, send the person a private message or a file, add the person to a list of friends, or ignore the person (prevent the person's messages from appearing on your screen).

➤ In the lower-left corner of the window is a list of tools. Click a tool to find out who's online, change to a different chat room, create your own room (public or private), surf the Web, get help, or exit. (You can edit your identity to provide additional information about yourself. Other chatters then see this information if they check your profile.)

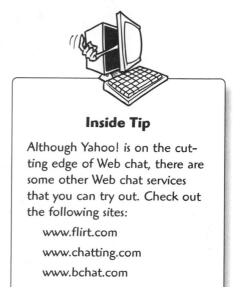

Inside Tip

Although Yahoo! is on the cutting edge of Web chat, there are some other Web chat services that you can try out. Check out the following sites:

www.flirt.com

www.chatting.com

www.bchat.com

Keeping in Touch with Friends and Family

Relatively recently, developers have come up with an innovative communications feature for the Web that allows people to create their own online community centers, family circles, or special-interest groups to keep in touch. For example, if you have a large extended family, you can create a family circle and have all your family members (at least those who have Internet access) join the circle. Members can then post messages, digitized photos, announcements, and calendar dates in a special area where everyone in the family can check them out. Many of these "community" centers also allow you to set up a members-only chat room and exchange electronic greeting cards and virtual gifts.

One of the best online community centers I know of is eCircles, which you can find at www.ecircles.com. When you first go to eCircles, click the **Sign Up** link and register, as shown in the following figure. You can then create your own circles or join existing circles, invite others to join, create your own online photo albums, enter important dates, post messages, and much more.

You must register for eCircles before you can join or create your own online community.

eCircles - Microsoft Internet Explorer

File Edit View Favorites Tools Help

Back Forward Stop Refresh Home Search Favorites History Mail

Address c/products/gate/login.cgi?DebugMSG=NoAuth&nextURL=/magic/products/circles/all.cgi%3Fdont=cache Go

Links Best of the Web Channel Guide Customize Links Free HotMail Internet Start Microsoft

eCircles is *the* great place to share with Family and Friends

Login Name

Password

Log In

☐ Save Login Info

Don't have a login name & password?
Sign up to create a new eCircle or to return to ones you've seen.

Sign Up

Sign Up

START a Private or Public eCircle
Start an eCircle & share your interests with others. You choose to make it private or list it in the Public Directory.

Start an eCircle

BROWSE our Public Directory
Search for eCircle with these keywords in their titles and descriptions:

Search Search Tips

Friends and Social Groups
Weddings, Organizations, Pen Pals...

School/Education
Universities, Greek, Alumni

Family and Genealogy
Parenting, Reunions, Baby...

Sports and Recreation
Travel, NBA, Wrestling...

eCircles News

Get 35mm-quality, Glossy Prints

Get 35mm-quality, glossy prints of your digital photos. Simply upload them, follow the easy ordering instructions, and your prints will be delivered right to your door. For a limited-time only,

(2 items remaining) Downloading picture http://static.ecircles.com/images, Internet

To send a greeting card or invitation to a friend or relative, check out the online virtual cards. There are hundreds of Web sites where you can create and send your own greeting cards via e-mail. Just connect to www.yahoo.com and search for virtual greeting cards. Here are a few sites to get you started:

www.mygreetingcard.com

www.pcgreetings.com

www.netgreeting.com

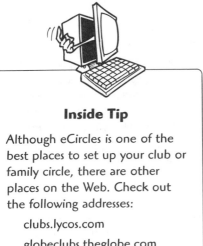

Inside Tip

Although eCircles is one of the best places to set up your club or family circle, there are other places on the Web. Check out the following addresses:

clubs.lycos.com

globeclubs.theglobe.com

groups.yahoo.com

Chatting Privately with Friends and Relatives on the Internet

Hanging out with strangers can be interesting, but if you'd like to chat with friends and relatives, spotting them in crowded chat rooms can be a bit difficult. To help track down individuals on the Internet, you can use an instant message program. You simply add the names and tracking information (typically an e-mail address) of each person you might want to contact, and the program lets you know when the person is online. Assuming that your friends and relatives run the same program (and are on-line), a dialog box pops up on your screen, indicating that the person is available. You can then start your own private chat with that person.

Where do you get such a program? You can pick up America Online's Instant Messenger at www.aol.com, grab a copy of Yahoo!'s Messenger (formerly known as Yahoo! Pager) at messenger.yahoo.com, or snatch MSN Messenger Service from Microsoft at messenger.msn.com. The following figure shows AOL's Instant Messenger in action.

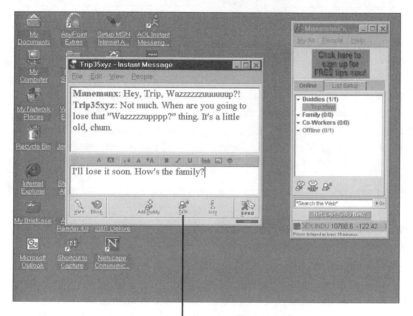

With AOL's Instant Messenger, you can keep in touch with your friends, colleagues, and relatives online.

If you and your buddy have a sound card, speakers, and a microphone, click here to establish voice contact.

What About Audio and Video?

You probably have heard about Internet phone programs that let you place toll-free long-distance calls over the Internet using your sound card and speakers. These programs typically use a special server to allow two computers to exchange audio signals.

I could tell you how to set up and use Microsoft NetMeeting (included with Internet Explorer) to place a call over the Internet, but there are easier ways to converse over the Internet without dealing with the complexities of Internet phone programs:

➤ Use Yahoo! Messenger, as explained in the preceding section. At the time I was writing this book, Yahoo! Messenger featured voice support, and I bet that by the time this book hits the shelves, most other instant message programs will offer voice support.

201

➤ Get your friends or relatives to join eCircles or a similar online community. When you choose the option for chatting, you are given the choice of text or voice chat. Choose voice chat to carry on an audio discussion.

Inside Tip

Some developers, including Microsoft and Yahoo!, have attempted to make their instant messaging programs work with each other so that a person using MSN Instant Messaging can chat with another person using Yahoo! Instant Messaging. However, during the writing of this book, the most popular instant messaging program, AOL's Instant Messenger, refused to play along. So, if all your friends and relatives use AOL Instant Messenger, you should use it, too.

For you to experience a high-quality audio connection over the Internet, your computer must be equipped with a full-duplex sound card (which can play and record at the same time), a fairly decent microphone, and a pair of speakers.

Videoconferencing requires additional equipment and a dedicated Internet phone program, such as Microsoft NetMeeting or CUSeeMe. Your computer must be equipped with a video capture card (some newer display cards support video input) and a digital camera. Even if your computer is properly equipped, don't get your hopes up. Over a 56Kbps connection, the video is typically fuzzy and jerky and might even slow down the audio portion of your conversation.

If you want to be able to use your computer to place free long-distance phone calls to real phones (instead of to other computers), you need special software and a special service, such as Net2Phone. (Of course, you still need a sound card, speakers, and a microphone on your end, but the person on the other end can talk to you on his or her phone.) For more information, check out Net2Phone at www.net2phone.com.

The Least You Need to Know

➤ America Online and Yahoo! are two of the many places to find hordes of eager chatters.

➤ To chat on America Online, click the **People** button, click **Find a Chat,** pick a chat room, and start typing.

➤ To "talk" in a chat room, type your message in the message text box and press **Enter** or click the **Send** button.

➤ To send another America Online member a private message, press **Ctrl+I** to send an instant message.

➤ You can create a virtual meeting place or community center on the Web at eCircles (www.ecircles.com).

➤ You can send private messages to your friends and family members over the Internet using a special message program.

➤ The easiest way to carry on voice conversations over the Internet is to use Yahoo! Messenger or select the voice chat option on the Web.

Chapter 19

Poking Around on the Web

In This Chapter

➤ Launching your Web browser on its virgin voyage

➤ Opening specific Web pages by entering addresses

➤ Skipping from one Web page to another with links

➤ Finding stuff on the Web

➤ Bookmarking Web pages for quick return trips

➤ Understanding cookies (pros and cons)

The single most exciting part of the Internet is the World Wide Web (or Web for short), a loose collection of interconnected documents stored on computers all over the world. What makes these documents unique is that each page contains a link to one or more other documents stored on the same computer or on a different computer (down the block, across the country, or overseas). You can hop around from document to document, from continent to continent, by clicking these links.

When I say documents, I'm not talking about dusty old scrolls or text-heavy pages torn from books. Web documents contain pictures, sounds, video clips, animations, and even interactive programs. When you click a multimedia link, your modem pulls the file into your computer, where the Web browser or another program plays the file. As you'll see in this chapter, the Web has plenty to offer, no matter what your interests—music, movies, finance, science, literature, travel, astrology, body piercing, shopping—you name it.

First, You Need a Web Browser

To navigate the Web, you need a special program called a Web browser, which works through your service provider to pull documents up on your screen. You can choose from any of several Web browsers, including the two most popular browsers, Netscape Navigator and Internet Explorer. In addition to opening Web pages, these browsers contain advanced tools for navigating the Web, finding pages that interest you, and marking the pages you might want to revisit.

Windows comes with Internet Explorer, which should already be installed on your computer. To keep things simple, we'll use Internet Explorer in our examples. However, if you're using a different browser supplied by your service provider, don't fret. Most browsers offer the same basic features and similar navigation tools. Be flexible, and you'll be surfing the Web in no time.

Whoa!

Your ISP might offer you its own custom Web browser, which is typically a waste of programming code. These custom browsers are usually customized to feed you more advertising from the ISP and are typically more difficult to navigate than popular browsers, such as Internet Explorer and Netscape Navigator. Stick with the popular browsers for now.

Steering Your Browser in the Right Direction

To run your Web browser, click or double-click its icon on the desktop or choose it from the **Start, Programs** menu. If you're using Internet Explorer, click the icon named **The Internet** or **Internet Explorer** on the Windows desktop.

When your browser starts, it immediately opens a page that's set up as its starting page. For example, Internet Explorer opens Microsoft's or MSN's (Microsoft Network's) home page. You can start to wander the Web simply by clicking links (typically, blue, underlined text; buttons; or graphic site maps). Click the **Back** button (on the button bar just above the page display area) to flip to a previous page, or click the **Forward** button (the button with the right-pointing arrow) to skip ahead to a page that you've visited but backed up from (see the following figure).

If you click a link and your browser displays a message that it can't find the page or that access has been denied, don't freak out. Just click the **Back** button and

Panic Attack!

If you're not connected to the Internet when you start your browser, it might display a message indicating that it cannot find or load the page. Open **My Computer,** double-click **Dial-Up Networking,** and double-click the icon for connecting to your ISP. (If Dial-Up Networking does not appear in My Computer, look on the **Start, Settings** menu or in the Windows Control Panel.)

then try the link again. If that doesn't open the page, try again later. In some cases, the Web page creator (Webmaster) might have mistyped the page address that the link points to or might have moved or deleted the page. On the ever-changing Web, this happens quite often. Be patient, be flexible, and don't be alarmed.

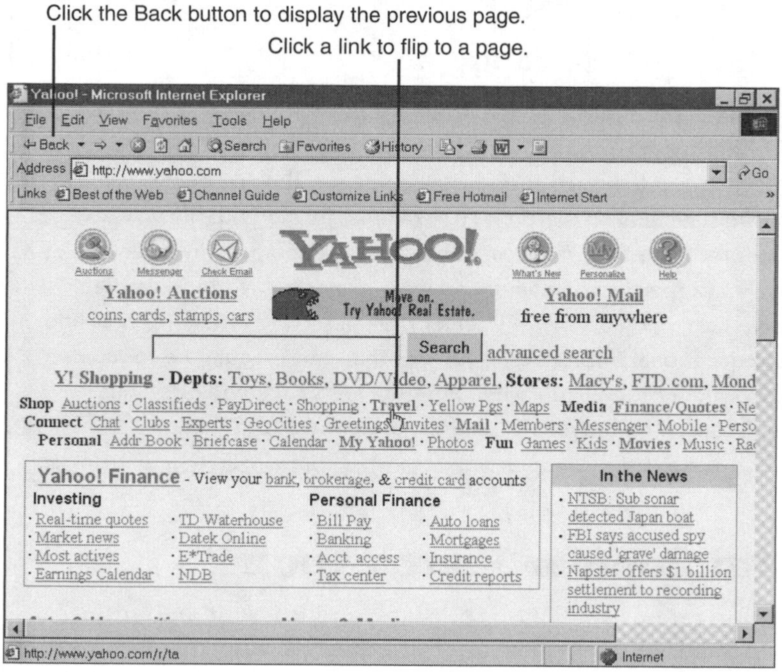

Click the Back button to display the previous page.
Click a link to flip to a page.
Yahoo! - Microsoft Internet Explorer
http://www.yahoo.com

A Web browser displays and helps you navigate Web pages.

A Word About Web Page Addresses

Every page on the Web has an address that defines its location, such as www.si.edu for the Smithsonian Institution or www.walmart.com for Wal-Mart. The next time you watch TV or flip through a magazine, listen and keep your eyes peeled for Web page addresses. Not only do these addresses look funny in print, but they sound funny, too; for instance, www.walmart.com is pronounced "dubbayou-dubbayou-dubbayou-dot-walmart-dot-kahm."

Web page addresses are formally called URLs (Uniform Resource Locators). They allow you to open specific pages. You enter the address in your Web browser, usually in a text box called **Go to** or **Address**, near the top of the window, and your Web browser pulls up the page.

All you really have to know about a URL is that if you want to use one, type the URL exactly as you see it. Type the periods as shown, use forward slashes, and follow the capitalization of the URL. If you make any typos, the browser either loads the wrong page or displays a message indicating that the page doesn't exist or that the browser cannot locate the specified page.

Inside Tip

All Web page addresses start with http://. Newsgroup sites start with news://. FTP sites (where you can get files) start with ftp://. You get the idea. HTTP (short for Hypertext Transfer Protocol) is the coding system used to format Web pages. The rest of the address reads from right to left (from general to specific). For example, in the URL http://www. mitsubishi.co.jp, .jp stands for Japan, co stands for corporation (a company in Japan), mitsubishi stands for Mitsubishi (a specific company), and www stands for World Wide Web (or Mitsubishi's Web server, as opposed to its FTP server or mail server). Addresses that end in .edu are for pages at educational institutions. Addresses that end in .com are for commercial institutions. You can omit the http:// when entering Web page addresses, but omitting ftp:// or news:// causes the browser to attempt to connect to a Web site.

Finding Stuff with Popular Search Tools

The Web has loads of information and billions of pages, and this vast amount of information can make it difficult to track down anything specific. The Web often seems like some big library that gave up on the Dewey decimal system and piled all its books and magazines in the center of the library. How do you sift through this mass of information to find what you need?

The answer: Use an Internet search tool. You simply connect to a site that has a search tool, type a couple of words that specify what you're looking for, and click the **Search** button (or its equivalent). The following are the addresses of some popular search sites on the Web:

www.yahoo.com

www.google.com

www.lycos.com

www.go.com

www.altavista.com

www.excite.com

Most Web browsers have a **Search** button that connects you to various Internet search tools. For example, if you click **Search** in Internet Explorer, Internet Explorer displays options that let you search for Web pages, people, businesses, maps, definitions, or even pictures. You simply pick the item you're looking for, type a word or two to describe the topic or item, and click **Search.**

The cool thing about the **Search** button is that it displays the search results in a separate pane. You can then click links in the left pane to open pages in the right pane without having to click the **Back** button to return to the search results (see the following figure).

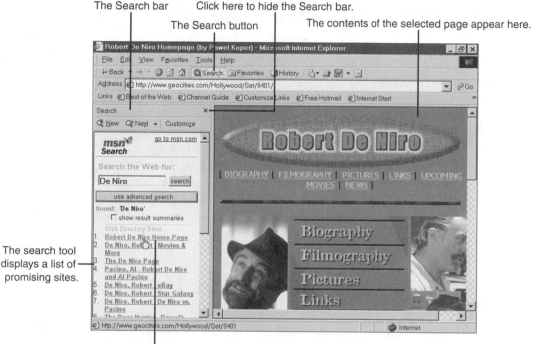

The Search bar lets you choose the search tool to use.

You can also use special search tools to find long-lost relatives and friends on the Internet. These search tools are like electronic telephone directories that can help you find mailing addresses, phone numbers, and even e-mail addresses. To search for people, check out the following sites:

people.yahoo.com

www.bigfoot.com

www.whowhere.lycos.com

www.infospace.com

Opening Multiple Browser Windows

You're hot on the trail of a fabulous Web site when you encounter a site that catches your eye. Do you stop and explore the site, forsaking the path to your original destination, or do you forge ahead and take the risk of never being able to return to the site?

Whoa!

Every program window you open consumes valuable system resources. When resources run low, your computer gets slow. If your computer seems to be slowing down, close some windows.

Neither. Your browser offers some better options:

➤ Bookmark the page, and quickly return to it later by selecting it from a menu (see "Marking Your Favorite Web Pages for Quick Return Trips" later in this chapter).

➤ Complete your journey to your original destination and then, later, use the history list to return to the site that caught your eye (see the next section).

➤ Open a new browser window, use it to complete your journey to your original destination, and then return to the other window when you have time. To open a new browser window in Internet Explorer, open the **File** menu, point to **New**, and click **Window** (or press **Ctrl+N**), or right-click the desired link and click **Open in New Window**.

Going Back in Time with History Lists

Although the **Back** and **Forward** buttons will eventually take you back to where you were, they don't get you there in a hurry or keep track of pages you visited yesterday or last week. For faster return trips and a more comprehensive log of your Web journeys, check out the history list:

➤ In Internet Explorer, click the **History** button to display the History bar on the left side of the window. Click the day or week during which you visited the Web site, and then click the Web site's name to see a list of pages you viewed at that site. To open a page, click its name, as shown in the following figure.

➤ In Netscape Navigator, open the **Window** menu and click **History** or press **Ctrl+H** to view the history list. Double-click the name of the page you want to revisit.

Click the day or week icon.

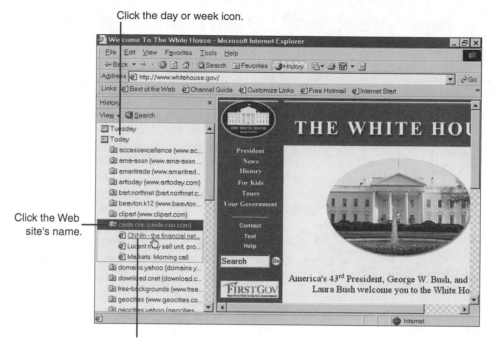

Click the Web site's name.

Click the page you want to revisit.

Use the history list to retrace your steps.

Whoa!

If you share your computer with someone, you might not want that person to know where you've been on the Web. To cover your tracks, clear the history list. In Internet Explorer, choose **Tools, Internet Options** or **View, Internet Options** (in earlier versions of Internet Explorer) and then click the **Clear History** button. In Netscape Navigator, choose **Edit, Preferences** and click the **Clear History** button.

Marking Your Favorite Web Pages for Quick Return Trips

As you wander the Web, you pull up pages that you know you want to return to in the future. When you happen upon such a page, flag it by creating a *bookmark* or marking the page as a *favorite*. This adds the page's name to the **Bookmarks** menu (in Netscape Navigator) or the **Favorites** menu (in Internet Explorer). The next time you want to pull up the page, you simply select it from your customized menu.

To mark a page, simply right-click a blank area of the page and select **Add Bookmark** (in Netscape Navigator) or **Add to Favorites** (in Internet Explorer).

Computer Cheat

Right-click a blank area of the page and click **Create Short-cut.** This places a shortcut icon for the page on your desktop.

In Internet Explorer, when you choose to add a page to the **Favorites** menu, the Add Favorite dialog box appears, asking if you only want to add the page to your **Favorites** menu or have Internet Explorer automatically download updates (*subscribe* to the page), making the page available offline (when you're not connected). If you choose to subscribe, Internet Explorer connects to the Internet at the scheduled times (typically when Internet traffic is light) and downloads the latest version of the page. When you choose to open the page, Internet Explorer quickly loads it from the cache rather than from the Web.

After you have added a page to the **Bookmarks** or **Favorites** menu, you can quickly open the page by opening the menu and clicking the name of the page.

Changing the Starting Web Page

Whenever you fire up your browser, it opens with the same page every time. If you have your own favorite page you'd like your browser to load on startup, just let your browser know:

➤ In Internet Explorer, open the page you want to view on startup. Choose **Tools, Internet Options** or **View, Internet Options.** On the **General** tab, under **Home page**, click **Use Current**, and then click **OK.**

➤ In Netscape Navigator, open the page you want to view on startup. Choose **Edit, Preferences.** Under **Navigator starts with**, be sure **Home page** is selected. Under **Home page**, click **Use Current Page**, and then click **OK.**

Can Cookies Hurt Me?

When you visit some Web sites, they automatically send an electronic passport, called a *cookie*, to your computer. As you browse the site, use its tools, or order products, the site "stamps" your passport to keep track of your interests, passwords, and any products you ordered. Whenever you revisit the site, the site can grab the cookie and immediately identify you. Think of it as living in a small town where everyone knows your business.

Because cookies are used to track your Web habits, they give many people the heebie-jeebies and inspire allusions to *1984*. Admittedly, cookies work behind the scenes to spy on you, but most cookies are designed to enhance your Web-browsing experience and allow companies to target advertisements to your tastes (rather than pitching products you probably wouldn't be interested in anyway).

In short, cookies are either good or bad, depending on how they're used and how you view them. If you love to shop on the Internet, cookies are a necessary evil, because they act as your shopping basket, keeping track of the items you ordered. On the other hand, if you're the kind of person who gets nervous around security cameras, cookies might bother you.

So, can you refuse a cookie when a site tries to send you one? Of course—you have the option of blocking all cookies or having your browser prompt for your okay before accepting a cookie. Here's what you do:

➤ In Internet Explorer, choose **Tools, Internet Options** or **View, Internet Options.** Click the **Security** tab. Click the **Custom Level** button. Scroll down to **Cookies**, and turn on the **Disable** option for both **Cookies** options. (Or, turn on **Prompt** to have Internet Explorer ask for your confirmation before accepting a cookie.)

➤ In Netscape Navigator, choose **Edit, Preferences.** In the **Category** list, click **Advanced.** Click **Disable cookies** or **Warn me before accepting a cookie,** and then click **OK.**

If you've done plenty of Web surfing with the cookies feature enabled, you probably have several cookies on your computer. To get rid of cookies in Internet Explorer, use My Computer to change to the Windows/Cookies folder, press **Ctrl+A**, press the **Delete** key, and click **OK.** To delete Netscape Navigator cookies, use the **Start, Find, Files or Folders** command to search for a file on your hard disk named Cookies.txt. Click it, press the **Delete** key, and click **OK.**

Inside Tip

For additional details about cookies, check out www. cookiecentral.com.

The Least You Need to Know

➤ To start Internet Explorer or Netscape Navigator, double-click its icon on the Windows desktop.

➤ Links typically appear as buttons, icons, or specially highlighted text (typically blue and underlined).

➤ Click a link to open the page that the link points to.

➤ If you know a Web page's address, type it in your browser's **Address** or **Go to** text box and press **Enter.**

➤ To search for a topic or site on the Web, use a search engine, such as www.yahoo.com, www.google.com, www.lycos.com, www.go.com, or www. hotbot.com, and enter one or two words to describe what you're looking for.

➤ To bookmark a page, right-click a blank area of the page and select **Add Bookmark** (in Netscape Navigator) or **Add to Favorites** (in Internet Explorer).

➤ If you're worried about cookies, disable the cookie feature in your Web browser.

Chapter 20

Shopping, Investing, Traveling, and Other Cool Web Stuff

In This Chapter

➤ Getting up-to-the-minute news, weather, and sports online

➤ Going shopping at the biggest mall on the planet

➤ Buying and selling stocks through an online broker

➤ Checking out some cool vacation spots

➤ Boning up on your movie trivia

➤ Downloading and playing your favorite audio clips

➤ Getting free technical support for your computer woes

Although the Internet hasn't changed anything we humans do, it has completely revolutionized the *way* we do everything. People still watch the news and read magazines and newspapers, but more and more folks are getting their news, weather, and sports on the Web. Investors still win and lose millions of dollars on their stocks and bonds, but now they can do it faster online. People still have affairs, but now they can ignite their passions in online chat rooms.

In short, the Web offers features that let you perform the same tasks you performed in the past, only more conveniently and (typically) at less expense. This chapter shows you how to take advantage of some of the Web's more practical real-life applications.

Keeping Up on News, Weather, and Current Events

TV stations can broadcast the news as it happens. You can watch live speeches, trials, and debates; view late-breaking reports from Washington; and watch Doppler radar track a storm as it moves through your town. The only trouble is that you're at the mercy of what the broadcasters want to show you. You need to wait for the news to come on and then wait for the reporters to get around to relating the information you want.

On the Web, news is slightly delayed. It takes a while for someone to format a story and place it on the Web. Even "live" video clips on the Web are delayed by the time it takes your modem to receive the data. However, the Web provides a self-directed approach to the news, so you don't have to sit through commercial breaks or wait for the story to air. You view only the information that interests you when you want it. In addition, Web news sites typically cover a story more thoroughly than on TV. Think of Web news as the ideal cross between a newspaper and TV news—it's fast and can provide audio and video coverage like TV, but it's thorough and scannable like a newspaper.

The following sections tell you where to find the best news, weather, and sports "channels" on the Web.

Checking Out Web Newsstands

Virtually every TV station and news publication has a Web site where you can find not only the major news stories, but also biographical information, health alerts, book and movie reviews, political analysis, travel information, and much more. Check out the following popular news sites:

➤ **CNN** at www.cnn.com. Even if you don't have cable TV, you can check out this award-winning news service online (see the following figure).

➤ **ABC News** at www.abcnews.go.com. If you missed the evening news, check out the ABC News site to view the latest stories. You'll also find links to the other ABC news shows, including *20/20* and *Nightline*.

➤ **CBS News** at cbsnews.com. This address takes you to the CBS News home page, where you'll find today's headline news plus links to CBS news specials, including *60 Minutes, 48 Hours, Face the Nation, CBS Sportsline,* and *MarketWatch.*

➤ **MSNBC News** at www.msnbc.com/news/. Although this site displays the standard "top stories" you find at most news sites, it's laid out a little differently, displaying a list of features from every NBC news show: *The Today Show, NBC Nightly News, Dateline NBC,* and *Meet the Press.*

➤ **Associated Press** at www.ap.org. Go to the source, and get the news from the place where the press gets its news: the Associated Press. When you get to the AP home site, click the **The Wire** link and then select your local news site from one of the available lists.

➤ **Yahoo!'s Daily News** at dailynews.yahoo. com. Although Yahoo! is a little light on news, it does provide an excellent starting point for your search. Here, you find plenty of links to other news sites that offer more thorough coverage.

If you've poked around at the news sites but you can't find the information you're looking for, use your favorite Internet search tool to search for the topic by name. If you're just browsing, go to Yahoo! (www.yahoo.com) and click the **News & Media** link on the opening page. You'll find links to thousands of news sites on the Web.

Computer Cheat

If you're ever unsure of where an organization's Web site is located (or if the organization even has a Web site), try guessing its address. For example, for *USA Today*, you might enter www.usatoday.com. You'll probably hit the right site more than 50 percent of the time.

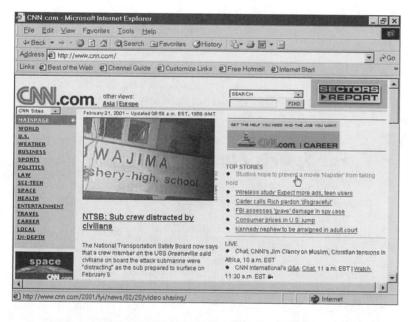

CNN offers the most thorough news coverage on the Web.

Getting the Latest Weather Reports

Sure, you can get a weather report at any of the sites mentioned in the preceding section, but why settle for second-rate weather forecasts when the best weather station in the world is on the Web? Check out the Weather Channel at www.weather.com.

The Weather Channel's opening page displays snippets from the big weather stories, along with any national weather alerts. For a specific local forecast, enter the name of the city or town or a ZIP code for the area in the **Local Weather** text box and press **Enter.** The local forecast appears, as shown in the following figure.

The Weather Channel can display local forecasts for any area in the world.

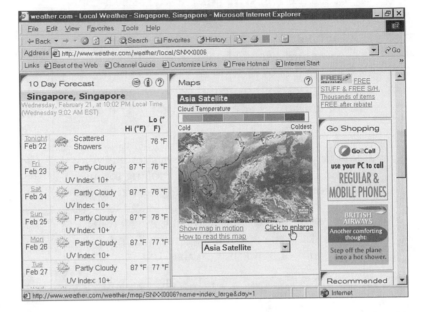

You can find hundreds of weather sites on the Web, including the National Weather Service (www.nws.noaa.gov) and EarthWatch Weather on Command (www. earthwatch.com). To find a more complete listing of sites, use any Internet search tool to search for sites.

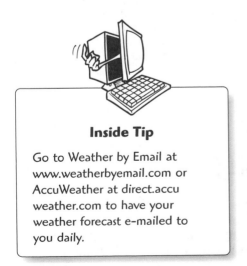

Inside Tip

Go to Weather by Email at www.weatherbyemail.com or AccuWeather at direct.accu weather.com to have your weather forecast e-mailed to you daily.

For Sports Fans Only

If you have cable TV, you can always find some sporting event to keep you entertained. But if you're flipping through stations and all you can find is the national Ping-Pong championships, you might want to take a break and check out a site for your favorite sport.

Given the current popularity of sports, you would expect to find plenty of sports sites on the Web, and the Web does not disappoint. Every sport you can think of, from archery to wrestling and everything in between, has at least one Web site devoted exclusively to it. In addition, all the major sports organizations and broadcasters have their own Web sites. Here are a few of my favorites:

➤ **ESPN** at espn.go.com. This site is a great place to go for a rundown of scores as well as in-depth coverage of sporting events and behind-the-scenes interviews with your favorite players and coaches.

➤ **CNN/SI** at sportsillustrated.cnn.com. This site is the Web home of *Sports Illustrated*. Although some of the articles at this site are mere teasers for the printed magazine, this site is packed with scores, team rankings, player statistics, and game analyses. You can even play fantasy sports and see how your teams stack up against those of fellow sports enthusiasts.

➤ **NFL** at www.nfl.com. This site is the official home of the National Football League. Do you have a favorite NFL team? Click its insignia at the top of the page to view the official team information, win/loss record, and statistics for your favorite players. (Go to www.nba.com for professional basketball, www. mlb.com for baseball [Major League Baseball], or www.nhl.com for hockey.)

➤ **CBS Sportsline** at www.sportsline.com. This site is the CBS sports center, where you can find coverage of the major professional and college sports. Sportsline offers a robust collection of photos and the latest point spreads (not that I'm saying gambling is okay).

➤ **Nando Times Sports** at www.nandotimes.com/sports/. This site is one of the best-established sports sites on the Web, offering quality sports reporting without the frills. Nando is also a great place to pick up the daily TV schedule for sporting events.

Mail-Order Paradise: Shopping on the Web

After businesses caught sight of the Internet, they began to realize the incredible opportunities it offered for advertising, marketing, and selling products directly to consumers. As more people purchased computers and started exploring online services and the Internet, businesses rushed to the Web to establish a presence, and many individuals created their own storefronts on the Web.

And boy, is business booming on the Web! Go to nearly any site, and an ad will pop up on your screen. Open any Internet search page, and you'll find thousands of links to retail stores, mail-order companies, manufacturers, online mega-malls, bookstores, music stores, and even mom-and-pop specialty shops. I'm not about to list all the great places to shop on the Web, because I'm sure you can find what you're looking for with your favorite search tool. However, before you do any serious shopping, you should be aware of the following shopping basics:

➤ When you find the desired product, you typically click a link for ordering it or placing it in your shopping basket. You can then click a link to keep shopping or to check out.

Tech Term

When you enter data using a **secure Web form,** your browser scrambles the data before sending it. When the Web server receives the scrambled data, it decodes it. This significantly reduces the possibility that someone can intercept the data en route to its destination and read it.

➤ Before you enter any personal information or your credit card number, be sure you are at a legitimate site and that the form you are about to fill out is a *secure Web form*. Internet Explorer displays a blue lock icon at the bottom of the window to indicate that a form is secure. If the form's page address starts with https:// instead of http://, it is stored on a secure server.

➤ When you're ready to place your order, you must fill out an order form, such as the form shown in the following figure. You'll be asked to select a payment method and enter billing and shipping data. Just pretend that you're entering information in a dialog box, and you'll do just fine.

➤ After you place your order, the site might display a confirmation page or send you a statement via e-mail. Be sure to print the statement. It typically contains a confirmation or order number that you can use to follow up on your order in case anything goes wrong.

https:// indicates that the site is secure.

Complete the online order form to place your order.

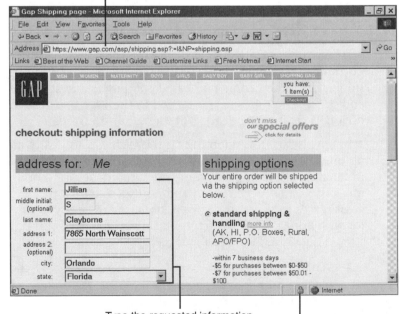

Type the requested information.

This icon indicates that the form is secure.

Becoming Your Own Stockbroker

Before state lotteries, bingo nights, and local casinos started becoming so popular, the stock market was the only game in town for legalized gambling. But even with the growing availability of lotteries and other betting venues, the stock market remains one of the most popular gambling institutions in the nation. And now, if you have Internet access and a little extra money, you too can place a bet on your favorite corporation.

Several Web-based stock trading companies allow you to buy and sell stocks online. You simply set up an account with the company and mail a check to cover your future transactions. After your account is set up, you can buy and sell stocks using the money in your account. These services typically charge a base fee per transaction (for instance, $8 per transaction). Most services also provide tools for tracking your investments and researching companies.

To see how this online investing thing works, check out the following online stock brokerages:

➤ **E*TRADE** at www.etrade.com. This site is one of the most popular stock brokerage firms on the Web, providing the tools you need to research companies, track your investments, and learn more about investing. You can open an account with a minimum of $1,000. Transactions cost about $15 to $20 per 1,000 shares, depending on whether the stock is listed on a major exchange or on NASDAQ.

➤ **Ameritrade** at www.ameritrade.com. This site is one of the least expensive brokerages, offering a flat fee of $8 for most transactions. Ameritrade also provides plenty of tools and data for researching and tracking investments.

➤ **CSFB Direct** at www.csfbdirect.com. This site is one of my favorite places to check on my stocks and mutual funds. In fact, I set up CSFB Direct as my home page, as shown in the following figure. I've never purchased stocks through CSFB Direct, but its services are competitive with the two brokerages just mentioned. CSFB Direct charges a little more per transaction than E*TRADE, but it provides more thorough information than both E*TRADE and Ameritrade.

➤ **Charles Schwab** at www.schwab.com. This site is a more full-service brokerage. As such,

Whoa!

To protect myself from lawyers and other whiners, I must say that I don't recommend using any of these online stock brokerages, purchasing stocks online, or even purchasing stocks offline. In short, I'm not responsible for anything you do with your money, your spouse's money, or the money in your kids' piggy banks.

it charges more than any of the other online brokerages described here—$30 per 1,000 shares plus $.03 per share for all shares over 1,000. If you're an active trader, the rates go down. For instance, if you make 61 or more trades, you pay $14.95 per trade. When you're first learning the ropes, getting professional advice might be worth the extra cost.

Online brokerages provide the information you need to invest wisely.

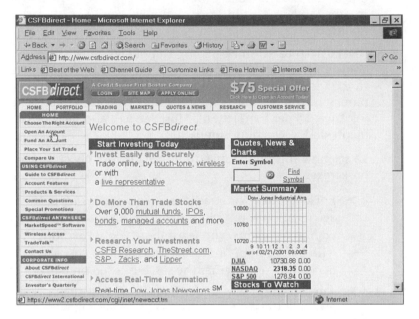

Inside Tip

Several sites, including Yahoo!, provide free quotes for airline tickets. You simply enter the dates on which you plan to travel and the departure and arrival locations, and the site displays a list of fares, typically from lowest to highest. For plane tickets and other vacation information, check out www.travelocity.com.

Planning Your Next Vacation

Whether you already have a vacation destination in mind or need a few ideas on where to go, the Web has plenty of tools for planning your vacation, buying tickets, and making reservations. If you want to go through a travel agent, you can find several travel agencies online. If you would rather plan the trip yourself, you can find thousands of links for travel bureaus, airlines, motels, campsites, tourist centers, and anything else you can imagine.

One of the best places to start planning your vacation is at Yahoo! (www.yahoo.com). On Yahoo!'s opening page, scroll down to the **Recreation & Sports** category and click the **Travel** link. Scroll down the page to view a list of travel subcategories, as shown in the following figure, and follow the trail of links to obtain the desired travel information.

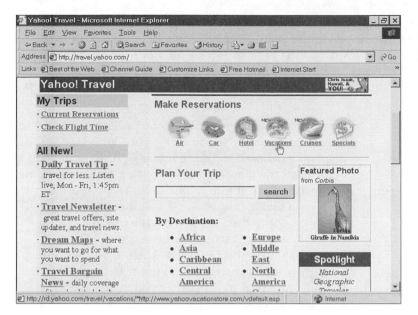

Yahoo! provides links to all the travel information you could possibly need.

For Movie Buffs Only

Whether you're at a party swapping movie trivia or at home trying to decide which movie to rent, a thorough, up-to-date movie database can come in handy. With a movie database, you can obtain a complete list of movies in which your favorite actor or actress appeared, quickly determine who directed a particular movie, or scan plots to decide which movie you want to rent.

One of the most thorough movie databases on the Web is the Internet Movie Database at us.imdb.com. The opening page displays a form that lets you search for movies based on the movie's title or the people involved in its creation (the actors, actresses, director, and so on). Simply type a person's last name or a portion of the movie's title and click the **Go!** button to start your search. Follow the trail of links to narrow your search and find the desired information.

Although the Internet Movie Database is one of the best places to go to answer trivia questions and research the careers of your favorite stars and directors, the Internet offers much more for film buffs. Most major movie studios have their own Web sites (for instance, Paramount at www.paramount.com) where they typically showcase new and future releases. Video rental stores (such as Blockbuster at www.blockbuster.com) have their own sites, which typically display a list of upcoming video releases along with any promotional deals. Magazines such as *The New Yorker* and *Time* have movie reviews. Many popular actors and actresses have their own "official" Web sites. You can even find shrines set up by devoted fans.

Use your favorite search tool to explore movies categories or search for a specific movie, director, actor, actress, movie studio, or other movie-related topic.

Many movie sites, especially sites set up by the film industry, contain links for *trailers* (short video clips that let you preview movies). Ideally, when you click a link to play a video clip, your computer downloads (copies) the video file from the Web site and starts to play it. If you're running Windows Me, for instance, and you click a link for playing an MPEG or AVI movie clip, Windows Media Player kicks into gear and starts playing the clip.

Inside Tip

Twenty-four hours a day, seven days a week, you can find movie chat rooms where fans meet to discuss movie facts and trade trivia questions. If you're looking for some friendly banter about the movies you like best, check out the chat rooms. For more about chat rooms, see Chapter 18, "Chatting with Friends, Relatives, and Complete Strangers."

Inside Tip

You can pick up a free QuickTime video player at www.apple.com/quicktime/download/. To download Windows Media Player, go to www.microsoft.com/windows/windowsmedia. You can find additional video players at www.tucows.com.

If your computer doesn't have the program required to play the clip and if you're lucky, your Web browser displays a dialog box asking if you want to download and install the player. Give your okay, and then follow the instructions. If you're not so lucky, your browser displays a dialog box asking if you want to open the file or save it to disk. Click the **Save to Disk** option, click **OK**, and then select the drive and folder in which you want the file saved. Then download the player you need, install it, and use it to open and play the file you saved to disk. After you've installed the appropriate player, your browser should automatically download and play clips without prompting you to open or save video files.

Creating Your Own Music Library

If you thought that the transition from LPs to CDs was revolutionary, the effect that the Internet has had on the music industry will make your head spin. As you would guess, every major label (and most minor labels) has its own Web site, where you can find out about your favorite recording artists, view video clips, and listen to sample audio clips. You can even find Web sites for lesser-known, independent artists who use the Web to distribute their music directly to fans. Check out the following sites:

➤ **Internet Underground Music Archive** at www.iuma.com. This site is just what its name describes—a music library where you can listen to bands you won't hear on the radio or see on MTV. If you're a musician yourself, you can create your own Web site and use it to chase your dream of signing that big record deal—or just have someone other than the neighbors listen to your tunes.

➤ SONICNET at www.sonicnet.com. This site is an online music network where you can get the latest news, music charts, reviews, and lists of events. SONICNET features in-depth coverage of the music industry and allows you to search for individual artists by name.

➤ CDNOW at www.cdnow.com. This site is a great place to pick up bargains on your favorite CDs and get some background information on your favorite artists.

➤ RollingStone.com at www.rollingstone.com. This site is the electronic version of the popular *Rolling Stone* magazine. Here you'll find plenty of reviews, industry news, and interviews. And if you have your own *MP3* clip, you can submit it to the editors for inclusion in their Top 10 list.

Most music sites have audio clips you can download and play. You simply click the link to play the clip, and your computer downloads (copies) the audio file from the Web site and starts to play it. If your computer doesn't have the program required to play the clip, your Web browser might display a dialog box asking if you want to download and install the player. Simply give your okay and follow the instructions.

If your browser doesn't offer to fetch the player for you, save the file to disk and then poke around on the Web to find a player. Windows Media Player, a part of Windows Me, can play MP3 clips as well as other types of audio and video files; you can download the latest version at www.microsoft.com/windows/windowsmedia. Another popular audio player is RealPlayer, which you can pick up at www.realaudio.com. For a wider selection of audio and video players, go to www.tucows.com.

Tech Term

MP is short for MPEG, which is short for Moving Picture Experts Group, an organization that develops standards for compressing audio and video files. The **MP3** standard improves file compression by stripping out data in audio signals that humans cannot hear anyway. This makes audio and video files much smaller so that they take up less storage space and download more quickly.

For more information on downloading and playing digitized music clips, copying clips to an MP3 player, and burning your own CDs, see Chapter 28, "Playing Digitized Music Clips."

Getting Technical Support for Your Computer

Nearly every computer hardware and software company has its own Web site, where you can purchase products directly and find technical support for products you own. If your printer is not feeding paper properly, if you're having trouble installing your sound card, if you keep receiving cryptic error messages in your favorite program, or if you have some other computer-related problem, you can usually find the solution on the Internet.

In addition, computer and software companies often upgrade their software and post both updates and fixes (called patches) on their Web sites for downloading. If you are having problems with a device, such as a printer or modem, you should check the manufacturer's Web site for updated drivers. If you run into problems with a program, check the software company's Web site for a *patch*—a program file that you install to correct the problem.

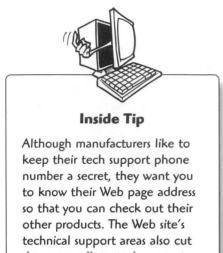

Inside Tip

Although manufacturers like to keep their tech support phone number a secret, they want you to know their Web page address so that you can check out their other products. The Web site's technical support areas also cut down on calls to tech support.

The following table provides Web page addresses of popular software and hardware manufacturers to help you in your search. Most of the home pages listed have a link for connecting to the support page. If a page does not have a link to the support page, use its search tool to locate the page. You might also see a link labeled **FAQ** (frequently asked questions), **Common Questions**, or **Top Issues.** This link can take you to a page that lists the most common problems that other users are having and gives answers from the company, as shown in the following figure.

Check out the FAQ or Top Issues link for answers to common questions.

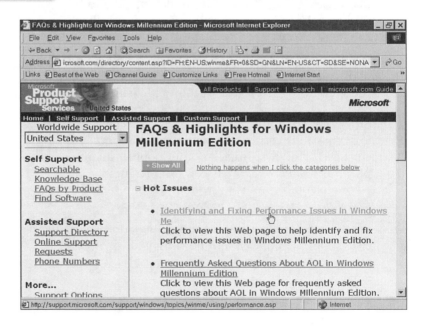

Computer Hardware and Software Web Sites

Company	Web Page Address
Acer	www.acer.com
Borland	www.borland.com

Company	Web Page Address
Broderbund	www.broderbund.com
Brother	www.brother.com
Canon	www.ccsi.canon.com
Compaq	www.compaq.com
Corel	www.corel.com
Creative Labs	www.soundblaster.com
Dell	www.dell.com
Epson	www.epson.com
Fujitsu	www.fujitsu.com
Gateway	www.gw2k.com
Hayes	www.hayes.com
Hewlett-Packard	www.hp.com
Hitachi	www.hitachipc.com
IBM	www.ibm.com
Intel	www.intel.com
Iomega	www.iomega.com
Lotus	www.lotus.com
Micron Electronics	www.micronpc.com
Microsoft	www.microsoft.com
Motorola	www.mot.com
NEC	www.nec.com
Packard Bell	www.packardbell.com
Panasonic	www.panasonic.com
Sony	www.sony.com
Toshiba	www.toshiba.com
3COM (U.S. Robotics)	www.3com.com

If the manufacturer you're looking for is not listed in the table, don't give up. Connect to your favorite Web search page and search for the manufacturer by name, or search for the problem you're having. You should also seek help from online computer magazines. Here are some excellent resources:

➤ **ZDNet** at www.zdnet.com. This site is the home of several quality computer magazines, including *PC Computing, Windows Sources,* and *ComputerLife.* Here you find articles on general computing, hardware and software reviews, tips, and answers to specific questions.

➤ **c|net** at www.cnet.com. This site is a great place if you need technical support for Internet problems. It's also a great place to check out gaming information, obtain shareware programs, and read hardware and software reviews. Although you don't find as much information about general computing issues as you find at ZDNet, the information you do find is very useful.

➤ **FixWindows.com** at www.fixwindows.com. This site is an excellent place to find answers to your Windows questions, learn about the latest improvements, and troubleshoot common problems in all versions of Windows.

The Least You Need to Know

➤ Thousands of Web sites are devoted to covering news, weather, and sports.

➤ Before you hand your credit card number to a company, be sure the company is legitimate and that the site is secure.

➤ You can research investments and buy and sell stocks on the Web for a fraction of the cost you would pay a stockbroker.

➤ One of the best places to start planning for your next vacation is on Yahoo!'s Travel page.

➤ Want to know the name of every movie in which Robert De Niro has appeared? Check out the Internet Movie Database at us.imdb.com.

➤ Most music Web sites are packed with links for downloading and playing audio and video clips.

➤ Virtually every computer and software company has a Web site where you can obtain technical support for products.

Chapter 21

Publishing Your Own Web Page in Ten Minutes or Less

In This Chapter

➤ Understanding how the Web works

➤ Sneaking a peek at the codes behind Web pages

➤ Slapping together your own cool Web page

➤ Using the Web to make money

➤ Finding free enhancements for your Web page

You wandered the Web. Perhaps you sent out a few electronic greeting cards, played some audio and video clips, and even ordered products online. You can use search tools to track down information about the most obscure topics, and you can monitor the progress of all your stocks and mutual funds.

But now you want more. You want to establish a presence on the Web, publish your own stories or poems, place pictures of yourself or your family online, show off your creativity, and communicate your ideas to the world.

Where do you start? How do you create a Web page from scratch? How do you insert photos and links? How do you add a background? And after you've created the page, what steps must you take to place the page on the Web for all to see?

This chapter shows you a quick and easy way to whip up your first Web page right online, without having to learn a special program or deal with any cryptic Web page formatting codes. And, because you create the page online, you don't have to worry about publishing your Web page when you're done.

What Makes a Web Page So Special?

Behind every Web page is a text document that includes codes for formatting the text, inserting pictures and other media files, and displaying links that point to other pages. This system of codes (*tags*) is called *HTML* (*Hypertext Markup Language*).

Most codes are paired. The first code in the pair turns on the formatting, and the second code turns it off. For example, to type a heading such as "Apple Dumplin's Home Page," you would use the heading codes like this:

<h1>Apple Dumplin's Home Page</h1>

The <h1> code tells the Web browser to display any text that follows the code as a level-one heading. The </h1> code tells the Web browser to turn off the level-one heading format and return to displaying text as normal. Unpaired codes act as commands; for instance, the <p> code inserts a line break or starts a new paragraph.

Web browsers use HTML codes to determine how to display text, graphics, links, and other objects on a page. Because the browser is in charge of interpreting the codes, different browsers might display the same page slightly differently. For example, one browser might display links as blue, underlined text, whereas another browser might display links as green and bold.

Inside Tip

Even if a browser is set up to display all level-one headings in a particular way, HTML codes can override the browser's setting and give the heading a different look. For example, they might make the heading appear in a different color or font.

Forget About HTML

A basic introduction to HTML is helpful in understanding how the Web works, troubleshooting Web page formatting problems, and customizing Web pages with fancy enhancements, but you don't need a doctorate in HTML to create your first Web page. Many companies have developed specialized programs that make the process of creating a Web page as easy as designing and printing a greeting card.

You can use programs such as Web Studio, FrontPage Express, Netscape Composer, and HotDog to create and format Web pages on your computer and then upload (copy) the pages from your computer to a Web server (typically your ISP's Web server). Or, you can create and format your Web pages right on the Web simply by specifying your preferences and using forms to enter your text. The next section shows you just how easy it is to create and publish your own Web page online at Yahoo! GeoCities.

Making a Personal Web Page Right on the Web

When it comes to publishing your own Web page, you have simple needs—a single Web page that lets you share your interests with others and express yourself to the world. For someone with such simple needs, the Web offers free *hosting* services, such as Yahoo! GeoCities. These services offer tools for building your Web page online, along with access to a Web server where you can publish your page.

Tech Term

A **Web host** is a server on which you can store your Web page and all files related to it, such as photos and other graphics. Think of it as a neighborhood in which you can build your home. Your ISP might provide free hosting services (typically with a limit of 5 megabytes), but in most cases you must create the Web page yourself and then upload it to the Web server.

So, let's get on with it and publish a simple Web page at Yahoo! GeoCities:

1. Run your Web browser, and go to geocities.yahoo.com.

2. Unless you registered with Yahoo! earlier (for example, for Yahoo! Chat), follow the series of links required to sign up as a new user. (Because Web sites are notorious for changing steps and commands, specific instructions would only confuse you. You have to wing it—trust me.)

3. Fill out the required form, read the legal agreement(s), and jump through whatever hoops you need to jump through to get your free membership. This gives you an ID (member name) and password so that you can sign in.

4. Use your ID and password to sign in to Yahoo! GeoCities. Your browser loads the Yahoo! GeoCities welcome page, as shown in the following figure.

Yahoo! GeoCities welcomes you.

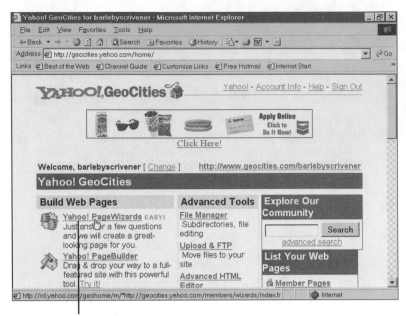

Click the Yahoo! PageWizards link.

5. Click the **Yahoo! PageWizards** link. Yahoo! GeoCities displays a list of pre-designed Web page templates you can use to get started.

6. Click one of the Page Wizard designs. Yahoo! GeoCities displays a brief introduction to the wizard, as shown in the following figure. (If you change your mind and decide to use a different template, click the **Back** button and choose another.)

7. Click **Launch Yahoo! PageWizard** to start the wizard with the selected design, or click one of the alternative color schemes or designs near the bottom of the page. The first Page Wizard dialog box appears, welcoming you to the wizard.

8. Click the **Begin** button. The wizard prompts you to select a color scheme.

9. Click the desired color scheme, and then click **Next >**. The wizard prompts you to enter your name and e-mail address as shown in the following figure.

10. Follow the wizard's instructions to complete your Web page and save it to the Yahoo! GeoCities Web server. (The steps vary, depending on which wizard you're running.)

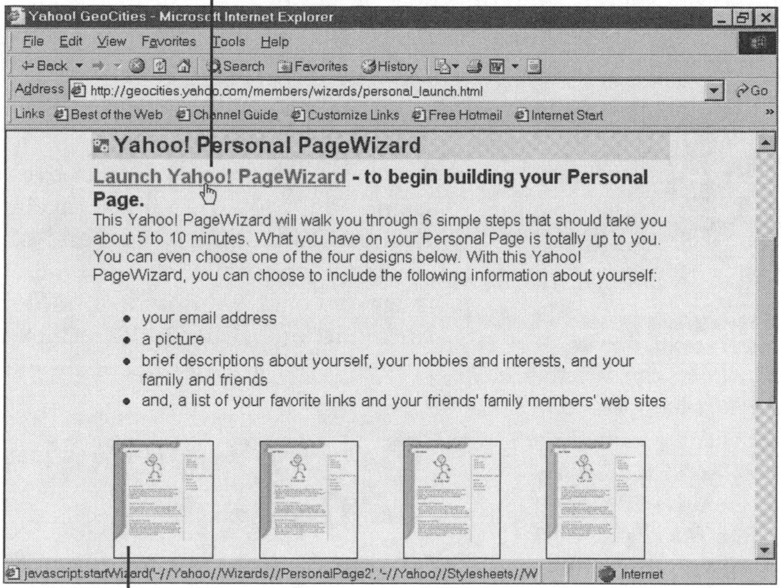

Click here to start the wizard.

Click an alternate design or color scheme to get started.

Yahoo! GeoCities provides a brief introduction to the selected wizard.

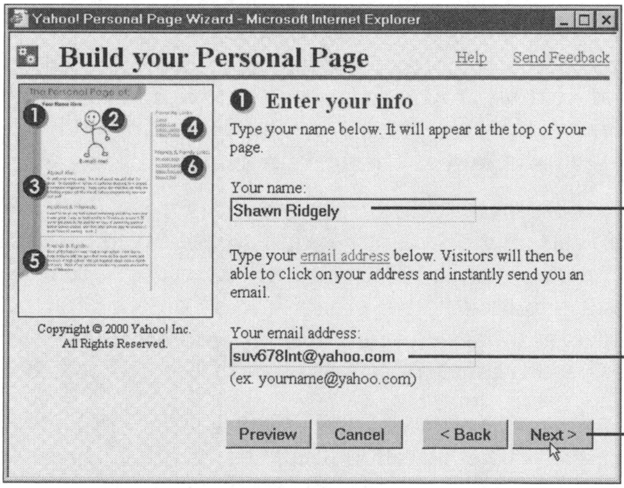

Type your name here.

Type your e-mail address here.

Click Next >.

*The Yahoo! Personal Page Wizard prompts you to type
your name and e-mail address.*

233

You can change your page at any time. Just go to Yahoo! GeoCities at geocities.yahoo.com, sign in, and run the Page Wizard. When the Page Wizard appears this time, it displays an option for editing an existing page. Click **Edit Existing Page**, open the drop-down menu, and click the name of the page you want to edit. Click **Next >** and follow the onscreen instructions to enter your changes.

For more options and control over your Web page design and layout, use Yahoo! PageBuilder. This is a full-featured Web page creation and editing tool. To run PageBuilder, simply open the Yahoo! GeoCities home page and click **Yahoo! PageBuilder**. This displays an introduction to PageBuilder. Click the **Launch PageBuilder** link to run the program.

Inside Tip

To delete a Web page, whether you created it with a wizard or with PageBuilder, you must use PageBuilder. Run PageBuilder, and then open the **File** menu and click **File Manager.** Click the check box next to the file you want to delete and then click the **Delete** button.

Placing Your Business on the Web

Of course, you didn't build that Web page to make money or pitch a pyramid scheme to your friends or relatives, but you can use your Web page to generate income and set up your own business or online store-front.

If you already have a page at Yahoo! GeoCities, one of the easiest ways to generate income from your page is to sign up for the Pages That Pay program. With this program, you insert advertisements and links for ordering products on your page. When someone orders the product through your page, you receive a sales commission from the manufacturer or dealer. You don't have to mess with creating order forms, tracking orders, or shipping products. You're just the middleman.

If you have more complex business needs (if you manufacture or ship your own product or provide a service), you might need more sophisticated Web-based business tools than those that Yahoo! GeoCities offers. You will need access to a secure Web server, a form for customers to use to place orders, and an online database that can receive and organize orders and track shipping information. In short, you need a more business-oriented Web hosting service. Check out the following sites:

➤ **Netscape Virtual Office** at www.nvo.com. This site costs $19.95 per month for about the same service you get at Yahoo! GeoCities for free. However, Netscape Virtual Office has more of a business slant and access to software for taking credit card orders over the Web. Of course, this comes at a price—starting at about $60 per month plus a $100 one-time setup fee for credit card transactions and 25 cents per transaction.

➤ **Yahoo! Small Business** at smallbusiness.yahoo.com. This site costs $100 per month for your own "small" online store, and you pay no per-transaction fee. (A "small" store consists of 50 items.) Yahoo! Small Business provides the basic tools you need to set up shop on the Web. For $35 a month, you can even get your own custom Web site address, and for a 2 percent sales commission, Yahoo! will advertise for you.

➤ **B-City** at www7.bcity.com. This site is a free Web site hosting service for businesses, entre-preneurs, and not-for-profit organizations. Its no-frills approach is refreshing, and you can't beat the price. (Advertisements are automati-cally added to your site to cover the cost of the free service.)

Inside Tip

When shopping for a Web host, compare costs and features care-fully. Check the amount of disk space you get and whether the service charges you extra every time someone visits your site. Also ask if any sales commissions are involved.

You can find hundreds of Web site hosting services on the Web that vary greatly in price and service. Use your favorite Web search tool to look for "Web hosting" or "free Web page." (Most services have trial offers that they advertise as "free." These sites typically are free only for 10 to 30 days and might include hidden costs for "special" business features, such as order forms and credit card pro-cessing.)

Finding Cool Stuff to Put on Your Page

You can decorate your Web page with everything from floral-print backgrounds to cartoon clip art. You can even add clocks, counters that mark the number of times people have visited your page, video clips, audio clips, and even small programs that allow visitors to perform calculations or play games.

Where do you find all this stuff? On the Web, of course. Check out the following Web sites for some cool free stuff you can use to enhance and enliven your Web site:

➤ **CLIPART.COM** at www.clipart.com. This site is one of the best places to go for Web graphics, photos, and animations. As shown in the following figure, you'll find dozens of free and *shareware* (try before you buy) clip art and animation li-braries.

➤ **ArtToday** at www.arttoday.com. This site offers a free membership that gives you access to more than 40,000 Web page graphics. Of course, that's just a teaser. Full membership (for $29.95 per year) gives you the good stuff—access to more than 1.4 million Web page images.

Download shareware and freeware clip art libraries.

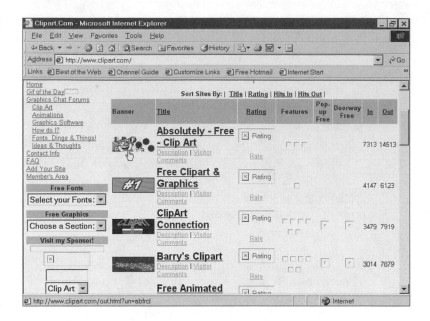

➤ **c|net** at download.cnet.com. This site provides plenty of free programs, ActiveX controls and Java applets (small programs you can place on your page), clip art, and audio and video clips. You'll need to poke around a little to find what you're looking for.

➤ **Free-Backgrounds.com** at www.free-backgrounds.com. This site specializes in custom background designs. New backgrounds are added every day. However, this is also a great place to pick up free clip art and animated graphics.

Computer Cheat

If you see something you like on a Web page, write to the Web page author via e-mail (if the person has his or her e-mail address on the page), and ask for permission to use the object. You can drag most clip art images, icons, and other objects right off a page displayed in your browser and drop them onto your page displayed in your Web page editor.

The Least You Need to Know

➤ HTML (Hypertext Markup Language) is a system of codes used to format Web pages.

➤ You don't need to master HTML in order to create your own attractive Web pages.

➤ To create and publish a simple Web page online, go to Yahoo! GeoCities at geocities.yahoo.com.

➤ The easiest way to create a page at Yahoo! GeoCities is to use one of the Yahoo! Page Wizards.

➤ To edit your Yahoo! GeoCities Web page, sign in at geocities.yahoo.com, and click the link for running the Page Wizard.

➤ For a more robust set of Web-based business tools, check out Netscape Virtual Office at www.nvo.com.

➤ For gobs of Web page clip art, go to www.clipart.com.

Part 5

Kids and Other Homey Stuff

Although you may think that your food processor is the most versatile tool in your home, your computer has it beat. With the right software, your computer can moonlight as a powerful game machine, reference library, interactive tutor, electronic photo album, family-tree maker, personal finance manager, and much more.

The chapters in this part introduce you to the most popular home-based computer software. Here, you learn how to manage your finances, shop for games and educational software, safely introduce your children to the Internet, organize and print photographs, and even research your lineage and create your own family tree.

Chapter 22

Managing Your Finances

In This Chapter

➤ Setting up checking, savings, and credit card accounts

➤ Entering transactions in your electronic checkbook

➤ Reconciling your checkbook balance and bank statement

➤ Creating and tracking your budget

➤ Doing your banking and tracking your investments online

The whole concept of money was supposed to simplify things, to make it easier to exchange goods. Instead of trading a fox pelt for a lobster dinner, you could sell the pelt for a handful of coins and then plop them down at your local seafood restaurant to pay for your lobster dinner.

Somewhere in the history of human existence, cash-based economies got all fouled up. We now store our money in banks and use checks to get at it, we have chunks of money removed from our paychecks before we've even touched it, and we invest money in companies hoping that we'll get even more money back.

To manage the complexities of our finances in these trying times, a personal finance program is essential. In this chapter, you learn how to pick a good personal finance program and use it to manage your checking and savings accounts, create and manage a budget, plan ahead with financial calculators, do your banking online, and even track your investments.

Choosing a Personal Finance Program

In the early days of personal finance programs, your choice was simple: Either you used Quicken to manage your finances, or you used a pencil and a calculator. There were no other personal finance programs on the market. As Quicken grew more popular (and profitable), other companies, including Microsoft, developed their own personal finance programs but they couldn't begin to compete with Quicken—until recently.

Just a couple years ago, Microsoft Money started to give Quicken a run for its … er … money. Now, Microsoft Money and Quicken are powerful competitors, each having its own unique strengths and weaknesses. Both programs offer basic tools for managing your accounts, budgeting, and paying bills; both include a set of financial planning calculators; and both have tools for tracking investments online.

Inside Tip

When a program is popular, it's more likely that someone you know owns and uses the program and can help you learn to use it. Books on popular programs are also more readily available. Look for *The Complete Idiot's Guide to Quicken 2000* (Alpha Books, 1999).

So, which is better? That depends on who you talk to or which review you read. Personally, I like Quicken, but I've been using it for nearly 10 years, and I'm not about to transfer all my accounts and transactions to Microsoft Money and relearn everything at the ripe old age of 41. If you're just starting out and you received a free copy of Microsoft Money with your new computer, don't run out and buy Quicken. Microsoft Money is an excellent personal finance program.

This chapter uses Quicken to illustrate the basic tasks you perform in a personal finance program. If you have Microsoft Money, use the steps and illustrations as an overview; although the steps might differ, the programs take a similar approach to most tasks.

Mastering the Basics

Before you can write checks or record transactions, you must create an *account,* specifying its opening balance and other important information. Most personal finance programs, including Quicken, let you create the following account types:

➤ **Checking.** Create a checking account to record written checks, deposits, withdrawals, and transfers.

➤ **Savings.** Create a savings account to record deposits, withdrawals, and transfers.

➤ **Credit card.** Create a credit card account to record your credit card charges and the payments you make when you receive your monthly statement.

➤ **Cash.** Create a cash account to track your cash expenditures.

➤ **Asset.** If you think you might want to determine your net worth sometime soon, you can create an asset account to track the value of big-ticket items, such as your home, car, boat, and RV.

➤ **Liability.** A liability is the flip side of an asset. Use a liability account to keep track of how much you still owe on those big-ticket possessions.

➤ **Investment.** If you've joined the wave of individual investors, you can use investment accounts to keep track of stock, bond, and mutual-fund transactions.

➤ **401(k).** If you're fortunate enough to have a 401(k) retirement plan through your employer, you can use a 401(k) account to track the amount of money you and your employer contribute to it with each paycheck.

➤ **Money market.** Create a money market account to track funds you have invested in a money market fund. A money market fund is similar to a savings account.

The following sections show you how to create an account in Quicken and then select an account to view or enter *transactions*.

Entering Account Information

You don't have to be a banker to create an account in your personal finance program. Both Quicken and Microsoft Money feature wizards that step you through the process. To run the Create New Account Wizard in Quicken and use it to create an account, here's what you do:

1. Press **Ctrl+A** to display the Accounts window, which lists all the accounts you have created. Assuming this is your first account, the list should be blank.

2. On the **Account List** menu bar, click **New**. The Create New Account Wizard pops up, as shown in the following figure, prompting you to specify the desired account type.

3. Click the desired account type and click the **Next** button.

4. Follow the onscreen instructions to enter the requested information.

Tech Term

A **transaction** is any activity that affects the balance of an account either positively or negatively. In a checking account, a written check and a deposit are both transactions.

Computer Cheat

When you start Quicken, it displays the My Finances screen, which contains an Accounts list. On the right end of the Accounts title bar, click **Actions** and then click **Create an account.**

Obviously, before you can enter a transaction, you must select the appropriate account—checking, savings, credit card, or other account. To change to a specific account, press **Ctrl+A** to display the Account List, and then double-click the desired account.

Select the desired account type.

Create New Account

Choose the type of account to create.

Banking & Cash	Investments	Household
⦿ Checking	○ Brokerage	○ House (with or w/o Mortgage)
○ Savings	○ IRA or Keogh	○ Vehicle (with or w/o Loan)
○ Credit Card	○ 401(k)	○ Asset
○ Money Market	○ Dividend Reinvestment Plan	○ Liability
○ Cash	○ Other Investment	

* If you are trying to set up a security such as a stock or bond, you should probably choose Brokerage. Click help for more information.

Cancel   Help   Next ——— Click the Next button.

The Create New Account Wizard steps you through the process.

Inside Tip

If you find yourself entering the same transaction on a regular basis (your paycheck deposit or mortgage payment, for instance), consider setting up the entry as a recurring (or scheduled) transaction. You simply tell Quicken the amount of the transaction and the frequency (weekly, every two weeks, every month), and Quicken automatically records the transaction for you. To set up a scheduled transaction, open the **Banking** menu, click **Scheduled Transaction List,** then click the **New** button, click **OK,** and enter the requested information.

Recording Transactions

Whenever you pay a bill, deposit your paycheck, or hit up the ATM for a wad of cash, you must record the transaction in Quicken, just as you record transactions in your checkbook. The process for recording transactions varies, depending on the account type. For all accounts, you must enter the transaction date, a description of the transaction, and the amount. Some accounts, such as checking accounts, require you to enter additional information (such as a check number). The following figure illustrates the process of entering a checking account transaction.

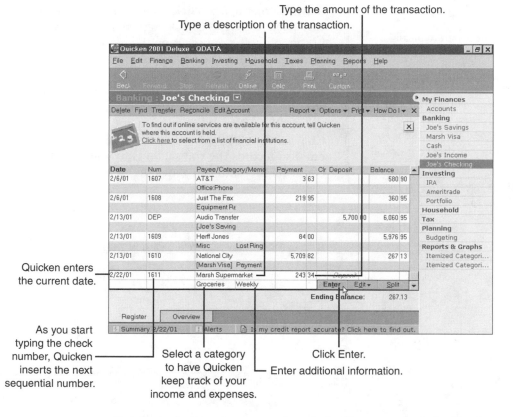

Type the amount of the transaction.

Type a description of the transaction.

Quicken enters the current date.

As you start typing the check number, Quicken inserts the next sequential number.

Select a category to have Quicken keep track of your income and expenses.

Click Enter.

Enter additional information.

Quicken's checking account register looks like a standard checkbook register.

Printing Checks

Most people use Quicken to help them budget and keep their accounts balanced. They tote around a checkbook so that they can write checks manually, and once a week or so they sit down and enter their transactions in Quicken. When they receive their monthly statement, they use Quicken to reconcile the statement with their records.

There's nothing wrong with using Quicken in such a limited way. However, if you're looking to further reduce your workload, consider having Quicken "write" (print) the checks for you. All you need to do is type the name of the payee and the amount of

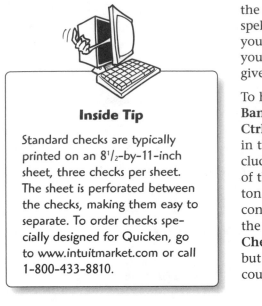

Inside Tip

Standard checks are typically printed on an 8¹/₂-by-11-inch sheet, three checks per sheet. The sheet is perforated between the checks, making them easy to separate. To order checks specially designed for Quicken, go to www.intuitmarket.com or call 1-800-433-8810.

the check. Quicken supplies the check number and spells out the amount based on the numerical entry you typed. When you're done "writing" the checks, you simply load blank checks into your printer and give Quicken the command to print them.

To have Quicken print your checks, first open the **Banking** menu, and click **Write Checks** (or press **Ctrl+W**). The Write Checks screen appears, as shown in the following figure. Type the required entries, including the date, the payee's name, and the amount of the check, and then click the **Record Check** button. This displays a new blank check so that you can continue writing checks. When you're ready to print the checks, open the **File** menu and click **Print Checks**. Quicken not only prints the checks for you but also records the transactions in your checking account register and calculates the new balance.

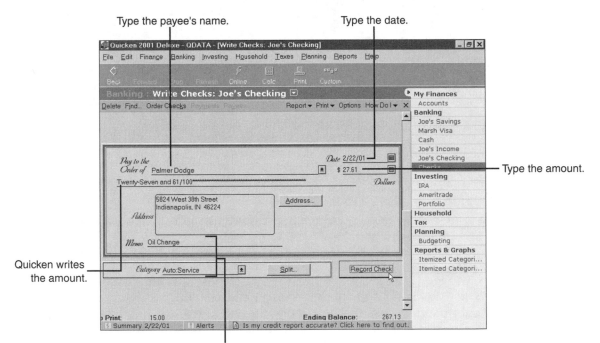

The Write Checks screen lets you type a check.

Reconciling Your Account and Bank Statement

In the old days, reconciling your checkbook balance with your monthly statement was an exercise in frustration. You calculated and recalculated until you started seeing double. With a personal finance program such as Quicken, reconciling your checkbook is no longer an ordeal. You simply mark the checks that have cleared, mark the deposits that appear on the bank statement, and enter any service charges, as shown in the following figure. Quicken performs the calculations and immediately determines whether your total matches the bank's total.

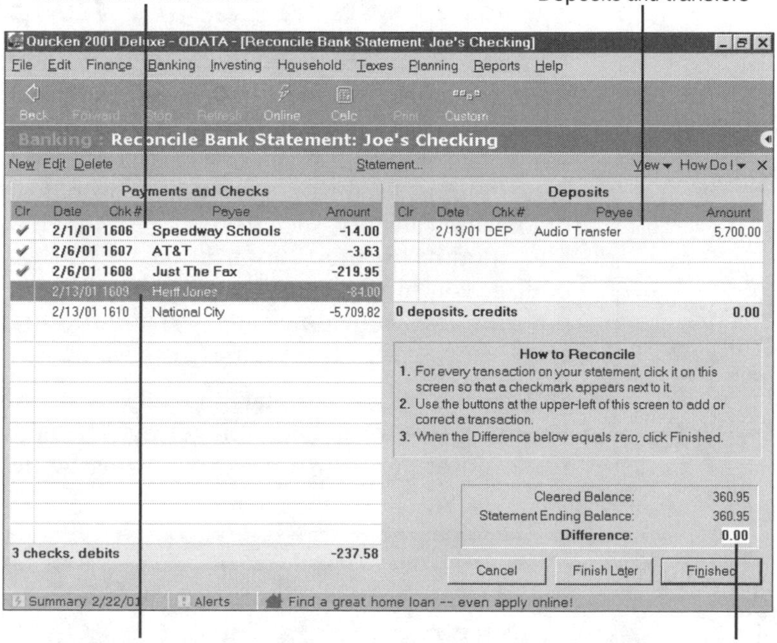

Withdrawals and checks

Deposits and transfers

Click a transaction to mark it as cleared.

When you're done, the difference should be 0.

Click the cleared transactions in the Reconcile window.

To display the Reconcile window, change to the account you want to reconcile, and then click **Reconcile** near the top of the account window. You must then enter the previous balance and any interest and service charges shown on your statement. After you enter this information and click **OK**, the Reconcile window appears.

Budgeting 101

Before you can take control of your personal finances, you must figure out where your money is coming from and where it's going. You can't decide if car repairs are costing more than a new-car payment unless you know how much you spend on car repairs each month. And you'll never have any money to invest unless you set realistic spending goals and stay within the limits. To take stock of your current financial status and start setting goals, draw up a budget.

But how do you draw up a budget? Most personal finance programs, including Quicken and Microsoft Money, have the required budget tools. You simply enter the budgeted amounts for each category: income, food, rent, entertainment, clothing, and so on. As you enter transactions in your account registers and assign categories, the program keeps track of your income and expenses by category. To see if you're on track, simply print a budget report. The following sections show you just what to do.

Panic Attack!

If your budget shows only the current month, open the **Options** menu (just above the budget window) and click **Display Months.**

Starting with a Budget Template

All personal finance programs, and even some spreadsheet programs, include a budget template that lets you create a budget simply by filling in the blanks. The template typically consists of a grid of intersecting rows and columns. Each row is devoted to a single income or expense category, such as food, rent, or clothing. The columns list the 12 months of the year. To create a budget, you simply enter the amount you earn each month (for each income category) and the amount you spend each month (for each expense category).

To view the budget template in Quicken, open the **Planning** menu and click **Budgeting**. The budget template appears, as shown in the following figure.

The budget template lets you enter monthly amounts for income and expense categories.

Category View	Jan	Totals
Equipment Repair	-100	-175
Medical		
Medical - Other	-250	-413
Office		
Phone	-40	-545
Office - Other	-2	-930
Online Service	-10	-110
Shipping	-20	-198
Software	-50	-753
Tax		
Fed	-3600	-21535
State	-400	-2054
Tax - Other	0	0
Tax Prep	0	-16
Upgrade	-100	-1781
TO Joe's Checking	0	-25300
TO Joe's Savings	0	-1400
Total Income	4300	106396
Total Expenses	-4922	-67141
Difference	-622	39255

Tweaking Your Budget

As you can see in the preceding figure, the budget template contains a comprehensive list of income and expense categories. Before you even think about entering numbers in the template, consider simplifying the budget by deleting some of the categories:

1. At the top of the Budget window, click **Categories.** The Select Categories to Include dialog box appears, displaying all available categories.

2. To remove a category from the budget, click its name to remove the check mark next to it. (To add the category back into the budget, click its name again.)

3. Repeat step 2 until only those categories you want included in the budget are checked.

4. Click **OK.**

Entering Income and Expenses

After you've established the categories for your budget, you can start entering income and expense amounts. You can enter amounts manually by typing them in or have Quicken automatically enter amounts based on transactions you've already entered. For instance, if you have several transactions showing paycheck deposits, you can have Quicken automatically enter your paycheck amount in the **Income** category.

To have Quicken automatically enter average amounts for each month, open the **Edit** menu at the top of the Budget window and click **Auto-create.** Enter your preferences, and then click **OK.**

Panic Attack!

You know you recorded your mortgage payments and the checks you wrote to pay your heating bills, but the budget dropped those categories or displayed a bunch of zeros. What's up? When entering transactions, it's easy to skip the step for selecting a category. Go back to your accounts (Checking, Savings, Credit, Cash) and be sure you have assigned a category to every transaction.

Making Adjustments

Now that your budget is complete, you can hang it on your refrigerator door and start saving money, right? Wrong. Before you use your budget, review it to be sure you can live with the numbers. If the monthly income value does not accurately reflect your current paycheck, you might need to adjust the amount. Likewise, if an expense seems too high or too low, you might need to enter a more realistic number.

Making changes to your budget is fairly easy. Use the **Tab** and arrow keys to highlight the desired value (or click the value), and then type the new value. To enter the same value for a category for every month, enter the value for January, then open the **Edit** menu, click **Fill Row Right**, and click **Yes.** To clone a column and use its values in all the columns to the end of the year, click any value in the column you want to clone, then open the **Edit** menu, click **Fill Columns**, and click **Yes**.

Inside Tip

If you're like me, you like to pay with cash. That's fine, but be sure to create a cash account in Quicken. Save your receipts and enter your cash transactions just as loyally as you enter transactions for your checking and savings accounts. (And don't forget to assign each transaction to a category.)

Panic Attack!

If you know how much you can afford to pay per month, work backwards with the Loan Calculator. Under **Calculate For,** click **Loan Amount.** Then enter the amount you can afford per month. The Loan Calculator determines the amount you can safely borrow at the specified interest rate and term.

Using Your Budget to Stay on Track

Face it—unless you're Bill Gates or Donald Trump, you have to stick to your budget in good times and bad. If you have $150 set aside each month for car repairs, and you don't touch that money for two months, don't spend it on anything else. Eventually, you will need that money for a repair or to purchase a new car. If, after three months or so, you see that your budgeted amount is way too high and another category's budgeted amount is way too low, adjust the numbers to set more realistic goals, but don't stray from your budget.

To print a copy of your budget, create a budget report. Display your budget, then open the **Report** menu, and choose **Budget Report**. Open the **Report Dates** list, and click the desired period for the report (for example, **Year to date**, **Current month**, or **Current quarter**). Or, type the desired dates in the **From** and **To** text boxes. Click the **Create** button. Click **Print** to print the report.

Planning Ahead with Financial Calculators

You're looking at a $17,000 car, and your bank is offering new car loans at 7.25 percent. How much is the monthly payment? If you invest $250 a month in a mutual fund and see an average annual return of 10 percent, how much money will you have in 30 years? At an inflation rate of 4 percent per year, how much will that money be worth? Would it pay to refinance your home? How much do you need to set aside for your kids' education?

Every personal finance program on the market, including Quicken, comes with a collection of financial calculators that can answer all these questions and help you plan for the future. To display one of Quicken's financial calculators, open the **Planning** menu, point to **Financial Calculators**, and click the desired calculator: **Loan, Refinance, Savings, College,** or **Retirement.**

When the calculator appears, simply fill in the blanks and click the **Calculate** button to get the answers you need. The following figure shows the Loan Calculator in action. By default, the Loan Calculator determines the payment amount per period based on the loan amount, interest rate, term, number of periods per year, and compounding period.

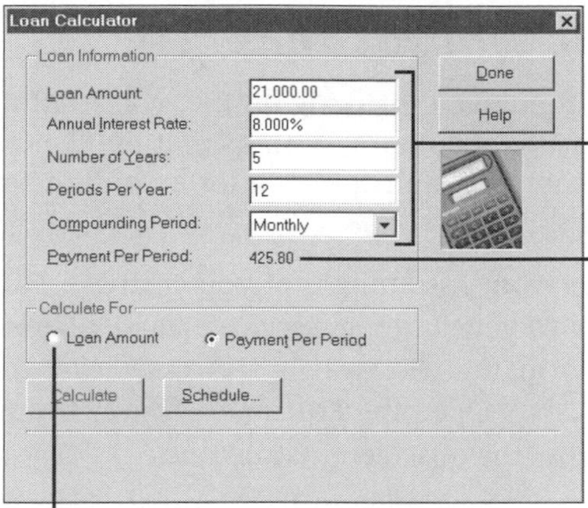

The Loan Calculator determines your monthly payment on the loan.

Enter the requested data.

The Loan Calculator displays the monthly payment.

Click here to calculate the total loan amount based on the monthly payment.

Electronic Banking 101

To make accounts even more accessible, many banks offer online banking services. Using your personal finance program or a specialized online banking program, you can access your account information 24 hours a day, seven days a week, without leaving your home or office. You can even use the service to pay your bills electronically and send printed checks to individuals and companies not equipped to accept electronic payments. In addition, if your credit card company offers online access, you can download up-to-date transaction details from the company to avoid typing the transactions manually.

That's what online banking is all about. It allows you to pay bills, transfer money, and get account information without filling out deposit slips and transfer requests and without writing or printing checks. And, if you're fortunate enough to have an online banking service that supports your personal finance program, you can immediately transfer transaction details from your bank to your computer, ensuring that you have the most up-to-date and accurate information.

How Much Will This Cost?

Online banking isn't free, but its cost is not out of line with the service fees that traditional banks charge. Many banks offer free-trial accounts for 6 to 12 months and might charge $5 per month after the free-trial period. Some banks offer free online banking for as long as you use the account. If you choose to use the bill-paying feature, expect to pay more (an extra $12 or more per month plus per-check fees for any printed/mailed checks). Make sure you read the agreement and understand the service fees before you open an account.

Signing Up for Electronic Transactions

Before you can even think about doing your banking online, you must lay the groundwork in Quicken. This consists of entering settings that tell Quicken how to connect to the Internet on your computer and applying for an online bank account. This is basically a four-step process:

➤ **Set up your Internet connection.** Assuming that you created a Dial-Up Networking icon for connecting to your Internet service provider (as explained in Chapter 16, "Finding an Information FREEway"), telling Quicken 2001 how to connect to the Internet is a snap. Open the **Edit** menu, select **Internet Connection Setup,** and follow the onscreen instructions.

➤ **Apply for an online bank account.** Call your bank and ask if they offer online banking and if they support the personal finance program you're using. If they do, you can sign up for online banking and receive a login name and password or PIN (personal information number). If your bank does not offer online banking, shop for a bank on the Internet or use your personal finance program to track down a bank. In Quicken, for instance, open the **Finance** menu, click **Online Financial Institutions List,** and follow the onscreen instructions.

➤ **Activate your online account in your personal finance program.** This process consists of entering the information your personal finance program needs to connect to the bank, log in, and interact with your online banking account. In Quicken, open the **Banking** menu and click **Online Banking Setup.** This starts the Online Account Setup Wizard, which leads you step-by-step through the process of creating a new account or entering online connection information for one of your existing accounts.

➤ **Enable online transactions for an account.** After you sign up for online banking and create a new account, you must edit the properties of

Whoa!

Many banks let you check your balance and download transaction details but do not allow you to pay bills online. In cases where online payment is unavailable, Quicken gives you the option of signing up for its online payment service. Before you attempt to pay a bill online, check with the payee to be sure the company or individual accepts online payments.

the accounts to enable online banking. In Quicken, press **Ctrl+A** to display the Accounts List. Right-click the account you want to use for online banking, and then click **Edit.** Click **Online Access** and follow the onscreen instructions to complete the process.

Paying Your Bills Electronically

With Quicken, paying bills electronically is a snap. You simply display the account register for your online bank account and enter the transaction information as you normally would. The only difference is that instead of entering a check number, you specify that you want to pay the bill electronically. Open the list in the **Num** column for the transaction and choose **Send Online Payment**, as shown in the following figure.

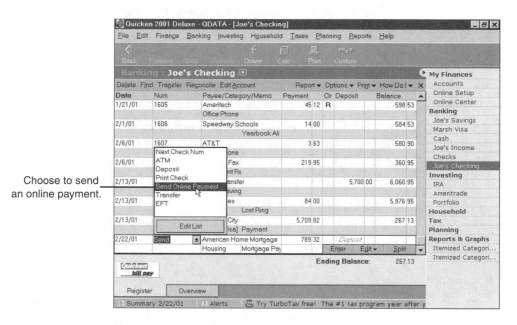

Choose to send an online payment.

Enter the transaction in your register just as you would enter a payment by check.

As you enter online transactions, Quicken keeps track of those transactions but does not immediately process them. To process the transactions and actually send the online payments, open the **Banking** menu, click **Online Banking**, and click **Update/ Send.** Follow the onscreen instructions to execute the transactions; for example, you might need to reenter your PIN.

Setting Up Automatic Recurring Payments

Nowadays, most banks, credit unions, and other financial institutions support automatic withdrawals. If you have a car loan or a mortgage, you can call the lender and have your payments automatically withdrawn from your savings or checking account on a specified day each month. You might even have payments automatically withdrawn and deposited in a mutual fund or used to pay your utility bills (if you're on a budget plan with the utility company).

For companies that do not support automatic withdrawals, you can set up Quicken to automatically send payments on a specified day each month. You simply set up a scheduled transaction. Here's what you do:

1. Open the **Banking** menu and choose **Scheduled Transaction List** (or choose **Lists, Scheduled Transactions** in Quicken 99).

2. If the transaction you want to schedule is already in the list, right-click the transaction and click **Edit.**

    If the transaction is not in the list, click **New** just above the scheduled transactions list.

3. Open the **Account to use** list, and click the online account from which you want the bill paid.

4. Open the **Type of Transaction** list and click **Online Pmt.**

5. Click the button next to the **Next Date** box and select the next date to send a payment. (Send the payment a few days before it's due to give your bank time to process the payment.)

6. Click in the **Amount** box and type the payment amount.

7. Open the **How often** list and click the desired frequency of the payments—for instance, monthly or yearly.

Inside Tip

You can set up scheduled transactions for depositing your paycheck and for printing checks. Their use is not limited to electronic payments.

8. Enter any other preferences and click **OK.** The Set Up Online Payee dialog box appears, prompting you to enter information about the payee.

9. Enter the requested information, including the payee's address and account number, and click **OK.** Another dialog box appears, asking you to confirm the information you entered.

10. Click **Accept.** Quicken might display additional dialog boxes if it detects that the payment will cause a problem with your budget or balance. Respond to the dialog boxes as needed.

When the specified payment date rolls around, Quicken automatically transfers the payment amount from your account to the payee's account as specified.

Transferring Cash Between Accounts

Online banking completely revolutionizes the way you transfer money from one account to another. Instead of filling out a transfer request, waiting in line, and then having the teller process the request and print a receipt, you simply transfer funds from one account to the other in Quicken. Quicken processes the transfer online, records the transaction, and recalculates the account balance.

To perform a transfer online, enter the transfer in the account register as you normally would—enter the date, a description of the transfer, and the amount to transfer. Open the list in the **Num** column and choose **Online Transfer.** Open the **Xfer Acct** list (just below the transaction description) and click the account to which you want the money transferred. Click the **Enter** button.

Downloading Transaction Records and Balances

Traditionally, you have to wait around for the mail carrier to deliver your monthly statement before you can find out if a check has cleared or if your balance is correct. With online banking, you don't have to wait. You can access your account any time, day or night, and download the latest record of your transactions and balances. To get the latest transaction details online with Quicken, follow these steps:

1. Open the **Banking** menu and click **Online Banking.**
2. Click the **Update/Send** button.
3. Be sure the **Download my latest online transactions and balances from** option is checked. Quicken might prompt you to enter your PIN if the bank requires you to enter it before performing the next step.
4. If prompted, enter your PIN and any other login information required by your bank, and then click **Send.** (Some banks might not prompt you to enter your PIN until you click **Send.**) Quicken downloads your transactions and updated balance and displays the Transaction Summary window.
5. Review the transactions to be sure they are correct, and then click **OK.**

Tracking Your Investments Online

In Chapter 20, "Shopping, Investing, Traveling, and Other Cool Web Stuff," you learned that you could open an account with an online stockbroker, such as E*TRADE or Charles Schwab, and trade stocks over the Internet.

So why do you need Quicken to manage your investments? Because Quicken can download all your investment data, consolidate it in a portfolio, help you analyze it, keep track of your capital gains and dividends for tax purposes, and even include the data in your reports.

Before you can process investment transactions online with Quicken, you must open an account with an online investment service and then enter the login information for your account in Quicken. If you already opened an account after reading Chapter 19, "Poking Around on the Web," you simply need to enter the login information.

The process for opening an account with an online broker is nearly identical to the process for opening an online bank account. Open the **Finance** menu and click **Online Financial Institutions List.** Under **Online Financial Services,** click **Investment Account Access.** Click the service you want to use, click **Apply Now,** and follow the onscreen instructions. For details, see "Signing Up for Electronic Transactions," earlier in this chapter.

After you have set up your investment account in Quicken, you can begin your life as a day trader, buying and selling stocks, downloading the latest numbers, and analyzing your portfolio's performance. Of course, this chapter isn't long enough to provide step-by-step instructions for using Quicken's investment tools, but here's an overview of what you can do in Quicken 2001:

➤ **Buy and sell stocks and mutual funds.** Open the **Investing** menu and click **Investing Center.** Open the **Easy Actions** menu (just above the transaction list) and click **Buy/Sell Shares.** Follow the onscreen instructions to complete the purchase.

➤ **Track your 401(k).** Open the **Investing** menu, point to **Investing Activities,** and click **Track My 401(k).** This starts the 401(k) Setup Wizard, which leads you through the process of entering details about your company's 401(k) plan.

➤ **Update your investment portfolio.** Go to Portfolio view by choosing **Investing, Portfolio View.** Click **Update,** select the type of information you want (for example, **Get Online Quotes** or **Get Asset Classes**), enter the requested information in the resulting dialog box, and click **OK.**

➤ **Research investments.** Select **Investing, Investment Research.** This displays the Quicken Investment Research window, which helps you track down the financial information you need to make well-informed investments.

Computer Cheat

Quicken's One Step Update lets you download all your online financial data at once, including bank transactions and investment share prices. Open the **Finance** menu and click **One Step Update.**

The Least You Need to Know

➤ Before you can enter transactions, you must create an account, specifying the starting date and current balance.

➤ To create a new account in Quicken, press **Ctrl+A,** click **New,** and follow the wizard's lead.

➤ To switch to an account in Quicken, press **Ctrl+A** and double-click the desired account.

➤ To record a transaction, enter the date, a transaction description, the amount of the transaction, and any other data in the corresponding boxes, and then click **Enter.**

➤ To begin reconciling an account in Quicken, first display the account's register and then click **Reconcile** near the top of the register.

➤ To display Quicken's Budget window, choose **Planning, Budgeting.**

➤ To access one of Quicken's financial calculators, choose **Planning, Financial Calculators,** and click the desired calculator.

➤ To apply for and enable online accounts in Quicken, choose **Banking, Online Banking Setup,** and follow the onscreen instructions.

➤ To schedule a regular payment, choose **Banking, Scheduled Transaction List,** click **New,** and enter the requested information.

➤ To download transaction details from an online bank, choose **Banking, Online Banking,** and click the **Update/Send** button.

Chapter 23

Finding and Playing Cool Games

In This Chapter

➤ Picking the right games for your computer system

➤ Checking out some essential game gear

➤ Finding and downloading free games from the Web

➤ Buying cool games online

➤ Getting game reviews, codes, and tips on the Internet

Many people buy a computer under the pretext that it will help them work more efficiently, organize their lives, or improve communication with friends, relatives, and colleagues. Two weeks after they get the computer home, they're plugging in a joystick and installing arcade games. Two months later, their eyes are glazed over, their thumbs are twitching, and they can't speak in complete sentences. Computer games can transform even the most disciplined worker, the most responsible adult, into a dysfunctional game junkie.

This chapter sets you on the path to your own computer game addiction. Here, you learn how to find the best computer games on the market, beef up your system with the latest game gear, get free games from the Web, and learn gaming tricks from the masters.

Shopping for the Right Games

The term computer game has different meanings for different people. For some people, computer game conjures up the image of old standards, such as Solitaire or Tetris. Other people envision action games, such as Mech Warrior and Doom. And still others think of strategy games, such as SimCity. The fact is that a computer game is any program that people play for fun.

Because the market is flooded with all sorts of computer games, dealers typically categorize games to help customers find what they like. Before you start shopping, familiarize yourself with these categories:

➤ **Action/fighting.** Whether you want to blast alien warships out of the sky or do a little kickboxing, this category is the one for you. If you're in a software store, just look for a group of angry boys, and you'll find the action games.

➤ **Adventure.** In an adventure game, you set out on a journey to complete a mission, discover something valuable, or solve a mystery. Adventure games typically give you clues and allow you to pick up helpful tools along the way, such as flashlights or keys. The adventure section is where the geeks usually hang out.

➤ **Arcade.** Think pinball, and you have a pretty good picture of the arcade game category. These are screen versions of games you typically play by feeding quarters into an arcade machine. Remember Pac-Man?

➤ **Sports.** This category is self-explanatory. Here you'll find games for playing football, baseball, basketball, golf, and any other popular sport whose athletes are overpaid. Sports is the category of choice for jocks and jock wannabes.

➤ **Driving/simulation.** Whether you want to drive the NASCAR circuit or pretend you're an F-16 fighter pilot, you'll find plenty of games to put you behind the wheel. This category appeals to everyone—young and old, male and female, geek and jock—anyone who likes to be in the driver's seat.

➤ **Role playing.** Do you want to be somebody else? Take a momentary break from reality? A role-playing game might be just the escape you need. You take on the role of one of the story's characters and then interact with other characters and your surroundings in an attempt to gain power. Of course, this might sound too much like reality.

➤ **Board games.** If you grew up playing Monopoly, Risk, checkers, chess, or other board games, you'll be happy to know that there's a computer version for nearly every traditional board game. Of course, there's no replacement for seeing the anguish on your opponent's face when he lands on a hotel-heavy Boardwalk, but with computer games, you never have trouble finding enough players.

➤ **Card games.** Tired of Solitaire and FreeCell? If so, maybe it's time to change games. Card game collections, such as Hoyle Card Games 2000, provide a robust selection of traditional card games, including Poker, Euchre, Gin Rummy, and even Old Maid.

➤ **Strategy.** Strategy games require thought and planning. You must be able to out-think your opponent and anticipate her every move. Although most strategy games are based on planning and executing attacks on the battlefield, some strategy games are rather peaceful. For instance, in The Sims, shown in the following figure, you must land a job, build your own home, and raise a family without ending up in bankruptcy court.

In The Sims, you build and furnish your own home—assuming you can hold down a job.

Additional Equipment You Might Need

First-time gamers can be pretty naive. They spend hours tracking down the coolest action game around and completely overlook the fact that their computer is ill-equipped to run it. Can you imagine flying a spaceship with a mouse or blasting enemy warships with a keyboard? Of course not!

To fully enjoy top-of-the-line action games or simulations, be sure your system is properly equipped:

➤ **SVGA video.** Most monitors manufactured in the last five years are SVGA, so this shouldn't be a problem for you. Although many good games require only VGA, graphics-heavy action games demand better monitors and video cards.

➤ **Special video card.** Some games require a special video card, such as the GeForce or Voodoo video card, with additional video RAM.

➤ **3D audio.** Sounds are unimportant for card games and some strategy games, but they can make or break an arcade game. If you're shopping for an arcade game, be sure the game supports the audio card installed in your computer. Some of the better computer games support 3D audio, which requires a special audio card along with speakers and a subwoofer.

➤ **Game controller.** Some games don't support a joystick or other game controller. You must use the keyboard and mouse to navigate and blast the alien enemies. That's no fun. Get yourself a joystick or other game controller, and if you're shopping for an arcade game, be sure it supports a joystick.

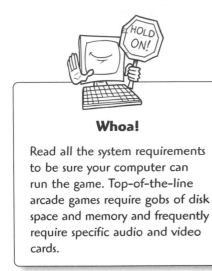

Whoa!

Read all the system requirements to be sure your computer can run the game. Top-of-the-line arcade games require gobs of disk space and memory and frequently require specific audio and video cards.

Whoa!

Some game installations can play havoc with your computer, completely rewriting the startup files and potentially disabling Windows. Consider consulting with a knowledgeable friend before installing a DOS game under Windows.

Running Stubborn DOS Games in Windows

Many computer games are designed to run on the operating system that preceded Windows. This operating system, called DOS (pronounced *Dawss*), isn't quite as intuitive as the Windows desktop. When you start a computer that runs DOS, the DOS prompt appears on-screen as C:\>. To run the game, you type the specified command at the prompt and press **Enter.**

Fortunately, you no longer need to know much about DOS to use a computer. You install a program and then click its icon or select it from a menu to run it. But when you're working with computer games, DOS is still boss. Many games still require you to run them under DOS. Although the game might run smoothly without your intervention, some games might cause problems or might not run at all under Windows. The following sections show you how to run games designed for DOS and make adjustments when you run into problems.

Running DOS Games and Other Programs

Windows is designed to run DOS games and other programs better than they run under DOS alone—in theory, anyway. To run the program, change to the disk and folder in which the program files are stored, and double-click the icon for running the program. (The files that execute DOS programs are typically displayed with an icon that looks like a tiny blank window.) You can add the DOS program to the **Programs** menu or create a shortcut to it, as explained in Chapter 3, "Launching Your First Program."

Running a DOS Game That Won't Budge

If you have trouble running a DOS game from Windows, create a shortcut icon for the game: Right-drag the game's program icon from My Computer onto the desktop, release the mouse button, and click **Create Shortcut(s) Here**. Right-click the shortcut and click **Properties**. In Windows Me, click the **Program** tab and click **Prevent MS-DOS-based programs from detecting Windows**, as shown in the following figure. In earlier versions of Windows, click the **Program** tab, click the **Advanced** button, choose **MS-DOS Mode**, and click **OK**. This gives the DOS game all available system resources, essentially "hiding" Windows from the program. Click **OK** to save your changes. Double-click the shortcut icon to run the game.

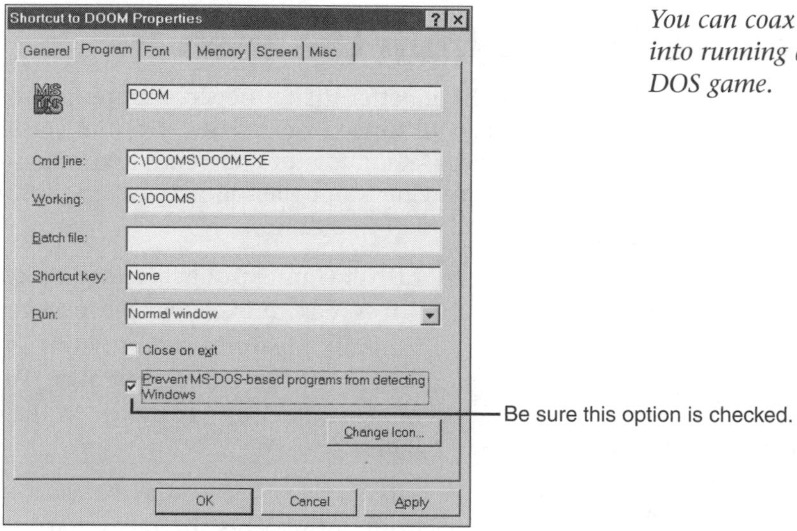

You can coax Windows into running a stubborn DOS game.

Be sure this option is checked.

If the game still does not run under a version of Windows before Windows Me, right-click the shortcut icon and choose **Properties**. Click the **Programs** tab, and then click the **Advanced** button. Click **Specify a new MS-DOS configuration**. Move the insertion point to the end of the DEVICE=C:\WINDOWS\HIMEM.SYS line, and press **Enter** to create a blank line. Type DEVICE=C:\WINDOWS\EMM386.EXE RAM. This provides expanded memory for running programs that require it. Click the **OK** button. When you return to the Properties dialog box, click **OK** to save your changes.

Still won't run? Try running the game from the DOS prompt using one of these methods:

➤ Click the **Start** button and click **Run.** Type command and press **Enter.** This displays a DOS window. Type cd\folder (where "folder" is the name of the folder in which the program's files are stored), and press **Enter.** Type the command for running the game (refer to the game's documentation), and press **Enter.**

➤ If you're using a version of Windows prior to Windows Me, click the **Start** button, choose **Shut Down**, choose **Restart in MS-DOS mode**, and click **OK.** Run the program from the DOS prompt as explained in the preceding item in this list.

➤ If that doesn't work, restart Windows. As soon as your computer beeps, press and release the **F8** key. This displays the Microsoft **Windows 98 Startup** menu. Type the number next to **Command Prompt Only.** Run the program from the DOS prompt as explained in the first item in this list.

Getting Free Games from the Web

For a dedicated gamer, the only thing better than a new computer game is a new *free* computer game. You can download all sorts of free games and trial versions from the Web—assuming, of course, that you know where to look. Check out the following Web sites for a great selection of free games:

➤ **ZDNet GameSpot** at www.zdnet.com/gamespot. This site is an excellent place to get started. GameSpot features not only one of the best selections of free games, but also game codes, tips, news, and demos, as shown in the following figure.

➤ **Ziff Davis** at www.zdnet.com/downloads/games.html. This site takes you to ZDNet's download site, where you'll find links to all sorts of freeware and shareware, including games, utilities, Internet programs, and educational software.

➤ **HotGames.com** at hotgames.com. This site offers a wide selection of game demos, along with tips and tricks for the most popular games.

➤ **The Games Network** at www.gamesnetwork.com or www.libertysurf.co.uk/sections/games.

Panic Attack!

Some games might require you to create a special floppy disk to use for starting your computer. Whenever you want to play the game, you must insert the disk and restart your computer. This starts the computer without running Windows, enabling the game to run in a pure DOS environment. Contact the game developer's technical support department for help.

This site is another excellent starting point for new and seasoned gamers. Here you'll find game reviews, previews, tips, and a wide selection of game demos. This site also covers popular video game systems, including Nintendo64 and Dreamcast.

➤ **Free Games Net** at www.free-games-net.com. This site offers free games in a wide variety of categories—from action and adventure to simulation and strategy.

➤ **Gamer's Inn** at www.gamersinn.com. This site offers more than a collection of computer games. Here you'll find an extensive list of free games, a message board where you can get help and trade tips, and a game room where you can test your skills against other gamers.

➤ **GameGenie.com** at www.gamex.net. This site is a great place to go for reviews and demos of the most popular games. Click the **Cheats** link to access a collection of tips, tricks, and codes from the masters.

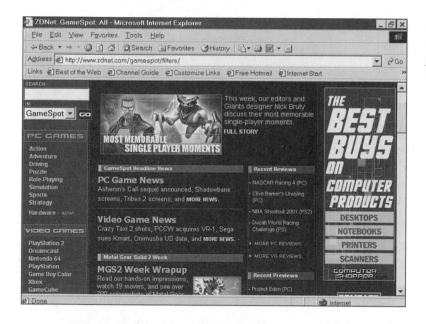

ZDNet GameSpot offers a wide selection of computer games, codes, tips, and news.

Many downloaded games are packaged as self-extracting, self-installing files. After downloading the file, you simply double-click its name in My Computer or Windows Explorer and follow the onscreen installation instructions.

Some downloaded games, however, arrive as compressed (zipped) files, which you must decompress before installation. These files typically have the .zip filename extension. You use a decompression program, such as WinZip, which you can get at www.winzip.com.

When you install WinZip, the installation routine associates WinZip with zip files. This makes it easy to decompress zip files. In My Computer or Windows Explorer, double-click the zip file to open it in WinZip. This displays a list of the files contained in the zip file. When you use WinZip to extract files, keep the following points in mind:

➤ If the zip file contains files for installing a program, you do not need to extract the files. Simply double-click the Setup.exe or Install.exe file in the WinZip window. WinZip will automatically extract the necessary files and run the installation. If you extract the files first, you'll have to delete them after you install the program.

➤ It's a good idea to extract files to a separate folder so that they don't get mixed up with your other files.

➤ If you click WinZip's **Extract** button before selecting a file, WinZip extracts all the files in the zip folder (which is what you usually want to do). If you select a file first, WinZip extracts only the selected file.

To extract files from a compressed file using WinZip, follow these steps:

1. In My Computer, click the icon for the zip file.
2. (Optional) To extract selected files, click a file and **Ctrl+click** any others you want to extract.
3. Click the **Extract** button.
4. Choose the disk and folder in which you want the extracted file(s) placed.
5. Click the **Extract** button.

Buying Games Online

Most of the "free" games you can download from the Web are trial versions (shareware). The developer might stipulate that you can play the game for free for 30 days and might even program in a routine that disables the game when the free trial period expires. In order to continue playing the game legally, you must purchase a copy.

You can purchase the most popular games at your local software store. For less-popular or newly released games, shop on the Web. Check out the following online game and software dealers:

➤ **gamestop** at www.gamestop.com

➤ **Outpost.com** at www.outpost.com

➤ **Beyond.com** at www.beyond.com/games.htm

➤ **Buy-Rite Video Games** at www.buyrite1.com

➤ **Buy.com** at www.buy.com/games

Finding Game Reviews and Tips

Tired of getting clobbered by meaner opponents wielding better weapons? Having trouble dodging fireballs? Do you keep running out of ammo in the middle of a battle? Then you probably need a few tips from the experts.

Fortunately, many of the same sites that offer game demos and shareware have links to game hints, cheats, strategies, and guides that can transform the greenest novice into a seasoned veteran. To start tracking down tips and tricks on the Web, revisit the sites you checked out in the earlier section "Getting Free Games from the Web." After you have exhausted those resources, check out the following Web sites dedicated to cheats:

➤ **CheatStation** at www.cheatstation.com. This site features tips and tricks for playing more than 1,400 PC games and most games designed for popular game systems, including Nintendo64 and Dreamcast.

➤ **Cheater's Guild** at www.cheaters-guild.com. This site offers a robust collection of tips organized by unique categories, such as Cheat Codes, Dirty Tricks, *Easter Eggs,* Hot Hints, and Level Codes.

➤ **Future Games Network** at www.fgn.com. This site is one of the largest and most well-established gaming networks. In addition to offering thousands of reviews, previews, and game tips, this site features plenty of links to other quality game sites.

Inside Tip

You don't need to find a store that specializes in games. Most Web-based software retailers and mega-stores carry a wide selection of games.

Tech Term

An **Easter Egg** is a hidden message, screen, or action in a game or other program. You initiate it by pressing keystrokes or buttons in a special sequence when a certain screen is displayed or by performing a weird series of steps you would never think of doing in real life. In late versions of Windows 95 and in Windows 98 and Me, for instance, set the screensaver to **3D Text,** click **Settings,** and type **Volcano** as the text you want the screen saver to display. The screensaver then cycles through the names of various volcanoes.

Computer Cheat

Use your favorite Web search tool to search for "game tips," "game cheats," or "game hints." To find tips and tricks for a specific game, search for the game by name; for instance, to find tips for playing Mech Warrior 2, search for "Mech Warrior tips."

➤ **IGN Guides** at guides.ign.com. This site is a great place to pick up detailed strategy guides for a variety of computer games. In order to download the free guides, you must register with IGN.

➤ **GameStats** at www.gamestats.com/tips. This site not only provides a comprehensive list of tips and tricks from real players, but also allows you to submit a tip or trick you have discovered while playing the game. At GameStats, you'll also find links to online forums where you can post questions, answers, and comments about your favorite games.

➤ **Super Games** at cheats.dreamhost.com. This site features tips and tricks for playing games designed for a PC, Mac, Nintendo64, Dreamcast, or other platforms. Simply click the desired platform and then click the game's name.

The Least You Need to Know

➤ The first step in choosing a computer game is to figure out which game category interests you: action, adventure, sports, strategy, and so on.

➤ Before you purchase a game, be sure your computer is properly equipped to run it.

➤ Many games require you to run the game from the DOS prompt.

➤ To display the DOS prompt in Windows 98, choose **Start, Programs, MS-DOS Prompt.**

➤ To go to the DOS prompt in Windows Me, choose **Start, Run,** type **command,** and press **Enter.**

➤ One of the best places to pick up free games and other programs is at ZDNet's download site (www.zdnet.com/downloads/games.html).

➤ Most Web-based software retailers and other online merchants carry computer games and allow you to order games online.

➤ If you're having trouble playing (or winning) a game, you might be able to find strategy guides, tips, tricks, and hints on the Web.

Chapter 24

Tapping the Power of Educational Software

In This Chapter

➤ Building your own computerized reference library

➤ Teaching your children reading, writing, and arithmetic

➤ Taking piano lessons with your computer

➤ Learning a foreign language from your computer

➤ Painting, drawing, and doing other creative activities

Face it—a computer can't make you smart. It can't pour knowledge or wisdom into your head. It can't stamp multiplication tables on your brain cells. It can't infuse your mind with an understanding of quantum physics. And it sure can't help you experience the pains and pleasures of real life.

What a computer can do (when equipped with the right software) is present a subject in an engaging format, complete with text, graphics, sounds, animation, and video. It can drill a student tirelessly to help him retain facts, equations, and rules. It can illustrate complex concepts. And it can test the student, provide immediate feedback, and help him determine which material he needs to review.

This chapter takes you on a tour of educational software and shows you how to use your computer as a tool for research and learning.

Researching Topics with Multimedia Encyclopedias

How would you like a 26-volume set of encyclopedias on a single disc? An encyclopedia that plays snippets of Mozart's symphonies, shows full-color pictures of world

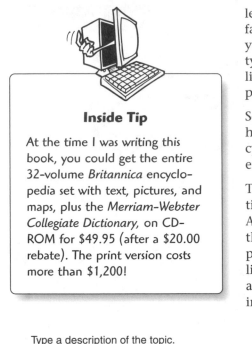

Inside Tip

At the time I was writing this book, you could get the entire 32-volume *Britannica* encyclopedia set with text, pictures, and maps, plus the *Merriam-Webster Collegiate Dictionary*, on CD-ROM for $49.95 (after a $20.00 rebate). The print version costs more than $1,200!

leaders and exotic animals, and displays video clips of famous speeches and historical events? How would you like to search the entire set of encyclopedias by typing a single word or phrase? And how would you like to save more than a thousand dollars on a complete set of encyclopedias?

Sound too good to be true? It's not. For less than a hundred bucks, you can purchase an entire set of encyclopedias on CD or DVD that gives you all the benefits just described.

The following figure shows Microsoft's Encarta in action. Here, I'm looking up an article about Wolfgang Amadeus Mozart. I click **Find**, type mozart, and click the entry for **Mozart, Wolfgang Amadeus.** This displays an article about Mozart's life, along with an outline of the article, a multimedia kiosk for playing audio clips and viewing pictures, and a link for viewing a timeline chart.

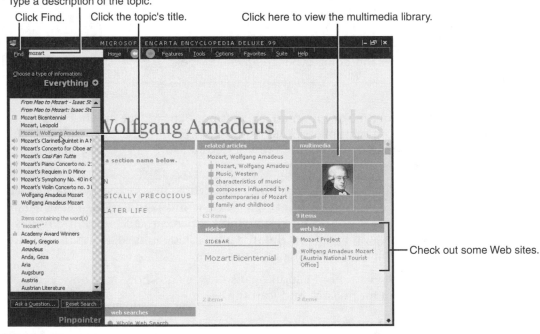

An encyclopedia on disc gives you instant access to the information you need.

More Books for Your Reference Library

If you do any writing for school, business, or pleasure, you probably use several reference books to develop your work. You might use a dictionary to verify spellings and check meanings, a thesaurus to find synonyms, and a book of quotations to give yourself the appearance of being well read.

Juggling these reference volumes and flipping pages to track down the information you want can be a daunting task and an inefficient way to find information. Consider placing a complete reference library on your computer. For example, Microsoft Bookshelf includes the following reference books:

➤ *The American Heritage Dictionary.* This contains definitions of more than 66,000 words. To find a definition, you simply type the desired word and press **Enter.** No more flipping pages.

➤ **Roget's Electronic Thesaurus.** Need another word for *lazy?* Simply press **Alt+E,** type lazy, and press **Enter.** The thesaurus gives you a list of suggestions. You can then choose a word from the list.

➤ *Columbia Book of Quotations.* This book offers 6,000 quotes that are appropriate for speeches and presentations. The quotes are organized by subject, so you can look up quotes for subjects such as War, City Life, and even Living Together.

➤ *Encarta Manual of Style and Usage.* This book can help you improve your grammar, punctuation, writing style, and diction (word choice).

➤ *Microsoft Press Computer and Internet Dictionary.* This quick reference brings you up to speed on computer terminology and concepts.

➤ *Encarta Desk Encyclopedia.* This encyclopedia is no match for *Britannica* or even the full-fledged version of *Encarta,* but it does have hundreds of pages covering historical topics, including everything from Greek mythology to the Iran-Iraq war.

➤ *Encarta Desk World Atlas.* If you're wondering where you stand in relation to the rest of the world, this book might come in handy. The atlas is packed with more than 135 full-color maps that include pop-up information boxes and links to articles in the encyclopedia and almanac.

Computer Cheat

Late in 1999, Britannica published the complete text of its encyclopedia on the Web. Of course, the Web version is slower than the disc version and excludes pictures and multimedia clips, but for free, up-to-date information, you can't beat it. Check it out at www.britannica.com. Perform a search to find links to encyclopedia articles as well as to other Web sites, or click the links under **Explore** to browse the collection.

Inside Tip

Several Web-based retailers specialize in educational software titles and typically offer better deals than the manufacturers. Check out SmarterKids.com at www.smarterkids.com, Fun School at www.funschool.com, SuperKids Education Software Review at www.superkids.com, and the Educational Software Institute at www.edsoft.com.

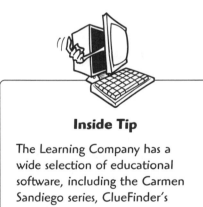

Inside Tip

The Learning Company has a wide selection of educational software, including the Carmen Sandiego series, ClueFinder's Math, Amazon Trail, All-Star Typing, Compton's Learning tools, and Dr. Seuss books. You can check out The Learning Company's complete selection of software at www.learningco.com, or call 1-800-821-5895.

➤ *The Encarta New World Almanac.* This electronic book contains a hodgepodge of information about the world, including census figures, U.S. economic data, employment figures, election results, offbeat news stories, scientific achievements, sports statistics, and much more.

➤ *The Encarta New World Timeline.* To trace important events in the history of the world, crack open the *New World Timeline*. It cross-references important historical events with happenings in the worlds of science, music, art, culture, technology, and other areas of human endeavor and interest.

Learning to Read with Your Computer

One of the greatest pleasures of parenthood is reading to your children and watching them learn to read on their own. No program can replace the quality time you spend reading with your children and encouraging them through your own desire to read. However, the techniques and patience required to teach your child how to read properly might be a bit beyond your abilities. You just don't know what kinds of exercises your child needs, and even when you do know, you might not have the patience to work through those exercises as often as needed. To help, purchase a reading readiness program for your child.

One of the most popular reading series on the market is the Reader Rabbit series from The Learning Company, shown in the following figure. In these reading programs, Reader Rabbit and friends demonstrate reading skills and teach basic phonics through engaging stories and games. The characters in the program provide plenty of positive feedback to reward and encourage beginning readers.

With Reader Rabbit and friends, students learn to read while they play.

(Screen shot courtesy of The Learning Company)

Reinforcing Math Skills

Ever since my kids began their formal education, I've been getting more and more homework. I'm expected to help them study their spelling lists, quiz them on making change, help them trace their family lineage, and drill them on their multiplication tables. Don't get me wrong. I love performing science experiments in the microwave oven and showing my kids how to make money on Wall Street, but when it comes to the basics, I think they should figure out how to study on their own. Of course, I do feel a little guilty when I see devoted parents flip through flash cards, build award-winning science projects, and take credit for their kids' spelling bee awards.

To alleviate my guilt, I purchased my kid a copy of Math Blaster (from Knowledge Adventure) and sat her down in front of the computer. She immediately began blasting numbers, never realizing that she was learning basic math skills in the process. Flash cards could never have inspired her to "study" so diligently and work so tirelessly. The following figure gives you a glimpse of just how much fun it can be to learn math.

Inside Tip

Knowledge Adventure's product line isn't limited to Math Blaster. It also includes the popular JumpStart series for preschool to sixth grade, Money Town, Reading Blaster, Spelling Blaster, Solar System Explorer, Typing Tutor, SmartStart Spanish, and much more. For product information, visit www.knowledgeadventure. com or call 1-800-545-7677.

Math Blaster teaches math through arcade-style games.

(Screen shot courtesy of Knowledge Adventure)

Encouraging Your Child to Play with Language

Kids love to create and print their own publications. They can spend hours composing and illustrating their own comic books or writing stories about their pets. They love to make signs for their bedrooms, write letters to their friends, keep journals, and even publish their own newsletters. Kids don't see this "play" as work. The fun they're having completely blinds them to the fact that they're learning how to write and how to present their ideas and opinions to an audience.

Inside Tip

If you have an Internet connection, visit Microsoft Kids at www.microsoft.com/kids and check out Microsoft's line of educational software. Here, you can download a shareware copy of Creative Writer and check it out for yourself. Better yet, have your kids check it out.

To encourage kids to write and to play with language and illustrations, several companies have developed writing/desktop publishing programs just for kids. One such program, Microsoft's Creative Writer, is set up like a desktop publishing program. On startup, the program provides options for creating a greeting card, viewing project ideas, printing banners, starting with an idea, or creating a Web page. The child picks the desired option, enters a few preferences, and then sits back and watches the program slap together a rough version of the publication. The child can then customize the publication with text, clip art, original drawings or paintings, borders, and other objects.

One of the coolest features of Creative Writer is that it can inspire creativity. The Splot Machine (a slot machine for words) displays random phrases that can

kick-start a story line, as shown in the following figure. If a child is more visually oriented, she might opt for the Story Starters—colorful graphics designed to get the creative juices flowing.

Click this button to have the Splot Machine combine phrases for you.

Click these buttons to cycle through phrases.

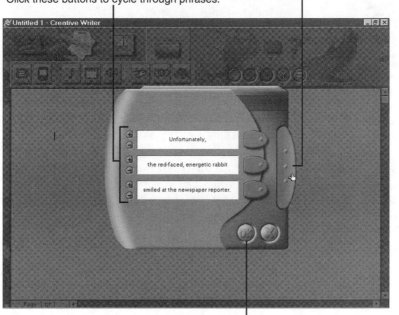

Click OK to insert the sentence.

*The Splot Machine combines phrases randomly to generate original
sentences.*

Learning to Play the Piano

With the right software and some fancy add-on devices, your computer can moonlight as a piano teacher. Voyetra's Teach Me Piano consists of a CD that works along
with a *MIDI* keyboard (sold separately) to teach students how to play popular piano
tunes and read music. The keyboard plugs into the MIDI port on your computer's
sound card, allowing you to perform hands-on, interactive exercises. The software includes video demonstrations of the exercises, along with narration. At the end of a
lesson, you are encouraged to put on a performance with full orchestra accompani-
ment. Of course, you're graded on your performance!

Although Teach Me Piano cannot replace a good piano teacher and formal lessons, it
functions as a great supplemental tool for teaching specific tunes and drilling students on the basics.

Learning a Foreign Language

Most students struggle and many flounder in standard foreign language classes. They like to learn common phrases, but when it comes to studying long lists of vocabulary words and learning how to conjugate irregular verbs, they lose their motivation. It's just too much work and not enough fun.

Of course, there's no replacement for motivation and hard work, but foreign language software can add a little fun to the drudgery by making your lessons more interactive. Learn to Speak Spanish, for instance, features a talking dictionary to teach you proper pronunciation, conversation simulations, and speech recording and playback tools to help you compare your pronunciation with that of native speakers. The program also contains more than 100 exercises to help you learn vocabulary, reading, writing, and grammar. You can even create your own study plan and track your progress.

A more down-to-earth foreign language program from Knowledge Adventure is JumpStart Spanish, shown in the following figure. For details about the JumpStart series and other language titles, go to www.learningco.com or www.knowledgeadventure.com, or use your favorite Web search tool to search for additional foreign language software.

Tech Term

MIDI (pronounced *middy*) is short for Musical Instrument Digital Interface. The music industry developed the MIDI standard to ensure uniformity among music devices, such as sound cards, synthesizers, keyboards, and other instruments. A MIDI keyboard has a MIDI port that you can connect to a standard sound card using a MIDI cable.

JumpStart Spanish helps students learn vocabulary and other essentials in "real-life" situations.

Bringing Out the Artist in Your Child

Now that our society is determined to specialize in science and math, language, music, and fine arts are quickly falling by the wayside. To help your child develop some artistic sensibilities, you must encourage your child on your own and provide the tools and opportunities for your child to develop his or her artistic talents.

Of course, crayons, paper, and watercolors are still the standard tools for a developing artist, but in order for an artist to make a living nowadays, some basic training in computer graphics is essential. Fortunately, several software companies have developed graphics programs just for kids. Check out the following offerings:

➤ **Art Dabbler** from Corel (newgraphics.corel.com/order/artdabbler.html or 1-800-846-0111). This package features the drawing and painting tools you'll find in professional graphics programs, along with online art lessons, traceable drawings, animation tools, photo-editing tools, flip-book animations, and much more.

➤ **Crayola Creativity Packs** from IBM (www.ibm.com/software/hke/ or 1-800-746-7426). These are a collection of software packages that encourage kids to color onscreen with computerized crayons. With Crayola Print Factory, for instance, kids can create banners, signs, greeting cards, reports, and other school-related publications.

➤ **Flying Colors** from Magic Mouse Productions (www.magicmouse.com or 415-669-7010). This package consists of a library of more than 3,000 color stickers and backgrounds, plus a complete set of professional paint tools. Kids can use the program to create their own paintings and greeting cards, signs, Web page graphics, and other publications (see the following figure).

➤ **ImaginAction** from Rose Studios (www.rosestudios.com or 1-888-543-7748). This package is more than just a paint program for kids. Here, kids must pay attention and use logic along with their artistic talents to understand spatial relationships, shapes, and their functions in the real world.

➤ **JumpStart Artist** from Sierra (shop.sierra.com or 1-800-757-7707). This package is an art/creativity program in which kids enter a tree house to experiment with various artistic media, including painting, collages, drawing, folk art, and crafts.

➤ **You Can Draw!** from Cognitive Technologies (www.cogtech.com or 301-581-9652). This package uses interactive lessons to teach kids how to draw everyday objects. This computerized art class covers six topics: gesture and expression, line, shape, value, volume, and perspective. The lessons engage students by using a good dose of animation, video, and audio.

Inside Tip

Several services specialize in reviewing, rating, and recommending educational software. Check out Children's Software Review at www.childrenssoftware.com.

277

Flying Colors helps bring out the artist in a child.

The Least You Need to Know

➤ To take advantage of your computer's power as a research tool, equip it with a good CD or DVD encyclopedia, dictionary, and other reference tools.

➤ Beginning readers can benefit from interactive reading programs, such as Reader Rabbit.

➤ Math programs, such as MathBlaster, are excellent for teaching students basic skills and concepts and for enforcing math skills by using arcade-style drills.

➤ Writing programs designed for kids, such as Creative Writer, encourage students to play with language and communicate clearly using their own publications.

➤ With a MIDI keyboard and music lessons on CD (such as Voyetra's Teach Me Piano), your computer can help you learn how to play your favorite tunes.

➤ If studying a foreign language seems like a drag, hire a foreign language tutor on CD, such as Learn to Speak Spanish.

➤ Although there's no replacement for paper, pencil, and watercolors, a good graphics art program, such as Art Dabbler, can help you learn basic techniques.

➤ For educational software reviews and ratings, check out Children's Software Review at www.childrenssoftware.com.

Chapter 25

Safely Introducing Your Child to the Internet

In This Chapter

➤ Being sure your child understands the rules

➤ Spying on ... er ... supervising your kids

➤ Blocking undesirable Web content with a censoring program

➤ Playing computer games against other people online

➤ Visiting educational sites on the Web

➤ Avoiding deviants in chat rooms and via e-mail

The Internet is a virtual city packed with shopping malls, libraries, community centers, museums, newsstands, meeting rooms, and other valuable offerings. But like any city, the Internet has its dark side—a section of town ruled by pornography, violence, bigotry, vandalism, and theft.

As a society, we want our children to have the freedom to explore the Internet, but we have the responsibility of protecting them from media and individuals who threaten their innocence. We want our children to visit museums online, communicate with students in other parts of the world, take classes, visit political institutions, and research topics of interest. We don't want our kids or students pulling up porno pages, reading racist propaganda, hacking the Pentagon's computer system, or sitting in the Hot Tub chat room conversing with a bunch of old guys and gals who should know better. And we sure don't want our 11-year-olds corresponding via e-mail with deviants twice or three times their age.

This chapter acts as a parent/teacher guide to the Internet. Here, you learn ways to introduce children to the Internet, help them fully explore its positive features, and prevent them from accessing undesirable content or falling prey to smooth-talking perverts.

Explaining the Rules of the Road

Most kids aren't rotten. They're confused, frustrated, careless, and selfish but not intentionally bad. A child usually makes a wrong choice or breaks a rule either because he doesn't understand the rule or he faces no consequence for misbehaving. So, before you let your child or student fire up the Web browser, lay down the rules and explain the consequences. Here are a few rules to pass along to your kids:

➤ **Keep passwords secret.** Anyone who knows your username and password can use your account, racking up connect time charges, placing orders, and performing illegal activities in your name.

➤ **Don't enter any personal information online without permission from a parent or guardian.** Using your real name, address, or phone number in your profile gives stalkers the information they want. Registering for contests and "free" stuff can make your private information public. And never tell someone your real name, address, or phone number in a chat room, where anyone can see it.

➤ **Don't use a credit card.** Leaving your teenager alone on the Web with your credit card can be a disaster. The Web is the biggest shop-at-home network in the world.

➤ **Don't run or install any programs without permission.** Downloading and running programs from unreliable sources can introduce computer viruses. You and your kids should also be careful with any program files you receive via e-mail.

➤ **Don't view sites that you wouldn't view with parents or guardians next to you.** Later in this chapter, I show you how to block undesirable content, but censoring programs do not block everything that's offensive. Be sure your kids know that you expect them to use good judgment.

➤ **Don't chat or correspond with creeps.** Some creepy adults use the Internet to prey on kids. Have your kids notify you immediately of any suspicious individuals or messages. Tell your kids not to send photos of themselves to strangers or post their photos on their Web pages. Let your kids know that people on the Internet can pretend to be anybody; the 14-year-old girl your daughter thinks she is chatting with actually could be a 35-year-old guy.

➤ **Don't meet anyone in person known only from online contact.** If your child wants to meet a friend from the Internet, have your child schedule a meeting in a public place and take you along.

In addition to laying down the rules, specify limits on Internet use, just as you would limit TV viewing. Specify the time of day your child can access the Internet and the amount of time he or she can spend at the keyboard. Although the computer and the Internet can be great tools for education and entertainment, they can also interfere with a child's education and social and physical development.

A Little Personal Supervision Goes a Long Way

When my kids started watching TV, I was pretty naive. I told my children to watch only those shows that they would feel comfortable watching with me or their mom. A couple days later, I walked into the den and caught my 13- and 10-year-old watching MTV's *Celebrity Death Match*. Of course, they saw nothing wrong with it.

As a parent, it's your obligation not to be stupid. Don't stick a computer in your kid's bedroom and then celebrate because you now have more quality time to spend with your spouse. The only reason your son isn't pestering you or picking on his kid sister is because he has found something much more sinister to do on the Internet.

Place the computer in a room that you can enter without looking like a spy. A room that's open to traffic, such as a living room or family room, is a good choice. If you have young children, spend some time exploring the Internet with them and supervising their activities. Your kids might balk and think you're a control freak, but that's your job.

Censoring the Internet

Over the years, people have debated whether the government should censor the Internet. As society wrestles with this issue, offensive material remains readily available. In the following sections, you learn what you can do on your end to prevent this material from reaching you and your children.

Inside Tip

Use computer time as a reward for proper behavior. If your child fails to follow the rules, reduce or eliminate the time your child spends on the computer. Your kid might claim that the punishment is harming his education. Don't buy it.

Whoa!

To be sure your kids can't surf the Internet without your permission, keep the password you use to connect to your ISP secret. Also, remove the check mark from the **Save password** check box in the Connect to dialog box. If you have a cable connection (which is connected all the time), this trick isn't an option.

Computer Cheat

View the history list to see where your kids have been. In Internet Explorer, click the **History** button to display the History bar. Click the folder for the week or day you want to check. The History bar displays a list of sites visited during the selected week or day. Click the site folder to view a list of pages that were opened at the site, and then click the page name to view the page. If your kids are wise to history lists, they might know how to clear the list, so if it's blank, suspect foul play.

Using America Online's Parental Controls

Without some level of censorship, America Online can be the most dangerous place for kids to hang out. Kids can access chat rooms such as The Flirts Nook and Chance Encounters, where chat topics are definitely adults-only and where chatters are likely to receive instant messages directing them to the latest porno site on the Web.

America Online's Parental Controls allow you to block access to the red-light districts on America Online and the Internet. Follow these steps to create a screen name for one of your children and set limits in America Online 6.0:

1. Sign on to America Online using your primary screen name. (You can add users to your account only by signing on with your primary screen name, the screen name you used when you first set up your America Online account.)

2. In the button bar (just below the menu bar), click **Settings,** and then click **Screen Names.** The AOL Screen Names dialog box appears, displaying a list of screen names for your account.

3. Click **CREATE a Screen Name.** The Create a Screen Name dialog box appears, asking if you're creating a screen name for a child.

4. Click **Yes.** America Online displays some important information for parents.

5. Read the information, and then click **Continue.** America Online displays a brief introduction to screen names.

6. Click **Create Screen Name.** AOL prompts you to type a screen name. (Try to use something unique. CutiePie, for instance, is no doubt already being used by someone, so you would need something to distinguish it, such as CutiePie1563xy.)

7. Type the name your child wants to use, and then click **Continue.** AOL prompts you to type a password.

8. Type a password for your child to use when logging on (six to eight characters), press **Tab,** type the same password again, and click **Continue.** AOL prompts you to select a Parental Controls setting.

9. Click the desired setting, as shown in the following figure, and click **Continue.** AOL prompts you to confirm or customize the settings.

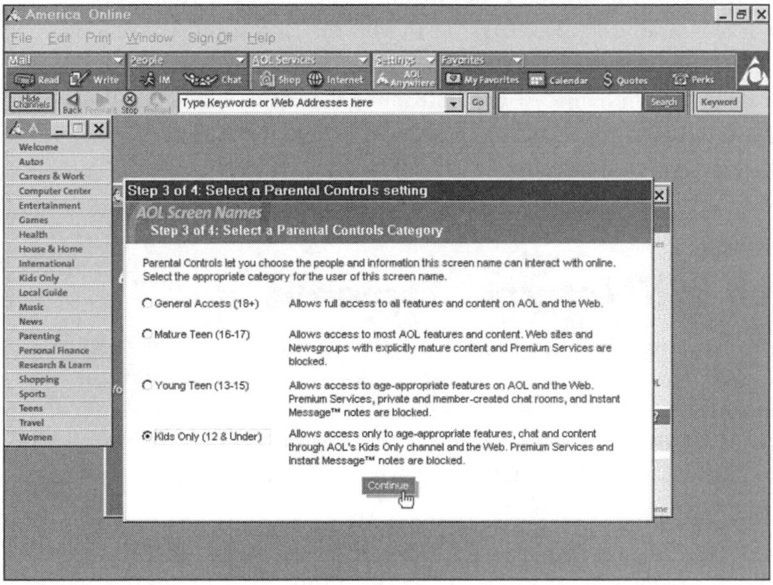

*Pick the desired age level, and then click **Continue.***

10. Click **Customize Settings** so that you can check the settings. The Parental Controls dialog box appears, listing the various groups of settings: E-mail control, Chat control, IM control, and so on.

11. Click the green check box next to the control group you want to check or modify. A dialog box pops up, showing your options.

12. Enter your preferences, and then click **Save** or **OK.** For example, if you chose E-Mail control in step 10, you can choose to block all e-mail messages, receive messages only from AOL members, or create a list of people from whom e-mail messages are to be accepted. Whether you click **Save** or **Cancel,** a confirmation message appears.

13. Read the confirmation message, and then click **OK.** You are returned to the window for customizing parental controls.

14. Repeat steps 10 through 13 to check or customize any other controls, and then click the close (**X**) button to exit the window.

Panic Attack!

If you already created a screen name for your child without specifying restrictions, you can specify restrictions at any time. Click **Settings** on the button bar, and then click **Parental Controls.** Click **Set Parental Controls,** and then open the **Edit Controls for** list, and click your child's screen name. At the bottom of the dialog box, click the button for the desired age group: General Access, Mature Teen, Young Teen, or Kids Only. You can then customize the settings if desired.

Censoring the Web with Internet Explorer

If you don't subscribe to America Online or some other commercial online service, you connect to the Internet through an ISP and are responsible for finding your own tools for censoring content. The next section reviews some of the specialized censoring programs currently available. In the meantime, if you use Internet Explorer as your Web browser, you can use its built-in Content Advisor to filter undesirable content.

Inside Tip

Unless you change the Content Advisor's settings, it'll block every unrated page on the Web—just about every page you try to pull up. To relax the ratings, open the **View** or **Tools** menu, click **Internet Options,** and click the **Content** tab. Click **Settings,** enter your password, and enter your preferences.

To censor sites with Internet Explorer, activate the Ratings feature. Open the **View** or **Tools** menu, click **Internet Options,** and click the **Content** tab. Under **Ratings** or **Content Advisor,** click the **Enable** button, and then click **OK.** The Create Supervisor Password dialog box appears. Type in both text boxes a password that you will remember but that your kids will have a tough time guessing. Click **OK** as many times as needed to save your changes and close the dialog boxes.

Don't set the kiddies in front of the screen just yet. Test your setup first. Try going to www.playboy.com. If you see hot babes in various stages of undress, the Content Advisor is disabled. Close Internet Explorer, run it again, and then try going to the nudie page. You should see the Content Advisor dialog box, shown in the following figure, displaying a list of reasons why you have been denied access to this site (as if you didn't know). Click **OK.**

The Content Advisor won't let you view the peep show.

Using Censoring Software

If your Web browser does not have a built-in censor, or if you want more control over the content and features your children can access, purchase a specialized censoring program. The following is a list of some of the better censoring programs, along with addresses for the Web pages where you can find out more about them and download shareware versions:

➤ **Cyber Patrol** (at www.cyberpatrol.com). The most popular censoring program on the market, Cyber Patrol uses a list of forbidden words to block access to objectionable material or uses a list of child-friendly words to block access to all Web pages except those that contain one of the specified words. Passwords let you set access levels for different users, and Cyber Patrol can keep track of the amount of time each user spends on the Internet. The one drawback of Cyber Patrol is that it doesn't keep track of the sites that your kids *try* to visit.

➤ **CYBERsitter** (at www.solidoak.com). Another fine censoring program, CYBERsitter is a little less strict than Cyber Patrol but is easier to

Whoa!

No censoring program is perfect. Some objectionable content can slip through the cracks, and the program can block access to un-objectionable sites. Use the censoring program only when you personally are unable to supervise your kids.

use and configure. CYBERsitter has a unique filtering system that judges words in context, so it doesn't block access to inoffensive sites, such as the Anne Sexton home page.

➤ **Cyber Snoop** (at www.pearlsw.com). Not the best content-blocker in the group, Cyber Snoop's claim to fame is that it can create a comprehensive log of a user's Internet activity. The best way to use Cyber Snoop is to install it and tell your kids that Cyber Snoop is recording everything they do on the Internet. You might not even have to buy the program—the threat might be deterrent enough.

➤ **Net Nanny** (at www.netnanny.com). Net Nanny is unique in that it can punish the user for typing URLs of offensive sites or for typing any word on the "no-no" list. If a user types a prohibited word or URL, Net Nanny can shut down the application and record the offense, forcing your child to come up with an excuse. To make the most of Net Nanny, however, you have to spend a bit of time configuring it; it's not the most intuitive program of the bunch.

Whoa!

Even something as apparently innocuous as a game room might pose a threat to your child's innocence. Many game rooms have a section of the screen devoted to chat, which your censoring software might not be able to filter or block. Check out the chat section before you let your kids loose in a game room.

Playing Games Online

Most kids need little encouragement to start exploring the Internet, but some kids might need a little push to get started. If your child seems reluctant to set out on her first journey, try introducing her to some online games. Yahoo! offers several two-player and multi-player games to encourage kids and adults alike to spend a little more time on the Web and generate a little human contact.

To get started, use your Web browser to go to games.yahoo.com and click the **Gameroom** link if it is not already selected (see the following figure). This displays a list of board games, card games, and other games you can play with other people at Yahoo!. Click the link for the desired game. You must then log in (if you already registered with Yahoo!) or register to obtain a screen name and password. Follow the onscreen instructions.

Inside Tip

For a long list of free games online, visit Web Games City at nxn.netgate.net/games.html. If that address doesn't get you there, try nxn.netgate.net and click the **Web Games City** link.

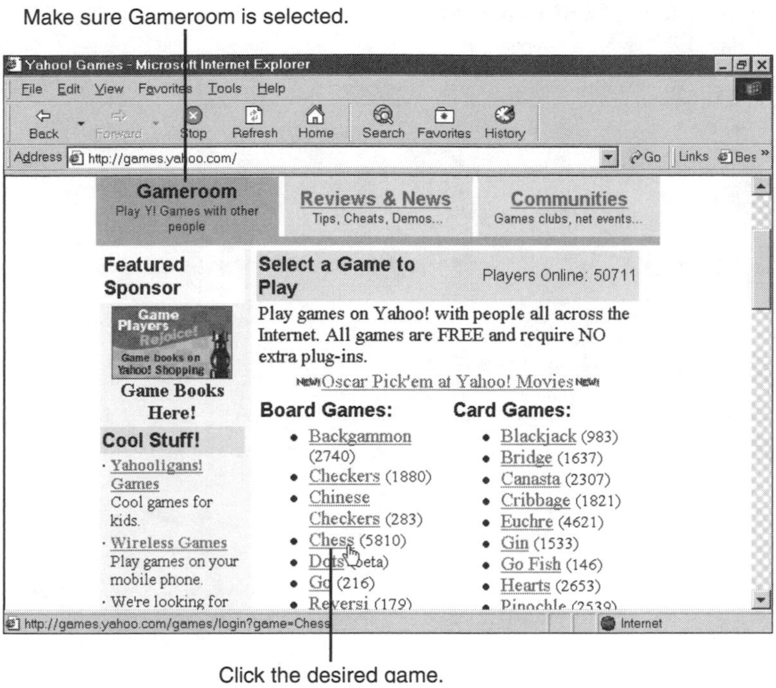

Make sure Gameroom is selected.

Check out Yahoo!'s game room.

Click the desired game.

After you sign in, Yahoo! attempts to send you the Java applet you need for playing the game. If your Web browser displays a dialog box asking you to confirm the download operation, give your okay to install the applet. Yahoo! then displays a list of game rooms where people are already playing the game you selected. To enter a game room, click its name. Yahoo! places you in a game room where several game "tables" are set up. Scroll down the list of tables until you find one that interests you. Then, click **Watch** to watch a game in progress or **JOIN** to sit down at a game table and play, as shown in the following figure.

If no open tables are available, you can click the **Create Table** button to create your own table or click **Play Now** to start playing a game. If you click **Play Now,** and an open "chair" is available at another table, you're automatically placed at the table and can start playing. Otherwise, a game table appears with two or more **Sit** buttons. Click one of the **Sit** buttons to sit down at the table and wait for an opponent to join you. As soon as someone chooses to join the game at your table (and be your opponent), you can start playing.

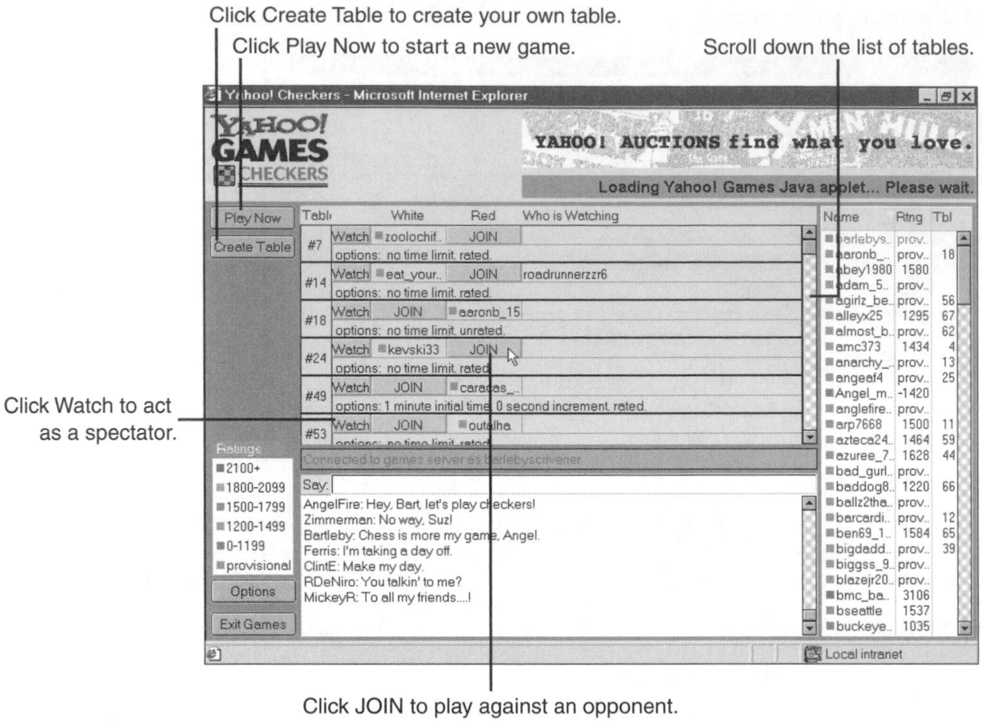

Click Create Table to create your own table.

Click Play Now to start a new game.

Scroll down the list of tables.

Yahoo! Checkers - Microsoft Internet Explorer					_ � X

YAHOO! AUCTIONS find what you love.

Loading Yahoo! Games Java applet... Please wait.

Play Now	Tabl	White	Red	Who is Watching		Name	Rtng	Tbl
Create Table	#7	Watch ▪zoolochif.. JOIN				▪arlebys.	prov..	
		options: no time limit. rated.				▪aaronb_	prov..	18
	#14	Watch ▪eat_your.. JOIN roadrunnerzzr6				▪abey1980	1580	
		options: no time limit. rated.				▪adam_5..	prov..	
	#18	Watch JOIN ▪aaronb_15				▪agirlz_be..	prov..	56
		options: no time limit. unrated.				▪alleyx25	1295	67
	#24	Watch ▪kevski33 JOIN				▪almost_b..	prov..	62
		options: no time limit. rated				▪amc373	1434	4
	#49	Watch JOIN ▪caracas_.				▪anarchy_.	prov..	13
		options: 1 minute initial time. 0 second increment. rated.				▪angeaf4	prov..	25
	#53	Watch JOIN ▪outalha				▪Angel_m..	-1420	
		options: no time limit. rated				▪anglefire.	prov..	

	▪arp7668 1500 11
	▪aztexa24. 1464 59

Connected to games server as arlebyscrivener

Ratings

▪ 2100+
▪ 1800-2099
▪ 1500-1799
▪ 1200-1499
▪ 0-1199
▪ provisional

Say:

AngelFire: Hey, Bart, let's play checkers!
Zimmerman: No way, Suz!
Bartleby: Chess is more my game, Angel.
Ferris: I'm taking a day off.
ClintE: Make my day.
RDeNiro: You talkin' to me?
MickeyR: To all my friends....!

▪azuree_7.	1628 44
▪bad_gurl.	prov..
▪baddog8.	1220 66
▪ballz2tha.	prov..
▪barcardi.	prov.. 12
▪ben69_1.	1584 65
▪bigdadd.	prov.. 39
▪biggss_9.	prov..
▪blazejr20.	prov..
▪bmc_ba.	3106
▪bseattle	1537
▪buckeye.	1035

Options

Exit Games

Local intranet

Click Watch to act as a spectator.

Click JOIN to play against an opponent.

In Yahoo!'s game rooms, you can sit and watch or join in the fun.

Visiting the White House

Most kids have their own agenda for using the Web. They want to play games, download the latest music clips, and do a little shopping. Adults, on the other hand, expect the kids to check out educational sites and build their knowledge base. So how do you steer kids in the right direction? Try pointing your kids to sites designed specifically for them, such as The White House for Kids.

Using your Web browser, you can visit the White House online at www.whitehouse.gov. Although you won't be able to make reservations to sleep in the Lincoln bedroom, you can read a brief biography of the President; read various press releases; access official White House documents; and learn more about the various federal agencies. On the left of the page is a link called **For Kids.** It leads to the White House for

Whoa!

Be sure you enter the White House Web site address as www.whitehouse.gov. If you mistakenly enter .com instead of .gov, you'll be kicking yourself for not installing Cyber Patrol! www.whitehouse.com is a very nasty (adult) site.

Kids page, as shown in the following figure. You can go directly to the White House for Kids page at www.whitehousekids.gov. (At the time I was writing this book, the site was still under construction.)

White House for Kids introduces children to United States government.

Visiting Museums and Libraries

You might not be able to fly your kids to the Louvre to see the Mona Lisa or drive to Washington, D.C., to visit the Smithsonian Institution, but you can do the next best thing: Visit the most famous museums and libraries and access the best educational resources online. Here's a short list of Web site addresses to get you started:

➤ **www.louvre.fr** takes you to the most famous art museum in the world—France's Le Louvre.

➤ **www.moma.org** opens the doors to the most famous modern art museum in the world— New York's Museum of Modern Art.

➤ **www.si.edu** carries you to the Smithsonian Institution's home page, where you'll find plenty of links to exhibits and special programs.

➤ **www.memphis.edu/egypt/main.html** connects you to the University of Memphis Institute of Egyptian Art and Archeology,

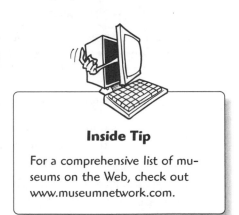

Inside Tip

For a comprehensive list of museums on the Web, check out www.museumnetwork.com.

where you can learn about ancient Egyptian history, take a tour of Egypt online, and find additional links to related sites.

➤ **www.adlerplanetarium.org** shifts your focus to the skies to study celestial bodies and astronomical figures from the Adler Planetarium in Chicago.

➤ **www.msichicago.org** displays the Museum of Science and Industry's most popular exhibits online. Take the submarine tour, do a little coal mining, or check out an online version of the International Space Station without ever leaving your home.

➤ **www.loc.gov** gives you a free ticket to the Library of Congress, the world's largest library. Here you can find an electronic version of the library's card catalog, hundreds of digitized photos, and a hefty collection of online journals, newspapers, and other publications.

➤ **www.libdex.com** gives you access to an index of libraries throughout the United States that allow you to search for books, audiotapes, videotapes, CDs, and other media online. Check it out—search for your local library.

Of course, this is an extremely short list of what's available on the Web. You can find thousands of museums and libraries throughout the world that have placed their most famous exhibits, collections, virtual tours, and interactive educational programs online. Use your favorite Web search tool to find additional sites.

Helping Your Child Find a Pen Pal

The best way to learn about the world and experience other cultures is to travel. The second-best way is to correspond with someone who lives in a different part of the country or in a foreign land. In addition to giving a child a different view of the world, having a pen pal encourages that child to use online resources and research tools to learn more about foreign lands and cultures.

Teachers have always encouraged their students to correspond with pen pals, but finding and connecting with a pen pal traditionally has been a long and complicated process. E-mail and the Web have simplified the process considerably. A student can use the Web to locate a pen pal in a matter of minutes and immediately send an e-mail message to his or her pal. To find a pen pal, check out the following sites:

➤ **epals.com** at www.epals.com. This site has the largest network of pen pals—more than three million students from more than 65,000 classrooms representing 134 different languages.

➤ **KeyPals** at www.mightymedia.com/keypals/. This site can't compete with epals.com when it comes to numbers, but it does provide another fairly safe and secure environment for connecting students and classrooms in different countries. KeyPals screens messages for obscene content and lets students keep their e-mail addresses private.

➤ **Kids' Space Connection Penpal Box** at www.ks-connection.org. This site offers the easiest way to find a pen pal. You simply click the **Penpal** box for the desired age group to view a list of kids looking for a pen pal and then click the kid's e-mail address to send a message. (Be careful using this site. The safeguards don't offer as much protection against undesirable e-mail correspondence as the other two sites listed here.)

The Least You Need to Know

➤ Before you unleash your kids on the Internet, lay down the rules you want them to follow.

➤ The most essential rule kids must follow is to never give out any personal or sensitive information, including passwords, phone numbers, addresses, credit card numbers, or even the name of the school they attend.

➤ No censor program can replace the supervision of a loving, caring parent.

➤ If you cannot supervise your kids every minute they're on the Internet (what parent can?), install Cyber Patrol or CYBERsitter and learn how to use it.

➤ If a child is reluctant to explore the Internet, try starting him out with some online games in Yahoo!'s Gameroom. Go to games.yahoo.com and click the **Gameroom** link.

➤ To encourage a child to explore educational Web sites rather than just play on the Web, have the child check out the White House online at www. whitehouse.gov.

➤ Let your kid's teacher know about epals.com. It's a great place for kids to learn about foreign cultures and peoples.

Chapter 26

Making a Family Photo Album

In This Chapter

➤ Storing your photos on CDs

➤ Scanning photos into your computer

➤ Adjusting the brightness, contrast, and colors

➤ Attaching photos to outgoing e-mail messages

➤ Taking instant photos with a digital camera

Do you have shoeboxes packed with undated photos of people you don't even recognize? Do you frequently find rolls of film you forgot to drop off for developing? Do you find dusty photo envelopes behind cabinets and dressers? Do rodents commonly chew up your photos and use them for bedding?

If you answered yes to any of these questions, consider changing the way you manage your photos. Instead of sticking with traditional negatives and prints, have your photos digitized and stored on a CD, or buy a digital camera and skip the film altogether! This chapter reveals your options and shows you how to use your computer to take control of your photos.

Getting a Kodak Picture CD

The easiest and cheapest way to go digital with your photos is to order a Kodak Picture CD when you drop off your next roll of film for developing. The developer creates the standard negatives and prints but also converts the photos to a digital format and saves each photo as a separate file on a CD.

The CD includes Kodak's digital image manager, a program that lets you view your pictures onscreen; adjust the brightness, contrast, and colors; sharpen photos; remove the red-eye effect (if present); send photos via e-mail; create your own photo albums; and print your photos.

Panic Attack!

The Kodak Picture CD installation routine might indicate that Windows needs to be set up to use small fonts. Right-click the Windows desktop, click **Properties,** click the **Settings** tab, and click the **Advanced** button. On the **General** tab, open the **Font size** list, and click **Small fonts.** You might need to restart Windows.

After you've brought your Kodak Picture CD home, take the following steps to view your pictures on your computer:

1. Pop the Kodak Picture CD into the CD-ROM drive. The Kodak Picture CD installation routine should start. If it doesn't, do the following:

   Double-click **My Computer.**

   Double-click the icon for your CD-ROM drive.

   Double-click the **Launch** icon.

2. Follow the onscreen instructions to install the Kodak Picture CD software. When the installation is complete, the Kodak Review magazine appears.

3. Click the arrow in the lower-right corner of the Kodak Review magazine cover to display the table of contents and thumbnail versions of your photos, as shown in the following figure.

4. To view a photo, click its thumbnail version.

After you install the Kodak Picture CD software for the first time, you can run the program at any time by selecting it from the **Start, Programs, Kodak Picture CD** menu option.

To view a full-screen slide show of your photos, click **View Your Pictures** on the Contents Page (the main menu). The Kodak Picture CD flips one-by-one through the entire "roll." After familiarizing yourself with the basic functions, you can move on to using the Kodak Picture CD software to create a photo album, enhance and print photos, and attach digitized photos to outgoing e-mail messages.

Thumbnail view of your photos

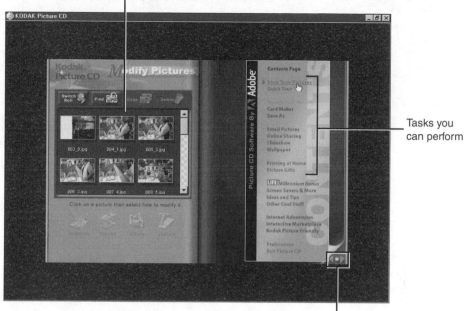

Tasks you
can perform

Click the arrows to navigate.

Kodak Picture CD displays your photos and lists the tasks you can perform.

Adding Photos from Another Kodak Picture CD

When you get your next Kodak Picture CD, you should register the photos with the Kodak Picture CD program to add the photos to your catalog. When the program catalogs your photos, it creates and stores a thumbnail version of the photo, which appears whether or not the CD is loaded. The program can then prompt you to insert the proper CD whenever you choose to view, enhance, print, or copy the photo.

To register a new Kodak Picture CD and catalog its photos, take the following steps:

1. Click **Start, Programs, Kodak Picture CD, Volume # Issue #,** where # represents the Picture CD Volume and Issue number shown on the CD label.

2. Click the arrow in the lower-right corner of the Kodak Review magazine.

3. Click the **Switch Roll** button just above the thumbnail preview window.

4. Insert the CD you want to register into your computer's CD-ROM drive.

5. Click **Get Kodak Picture CD.** Picture CD registers the new CD and creates thumbnail versions of all the photos on the CD. These appear in the thumbnail preview window.

To switch from one roll of pictures to another, click the **Switch Roll** button to view a list of all the Picture CDs you have registered. Click the name of the desired roll.

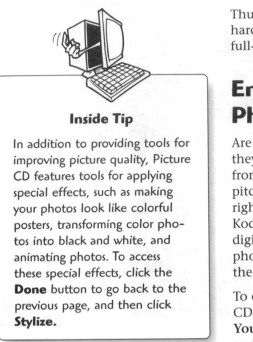

Thumbnail versions of all the photos stay on your hard drive, but if you try to edit a photo or display it full-size, the program prompts you to insert the CD.

Enhancing and Editing Photos

Are your photos too dark? Are some too light? Are they fuzzy and out of focus? Do your portraits all suffer from the red-eye effect? If so, you might be tempted to pitch that Picture CD and the accompanying prints right in the trash. Resist the temptation. With the Kodak Picture CD software, you can touch up your digitized photos by increasing the brightness for dark photos, sharpening blurry images, and even removing the red-eye effect.

To edit and enhance your photos, run Kodak Picture CD, navigate to the main menu, and click **Modify Your Pictures.** Click the desired image, click **Enhance,** and use the following tools to touch up the photo:

Inside Tip

In addition to providing tools for improving picture quality, Picture CD features tools for applying special effects, such as making your photos look like colorful posters, transforming color photos into black and white, and animating photos. To access these special effects, click the **Done** button to go back to the previous page, and then click **Stylize.**

 instant fix automatically adjusts the brightness, color, and contrast and sharpens out-of-focus photos. Instant fix does not remove the red-eye effect.

 brightness contrast lets you brighten dull pictures and lighten dark pictures.

 sharpen corrects shots that are slightly out of focus. Don't get your hopes up; you can't do much to improve photos that are seriously blurry.

 trim zooms in on the most important area of the photo and crops extraneous details from the borders. If you've ever taken a picture of your dog only to have it appear as a dot on the print, you'll love this feature.

 remove red eye eliminates the red-eye effect that crops up in pictures of humans and other animals. When all your subjects look like vampires, it's a good sign that you need to remove the red-eye effect.

 remove all changes returns the image to its original, mint condition. If you get carried away with your "enhancements," this button can be a lifesaver.

done accepts your changes and returns you to the previous page, where you can select other options for modifying the photo.

Typing Your Own Captions

The adage "A picture's worth a thousand words" might be true, but a few select words (a caption) can enhance even the most detailed picture. A caption might specify the date and location, name the people in the photo, or even insert a witty remark. Although captions do not appear on printouts, they do appear below the photos if you arrange them in a slide show. Captions also make it easier to locate a photo later using the search feature.

To add a caption to a photo in Kodak Picture CD, click **Modify Your Pictures**, click the picture below which you want to add a caption, and click the **caption** button. Type the caption in the text box below the photo, as shown in the following figure.

Panic Attack!

The text that appears below a photo in thumbnail view is the photo's filename, which you cannot change. In order to add or modify a caption, you must use the **caption** button.

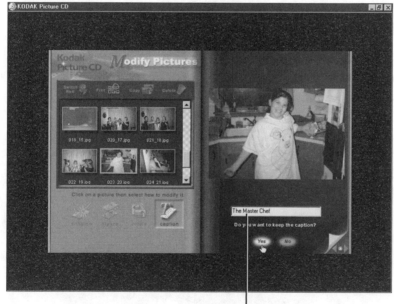

Add your own comments and other details with captions.

Type your caption here.

Printing Your Photos on Photo-Quality Paper

Digitized photos are great for sending via e-mail and posting on the Web, but you might still want some old-fashioned prints. Of course, you can print your photos on standard inkjet or copy machine paper, but this cheaper paper stock tends to bleed, making photos and other graphics appear fuzzy.

Inside Tip

Several companies on the Web can transfer digital photos to T-shirts and make mugs, coasters, boxer shorts, and other products with your photos. Check out Zing Networks, Inc., at www.pix. com.

For best results, purchase some photo-quality paper. This paper can be quite costly, but if you want photos that look like bona fide photo prints, don't go cheap. In addition, just before you give your final okay to start printing, double-check your print settings to be sure your printer is set for the highest-quality output. If you print photos in draft mode on photo-quality paper, they will come out dingy, no matter how good the paper is (not to mention wasting expensive paper).

When you're ready to print your photos from Kodak Picture CD, take the following steps:

1. Display the main menu by clicking the back arrow button to flip back through the option pages or by clicking the dot between the arrow buttons. (Clicking the dot displays a pop-up menu with all the available options.)

2. On the main menu, click **Printing at Home.** The Printing at Home page appears, as shown in the following figure.

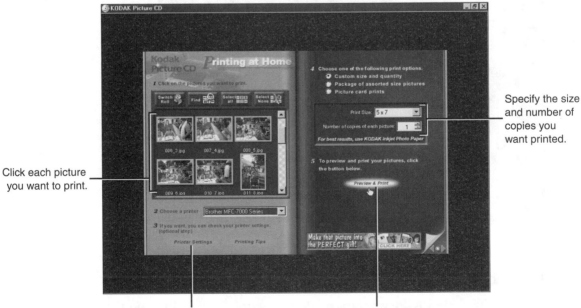

Specify the size and number of copies you want printed.

Click each picture you want to print.

Enter settings for your printer.

Click Preview & Print.

With Kodak Picture CD, making additional prints is a snap.

3. Click each photo you want to print. (To deselect a picture, click it again.) A yellow box appears around each picture you select, indicating that it will be printed.

4. Click the **Printer Settings** button and use the resulting dialog box to enter quality preferences for your printer. You might need to click the **Properties** button in the dialog box to access additional preferences. (The steps for entering printer settings vary from printer to printer.)

5. In step 4 onscreen, click **Custom size and quantity** and enter the desired print size and number of copies. (Check out the other two options under step 4 for some predesigned print layouts.)

6. Click **Preview & Print.** The Print Preview dialog box appears, showing the first photo.

7. Click the plus (+) and minus (–) buttons to flip through the photos if desired.

8. Click **Print** to start printing.

Tech Term

A **digital camera,** like a scanner, is built around a CCD (charge-coupled device). When you snap a picture, the shutter opens and bombards the CCD with light. The CCD converts the light into electrical impulses, which are then applied to a magnetic storage medium, such as a disk or PC card.

Sharing Photos Via E-Mail and Disk

You don't have to print your digitized photos in order to share them. Kodak Picture CD offers several tools that let you attach photos to outgoing e-mail messages, make your own 3$\frac{1}{2}$-inch Kodak Picture Disk, create an onscreen slide show, and even order photo coffee mugs and other products.

To transmit your photos via e-mail, display the main menu and click **Email Pictures.** The Email Pictures screen appears, as shown in the following figure. Click each picture you want to send and then address and compose your message as you normally do. Click the **Send Pictures** button.

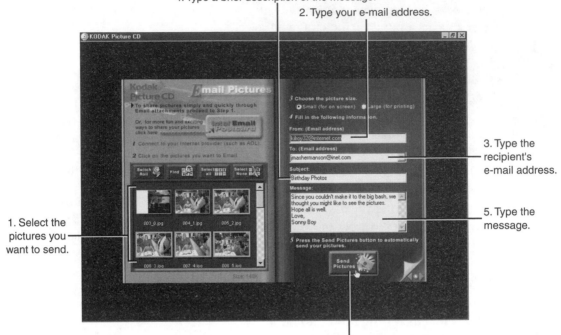

The Email Pictures screen makes it easy to send a single picture or an entire photo album.

Avoiding the Middleman with a Digital Camera

Although *digital cameras* are one of the most popular computer toys around, they're not the most affordable cameras on the market. You can get a 35mm box camera at your local drugstore that can take better snapshots than a $200 digital camera. For another $80, you can get a 600×600dpi 24-bit color scanner that produces better digitized images.

So why are so many people buying digital cameras? Several reasons come to mind:

➤ They're fun. Take a digital camera with an LCD viewfinder to a party, and you'll be the center of attention—or at least your camera will be.

➤ They provide instant gratification. With a digital camera, you don't even have to wait for one-hour film developing service. You plug the camera in to your computer, download the images, and print as many copies as you like.

➤ They let you create digital photo albums that you can write to CDs or DVDs for easy storage and management.

➤ They save you money on film and developing.

➤ They make it easy to post pictures on Web pages and send photos via e-mail.

Shopping for a digital camera is nearly as complicated as shopping for a computer. Prices range from $100 to more than $1,000, and features vary widely. You need to consider resolution, color depth, memory, flash options, battery life, storage options, zoom features, and the method used to download photos to a computer. Special features, such as voice annotation, an LCD viewfinder, and optical zoom, come at a premium price. As with any big-ticket item, try before you buy, and read current reviews.

Taking Pictures

Because digital cameras are modeled off of standard 35mm cameras, snapping a picture is easy. You just point and shoot. However, before you snap too many pictures, you should check the camera settings.

Most digital cameras have two buttons: one for changing modes (such as flash, image quality, timer, and audio) and another for changing the mode settings. You change to the desired mode (for instance, Flash) and then press the other button to change the setting (for instance, Auto Flash or Flash On). Check the following settings before taking a picture:

➤ **Resolution.** To fit more pictures in storage, crank down the resolution setting. For higher-quality pictures, choose a higher setting.

➤ **Flash.** In most cases, leave the flash setting on Auto. If you're taking all your pictures outside, turn off the flash. For backlit scenes, turn on the flash if this option is available on your camera.

➤ **Audio.** If your camera supports audio input, turn on Audio if desired. Keep in mind that audio recordings consume quite a bit of storage space.

Whoa!

As you snap pictures, keep track of the amount of storage remaining. Most cameras have a small LCD display (not to be confused with the LCD viewfinder) that shows the number of pictures you've taken and the available storage.

Copying Pictures to Your Computer

Digital cameras come with their own software that transfers the image files from the camera to your computer. In addition, the camera should include a cable for connecting to one of the ports on your PC (typically the serial, USB, or FireWire port). Some digital cameras require a PC card reader.

To transfer the images, connect the cable to your camera and to the specified port. Refer to the camera and software's documentation to run the photo transfer utility, and then enter the command to retrieve the images. The program retrieves the images from the camera and displays them onscreen. The program then deletes the images from the PC card or other storage area or gives you the option of having the images deleted.

Inside Tip

Scanner types include handheld, which you drag over a picture manually; sheet-fed, in which you feed the photo into the scanner as you would feed paper into a printer; and flatbed, which has a glass surface on which you lay the photo. Scanners's resolution, color depth, speed, connection type, and other features also vary. Shop carefully.

Ordering High-Quality Photo Prints Online

Of course, you can print your pictures using the software that came with your digital camera or with special photo-management software, but what do you do if you want some high-quality 5×7-inch prints?

Fortunately, you can drop off your "film" online at any of several online film developers, such as Shutterfly (www.shutterfly.com) or Snapfish (www.snapfish.com). The process is pretty simple. You can either e-mail your photo files to the online photo shop or use the online photo shop's software to upload your photo files to the service. For example, at Shutterfly, you simply drag your photos from your digital camera's program into a special Shutterfly window, as shown in the following figure. You then complete an order form, specifying the size and number of prints you want and your billing and delivery information. Shutterfly processes your pictures and then mails them to you.

If you're in a big hurry and need one-hour processing (or faster), take your digital camera to a professional photo shop. Most photo shops have special printers that can transfer your digital photos into high-quality prints in a matter of minutes.

At Shutterfly, you drop off your "film" by dragging and dropping the photos you want developed.

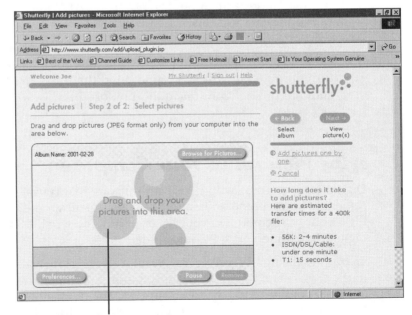

Drag your photos into this window.

Scanning Photos

Now, about those boxes of old photos stashed in the attic: How do you digitize them? Get a scanner. With a high-quality scanner and the accompanying software, you can pull photos and other images off prints and store them on your hard drive.

If you have a *flatbed* scanner, first position the image face-down on the glass as specified in the scanner's documentation. Run the scan program that came with your scanner, and click the button for initiating the scanning operation. This typically calls up a dialog box that lets you enter color settings, specify the resolution, and mark the area you want to scan (see the following figure).

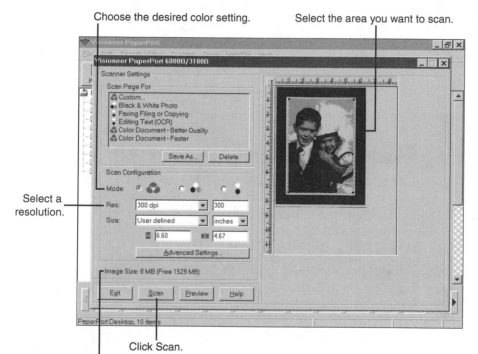

Choose the desired color setting.

Select the area you want to scan.

Select a resolution.

Note the amount of disk space the image requires.

Click Scan.

Before you scan an image, select the area you want to scan, and enter preferences for color and resolution.

If the dialog box has a button for previewing the image, click the button so that you can select the area you want to scan. Don't be shocked if the preview looks bad; the preview area typically shows a low-resolution version of the image. Enter your preferences, and then click the **Scan** button to start scanning. The scanner digitizes the image and typically displays a thumbnail view of the image onscreen.

Some scan programs include tools for editing and enhancing the photos. If the program does not feature photo-editing tools, or if the tools are poorly designed, purchase a separate photo editor, such as Paint Shop Pro. You can download a share-ware version of Paint Shop Pro from Jasc Software at www.jasc.com/download.asp.

Computer Cheat

If you don't have a scanner, don't fret. You can take your photos to almost any photo shop or other store that develops film and scan them at the store. The scanner typically has a floppy drive or CD-RW, which can store the scanned images on a floppy disk or CD. Most of these photo scanners have built-in software for enhancing and editing the photos and a printer for creating high-quality prints.

Creating Your Own Digital Photo Album

Kodak Picture CD is a great tool for managing your *new* photos, but if you're scanning old prints, Picture CD offers little help. It doesn't allow you to import scanned images, enhance them, and combine them with Picture CD prints to create custom photo albums. To gain complete control over your photos, obtain a quality photo management program, such as PhotoRecall.

With PhotoRecall, shown in the following figure, you can create virtual photo albums and flip the pages onscreen. To pick up a free 30-day demonstration copy of PhotoRecall, go to www.photorecall.com.

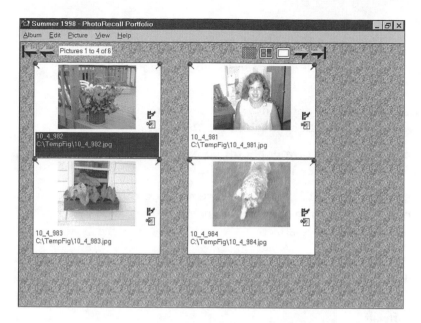

With PhotoRecall, you can create and print your own custom photo albums.

Changing Yourself and Others with Morphing

Are you feeling blue? Do you feel as though you need to do something drastic, like chop off your hair or run off with the UPS driver? Then maybe you need a change. With a good morphing program, you can experience a complete body makeover without the risks of surgery. You simply take two pictures—before and after—and then tell the morphing program to morph the before picture into the after picture. You can then sit back and see your dumpy old self transformed into Brad Pitt or Cindy Crawford. Of course, you won't actually feel the change, but after you see the results, you might be happy just to be yourself.

Some photo-editing programs include morphing tools, but if you're looking for professional results, try the following dedicated morphing programs:

➤ **BitMorph** by DC's Creation Software (www.people.cornell.edu/pages/dmc27/). This software is an easy-to-use morphing program that allows you to bend, stretch, and distort objects in an image, in addition to the standard morphing of one image into another. Get a shareware version of the program at DC's Web site.

➤ **Elastic Reality** by SoftImage (www.softimage.com). This software is one of the most powerful and precise morphing programs on the market. Although you might not be able to download a shareware version from this Web site, you can obtain additional information about the software and find out where you can purchase a copy.

➤ **Morph Man** by STOIK Software (www.stoik.com). This software not only morphs one image into another but can also morph an entire video clip into another video sequence. The shareware version, which you can download from STOIK's Web site, has the Save feature disabled, but it's fun to play with anyway.

The Least You Need to Know

➤ When you drop off your next roll of film for developing, request a Kodak Picture CD.

➤ To run your Kodak Picture CD, pop it into your computer's CD-ROM drive and follow the onscreen instructions to install the software.

➤ To view a full-screen slide show of your photos on a Kodak Picture CD, run the Picture CD software and click **View My Pictures.**

➤ You can use the Kodak Picture CD photo enhancement tools to adjust the brightness and contrast, sharpen the photo, trim extraneous areas of the photo, and eliminate the red-eye effect.

➤ A digital camera stores pictures on a memory card or disk instead of on film and lets you copy the images to your computer.

➤ To digitize existing photo prints, scan the images using a color scanner and its accompanying software.

➤ To create and print custom photo albums, get a photo management program such as PhotoRecall.

Chapter 27

Drawing Your Family Tree

In This Chapter

➤ Buying the best genealogy program on the market

➤ Plugging in the information you know about your family

➤ Digging up more data from the CD-ROM collection

➤ Researching your roots on the Web

➤ Finding your long-lost relatives

➤ Getting help from other genealogy buffs

Although technology and industrialization have helped our society progress in many ways, they have weakened our family structure. We leave the towns and communities in which we grew up, dilute our cultures, and cut the ties that bind us to our closest relatives—all in the name of progress and independence. The nuclear family is set adrift, completely alienated from any sense of an extended family.

Sensing this loss, people increasingly have become more motivated to research their family history and trace their lineage. We want to know more about our parents, their siblings, and our parents' parents. We want to know what roles they played in human history. We're curious about how our ancestors lived and what they did. We crave to learn more about our heritage and better understand ourselves.

In the past, if you wanted a thorough report of your family's history, you needed to hire a professional genealogist to help. Now, with the assistance of a good genealogy program, you can perform the research yourself and reconstruct a detailed account of your family history for as far back as humans have been keeping records. This chapter shows you how to get started.

Picking a Good Genealogy Program

Not long ago, the genealogy software market consisted of one program—Family Tree Maker, which is still king of the hill. But is it still the best? That depends on what's most important to you: powerful research tools, ease of use, or low cost. When you look at these features, the choices become clear:

➤ **Family Tree Maker.** This software offers the most robust collection of research tools and genealogy databases. This makes Family Tree Maker the top choice of serious genealogists. Because Family Tree Maker is the most popular genealogy program around, you can share data with a large population of users and work together to complete your tree. However, Family Tree Maker has a few drawbacks, including a poorly designed interface, poor handling of digitized photos, and additional expenses to access online genealogy services. Get more information at www.broderbund.com.

➤ **Generations Family Tree.** This software is a user-friendly family tree program that provides simple tools for constructing and printing your family tree and incorporating photos. Family Tree's genealogy database is a little weak, however, making it more suitable for the weekend genealogist than for professional researchers. Learn more about Generations Family Tree at www.sierra.com/sierrahome/familytree/.

➤ **Ultimate Family Tree.** This software is another powerful yet user-friendly genealogy program that's excellent for laying out and printing a family tree. Ultimate Family Tree also makes great use of Internet tools to help you trace your lineage. Learn more about Ultimate Family Tree and pick up a free trial version at www.uftree.com.

➤ **Shareware programs.** Software such as My Family Tree (huhnware.com/genealogy.htm) and Fzip Family Tree (www.ozemail.com.au/~acroft/) are great if you have all the information you want to include in your family tree but need a tool to organize it.

Because Family Tree Maker is the most powerful and popular genealogy program on the market, this chapter uses it to illustrate the basic tasks you must perform to create your own family tree and map your family history.

Computer Cheat

If you decide to save money and use a shareware program, you can find plenty of research tools on the Internet, as explained later in this chapter.

Plugging in Names, Dates, and Relationships

The first step in creating a family tree is to enter data you already know. In most cases, you can safely enter your name, the names of your parents, and the names of your grandparents. Most genealogy programs lead you through the process. Family Tree Maker, for instance, prompts you for some basic information the first time you start the program. As shown in the following figure, you must enter at least your own name to get started. Enter the requested information and click **Next >**.

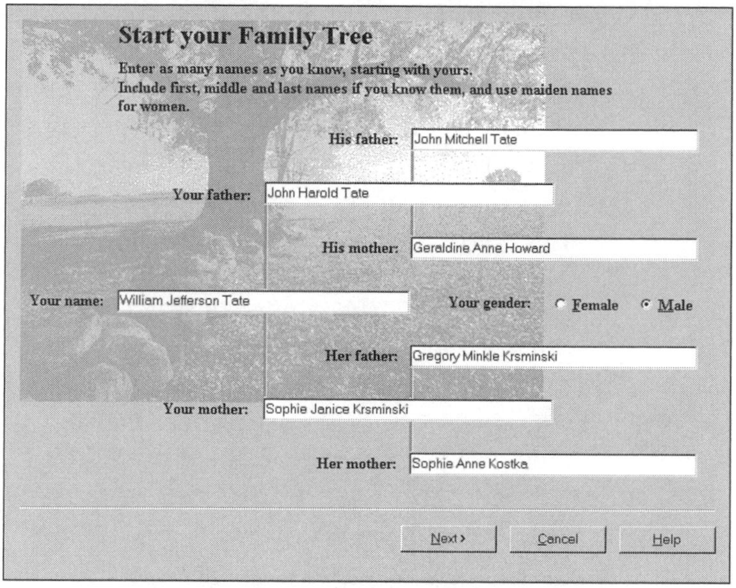

Start your Family Tree

Enter as many names as you know, starting with yours.
Include first, middle and last names if you know them, and use maiden names for women.

His father: John Mitchell Tate

Your father: John Harold Tate

His mother: Geraldine Anne Howard

Your name: William Jefferson Tate   Your gender: ○ Female ● Male

Her father: Gregory Minkle Krsminski

Your mother: Sophie Janice Krsminski

Her mother: Sophie Anne Kostka

Next >   Cancel   Help

Start your family tree with a few simple entries, and then watch it grow.

After you enter a few names, click **Next >**. Family Tree Maker prompts you to enter additional information about each person dangling from your tree, including each person's birth date and the geographical location in which they were born. You might be able to pick up some of this information by interviewing your living relatives, but if you can't find the information, don't worry—just fill in what you know. In the next few sections, you learn how to gather additional information.

Digging Up Your Roots with CD-ROM Databases

The top genealogy programs include 10 or more CDs packed with indexes, birth and death records, biographies, genealogies, military records, marriage indexes, immigration lists, land records, and even probate data. The Collector's Edition of Family Tree Maker comes with more than 30 CDs! The first step in fleshing out your family tree is to search these CDs for information about the family members you have added to your family tree so far.

Of course, you can't shove the entire stack of CDs into your CD-ROM drive at one time. To make the stack of CDs more manageable, the first couple of CDs include an index of everything on the CD collection. You pop in one of the index CDs and enter the search command. The program uses the index to generate a catalog of pertinent information and prompts you to enter the other CDs in the collection as needed. Here's what you do in Family Tree Maker:

Inside Tip

After you have added four or five more people to your family tree, perform the FamilyFinder search again. The search is likely to return a list of additional matches.

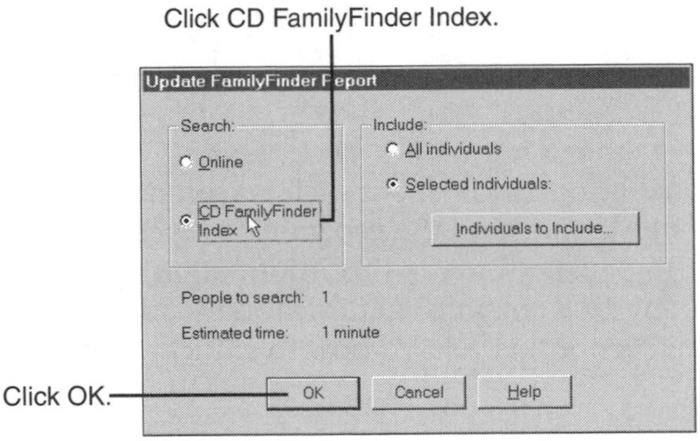

1. Click the **FamilyFinder Center** button on the Family Tree Maker toolbar. This displays the FamilyFinder page with links to several research tools.

2. Click **Run a FamilyFinder Search**. A Family-Finder Cue Card appears, providing some tips on using FamilyFinder.

3. Read through the tips, if desired, and click **OK**. The Update FamilyFinder Report dialog box appears, as shown in the following figure. It asks if you want to search online or search the FamilyFinder Index on CD.

4. Click **CD FamilyFinder Index**, and then click **OK**. Family Tree Maker starts the search and prompts you to insert one of the index CDs.

FamilyFinder can search online or through the FamilyFinder Index.

Click CD FamilyFinder Index.

Update FamilyFinder Report

Search:
○ Online
◉ CD FamilyFinder Index

Include:
○ All individuals
◉ Selected individuals:

Individuals to Include...

People to search: 1
Estimated time: 1 minute

Click OK.───── OK   Cancel   Help

5. Follow the onscreen instructions, inserting and swapping CDs as instructed. When you have fed Family Tree Maker all the CDs it asks for, the FamilyFinder Index returns a list of names that match the names you entered in your tree. (FamilyFinder ranks the matches with stars. A five-star match is the most promising.)

6. Click a name to view additional information.

Researching Your Family Tree Online

Swapping 30 CDs in and out of your CD-ROM drive is no fun. Besides, by the time the company burns those CDs, they're already old and outdated. Where can you obtain the most comprehensive, up-to-date data? On the Web, of course. Many companies, including Broderbund and Sierra, have online databases to aid you in your search. In addition, many genealogy organizations and services maintain Web sites, bulletin boards, chat rooms, and other resources for genealogy buffs.

Searching Online with Family Tree Maker

The best way to search online is to go through your genealogy program. In most programs, you enter a single search instruction to search through multiple databases. In Family Tree Maker, for instance, you follow these steps to perform a thorough Web search:

1. Click the **FamilyFinder Center** button on the Family Tree Maker toolbar. This displays the FamilyFinder page with links to several research tools.

2. Click **Run a FamilyFinder Search.** A FamilyFinder Cue Card appears, providing some tips on using FamilyFinder.

3. Read through the tips, if desired, and click **OK.** The Update FamilyFinder Report dialog box appears, asking if you want to search online or search the Family-Finder Index on CD.

4. Click **Online,** and then click **OK.** Family Tree Maker starts the search and might prompt you to establish an Internet connection. After connecting to the Internet, Family Tree Maker displays your browser window and then a dialog box showing the progress of the search. When the search is complete, the Search Results dialog box appears, displaying a summary of the results.

5. Click **OK** to close the Search Results dialog box and return to the main screen. If you performed a CD Index search earlier, the Internet search results are tacked onto the bottom of the report as shown in the following figure.

6. Click the link to the far right of an entry to view information about the person. Family Tree Maker opens the corresponding page in your Web browser. (Most pages consist of information submitted from other Family Tree Maker users.)

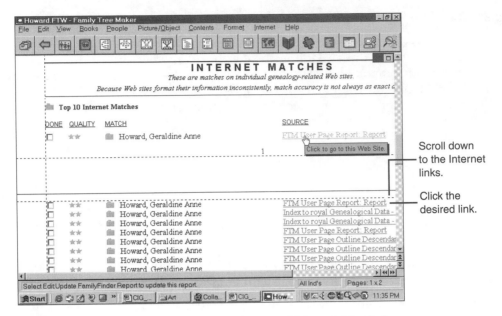

Family Tree Maker displays links to Web pages with matching information.

Visiting Genealogy Web Sites

Even if you don't have a fancy family tree program, you can research your lineage on the Web. Many genealogy organizations and government agencies provide access to electronic databases that are publicly accessible. Some are even free. To take advantage of the Internet for family research, check out the following sites:

➤ **Ancestry.com** at www.ancestry.com. This site is one of the best places to start your search. The home page greets you with a simple search form that prompts you to enter a name. The search pulls up links to several free databases (such as a social security death index and telephone number/address listings), as shown in the following figure.

➤ **Genealogy.com** at www.genealogy.com. This site is a great place to dig up information. Here you can perform a search that sifts through several online databases and points you to the sources. This site also offers links to additional genealogy guides, tips, message boards, and other resources.

➤ **Gensource.com** at www.gensource.com. This site provides another search tool that's a little less comprehensive. It returns a list of links that point you to other people on the Web who might be researching the same lineage. You might connect with someone who has already done much of your homework.

➤ **FamilySearch** at www.familysearch.org (developed and maintained by The Church of Jesus Christ of Latter Day Saints). This site has the most interesting search form of the bunch, allowing you to type entries for an entire branch of your family tree. If the search returns no matches, try entering only a last name.

➤ **GENDEX** at www.gendex.com. This site is a genealogy site that indexes entries for numerous genealogy databases and makes the entries available via a single search. GENDEX offers free and members-only search options.

➤ **GenExchange & Surname Registry** at www.genexchange.com. This site is one of the largest noncommercial genealogy database organizations on the Web. GenExchange is maintained and developed by volunteers to make genealogical data freely available to any and all researchers. After you reach the home page, click the link for performing a search, and then click the state you want to search.

➤ **The Genealogy Home Page** at www.genhomepage.com. This site is a great place to go when you've hit a dead end or exhausted the resources listed here. This site features links to hundreds of helpful genealogy guides, mailing lists, search tools, organizations, maps, commercial services, and much more.

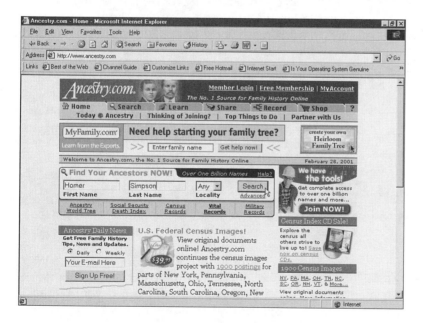

Ancestry.com can give you a good collection of leads.

Getting Advice Via Newsgroups and E-Mail

A good genealogist is a good detective, and a good detective talks to people. If you're lucky, you'll find all the information you need by poking around on a few CDs and cruising genealogy sites on the Web. In most cases, however, you need to do some interviews and track down people who have better records (and a better memory) than you do.

Although the phone is still an excellent tool for contacting people directly, newsgroups (message boards) and e-mail provide another avenue. As you research your family lineage, record e-mail addresses you encounter and write to people who are researching the same surname (last name) or lineage. You should also check out the following newsgroups: soc.genealogy.misc, soc.genealogy.methods, soc.genealogy.surnames.usa, and soc.genealogy.surnames.misc. You can use Outlook Express, Netscape Messenger, or another newsreader to connect to these newsgroups.

Another great way to keep up on the latest information is to subscribe to Internet mailing lists. Go to The Genealogy Home Page at www.genhomepage.com for information on how to subscribe to hundreds of mailing lists. Many mailing lists are maintained by individuals who are searching for information about a particular surname. If you're lucky, you'll find a mailing list devoted specifically to the family you're researching.

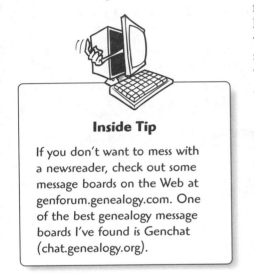

Inside Tip

If you don't want to mess with a newsreader, check out some message boards on the Web at genforum.genealogy.com. One of the best genealogy message boards I've found is Genchat (chat.genealogy.org).

You can also learn more about genealogy and make some contacts through chat rooms and online clubs. America Online and other commercial online services host chat rooms devoted to genealogy topics. Yahoo! hosts more than 1,000 genealogy clubs at dir.clubs.yahoo.com/family_ _ _home/genealogy/ (that's three underscore characters between family and home). Also, check out the chat rooms at GenForum (chat.genforum.com). To find additional chat sites, use your favorite Web search tool to look for "genealogy chat."

Tracking Down Lost Relatives

When you lose contact with your relatives through divorce, adoption, or just plain lack of trying, you might need to do a little good old-fashioned detective work. Keep in mind that most telephone books are accessible on the Internet. If you have a unique last name, go to people.yahoo.com or another people search page on the Web and search e-mail and phone book listings for your last name. Try contacting prospective relatives individually. You might just find someone who knows your family! (See Chapter 19, "Poking Around on the Web," for more information.)

If you're having little luck on your own, get some professional help. Private eyes and genealogy researchers abound on the Internet. For about $40, you can hire a firm such as Find People Fast (www.fpf.com) or USSearch.com (www.1800ussearch.com) to do an individual or family name search for you.

Growing Your Family Tree

As you gather data and shake a few more individuals out of your family tree, you can start expanding your tree. Your genealogy program has the tools you need to add entries. In Family Tree Maker, for instance, you follow these steps to add entries to your family tree:

1. Click the **Family Page** button. A tabbed "book" appears displaying the names of the people already entered in your family tree as shown in the following figure.

Click the Parents of tab to enter ancestors.

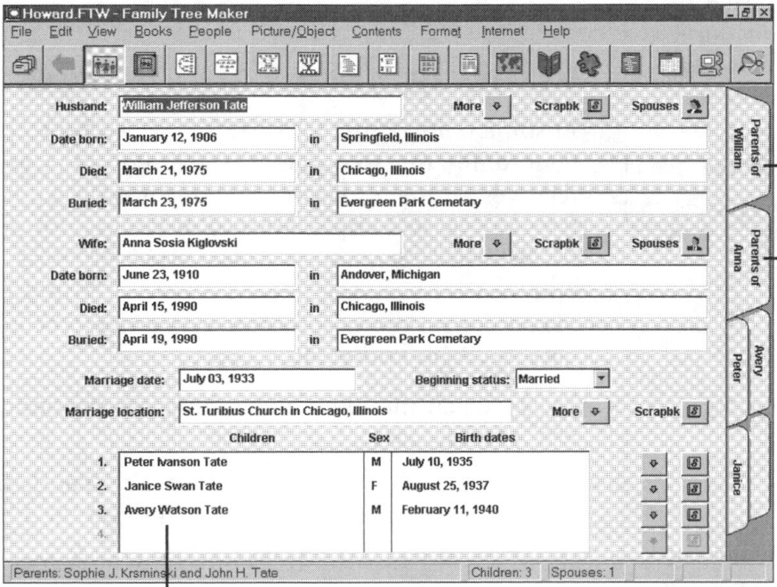

Enter direct descendents (children) here.

You typically enter additional people by adding parents or children of existing individuals.

2. Click a person's name to display the page of information about that person. The person's information page appears.

3. To enter additional information about the selected individual, type the information in the appropriate text boxes.

4. To add information about the parents of the individual, click the **Parents of** tab, and type the information you have obtained. (This allows you to add people to the tree.)

As you research your family history, you might meet someone who has a branch of your family tree that feeds into your own tree. In such a case, you can graft (append) that branch to your tree—assuming that you can get the person to send you his or her Family Tree Maker file.

To append a branch, open your family file, and then choose the **File, Append/Merge Family File** command. This displays a dialog box prompting you to select the file. Change to the disk and folder in which the file is stored, and then double-click its name. Follow the on-screen instructions to complete the process.

Whoa!

Before you append or merge family trees, back up your original file using the **File, Backup Family File** command. Grafting a branch to another family tree has been known to cause problems.

Inside Tip

Cramming a large family tree on 8$^1/_2$-by-11-inch sheets of paper is like growing an oak tree in a glass house. To make your family tree fit, consider printing it as a banner or taking your file to a professional printer to have it rendered by a plotter. If you choose to print on a banner, you must change the print settings for your printer. To access your printer settings, choose **Start, Settings, Printers,** right-click the icon for your printer, and choose **Properties.**

Printing Your Family Tree

At some point in the process, you will want to print your family tree to frame it, pass it along to interested relatives, or file it for your own records. Because family trees can be so complex, not to mention enormous, the printing operation is critical and contains several options for fitting the tree on paper. In Family Tree Maker, for instance, you must pick a tree type and then give the **Print** command:

1. Open the **View** menu and click the desired family tree type:

   All-in-one Tree displays you and all your relatives in one continuous tree.

   Ancestor Tree shows the pedigree of the selected individual (the person's parents, grandparents, great-grandparents, and so on, omitting brothers, sisters, uncles, and aunts).

   Descendant Tree shows the selected individual's children, grandchildren, great-grandchildren, and so on.

   Hourglass Tree shows the upward and downward lineage of the selected individual. In other words, the selected individual appears in the center with parents, grandparents, and so on branching out from the top and children, grandchildren, and so on branching out from the bottom.

Outline Descendant Tree is a space-saving descendant tree. Instead of displaying a box for each person, the tree displays offspring in text-only outline view.

2. To include information other than each person's name, birth date, and date of death, open the **Contents** menu, click **Items to Include in each Box**, and use the resulting dialog box to specify the data you want to include in your family tree.

3. To limit the number of generations included in your tree, open the **Contents** menu, click **# of Generations to Show**, and specify the desired number of ancestors and descendants.

4. Use options on the **Format** menu to enter the desired formatting preferences for your family tree, including the font and box border type. You can even choose to include a background picture.

5. When you're ready to print your family tree, open the **File** menu and click **Print.** The Print dialog box appears.

6. Enter the desired print options, including the print quality and number of copies, and click **OK.**

The Least You Need to Know

➤ Get a good genealogy program, such as Family Tree Maker, and learn how to use it.

➤ When you first start Family Tree Maker, it leads you through the process of recording information about a few of your closest relatives.

➤ Use the search tools in your genealogy program to search through the database CDs included with most programs.

➤ Use the Internet search commands in your genealogy program to perform more thorough searches of up-to-date databases.

➤ Even if you don't have a fancy genealogy program, you can explore your roots at such sites as www.ancestry.com.

➤ If you're having trouble tracking down long-lost relatives, try a professional service such as www.1800ussearch.com.

➤ Before you print your family tree in Family Tree Maker, check out the options on the **View, Contents,** and **Format** menus for options on laying out your family tree.

Part 6

Tinkering with Computer Gadgets and Gizmos

Were you the last one on the block to buy a computer? Do you still use Post-it notes for grocery and to-do lists? Do you have a paper address book? Do you have stacks of unlabeled camcorder tapes? Do you still have to hunt for your TV's remote control?

If so, the latest technology has skipped your generation. Fortunately, the chapters in this part will bring you up to speed. Here, you learn how to copy and play digital music clips from the Internet, manage your life with a palm computer, watch TV and DVD movies on your computer, edit your camcorder videos and copy them to CDs or tapes, and even upgrade your computer to accept voice commands and dictation!

Chapter 28

Playing Digitized Music Clips

In This Chapter

➤ Playing your favorite audio CD tracks on your computer

➤ Finding and installing a free MP3 audio player

➤ Copying and playing MP3 audio clips from the Web

➤ Copying MP3 audio clips to a portable MP3 player

➤ Burning your own audio CDs

If you thought the move from LPs to CDs was impressive, you're going to love the latest in audio technology. With your computer and a CD-ROM drive, a sound card, and a decent set of speakers, you can create your own computerized jukebox that can play hundreds of your favorite songs. Add an Internet connection, and you can download free MP3 music clips to add to your collection. With a portable MP3 player, you can take your favorite tunes wherever you go. And, if you have a CD-R or CD-RW drive, you can even "burn" your own custom CDs and play them on any CD player! This chapter steps you through the process of building your own "recording studio" and points out the best places on the Web to get free MP3 players and music clips.

Understanding CD and MP3 Audio Basics

To understand CD and MP3 audio basics, you must first know that standard audio CD players and computers differ in how they store and play audio clips. On an audio CD, data is stored in a format called "Red Book," which has been the standard format for more than 20 years. Computers, on the other hand, store audio data in various formats, the most popular of which is MP3, a format that compresses an audio clip to about one twelfth its size with an imperceptible loss of quality. MP3 lets users download audio clips more quickly over the Internet and store them in less space on their computers' hard drives.

The only trouble is that a standard audio CD player cannot play MP3 files, and a computer cannot process audio data stored on an audio CD in the Red Book format (although all newer CD-ROM drives can play audio CDs through an earphone jack or through your computer's sound card). Fortunately, specialized programs can handle the required format conversions for you:

➤ **MP3 player.** An MP3 player lets your computer play MP3 audio clips. You can copy MP3 clips from Web sites or convert audio clips from your CDs into MP3 files with a CD ripper, described next. An MP3 player converts MP3 files into a standard digital audio format (typically a WAV format) that your computer can play through its sound card and speakers.

➤ **CD ripper.** A CD ripper converts audio clips from a CD into the MP3 format or another format that a computer equipped with the required software can play. A CD ripper is commonly called a *jukebox* because it stores all the clips you record and lets you play each clip simply by selecting it from a list.

➤ **CD burner.** A CD-R (CD-Recordable) or CD-RW (CD-Rewritable) drive writes data to a CD by using a tiny laser. A CD burner utility converts MP3 audio clips stored on your computer into the standard Red Book format used to store audio data on CDs and controls the process of recording the audio clips to the CD. You can then play the CD in a standard audio CD player.

Before you run out and buy a case of CD-R or CD-RW discs, you should understand the difference between the two types of discs. CD-R discs let you write to the disc only once; you can't erase the data on a CD-R disc and then record over it. With a CD-RW disc, you can record data to the disc, erase the data, and write new data to the disc. This makes CD-RW discs an excellent storage medium for backing up files. However, CD-RW discs are typically less reflective than CD-R discs, making them a poor choice for recording audio CDs.

The surface of a compact disc has smooth, reflective areas and pits or dyed areas that refract rather than reflect light. A CD drive or player reads data from a disc by bouncing a laser beam off the surface of the disc and interpreting differences in the intensity of the returning beam. On CD-RW discs, the contrast between the reflected areas and the dyed areas is less than the contrast found on CD-R discs. Some audio CD players have a tough time reading a CD-RW disc. When you're burning audio CDs, stick with CD-R discs.

Some newer audio CD players can play MP3 files stored on CDs, making it unnecessary to convert MP3 clips into the Red Book format before burning them on a CD.

This allows you to store more than 10 times as much music per CD. However, the first batch of these CD players had some glitches, making it tough for them to find all the songs on a CD.

Although MP3 gets all the press, you'll encounter many other audio formats on the Web. Some audio formats are designed specifically for streaming audio; that is, they are designed to start playing an audio clip as soon as your computer starts receiving it. Streaming audio, such as RealAudio, is commonly used for online radio stations and "live" broadcasts. Liquid Audio is a newer audio format that's designed to prevent unauthorized copying and distribution of audio clips. If you encounter an audio clip you want to hear in the Liquid Audio format, you might need to download a new audio player.

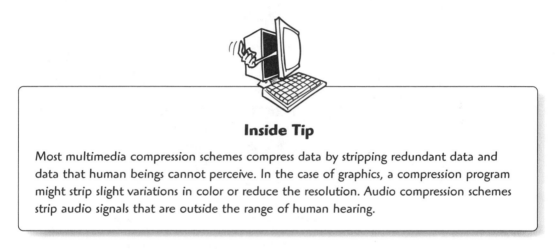

Inside Tip

Most multimedia compression schemes compress data by stripping redundant data and data that human beings cannot perceive. In the case of graphics, a compression program might strip slight variations in color or reduce the resolution. Audio compression schemes strip audio signals that are outside the range of human hearing.

Using Your Computer as a Jukebox

In Chapter 6, "Making Your Computer Play Cool Sounds," you learned how to play audio CDs through your computer's CD-ROM drive, sound card, and speakers. This makes your computer little more than an overpriced audio CD player. To make your computer a superior overpriced CD player, record your favorite audio clips to your computer's hard drive as MP3 files. This provides you with a virtual jukebox, which you can program to play only the songs you want to hear in the order in which you want to hear them.

Media Player, included as part of Windows Me, not only plays audio CDs but also can copy entire CDs or selected tracks to your computer's hard drive to create custom *playlists*. To see if Media Player is installed on your computer, check the Windows **Start, Programs** menu option or **Start, Programs, Accessories, Entertainment.** If Media Player is not installed, you can install it from the Windows Me CD or, if you have an earlier version of Windows (and you have an Internet connection), pick up a copy of Windows Media Player at www.microsoft.com/windows/windowsmedia/en/ and install it.

Creating a Custom Playlist with Windows Media Player

Using Windows Media Player, take the following steps to record your favorite CD tracks to your computer's hard drive and create a custom playlist:

1. Run the Windows Media Player by selecting **Start, Programs, Windows Media Player** or **Start, Programs, Accessories, Entertainment, Windows Media Player**.

2. Insert a CD that has one or more tracks you want to record. (Your computer might have a CD player other than Media Player that runs when you insert an audio CD. At this point, you can either use the player that appears or close the player and proceed with these steps.)

3. In Media Player, click the **CD Audio** button. After some time, Windows displays a list of the tracks stored on the CD, as shown in the following figure.

Inside Tip

To check out another popular virtual jukebox, go to www.re-alaudio.com and click the link for downloading RealJukebox. The basic, free version lets you record audio clips from CDs to your hard drive and create custom playlists. With the Plus! version ($29.99), you can record your playlist to a CD—assuming, of course, that you have a CD-R or CD-RW drive.

A check mark indicates that the track is selected for recording.

Click Copy Music to copy the selected tracks to the media library.

Windows Media Player makes it easy to copy individual tracks from a CD.

	Name	Length	Copy Status	Artist	Genre	Style
☑	Underground	2:00		Tom Waits	ROCK	Singer-So
☑	Shore Leave	4:18		Tom Waits	ROCK	Singer-So
☑	Dave The Butcher [Instrume...	2:20		Tom Waits	ROCK	Singer-So
☐	Johnsburg, Illinois	1:33		Tom Waits	ROCK	Singer-So
☑	16 Shells From A Thirty-Oug...	4:33		Tom Waits	ROCK	Singer-So
☑	Town With No Cheer	4:28		Tom Waits	ROCK	Singer-So
☑	In The Neighborhood	3:07		Tom Waits	ROCK	Singer-So
☐	Just Another Sucker On The...	1:46		Tom Waits	ROCK	Singer-So
☑	Frank's Wild Years	1:53		Tom Waits	ROCK	Singer-So
☐	Swordfishtrombone	3:06		Tom Waits	ROCK	Singer-So
☑	Down, Down, Down	2:16		Tom Waits	ROCK	Singer-So
☑	Soldier's Things	3:20		Tom Waits	ROCK	Singer-So
☑	Gin Soaked Boy	2:24		Tom Waits	ROCK	Singer-So

4. If the track names do not appear and you have an Internet connection, click the **Get Names** button above the track list to obtain the track names and other information from the Web. (Assuming that Media Player finds the information for the right CD, click the **Confirm** button to copy the information.)

Whoa!

If the track names still do not appear, manually label each track. Click the track number to select it, click it again to highlight the track number, and then type the track name. (If the tracks have no names, identifying the tracks later is nearly impossible.) You can enter artist names for each track as well. To enter the same artist for every track, click the first track, **Shift+click** the last track, right-click **Unknown Artist,** and click **Edit Selection.**

5. Click the check box next to each track you do *not* want to record, to remove the check mark from the box.

6. Click the **Copy Music** button. Media Player displays the progress of the copy operation next to each track as it records the track.

7. Repeat steps 2 through 6 for each CD that has one or more tracks you want to record.

8. Click the **Media Library** button so that you can create a custom playlist.

9. Click the **New Playlist** button. The New Playlist dialog box appears, prompting you to type a name for the playlist.

10. Type a descriptive name for the playlist, such as Exercise Warmup, and click **OK**. A new folder with the name you typed appears below **My Playlists**, as shown in the following figure.

11. If a plus sign appears next to **Album**, click the plus sign to display a list of CDs from which you recorded clips.

12. Click the icon for the CD that has the song you want to add to your playlist. The tracks you recorded from the CD appear in the window on the right.

Inside Tip

Windows Media Player isn't the only CD player/ripper on the market. Check out these other players on the Web: RealJukebox (www.real.com/jukebox), Audiograbber (www.audiograbber.com-us.net/), and Audio Catalyst (www.xingtech.com/mp3/audiocatalyst/).

Click the icon for the
CD that contains the
recorded track.

*Drag and drop the audio
tracks you recorded to
your playlist.*

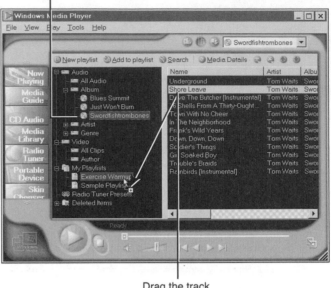

Drag the track
and drop it on the
icon for your playlist.

13. Drag the desired track over the icon for the playlist you created, and then release the mouse button. The track is added to your playlist.

14. Repeat steps 12 and 13 for the remaining tracks you want to add to your playlist.

Inside Tip

If you don't like the selection of skins, click the **More Skins** button (just to the right of **Apply Skin**). This connects you to Microsoft's Web site, where you can download additional skins.

15. To display your playlist, click its icon.

16. To move a song up or down on the playlist, click its name, drag it up or down in the list to the desired location, and release the mouse button.

17. To play your clips, click the clip you want to start playing and then click Media Player's **Play** button. Media Player plays the selected song and then the remaining songs in your playlist.

Changing Media Player's Skin

Many cell phones, handheld computers, and other trendy electronic devices now come with thin, detachable covers called *skins*. Likewise, most onscreen MP3 players come with their own virtual skins. You simply pick the desired skin from a list to personalize the appearance of your player.

To change skins in Media Player, click the **Skin Chooser** button, as shown in the following figure, and then click the name of a skin to preview it. When you find a skin you like, click its name and then click the **Apply Skin** button.

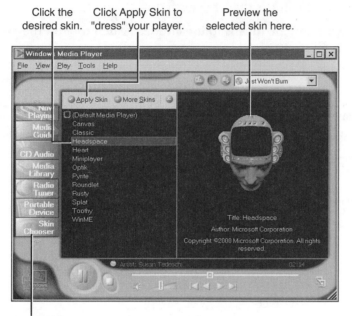

Click the   Click Apply Skin to   Preview the
desired skin.   "dress" your player.   selected skin here.

Give Media Player a new skin to completely re-design it.

Click the Skin
Chooser button.

I Want My MP3: Downloading Music Clips from the Web

You've probably heard of a company called Napster, which allowed users to freely share their MP3 audio recordings over the Internet. You also might have heard that the courts ruled against Napster and slapped some serious restrictions on this free music distribution center. Apparently, a few musicians were upset that they weren't getting paid for their work.

At any rate, many legal MP3 distribution sites remain up and running. Some charge a subscription fee to download a certain number of recordings per month. Others charge per recording. And some allow you to download some free tracks or samples of tracks in the hope that you'll purchase a CD online.

The following sections take you on a brief tour of MP3 sites and show you how to download and play MP3 clips using Internet Explorer and Windows Media Player.

You also learn how to copy your clips to a portable MP3 player to take them with you wherever you go.

Finding and Downloading Music Clips

Downloading any file is pretty easy. You click a link and follow the onscreen instructions to tell your browser where to save the file. However, before you can download MP3 clips, you have to find some tunes that are worth downloading.

The best way to track down a specific tune is to use an MP3 search tool on the Web. Here are some sites to get you started:

➤ AudioGalaxy (www.audiogalaxy.com)

➤ Gigabeat (gigabeat.com)

➤ Palavista (www.palavista.com)

➤ Look4MP3 (www.look4mp3.com)

➤ MP3Board (www.mp3board.com)

➤ Audiofind (www.audiofind.com)

➤ MusicMatch (www.musicmatch.com)

➤ MP3Search (www.mp3search.nu)

Panic Attack!

Although MP3 audio clips are smaller than their audio CD counterparts, they're still fairly large. A four-minute music clip can be more than 4 megabytes, which can take nearly half an hour to download over a 28.8Kbps modem connection. If you plan to download MP3s on a regular basis, you should have a 56Kbps modem or faster connection.

If you're just browsing or if you're looking for a more commercial site where you can download clips legally, check out the following MP3 distribution centers on the Web:

➤ **MP3.com** (www.mp3.com). This site has one of the most complete collections of MP3 audio clips on the Web, along with links for free MP3 players, rippers, portable players, and other MP3 gear. You can spend days at this site.

➤ **Amazon** (www.amazon.com). This site is the world's largest online bookstore but also distributes MP3 audio clips. After pulling up Amazon's home page, click the **Music** link, and then click **Free Downloads** in the banner at the top of the Music page.

➤ **IUMA**, the Internet Underground Music Archive (www.iuma.com). This site offers clips from independent artists. Many songwriters and musicians upload their music clips to this site, hoping to be discovered or at least generate some fan enthusiasm.

➤ **TUCOWS** (music.tucows.com). This site is an offshoot of one of the most popular shareware sites on the Web. This site offers hundreds of links to the latest tunes and hottest artists. You can also browse for music by category or search for specific tunes.

➤ **RollingStone.com** (www.rollingstone.com). This site is the official Web site of the popular rock magazine. After you reach the home page, click the **MP3** link to view a list of available tunes. Some are free downloads, and others cost a buck or more.

For more MP3 download sites, use your favorite Web search tool to search for "mp3" or "free mp3" or "free mp3 download."

Whoa!

At this point, you might be wondering if it's legal to copy commercial audio clips. If you're copying tracks from CDs you purchased for your own personal use, you're not breaking any laws. You cannot copy tracks for distribution to your friends and family or to strangers over the Internet. Of course, if the artist gives permission to freely copy and distribute his or her music, you're safe.

Playing Your Clips

As soon as you find a clip you want to download, simply click its link to play it. After your computer is finished downloading the clip, it should run your MP3 player, which typically starts playing the clip. If the clip doesn't start, click the **Play** button.

If your MP3 player does not start automatically, it might not have a *file association* with MP3 files. Here's what you do to check the MP3 file association and change it, if necessary:

1. Click the **My Computer** icon on the Windows desktop.

2. Open the **Tools** menu and click **Folder Options.**

3. Click the **File Types** tab to view a list of file types and the programs associated with them.

4. Scroll down the **Registered file types** list and click **MP3.** (If MP3 is not in the list, click the **New** button, type mp3, and click **OK.**) The **Details** box near the bottom of the dialog box displays the icon for the program set up to play MP3 files.

5. To associate a different player with MP3 files, click the **Change** button to display a list of programs installed on your system, and continue with step 6. Otherwise, click **OK** and skip the next step; you're done.

6. Click the program you want to use to play MP3 clips, as shown in the following figure, and then click **OK.**

Click the name of
your MP3 player.

*Associate your MP3
player with MP3 files.*

Click OK.

Copying MP3 Clips to a Portable MP3 Player

Building a huge music library on your computer is cool, but a computer is a bit too bulky to replace your Walkman. How do you take your music collection, or at least a portion of it, on the road? The easiest way is to purchase a portable MP3 player, as shown in the following figure. Portable MP3 players typically come equipped with 32 to 128 megabytes of RAM, enough to store 4 to 8 hours of music clips.

*A portable MP3 player
lets you take your MP3
collection on the road.*

(Photo courtesy of Rio, Inc.)

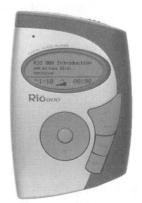

Portable MP3 players include a serial, parallel, or USB cable connection that plugs into your computer. Players typically come with their own software for copying files between your computer and the player, but Windows Media Player can handle the job:

1. Connect your portable MP3 player to your computer as instructed in the portable MP3 player's documentation. (If you connect the device using a USB cable, you need not turn off your computer to make the connection; otherwise, you might need to shut down the computer.)

2. Run the Windows Media Player by selecting **Start, Programs, Windows Media Player** or **Start, Programs, Accessories, Entertainment, Windows Media Player.**

3. Click the **Media Library** button.

4. Click the CD or playlist that contains the clips you want to transfer to your portable MP3 player.

5. Click the **Portable Device** button. Media Player displays two windows. The window on the left displays a list of audio clips in the selected CD or playlist, and the window on the right displays the names of any audio clips already stored on your portable MP3 player.

6. In the window on the left, be sure there is a check mark next to each audio clip you want to copy to your portable MP3 player.

7. Click the **Copy Music** button.

8. Repeat steps 3 through 7 to copy additional audio clips to your portable player.

9. Exit Media Player and disconnect your portable MP3 player as instructed in its documentation.

Burning Your Own Audio CDs

Ever since companies placed the power of recording technology in the hands of the people, people have copied albums, CDs, audiotapes, TV shows, movies, and anything else they can get their hands on. CDs are no exception. As soon as audio CD burners hit the market, people started their own bootleg operations, churning out free CDs for themselves, their friends, and their family.

Some of this copying is acceptable. For instance, if you purchased the entire collection of Beatles CDs and you want to create your own "favorites" CD to play in your car, you won't be prosecuted for copying songs you paid for to another disc for your own use. However, if you copy your entire collection to give as Christmas gifts, you're crossing the line.

Computer Cheat

Although Windows Media Player features no command for copying an audio CD, you can copy all the songs from the CD, save them in a separate playlist, and then copy the playlist to a CD. See the next section for details.

Be that as it may, the technology is available for copying CDs and for transferring your collection of MP3s (however you obtained it) to CDs, and I'll show you how to do it. I'll leave the legal and ethical decisions up to you, the courts, and the music industry.

Duplicating CDs

If your computer is equipped with a CD-R or CD-RW drive and a program for copying CDs, you can duplicate your audio CDs. Most computers that come with CD-R or CD-RW drives have a program for copying CDs. If you don't have a CD copy program, check out Adaptec's Easy CD Creator at www.roxio.com (Roxio is a spin-off of Adaptec). At $79.95, it's a little pricey, but Easy CD Creator can help you make the most of your CD-R or CD-RW drive. It includes features for backing up your computer's hard drive to CDs, recording video clips to CDs, transferring MP3 clips to CDs, and much more.

The following figure shows just how easy it is to duplicate a CD with Easy CD Creator. You simply insert the CD you want to copy, run Easy CD Creator, and click the **Copy** button. Easy CD Creator copies everything on the CD and then displays a dialog box telling you to insert a blank CD-R or CD-RW disc. After you insert the disc, Easy CD Creator transfers everything it copied from the original disc to the blank disc.

Whoa!

If you insert a CD and no CD title, artist name, or track names appear, enter this information yourself. Otherwise, you won't know which CD to insert during the copy operation, and you risk overwriting tracks with tracks of the same name.

The original CD

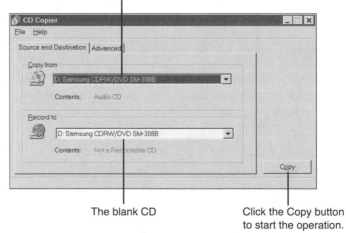

Adaptec's Easy CD Creator can copy CDs as easily as Windows can copy floppy disks.

The blank CD

Click the Copy button to start the operation.

Recording a Custom Mix to a CD

Besides the Counting Crows' *August and Everything After* and Tom Waits's *Swordfish Trombones,* I haven't encountered a CD that contains more than three songs I like. Fortunately, with a CD-R or CD-RW drive and the right program, you can pull one or more of your favorite songs off each CD to create and record your own custom mix to a blank CD. You can even add to the mix MP3 clips you downloaded from the Internet.

Again, several programs on the market let you copy tracks from one CD to another and burn MP3 clips to CDs, but Adaptec's Easy CD Creator is one of the cleanest tools for the job. As shown in the following figure, Easy CD Creator makes recording tracks as easy as copying files in Windows Explorer.

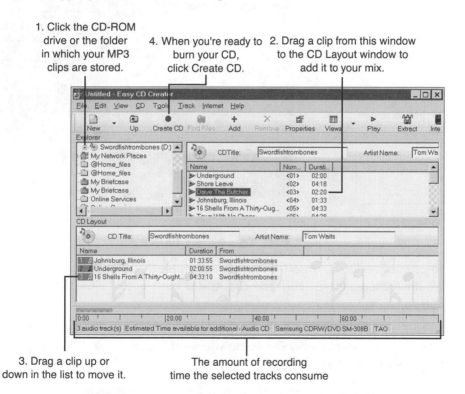

Adaptec's Easy CD Creator can burn MP3 clips and CD tracks to a blank CD.

After you click the button to create your CD, the program displays onscreen instructions telling you which CDs to insert.

If you didn't run out and buy Adaptec's Easy CD Creator after reading about how wonderful it is, Windows Media Player can do a fine job of transferring tracks to a CD-R or CD-RW disc. First, record the desired tracks and copy them to a separate playlist, as explained earlier in this chapter. Then insert the disc, open Media Player's **File** menu and choose **Copy to CD.** This displays the Playlists dialog box, as shown in the following figure. Click the playlist that has the audio tracks you want to write to the disc, and then click **OK.**

Windows Media Player can write the tracks in a playlist to a disc.

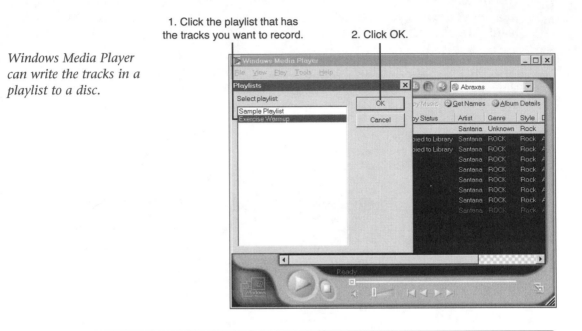

1. Click the playlist that has the tracks you want to record.

2. Click OK.

The Least You Need to Know

➤ To play an audio CD, insert it into your computer's CD-ROM drive, run Windows Media Player, click the **CD Audio** button, and click the **Play** button.

➤ To copy tracks from the CD to the Windows Media Library, be sure a check mark appears next to only the tracks you want recorded, and then click the **Copy Music** button.

➤ To create a new playlist in Media Player, click the **Media Library** button and then click the **New playlist** button.

➤ Go to www.mp3.com for a wide selection of MP3 music clips and links to players, rippers, and MP3 gear.

➤ To take your tunes on the road, copy them to a portable MP3 player.

➤ You can use a CD burner program, such as Adaptec's Easy CD Creator, to duplicate audio CDs or to copy MP3 clips to a blank CD to create your own mix.

Chapter 29

Managing Your Life with a Palm Computer

> **In This Chapter**
>
> ➤ Understanding handheld and pocket computers
>
> ➤ Entering commands and options with a stylus
>
> ➤ "Typing" on a handheld computer
>
> ➤ Transferring data between your desktop and handheld computers
>
> ➤ Downloading additional software for your handheld computer

Before I purchased my first handheld computer, I wasn't the most organized person. I had an address book in a kitchen drawer, a phone list taped to the inside of one of my kitchen cabinets, a list of birthdays and anniversaries on the refrigerator, a calendar on the wall, a calendar in my pocket, a calculator that never was where I thought it would be, and a pocketful of lists and Post-it Notes. Now I carry all this stuff around on a handheld computer that's slightly larger than my wallet. If you're interested in trading in your loose collection of addresses, dates, and notes for a compact personal organizer, read on.

Understanding Subcompact Computers

In the 1990s, you weren't considered a "professional" unless you lugged around a Franklin Day Planner packed with all the information you needed to survive your professional and personal life. Many people still rely on these dinosaurs to stay organized, but these day planners are heavy and bulky and require a great deal of manual labor. And if you want to transfer your handwritten notes or contact information to your computer later, you must reenter all the information.

Subcompact computers (palm, handheld, and pocket computers) are essentially condensed, computerized day planners. Most come complete with their own software, including an address book, calculator, calendar, to-do list, e-mail program, and memo pad. Using a special stylus that is included with the handheld device, you tap a touch screen to run programs and select menu commands, as shown in the following figure. You also use the stylus to jot down notes or tap the keys of an onscreen typewriter to enter text.

Tap and draw on the touch screen to enter commands and "type."

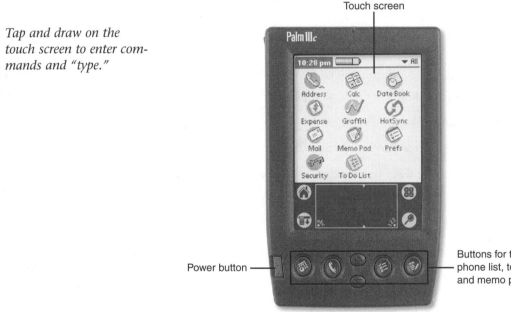

If you prefer to type appointments and contact information on your desktop computer, you can enter the information on your desktop computer and then *synchronize* your handheld device with the desktop computer to copy the information. You can also copy information from your handheld device to your desktop computer to use as a backup, just in case you ever lose your handheld device. Most handheld devices include a *cradle*, which plugs into a power source and connects to a serial or USB port on a desktop computer. You plug the handheld device into the cradle to recharge its battery, install software, and synchronize data between the handheld and desktop computers.

Handheld computers are much more than overpriced day planners. With additional software and add-on devices, you can use your mini-computer to play games, download stock quotes, browse the Web, scan business cards, read the latest news, navigate roads and highways, and even take photos! Most subcompact computers also have an infrared port that lets you beam files and software from one compact computer to another, making it easy for you and your friends and colleagues to share programs and files.

Palm Data Entry 101

"Typing" on a handheld device isn't the most intuitive activity. You usually have two options. You can scribble characters in the corner of the screen and trust that the handwriting recognition feature will transform your chicken scratching accurately into typewritten text. Or, you can tap the **abc** dot on the screen to display an on-screen keyboard and then hunt and peck to "type" onscreen.

I prefer the hunt-and-peck technique, but if you want to try your hand at scribbling on the screen, you should know what's involved. Handheld devices typically set aside a 1-by-2-inch portion of the screen for you to scribble on. That's just enough room to write a single character or numeral. And, unlike most handwriting recognition software, which you can train to interpret your handwriting, most handheld devices require that you train yourself to write properly.

In most cases, you must define each character with a single stroke of the stylus. For example, to type an "A," you place the stylus where you want the bottom-left leg of the "A" to start, and then you drag the stylus up to the top of the "A" and then down to the bottom of the right leg. You don't draw the crossbar. Likewise, you don't draw the crossbar on an "F." The following figure shows the alphabet quick reference for drawing characters on a Palm computer.

Inside Tip

Some handheld and pocket computers offer an optional keyboard into which you can plug the device.

Connecting Your Palm Computer to Your Desktop Computer

Whether you hunt and peck or scribble on the screen, typing on a handheld or pocket computer is no fun. You can jot down your grocery list on a piece of paper in much less time than you can type it on a handheld computer.

You must train yourself to jot down notes on a handheld computer.

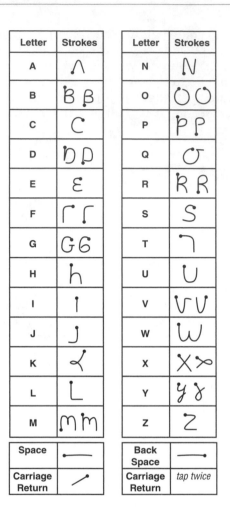

Letter	Strokes	Letter	Strokes
A	∧	N	N
B	B B	O	O O
C	C	P	P P
D	D D	Q	σ
E	ε	R	R R
F	ſ ſ	S	S
G	G 6	T	⌐
H	h	U	U
I	↑	V	∨∨
J	J	W	W
K	≺	X	X⤳
L	L	Y	y ɣ
M	m m	Z	Z
Space	•—	Back Space	—•
Carriage Return	⟋	Carriage Return	*tap twice*

Fortunately, these subcompact computers come with desktop software that you can use to enter your dates, contact information, to-do lists, and other information, as shown in the following figure. If you use a popular personal information manager (PIM), such as Microsoft Office, you can use the PIM instead of the handheld computer's desktop software to enter the information.

After you have entered the information you want to transfer to your portable device, or after you enter information on your portable device that you want to transfer to your desktop computer, you must connect the computers and *synchronize* the data. Although the process differs depending on the connection type and the software you're using, the following steps provide an overview:

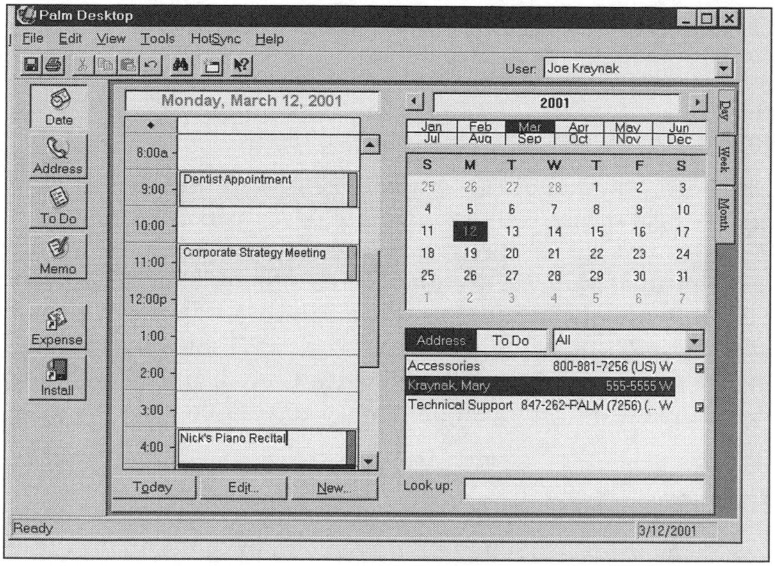

The Palm IIIc includes desktop software for entering appointments, events, to-do lists, and other information.

1. Plug your portable device into its cradle.

2. Start the synchronization manager if it is not already running. (Most handheld devices run the synchronization manager in the background after you install the desktop software and display an icon for the synchronization manager in the Windows system tray.)

3. Make sure the synchronization manager is set up for a local connection (via the cradle). (Most handheld devices allow you to synchronize locally, via modem, or over a network.)

4. Press the synchronization button on the cradle or enter the command in the synchronization dialog box for initiating the synchronization. The synchronization manager typically displays the progress of the operation, as shown in the following figure.

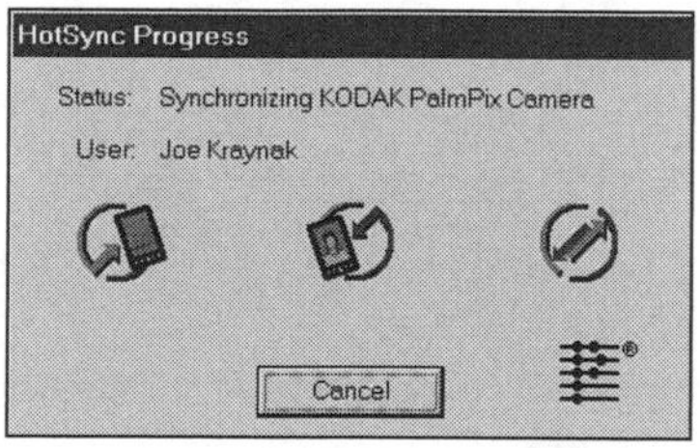

The synchronization manager displays the progress of the synchronization operation.

339

Getting Additional Software and Games

How would you like to play chess on your handheld? View photos of your family and friends? Calculate loan payments? Create your own flash cards? Keep track of movies you want to see? Record your golf scores and track your handicap?

With some additional software, your handheld computer can do all this and much more. In fact, the Palm handheld device is so popular that developers have created hundreds of shareware programs designed specifically for Palm computers. To check out a great collection of Palm shareware, use your desktop computer to go to ZDNet at www.zdnet.com, click the **Downloads** link, and click the **Palm OS** link (for Palm software) or the **CE & Pocket PC** link (for Windows CE and Pocket PC software). Click the link for the desired software category (Utilities, Productivity, Games, and so on) and follow the trail of links to download the desired program(s) to your desktop computer.

Installing Add-On Programs

If the program you downloaded is in a compressed format, you must decompress the program, as explained in Chapter 23, "Finding and Playing Cool Games," in the section "Getting Free Games from the Web." After you decompress the program, you can use your handheld computer's installation utility (on your desktop computer) to transfer the program to your handheld computer. Although the steps vary depending on the handheld computer you have, the following steps show how easy the process is on a Palm computer:

1. Plug your portable device into its cradle.

2. On your desktop computer, open the Windows **Start** menu, point to **Programs, Palm Desktop,** and click **Install Tool.**

3. Click the **Add** button. The Open dialog box appears, showing the contents of the C:\Palm\ Add-ons folder on your desktop computer.

4. Change to the drive and folder that store the program file you want to install, and click the program's name.

5. Click the **Open** button. The Install Tool displays the name of the selected program in the list of programs it will install, as shown in the following figure.

6. Repeat steps 3 through 5 to install additional programs.

7. Click the **Done** button. A dialog box appears, informing you that the program will be installed the next time you synchronize your Palm and desktop computers.

Inside Tip

If your handheld computer came with a CD, check the CD for additional programs. Palm computers and other handheld and pocket computers typically come with some add-on programs that are not installed on the computer.

8. Synchronize your Palm and desktop computers, as explained earlier in this chapter.

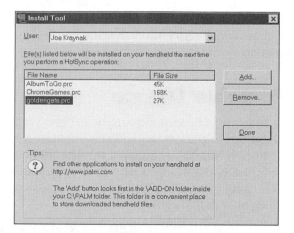

Palm's Install Tool can transfer Palm OS programs from your desktop computer to your Palm computer.

Beaming Programs and Data over an Infrared Connection

Most handheld computers have a built-in infrared port that can establish a wireless connection with other handheld computers over short distances (about 1 meter). This provides a convenient way to exchange data between handheld computers. If you and a business associate have compatible handheld computers, for instance, you can exchange contact information electronically rather than by trading business cards. You can even share programs by beaming a program from one handheld device to another.

To beam a record, file, or program, first you point the infrared ports on the two devices directly at each other. The ports should be about 4 to 36 inches apart. You then set up one of the handheld computers to receive the beamed information. On a Palm computer, you simply point the infrared port at the infrared port on the other Palm computer and turn on the computers. When the other Palm computer starts sending the data, a dialog box appears on the receiving computer, prompting you to specify where you want the data or program filed.

The steps for beaming data vary, depending on the handheld operating system you're using and the type of data you're sending. To beam a business

Whoa!

Not all handheld and pocket computers are as expandable as others. The newer portable devices have an open slot that acts as a serial port into which you can plug add-on devices. Before you purchase a handheld device, find out how add-on devices connect to it and determine the types of add-on devices that are available.

card from a Palm IIIc, for example, you first display the address book entry you want to beam and then open the **Record** menu and tap the **Beam Business Card** command. To beam a program, you open the **App** menu, click **Beam**, click the name of the program you want to beam, and click **Beam.** As soon as you give the **Beam** command, the sending computer searches for a recipient beam, establishes a connection, and sends the record, file, or program to the receiving computer.

Accessorizing Your Portable Device

Some of the coolest features of a subcompact computer are the gadgets you can purchase to accessorize and add capabilities to the device. You can purchase a full-size keyboard to make typing a little more comfortable, attach a wireless modem so that you can check your e-mail on the road, add a business card scanner to quickly add new contacts to your address book, plug in a GPS (global positioning system) to help you navigate the globe, or even slip on a digital camera.

The best way to shop around for the latest selection of gadgets and gizmos is to hit the Web. For Palm gadgets, start at Palm's Web site at www.palm.com, but don't purchase anything just yet. If you find something you like, go to clnet at www.cnet.com and search for the product by name. This returns a list of online stores that offer the same product for the lowest prices. During the writing of this chapter, I found a PalmPix snap-on camera from Kodak for $179 at one store and $84 at another. Be a savvy shopper.

The Least You Need to Know

➤ You enter text on a portable device by using an onscreen keyboard or by handwriting your entries on the touch screen.

➤ To ensure that your desktop computer and portable device have the same up-to-date data, you must synchronize the devices.

➤ To obtain additional software for your portable device, go to ZDNet at www.zdnet.com, click the **Downloads** link, and click the **Palm OS** link (for Palm software) or the **CE & Pocket PC** link (for Windows CE and Pocket PC software).

➤ After downloading and decompressing a program to your desktop computer, you must run your portable device's program installation utility to transfer the program to your portable device.

➤ You can beam records, folders, and programs from one portable device to another via their infrared ports.

➤ Many companies have developed add-on devices for handheld and pocket computers to allow them to perform additional tasks.

Making Your Computer Act Like a TV

Most computers are not cable-ready. They have no jack for connecting a TV cable or antenna. To add TV capabilities to a computer, you must install a TV tuner card, a circuit board that plugs into your computer's motherboard.

When shopping for a TV tuner card, don't buy the first card you see. If you have an older computer, use this purchase as an opportunity to upgrade your display card as well. With an ATI All-in-Wonder card, shown in the following figure, you can replace your old display card with a new card that offers faster video, TV tuner capabilities, and video capture support so that you can record and edit your video clips (as explained in the next chapter). If you have a newer computer, you don't need to shell out more money for a new display card, but consider buying a TV tuner card that includes a video capture port in case you decide to record and edit videos later.

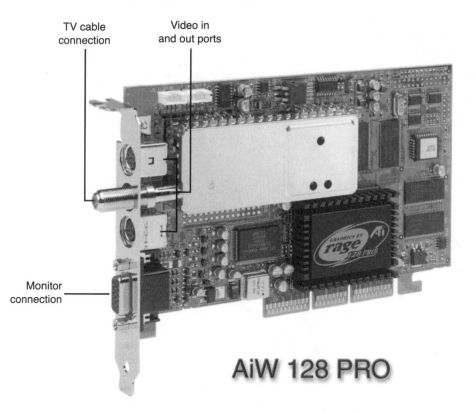

The ATI All-In-Wonder video card supports a monitor, camcorder and VCR input, and TV cable connections.

(Photo courtesy of ATI Technologies, Inc.)

Installing the video card is pretty easy, but if you've never installed a circuit board, obtain help from a friend or colleague who has experience. Carefully read and follow the installation instructions and safety precautions. The procedure typically consists of opening the system unit case, removing an expansion board cover from the back of the computer (one screw), and plugging the expansion board into an open expansion slot. The card should come with a cable that connects the audio output jack on the TV tuner card to the audio input jack on your sound card. Make the other cable connections as instructed in the installation guide.

Tuning in with Windows

Although your TV tuner probably came with its own program for flipping stations, Windows 98 and Windows Me include WebTV, an excellent program for flipping channels and controlling the TV window. WebTV also allows you to download programming information from the Web, placing a TV guide right on your screen, where you'll never misplace it.

WebTV is not installed during a typical Windows installation. To install WebTV, follow these steps:

1. Open the Windows **Start** menu, point to **Settings**, and click **Control Panel**.

2. Click or double-click the **Add/Remove Programs** icon.

3. Click the **Windows Setup** tab.

4. Click the plus sign next to **WebTV for Windows**.

5. Click **OK**.

6. When prompted, insert the Windows CD, and follow the onscreen instructions to complete the installation.

Inside Tip

You don't need a TV tuner card in order to get the TV listings for your area. If you have an Internet connection, you can use WebTV for Windows to download the listings.

After WebTV is installed, click the **Launch WebTV** icon in the Quick Launch toolbar to run it. WebTV runs through some standard introductory screens to welcome you to WebTV and explain some of its features. At the end of the introduction, WebTV prompts you to scan for channels. Click the **Scan** button. WebTV flips through the available stations and adds the numbers of any stations that provide signals of sufficient strength.

To preview a channel, click its number. WebTV displays the program in a small box in the upper-right corner of the screen. To display the channel in its own window, click **WATCH**, as shown in the following figure.

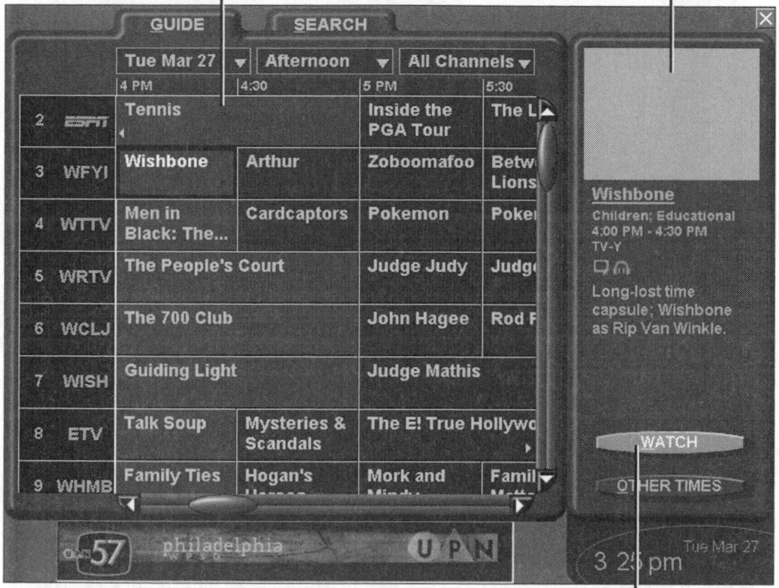

Click a channel to preview the program.　　　The program preview area.

GUIDE	SEARCH				✕

Tue Mar 27 ▼　Afternoon ▼　All Channels ▼

	4 PM	4:30	5 PM	5:30
2 ESPN	Tennis		Inside the PGA Tour	The L
3 WFYI	Wishbone	Arthur	Zoboomafoo	Betw Lions
4 WTTV	Men in Black: The...	Cardcaptors	Pokemon	Poke
5 WRTV	The People's Court		Judge Judy	Judg
6 WCLJ	The 700 Club		John Hagee	Rod F
7 WISH	Guiding Light		Judge Mathis	
8 ETV	Talk Soup	Mysteries & Scandals	The E! True Hollywo	
9 WHMB	Family Ties	Hogan's Heroes	Mork and Mindy	Famil Matt

Wishbone
Children; Educational
4:00 PM - 4:30 PM
TV-Y

Long-lost time
capsule; Wishbone
as Rip Van Winkle.

WATCH

OTHER TIMES

57　philadelphia　U P N

3 25 pm　Tue Mar 27

*WebTV displays an
electronic channel
changer.*

Click WATCH to display the program in its own window.

Can I Play Interactive Games?

If you have an Internet connection via modem or
cable, you can play along with contestants on interactive TV game shows, cast votes on news
shows and other programs that support online bal-
lots, and even chat with other viewers while
watching your favorite show. The following figure
shows an interactive TV show in action. As you
can see, you can cast your ballot by clicking **Poll**
or submit your opinion by clicking **E! Mail.**

Panic Attack!

If you receive an error message
concerning the display resolution, you might need to adjust
your display settings. Right-click
a blank area of the Windows
desktop and click **Properties.**
Click the **Settings** tab and set
the **Screen area** to **800×600**
and **Colors** to **High color.**
Click **OK** and restart the computer if necessary.

With WebTV for Windows and an Internet connection, you can interact with your favorite TV Shows.

(Screen shot courtesy of E! and WebTV)

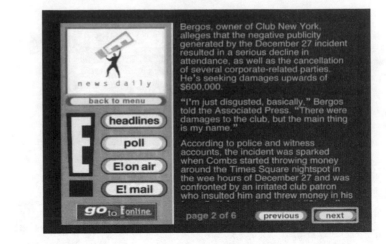

Playing DVD Videos on Your Computer

There's no trick to playing DVD videos on your computer assuming that it is equipped with a DVD drive. The DVD drive typically comes with a DVD video player that has its own set of onscreen controls. Simply run the DVD player, pop the DVD disc into your computer's DVD drive, and click the **Play** button as shown in the following figure. The only controls that might cause some confusion are the chapter buttons (**Previous Chapter** and **Next Chapter**). Just think of a chapter as a scene. To move to the previous scene, click the **Previous Chapter** (or **Backward Chapter**) button; to move to the next scene, click the **Next Chapter** (or **Forward Chapter**) button.

Each DVD video has a built-in menu system for choosing a particular scene (chapter), viewing outtakes and deleted scenes, flipping through production photos, listening to interviews, and accessing other bonus material on the disc. The procedure for accessing the menu varies, depending on the DVD player you're using. If you see no obvious button or command for displaying the menu, try right-clicking the movie. This should display a context menu with a command for viewing the DVD's menu.

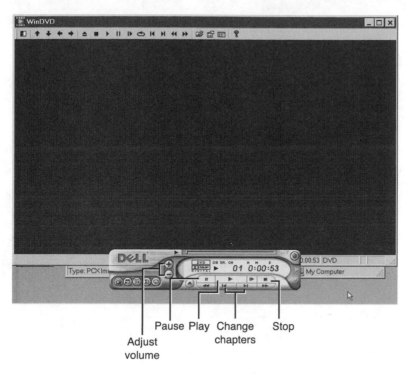

A DVD video player displays onscreen controls for playing and pausing the video.

Adjust
volume

Pause Play Change Stop
chapters

The Least You Need to Know

➤ To tune in television stations, your computer needs a TV tuner card.

➤ To allow the computer to output the audio as well as the video portion of a TV show, you must connect the audio-out jack on the TV tuner card to the audio-in jack on the sound card.

➤ If your TV tuner did not come with its own tuning software, use WebTV for Windows to flip channels.

➤ To take advantage of interactive TV shows, your computer must have an Internet connection.

➤ To play a DVD video, run your DVD player, insert the DVD disc into your DVD drive, and click the **Play** button.

Chapter 31

Playing Film Editor with Digital Video

In This Chapter

➤ Transferring video from a camcorder or VCR to your computer

➤ Working with digital camcorders

➤ Editing your video recordings

➤ Adding professional transitions between video clips

➤ Recording video clips to CDs or VHS tapes

Back in the 1960s and 1970s, 8mm film was the medium of choice for amateur movie makers. I know people who still have boxes of 8mm film cans in their attics and basements. In the 1980s and 1990s, people traded in their 8mm cameras and projectors for VHS and 8mm camcorders. These relatively compact devices made it easy to record video and play it back on a television set, but the tapes were still bulky, and you had to fast-forward through several minutes of tape to find your favorite clips. The new millennium has introduced a new video technology, digital video, allowing us to transfer, edit, and catalog our video clips using a computer. In this chapter, you learn how to take advantage of digital video.

What You Need to Get Started

You can approach digital video from two different directions, depending on how much you have invested in an older camcorder, how many old tapes you have, and how much money you're willing to spend. If you don't have a camcorder or old tapes and you have some cash on hand, purchase a digital camcorder and start filming. Digital camcorders record video in a much higher resolution than analog VHS or 8mm camcorders, and the digital clips won't lose quality when copied to your computer. (The quality of video clips recorded with analog camcorders suffers when they are converted from an analog to a digital format.)

When shopping for a digital camcorder, you need to think about how you will connect the camcorder to your computer. Most digital camcorders have an *IEEE-1394* (FireWire) or USB connector. If your computer does not have an IEEE-1394 or USB port, you need to install an expansion board to add the required port.

Tech Term

IEEE-1394 is a standard for transferring data between devices very quickly—at a rate of 400Mbps (megabits per second). Compare that to the USB standard of 12Mbps, and you can see why IEEE-1394 is the preferred method of transferring video to a computer. IEEE-1394 goes by many names, the most common of which is Apple's FireWire. You might also see IEEE-1394 labeled i.link or Lynx.

If you already have an analog camcorder and plenty of old tapes, or if your computer budget is already strained, consider adding a video capture device to your computer. You have several options here. The most convenient way to go is to purchase an external unit that connects to your computer's parallel, USB, or IEEE-1394 port. The following figure shows the Dazzle Hollywood DV-Bridge. Note that you plug the cables from the camcorder or VCR into the jacks on the front of the unit. For a more permanent addition, purchase a video capture board, which plugs into an expansion slot inside your computer.

Video capture boards and external units have special ports that let you connect your camcorder to your computer. They typically capture video at a rate of 15 or more frames per second, and they do a fairly good job of converting your analog clips into a digital format. If you're looking for a way to convert your collection of old camcorder or VHS tapes into a digital format and store them on CDs, this is the way to go.

An analog-to-digital converter lets you connect a camcorder or VCR to your computer.

(Photo courtesy of Dazzle, Inc.)

Setting Up Your Audio-Video Equipment

If you're preparing to record and edit video from a digital camcorder, there's not much to setting up your equipment. You simply connect the USB or IEEE-1394 cable to the USB or IEEE-1394 ports on the camera and your computer, and you're ready to roll.

If you're recording from a VCR or analog camcorder, on the other hand, the setup is a bit more time-consuming. You must first install the video capture device and then connect the VCR or camcorder using several cables. The procedure for installing the video capture card or external device varies. The setup might be as simple as plugging the external device into your computer's USB port, or it might require you to install an expansion board inside the system unit. Read and follow the instructions and safety precautions that came with the card or device.

After the video capture device is installed, you can connect your VCR or camcorder to it. The audio and video connections vary, depending on the video capture card, the cables included with it, and the VCR or camcorder. On an external unit, such as Dazzle's Hollywood DV-Bridge, the jacks are color-coded and match up with the standard A/V jacks found on most camcorders and VCRs.

Video capture cards typically have a single A/V input jack for audio and video input. You need a *four-headed input adapter* to make the necessary connections. This adapter contains a single plug for the A/V input jack on your video capture card and four connectors for the camera: one for left audio, one for right audio, one for S-video, and one for composite video. You use either the S-video or composite video connector, depending on the camera. (S-video produces higher-quality recordings.) See the following figure.

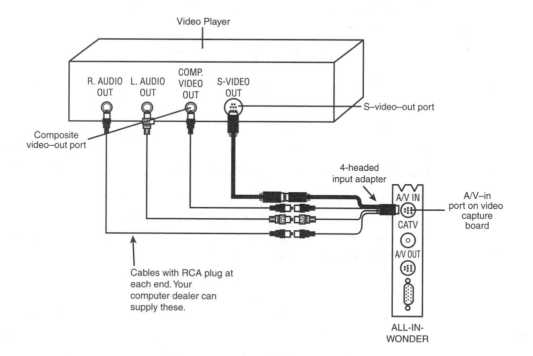

Use the proper cables to connect the video player to the A/V-in port on your video capture card.

Capturing and Saving Your Clips

Your digital camcorder or video capture device probably came with its own program for recording and editing your video footage. Most of these programs are similar and follow the same overall procedure for recording and editing video. Here's a quick overview of the process:

1. Connect your camcorder or VCR to the video capture device.

2. Run your video recording program and enter the command to start recording.

3. Use your camcorder or VCR controls to play the video you want to record.

4. When you're ready to stop recording, enter the command to stop recording, and then press the **Stop** button on the camcorder or VCR. The video recording program chops the recording into *clips* to make them more manageable. It displays a thumbnail view of each clip.

5. Trim the clips. You can trim sections of any clip.

6. Arrange the clips in the order in which you want them played.

7. Add background music.

8. Add transitions between clips. For example, you can have a clip fade out at the end and fade into the next clip.

9. Save your movie to your hard drive.

10. Record your movie to a CD or tape or e-mail the movie clip.

Windows Me includes its own video recording and editing software (Windows Movie Maker), so let's use it to run through the basics. If you have Windows Me, open the **Start, Programs, Accessories** menu, and then click **Windows Movie Maker**. Windows Movie Maker appears, as shown in the following figure. If you don't have Movie Maker, read along to learn the basics.

To start recording clips in Movie Maker, follow these steps:

1. Connect your VCR or camcorder to the video capture device.

2. In Movie Maker, click the **Record** button. The Record dialog box appears.

3. Open the **Record** drop-down list, and choose the medium you want to record: **Audio and Video**, **Video Only**, or **Audio Only**.

4. Use the controls on your VCR or camcorder to locate the beginning of the clip you want to record.

5. Click the **Record** button. "Recording" blinks to indicate that Movie Maker is now recording.

6. Use the controls on your VCR or camcorder to play the clip. As you play the clip, Movie Maker displays it onscreen.

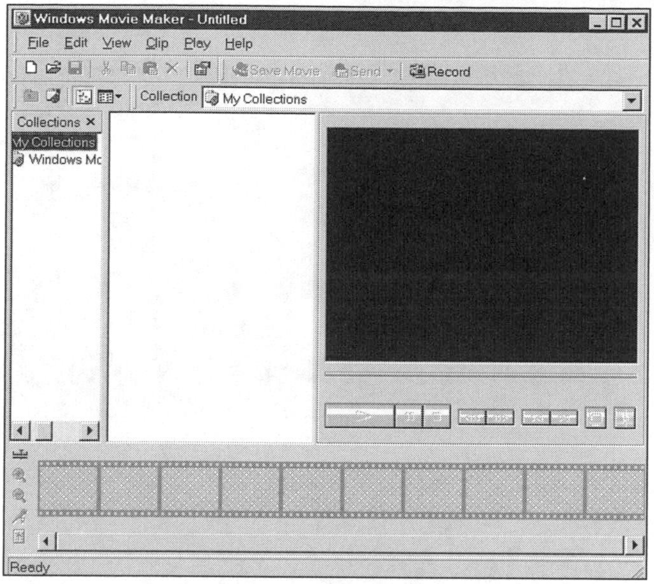

Windows Movie Maker.

7. When you have reached the end of the clip, click the **Stop** button to stop recording, and press the **Stop** button on your VCR or camcorder. A dialog box appears, prompting you to save your movie.

8. Choose the folder in which you want your movie saved, type a name for the movie in the **File Name** box, and click **Save**. Movie Maker automatically chops the footage you recorded into smaller clips to make them more manageable. It also displays a thumbnail view of each clip, as shown in the following figure.

9. If desired, repeat steps 2 through 7 to add additional film footage to this movie. (You don't need to perform step 8 again, because you already saved your file. Open the **File** menu and select **Save** at any time to save your changes.)

The procedure for recording from a tape in a digital video (DV) camcorder is a little different, because you can control the camera from Movie Maker. Simply connect the DV camcorder to your computer and set the mode to play your video. When the Windows Movie Maker dialog box appears, click **Begin recording my video from the current position on my tape,** and then click **OK**. Use the controls in the **Digital video camera controls** area to play and record the tape.

355

Movie clips   Preview area

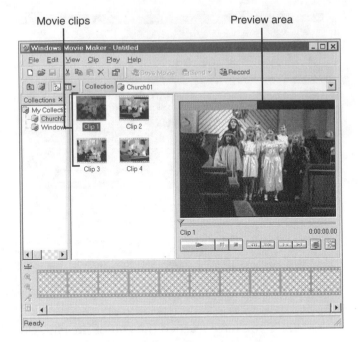

Windows Movie Maker chops your film footage into smaller clips.

Splicing Your Clips into a Full-Length Movie

As soon as you have a few clips to work with, you're ready to start your new career as a professional film editor, cutting undesirable footage, trimming clips, and rearranging clips to create your own feature film. The editing procedure is surprisingly simple. You drag and drop thumbnails of your clips onto the virtual film strip at the bottom of the Movie Maker window, as shown in the following figure.

If a portion of a particular clip is out of focus or contains material you do not want to include in your video, you can trim the clip. This process consists of designating a start and end trim point. Movie Player then cuts the video between those two points. Here's what you do:

1. Click the clip you want to trim.

2. Open the **Play** menu and click **Play/Pause**. Movie Player starts playing the clip.

3. When the clip gets to the point at which you want to trim it, open the **Clip** menu and click **Set Start Trim Point**. Movie Player marks the starting trim point and continues to play the clip.

4. When the clip gets to the point at which you want to stop trimming, open the **Clip** menu and click **Set End Trim Point**. Movie Player chops the designated section from the clip.

Drag a clip from this
list to the film strip.

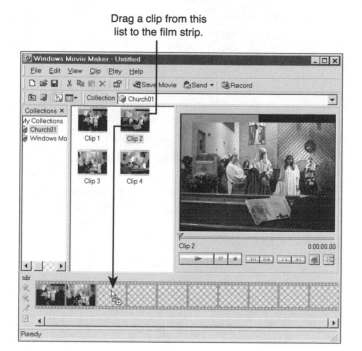

Drag and drop your clips onto the film strip.

Inside Tip

You can add a title frame to your video. Choose **Start, Programs, Accessories, Paint** to run the Windows graphics program. Open the **Image** menu and click **Attributes.** Type 320 for the width and 240 for the height. Make sure **Pixels** is selected under **Units,** and then click **OK.** Use Paint to draw your title frame, and then save it as a .BMP graphics file. Use the **File, Import** command in Movie Maker to bring the file into Movie Maker, and then drag it to the first frame on the film strip.

Adding an Audio Background

To give your video another dimension, consider recording some background music or narration. To record narration, open the **View** menu and click **Timeline.** Open the **File** menu and click **Record Narration.** Click the **Record** button and start talking into

Panic Attack!

Movie Maker might have trouble importing audio clips recorded with Windows Media Player. If you receive error messages when trying to import these clips, try recording your audio clips with a different CD ripper.

your microphone. When you're finished, click **Stop** and then name and save your narration.

The easiest way to add background music, assuming you have a CD-ROM drive, is to record tracks from your audio CDs or download some MP3 audio clips, as explained in Chapter 28, "Playing Digitized Music Clips." You can then use Movie Maker's **File, Import** command to import the audio clips into Movie Maker.

After you have imported audio clips into Movie Player, adding them to your video is a snap. First, display the timeline by opening the **View** menu and selecting **Timeline**. Next, drag and drop the desired audio clip over the audio bar, as shown in the following figure.

Drag and drop your audio clips onto the audio bar.

Drag an audio clip from this list to the audio bar.

Smoothing Out Your Transitions

When you splice clips and trim sections of clips, some of the transitions might seem a little abrupt and surreal. To reduce the shock, add smooth transitions between clips. With Movie Maker, you can create a transition that makes the end of one clip fade out and the beginning of the next clip fade in. (Other video recording programs feature collections of cool transitions.)

To create a transition, you overlap the two clips between which you want the fade effect. First, make sure you're in Timeline view; open the **View** menu and click **Timeline.** In the timeline, drag the second of the two clips to the left so that it slightly overlaps the previous clip. You also can create a transition between audio clips by overlapping them in the audio bar. To preview your movie with the added transitions, open the **Play** menu and click **Play Entire Storyboard/Timeline.** To view the movie in full-screen mode, open the **Play** menu and click **Full Screen.**

Saving Your Movie

When your movie is complete, save it to your computer's hard drive. During the save operation, Movie Maker transforms your collection of clips into a single Movie Maker file, which you can then e-mail, save to a Web server, or copy to a CD (assuming you have a CD-R or CD-RW drive). To save your movie, follow these steps:

1. Open the **File** menu and click **Save Movie.**

2. Open the **Setting** drop-down list and select the desired quality setting. **Medium Quality** is recommended for most purposes.

3. In the **Display Information** area, enter the information you want people to see when they open the file in Windows Media Player.

4. Click **OK.** The Save As dialog box appears, prompting you to name the file and pick a folder.

5. Select the drive and folder in which you want to save the file.

6. Click in the **File Name** text box and type a name for the file.

7. Click the **Save** button. The Windows Movie Maker dialog box appears, asking if you want to view your movie in Media Player.

8. Click **Yes** to play the movie or **No** to skip this step.

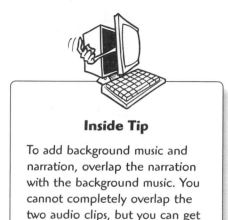

Inside Tip

To add background music and narration, overlap the narration with the background music. You cannot completely overlap the two audio clips, but you can get pretty close.

Sharing Your Movies with Friends and Relatives

Movie Maker provides several options for sharing your movies with others. If you have a CD-R or CD-RW drive, you can copy the movie file you created in the preceding section to a CD. Anyone with a computer, a CD-ROM drive, Windows 95 or a later version, and a multimedia player, such as Windows Media Player, can watch the movie on his or her computer. You can also e-mail your movie as an attachment or save it to a Web server, where people can download it and view it online. Simply open Movie Maker's **File** menu, point to **Send Movie To**, and click **E-Mail** or **Web Server**.

If you want to copy your movie to a VHS tape to share it with people who don't have computers, good luck. Most video recording devices and programs are much better at pulling video off tapes than recording edited video back to tapes. If your video capture card has an A/V output port, you can connect the card to a VCR to record to tape or a TV set that has RCA jacks. To make the connections, you need an adapter that plugs into the A/V output port on the video capture board and that has the proper connectors for the S-video-in or composite-in jacks on your VCR or TV set. See the following figure.

Some video capture cards allow you to output recorded clips to a TV set or VCR.

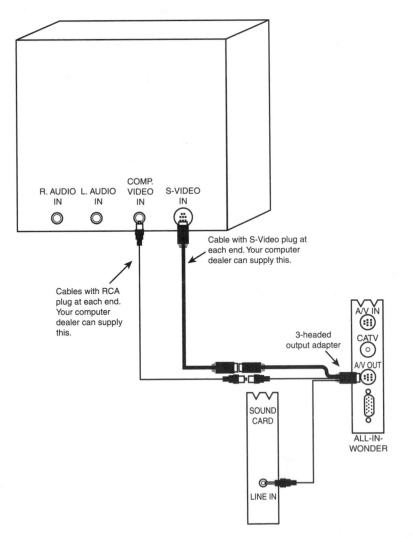

Now that you've made the physical connection between the computer and the VCR or TV, how do you play the video? Movie Maker has no command for sending the video to a VCR or TV. However, if your video card has an option for using a TV as a display device, here's a little trick you can do to record your movie on a tape using your VCR:

1. Connect your VCR to the A/V-out port on your video card.

2. Right-click a blank area of the Windows desktop and click **Properties.**

3. Click the **Settings** tab and then click the **Advanced** button. This displays advanced options for your particular video card.

4. If you see a **Television** option, turn it on. If no **Television** option is available, this feature might not be available for your video card. Check the card's documentation to be sure.

5. Run Windows Media Player, as explained in Chapter 28.

6. Use the **File, Open** command to open the movie file you created.

7. Press the **Record** button on your VCR, and then perform the next two steps as quickly as possible.

8. Click Media Player's **Play** button.

9. Press **Alt+Enter** to change to full-screen mode.

Panic Attack!

Some video cards have a very odd configuration. Some cards have a video–out connector that hooks up to the video–in port on a VCR, but the audio–out jack plugs into the sound card on a computer. So you play the video into the VCR and the audio into the computer, making it impossible to record both the audio and video portions to a tape!

The Least You Need to Know

➤ You can connect a digital camcorder directly to your computer via an IEEE-1394 port.

➤ To connect an analog camcorder or VCR to your computer, you must install an internal video capture card or an external video capture device.

➤ To run Windows Movie Maker, open the **Start** menu, point to **Programs** and then **Accessories,** and then click **Windows Movie Maker.**

➤ To start recording video in Movie Maker, click the **Record** button.

➤ To create transitions between video clips, drag the clips on the timeline to the left to make them overlap.

➤ To save your movie as a file, open the **File** menu and click **Save Movie.**

Chapter 32

Upgrading for Voice Commands and Dictation

In This Chapter

➤ Equipping your computer for speech recognition

➤ Installing speech recognition software

➤ Training the software to understand your spoken words and commands

➤ Look, Ma, no hands—typing via dictation

➤ Entering commands without touching your keyboard or mouse

Are you a hunt-and-peck typist? Are you looking for a more efficient way to enter text? Are you concerned about carpal tunnel syndrome? If you answered "Yes" to any of these questions, consider installing speech recognition software. With a good microphone and the right program, your computer can recognize voice commands and take dictation. Instead of clicking through a stack of menus and dialog boxes to get what you want, you simply *tell* your computer what to do, and it carries out your every command. Do you want this document printed? Say, "Click File, click Print, click OK," and your printer spits out the document. Do you need to type a document while you're getting your weekly manicure? Switch to dictation mode and start talking. In this chapter, you learn how to set up your computer and train it to recognize your voice and carry out your commands.

What You Need to Get Started

Although you don't need a professional recording studio to take advantage of speech recognition, you do need a fairly powerful computer equipped with a sound card and a high-quality microphone. The following checklist describes the minimum requirements for a typical speech recognition program. Some programs have additional requirements.

> ➤ **Processor.** A Pentium 200MHz or faster or an equivalent processor (such as an AMD K6-3). Speech recognition requires a fairly powerful processor. On a slower computer, the speech recognition software will bog down the computer.

> ➤ **Memory.** 64MB of RAM. Don't even try to run speech recognition if your system has 32MB of RAM or less.

> ➤ **Sound card.** Most computers come equipped with a 16-bit SoundBlaster-compatible sound card or better. A 16-bit sound card is sufficient for voice commands and dictation.

> ➤ **Close-talk microphone.** Your Karaoke microphone might work fine for belting out a few bars of "Let It Be," but it's probably not the best choice for speech recognition. You need a close-talk microphone that's designed to block out background noise. Otherwise, your speech recognition software won't be able to understand a word you say. If your system has a built-in microphone or a microphone that sits on your desk, you must buy a new microphone that can handle dictation.

Inside Tip

Get a microphone with a head-set mount, and position the microphone about one inch from the corner of your mouth. Don't position the microphone directly in front of your mouth, or your breathing might be interpreted as speech. Try to mount the microphone in the same position each time you use it.

"Testing, One, Two, Three": Checking Your Sound System

Before you start talking to your computer, you should ensure that your sound system is working properly. First, make sure none of your devices are muted or have their volume turned way down in Windows. For details, refer to "Adjusting the Volume" in Chapter 6, "Making Your Computer Play Cool Sounds."

Now, plug your close-talk microphone into your sound card's microphone jack, and test your microphone to see whether it's working. Open the Windows **Start** menu and point to **Programs, Accessories, Entertainment, Sound Recorder.** This starts the Windows audio recorder. Click the **Record** button (the one with the big red dot on it) and say a few words into your microphone. Then click the **Stop** button (the square block next to the **Record** button) and click the **Play** button (the single pointer). If you hear your computer talking back to you in your own voice (through its speakers), your microphone is working properly.

If you don't hear your voice, check the following:

➤ Make sure your microphone and speakers are plugged in to the correct jacks on your sound card. It's easy to get the connections mixed up.

➤ If your sound card has a volume control, make sure it's cranked up.

➤ If your microphone has a power switch, make sure the switch is in the on position. (Some close-talk microphones have an on/off switch and a volume control on the cable.)

➤ If your speakers have a power switch, make sure the switch is in the on position.

➤ If your speakers have a volume control, make sure the volume is turned up.

Installing Your Speech Recognition Software

Of course, before you can start barking orders at your computer, you must install a speech recognition program. Dragon NaturallySpeaking and IBM ViaVoice are the market leaders in this area, and both programs offer excellent voice command and dictation features. The examples in this chapter use NaturallySpeaking, but the steps you take to train the software and use it are similar in all speech recognition software.

To install the software, follow the same steps you would to install any program. (See Chapter 9, "Installing and Removing Programs.") After you install the program, or the first time you run it, the program leads you through a brief training session, as explained in the following section.

Training the Software to Recognize Your Voice

To achieve success with speech recognition, you must train the program to recognize your voice and train yourself to speak clearly and consistently into the microphone. If you mumble through the training session, don't expect the speech recognition feature to translate your grunts into coherent text. That having been said, let's start the training session.

If you just installed the program and the training dialog box is onscreen, you can begin immediately. If the training dialog box is not onscreen, run your speech recognition program and then enter the command for starting a training session. (Most programs allow you to run through the training program at any time to fine-tune it or to train it for multiple users.)

The training utility typically consists of a two-step process. The first step leads you through the process of positioning the microphone correctly. The second step prompts you to read a script into the microphone, as shown in the following figure, so that the program can "learn" how you pronounce certain words and sounds. The entire training session takes 30 to 45 minutes. Here are some tips to make the training session a little more successful:

➤ Shut yourself in a quiet room, turn off the radio, unplug the phone, and tell your roomies to leave you alone for an hour.

➤ Speak in a level tone. Don't whisper, yell, or use a great deal of intonation.

➤ Read the sentences at a consistent rate of speed. Don't pause between words; the speech recognition program can translate phrases more accurately than single words.

➤ Articulate (sound out) the words clearly, but don't go overboard. The speech recognition feature has an easier time if you say "enunciate" as you normally would rather than saying "*EEE-nun-seee-ate.*"

➤ Keep the microphone in a consistent position, no matter how much the headset tries to slide around.

During the training session, you read a script aloud.

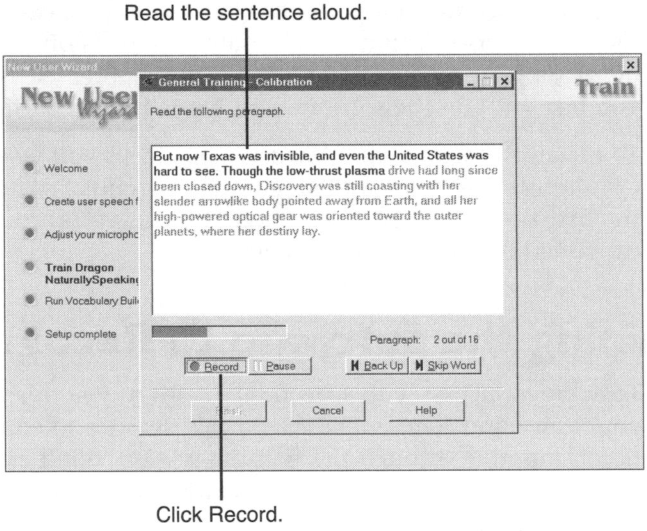

Read the sentence aloud.

New User Wizard

New User

● Welcome

● Create user speech

● Adjust your microphc

● **Train Dragon NaturallySpeakin**

● Run Vocabulary Buil

● Setup complete

Train

General Training - Calibration

Read the following paragraph.

But now Texas was invisible, and even the United States was hard to see. Though the low-thrust plasma drive had long since been closed down, Discovery was still coasting with her slender arrowlike body pointed away from Earth, and all her high-powered optical gear was oriented toward the outer planets, where her destiny lay.

Paragraph: 2 out of 16

◉ Record   ‖ Pause   ⏮ Back Up ⏭ Skip Word

Cancel   Help

Click Record.

If you share a computer with other users, a computer trained for your voice obviously will be less responsive to other voices. Fortunately, each user can train speech recognition for his or her own voice by creating a separate profile, as shown in the following figure. After you have set up two or more recognition profiles, you can switch from one profile to another. To set the program to recognize your voice, enter the command to switch profiles, and then click your user name and click **OK**.

Create a separate profile for each person who uses the computer.

No-Hands Typing with Dictation

After you have trained speech recognition, it's a snap to use this feature to convert your spoken words into typed text. Here's what you do:

1. Strap on your microphone and adjust the microphone to place it in the same position as you had it during the training session.

2. Click the **Start** menu, point to **Programs**, and click the command for running your speech recognition program. This typically displays a toolbar or an icon in the Windows taskbar for accessing program options.

3. Start the program in which you want to type. For example, choose **Start**, **Programs**, **Accessories**, **WordPad** to type in the Windows word processing program.

4. Enter the command for turning the microphone and dictation feature on. In NaturallySpeaking, you click the microphone icon on the Windows taskbar to toggle the microphone on or off. (If your microphone has a switch on it, make sure it is in the on position, too.)

5. Click inside the window where you want your text to appear.

6. Start talking. As you talk, words pop up on your screen, just as if you had typed them.

The program can take several seconds to convert your spoken words into text. Fortunately, most speech recognition programs display a small text box or other indicator onscreen, showing you that the program is processing your speech. The box might even display the program's first-guess interpretation of what you just said. Even though you might not immediately see what you're saying, just keep talking.

To add punctuation, speak the name of the punctuation mark you want to insert. For instance, say "Period" to insert a period or "Comma" for a comma. To start a new paragraph, say "New Paragraph" or "Enter." Most programs include a quick reference

Inside Tip

Try to keep your microphone as far away from other electrical devices as possible, including your computer. These devices emit EMF noise (electromagnetic frequencies), which can cause a low hum that might interfere with your dictation. Special noise-reduction microphones also can help reduce background noise. You might want to stay clear of chatty officemates as well.

card that lists commands for inserting punctuation marks and special characters, moving the cursor, and editing text.

Even the best speech recognition program will occasionally misinterpret a word or phrase. In most cases, you can enter a command (via keyboard, mouse, or speech) for viewing a list of alternate interpretations. Then you click the correct interpretation, assuming it is in the list (see the following figure). Click **OK** to replace the original interpretation with the correction.

To fine-tune your speech recognition program as you use it, whenever the program misinterprets you, use the error as an opportunity to train the program. In the following figure, for example, instead of simply clicking the correct phrase and then clicking **OK**, click the **Train** button. This displays the Train Words dialog box, shown in the figure on the next page, which allows you to record yourself saying the misinterpreted phrase and the correct phrase. This helps the speech recognition program distinguish the difference in the future.

You can correct misinterpretations as you "type."

Click the correct phrase.

Click OK.

The Train button lets you retrain speech recognition on-the-fly.

3. Read aloud the
text as it is displayed.

You can clarify misunderstandings between you and the speech recognition program.

1. Click the phrase
you want the program
to recognize.

2. Click the
Record button.

Entering Voice Commands

Your new virtual secretary is very impressive when it comes to dictation, but what about carrying out simple commands, such as saving files and printing documents? Assuming you did a good job of training your secretary to recognize your voice, the secretary will carry out your every command.

To enter a command, you must switch from dictation mode to command mode. In NaturallySpeaking, you simply pause a second and then speak your command, such as "Click Edit, click Copy." In other programs, you might need to press a hotkey or click a button to toggle between voice-command and dictation modes.

The Least You Need to Know

➤ Plug a close-talk microphone into your sound card's microphone jack.

➤ Purchase and install a speech recognition program.

➤ Train the speech recognition program to correctly interpret your speech.

➤ Correct the speech recognition program when it enters an erroneous interpretation of a word or phrase.

➤ Switch to command mode to enter spoken commands.

Part 7

Maintaining Your Investment

You don't need to be a mechanic to use a computer, but you should perform some basic maintenance tasks on a regular basis to keep your computer in tip-top condition.

This part acts as your computer maintenance manual. Here you learn how to clean your monitor, keyboard, mouse, printer, and system unit and give your computer a regular tune-up to keep everything running at top speed.

Chapter 33

Keeping Your Computer Clean

In This Chapter

➤ Sucking the dust from your computer

➤ Squeegeeing your monitor

➤ Picking hair and other gunk out of your mouse

➤ Keeping your printer shiny and new

➤ Spin–cleaning your disk drives

One of the best clean-air machines on the market is a computer. The cooling fan constantly sucks in the dusty air and filters out the dust. A monitor acts like a dust magnet, pulling in any airborne particles unfortunate enough to get close to it. And the keyboard and mouse act like vacuum cleaners, sucking crumbs and other debris from your desk. Unfortunately, the dust and smoke that your computer filters out eventually build up on the mechanical and electrical components inside it. When enough dust and debris collect on your computer and accessories, it's time for a thorough cleaning.

Tools of the Trade

Before you start cleaning, turn off your computer and any attached devices, and gather the following cleaning equipment:

➤ **Screwdriver or wrench** for taking the cover off your system unit. (If you don't feel comfortable going inside the system unit, take your computer to a qualified technician for a thorough annual cleaning. It really does get dusty in there.)

➤ **Computer vacuum.** Yes, there are vacuum cleaners designed especially for computers.

➤ **Can of compressed air.** You can get this at a computer or electronics store. Compressed air is great for blowing the dust out of tight spots, such as between keyboard keys.

➤ **Soft brush** (a clean paintbrush with soft bristles will do). Use the brush to dislodge any stubborn dust that the vacuum won't pick up.

➤ **Toothpicks** (the only tool you need to clean your mouse).

➤ **Cotton swabs.**

➤ **Paper towel.**

➤ **Alcohol** (not the drinking kind; save that for when you're done).

➤ **Distilled water.** (You can get special wipes for your monitor, but paper towels and water do the trick.)

➤ **Radio or CD player.** (When you're cleaning, you need music.)

Don't run out and buy a floppy disk or CD-ROM cleaning kit. If your drive is having trouble reading disks, clean it. If it's running smoothly, let it be.

Vacuuming and Dusting Your Computer

Work from the top down and from the outside in. Start with the monitor. (You can use your regular vacuum cleaner for this part; if you have a brush attachment, use it.) Get your vacuum hose and run it up and down all the slots at the top and sides of the monitor. This is where most of the dust settles. Work down to the tilt-swivel base and vacuum that (you might need a narrow hose extension to reach in there). Now, vacuum your printer, speakers, and any other devices. If dust is stuck to a device, wipe it off with a damp (not soaking wet) paper towel.

Now for the system unit. When vacuuming, make sure you vacuum all the ventilation holes, including the floppy disk drive, power button, CD-ROM drive, open drive bays, and so on. If you have a CD-ROM drive, open it and gently vacuum the tray.

Now for the tough part—inside the system unit. Before you poke your vacuum hose in there, you should be aware of the following precautions:

➤ Use only a vacuum designed for computers. Don't use a Dust Buster, your regular vacuum cleaner, or your ShopVac. These can suck components off your circuit boards and can emit enough static electricity to fry a component. A computer vacuum is gentle and grounded. You can use a can of compressed air to blow dust off external peripheral devices, such as your keyboard and speakers, but be careful spraying the air against internal components. Compressed air can be very cold and can cause condensation to form on sensitive electrical components.

➤ Be careful around circuit boards. A strong vacuum can suck components and jumpers right off the boards. Also be careful not to suck up any loose screws.

➤ Touch a metal part of the case to discharge any static electricity from your body, and keep your fingers away from the circuit boards.

Inside Tip

Some PCs have a fan that pulls air from the outside and pushes it through the ventilation holes. If the system unit case has openings near the fan, cut a square of sheer hosiery fabric, stretch it over the openings, and tape it in place with duct tape, keeping the tape away from the openings. Check the filter regularly, and replace it whenever dust builds up.

Now, take the cover off the system unit and vacuum any dusty areas. Dust likes to collect around the fan, ventilation holes, and disk drives. Try to vacuum the fan blades, too. If you can't get the tip of the vacuum between the blades, gently wipe them off with a cotton swab. Some fans have a filter where the fan is mounted. If you're really ambitious, remove the fan (be careful with the wires) and clean the filter.

WASH ME: Cleaning Your Monitor

If you can write "WASH ME" on your monitor with your fingertip, the monitor needs cleaning. Check the documentation that came with your computer or monitor to see if it's okay to use window cleaner on it. The monitor might have an antiglare coating that can be damaged by alcohol- or ammonia-based cleaning solutions. (If it's not okay to use a cleaning solution, use water.) Spray the window cleaner (or water) on a paper towel, just enough to make it damp, and then wipe the screen.

Inside Tip

If you don't want to spend money on antistatic wipes, wipe your monitor with a used dryer sheet. (A new dryer sheet might smudge the screen with fabric softener.)

Don't spray window cleaner or any other liquid directly on the monitor; you don't want moisture to seep in. You can purchase special antistatic wipes for your monitor. These not only clean your monitor safely, but they also discharge the static electricity to prevent future dust buildup.

Shaking the Crumbs Out of Your Keyboard

Your keyboard is like a big place mat, catching all the cookie crumbs and other debris that fall off your fingers while you're working. The trouble is that, unlike a place mat, the keyboard isn't flat; it's full of crannies that are impossible to reach. And the suction from a typical vacuum cleaner just isn't strong enough to pull up the dust (although you can try it).

The easiest way I've found to clean a keyboard is to turn it upside down and shake it gently. Repeat two or three times to get any particles that fall behind the backs of the keys when you flip it over. If you don't like that idea, get your handy-dandy can of compressed air and blow between the keys.

For a more thorough cleaning, shut down your computer and disconnect the keyboard. Dampen a cotton swab with rubbing alcohol and gently scrub the keys. Wait for the alcohol to evaporate before reconnecting the keyboard and turning on the power.

Thrills and Spills

If you spill a drink on your keyboard, try to save your work and shut down the computer fast, but properly. Flip the keyboard over and turn off your computer. If you spilled water, just let the keyboard dry out thoroughly. If you spilled something sticky, give your keyboard a bath or shower with lukewarm water. Take the back off the keyboard, but do not flip the keyboard over with the back off, or parts will scurry across your desktop. Let it dry for a couple of days (don't use a blow-dryer), and put it back together. If some of the keys are still sticky, clean around them with a cotton swab dipped in rubbing alcohol. If you still have problems, buy a new keyboard; they're relatively inexpensive.

Making Your Mouse Cough Up Hairballs

If you can't get your mouse pointer to move where you want it to, you can usually fix the problem by cleaning the mouse. Flip the mouse over and look for hair or other debris on the mouse ball or on your desk or mouse pad. Removing the hair or wiping off your mouse pad fixes the problem 90 percent of the time.

If that doesn't work, remove the mouse ball cover (typically, you press down on the cover and turn counterclockwise). Wipe the ball thoroughly with a moistened paper towel. Now for the fun part. Look inside the mouse (where the ball was). You should see three rollers, each with a tiny ring around its middle. The ring is not supposed to be there. The easiest way I've found to remove these rings is to gently scrape them off with a toothpick. You have to spin the rollers to remove the entire ring. You can also try rubbing the rings off with a cotton swab dipped in rubbing alcohol, but these rings are pretty stubborn. When you're done, turn the mouse back over and shake it to remove the loose crumbs. Reassemble the mouse.

Cleaning Your Printer (When It Needs It)

Printer maintenance varies widely from one printer to another. If you have a laser printer, you need to vacuum or wipe up toner dust and clean the little print wires with cotton swabs dipped in rubbing alcohol. For an inkjet printer, you might have to remove the print cartridge and wipe the print heads with a damp cotton swab. If you have a combination scanner/printer, you might have to wipe the glass on which you place your original. Be sure to check the documentation that came with your printer for cleaning and maintenance suggestions.

You also need to be careful about the cleaning solution you use. Most printer manufacturers tell you to use only water on the inside parts—print rollers, print heads, and so on. In other cases, you can use a mild cleaning solution. Some manufacturers recommend using rubbing alcohol on some but not all parts.

Even with these variables, there are a few things the average user can do to keep the printer in peak condition and ensure high-quality output:

➤ When turning off the printer, always use the power button on the printer (don't use the power button on your power strip), or press the **Online** button to take the printer offline. This ensures that the print head is moved to its rest position. On inkjet printers, this prevents the print head from drying out.

➤ Vacuum inside the printer. Open any doors or covers to get inside.

➤ If the ink starts to streak on your printouts (or you have frequent paper jams in a laser printer), get special printer-cleaner paper from an office supply store and follow the instructions to run the sheet through your printer a few times.

Whoa!

Rubbing alcohol is an excellent cleaning solution for most electronic devices, because it cleans well and dries quickly. Use it for your keyboard, plastics, and most glass surfaces (except for some monitors). Avoid using it on rubber (for example, your mouse ball), because it tends to dry out the rubber and make it brittle.

➤ Using a damp cotton cloth, wipe paper dust and any ink off the paper feed rollers. Do not use alcohol. Do not use a paper towel; fibers from the paper towel could stick to the wheels.

What About the Disk Drives?

Don't bother cleaning your floppy, CD-ROM, or DVD-ROM drives unless they're giving you trouble. If your CD-ROM or DVD-ROM drive is having trouble reading a disc, the disc is usually the cause of the problem. Clean the disc and check the bottom of the disc for scratches. If the drive has problems reading every disc you insert, try cleaning the drive using a special drive-cleaning kit. The kit usually consists of a disc with some cleaning solution. You squirt the cleaning solution on the disc, insert it, remove it, and your job is done.

If you have a floppy disk drive that has trouble reading any disk you insert, you can purchase a special cleaning kit that works like the CD-ROM drive-cleaning kit. Although cleaning the disk drive might solve the problem, the problem can also be caused by a poorly aligned read/write head inside the drive, which no cleaning kit can correct.

The Least You Need to Know

➤ Vacuum your system, especially around its ventilation holes.

➤ Wipe the dust off your screen using a paper towel and the cleaning solution recommended by the manufacturer.

➤ Blow the crumbs out of your keyboard with compressed air.

➤ Remove those nasty mouse rings with a toothpick.

➤ Vacuum any ink dust that accumulates inside your printer.

➤ Clean your floppy or CD-ROM drive if it is having trouble reading disks.

Chapter 34

Giving Your Computer a Tune-Up

In This Chapter

➤ Clearing useless files from your hard disk

➤ Streamlining the Windows startup

➤ Repairing hard disk storage problems with ScanDisk

➤ Doubling your disk space without installing a new drive

➤ Getting more memory without installing more RAM

Over time, you will notice that your computer has slowed down. Windows takes a little longer to start up. Programs that used to snap into action now seem to crawl. Scrolling becomes choppy. Your computer locks up almost every day. You might begin to think that you need a new processor, more RAM, a larger hard disk drive, or even a whole new computer.

Before you take such drastic action, work through this chapter to give your computer a tune-up. By clearing useless files from your disk drive, reorganizing files, and reclaiming some of your computer's memory, you can boost your computer's performance and save a lot of money at the same time.

One-Stop Optimization with the Maintenance Wizard

The Windows Maintenance Wizard (included with Windows 98 and Windows Me) can help you keep your computer in tip-top condition. It automatically performs a series of tests and corrections at a scheduled time to check for problems on your hard disk, defragment files, delete temporary files, remove programs from the **StartUp** menu, and optimize your hard disk.

With the Windows Maintenance Wizard, you rarely have to go behind the scenes to perform these tasks manually. In this chapter, you learn how to use the Maintenance Wizard to delete temporary files and Web files from your hard disk and to optimize your hard disk and check it for errors. If you prefer to perform these maintenance tasks individually, without the help of the wizard, skip ahead to the following sections in this chapter:

➤ To find and delete temporary files from your hard disk, see "Clearing Useless Files from Your Hard Disk."

➤ To check your hard disk for damaged files and folders, see "Checking for and Repairing Damaged Files and Folders."

➤ To optimize the storage on your hard disk, see "Defragmenting Files on Your Hard Disk."

To run the Maintenance Wizard, follow these steps:

1. Click the **Start** button, point to **Programs, Accessories, System Tools,** and click **Maintenance Wizard.**

2. Click **Express,** and then click **Next.** Express tells the wizard to delete temporary files and Web files from your hard disk, optimize your hard disk, and check it for errors, but Express does not tell the wizard to remove programs from the **StartUp** menu. The next dialog box prompts you to specify the time of day you want the wizard to run.

3. Click the desired time (a time when you normally have your computer on but are not using it), and then click **Next.** The wizard displays a list of optimization activities it will perform at the scheduled time(s), as shown in the following figure.

4. To have the wizard perform the selected activities now, choose **When I click Finish, perform each scheduled task for the first time.**

5. Click the **Finish** button. Be sure to leave your computer on at the scheduled time so that Windows can perform the optimization activities at the scheduled time(s).

The Windows Maintenance Wizard optimizes your system on schedule.

Clearing Useless Files from Your Hard Disk

Your hard disk probably contains temporary and backup files that your programs create without telling you. These files can quickly clutter your hard disk drive, taking room that you need for new programs or new data files you create. You can easily delete most of these files yourself.

The first candidates for removal are temporary (.TMP) files. These are files that your programs create but often forget to delete. Think of temporary files as notes you take when researching a topic. After you complete the project, you can throw your notes in the trash. Unfortunately, Windows and your Windows applications frequently forget to clean up after a project, leaving useless temporary files to clutter your computer's hard disk.

You can safely delete all temporary files from your hard drive. In Windows Me, click the Windows **Start** menu, point to **Search,** and click **For Files or Folders.** In earlier versions of Windows, click the Windows **Start** button, point to **Find,** and click **Files or Folders.** Type *.tmp and press **Enter.** Press **Ctrl+A** to select all the files, and then press **Shift+Delete** and click **OK** to confirm. Gone! You should now have an extra megabyte or more of disk space. (Windows might not be able to delete some .TMP files that it is currently using.)

To remove temporary files that your Web browser saves, clear the disk cache in your browser. To clear the disk cache in Internet Explorer, open the **View** or **Tools** menu and click **Internet Options.** Under **Temporary Internet Files,** click the **Delete Files** button and then click **OK** to confirm. In Netscape Navigator, open the **Edit** menu, click **Preferences,** click the plus sign next to **Advanced,** click **Cache,** and click the **Clear Disk Cache** button.

While you're at it, open your e-mail program and delete any e-mail messages you no longer need. When you delete e-mail messages, some e-mail programs, such as Outlook Express, stick the deleted messages in a separate folder (called Deleted Items in Outlook Express). Be sure to delete the messages from that folder as well.

Inside Tip

When you save a file you created, most programs create a backup file that contains the previous version of the file. These files typically have the .BAK extension. If you mess up the original file, you can open the backup file instead. To find backup files, check the folder(s) in which you save your documents; most programs save backup files in the same folder as the original files. Before deleting backup files, make sure you don't want the previous versions of your files.

Most of the stuff you deleted is now sitting in the Recycle Bin, where it is still hogging disk space. Open the Recycle Bin, and scroll down the list of deleted files to make sure you will never again need anything in the Bin. If you find a file you might need, drag it onto the Windows desktop for safekeeping, or right-click the file and select **Restore** to restore the file to its original location. Now, open the **File** menu and click **Empty Recycle Bin**.

Panic Attack!

If Windows shuts down improperly (if you press the power button on your system unit before Windows is ready, if the power goes out, or if Windows locks up), Windows might run ScanDisk automatically when you restart your computer. It reminds you to shut down properly next time, even though this probably wasn't your fault.

Checking for and Repairing Damaged Files and Folders

Windows comes with a utility called ScanDisk that can test a disk (hard or floppy), repair most problems on a disk, and refresh the disk if needed. What kind of problems? ScanDisk can find defective storage areas on a disk and block them to prevent your computer from using them. ScanDisk can also find and delete misplaced (usually useless) file fragments that might be causing your computer to crash.

You should run ScanDisk regularly (at least once every month) and whenever your computer seems to be acting up (crashing for no apparent reason). Also, if you have a floppy disk that your computer cannot read, ScanDisk might be able to repair it and recover any data from it. To run ScanDisk, follow these steps:

1. Open the **Start** menu, point to **Programs, Accessories, System Tools,** and then click **ScanDisk.** The ScanDisk window appears, as shown in the following figure.

Pick the disk you
want to check.

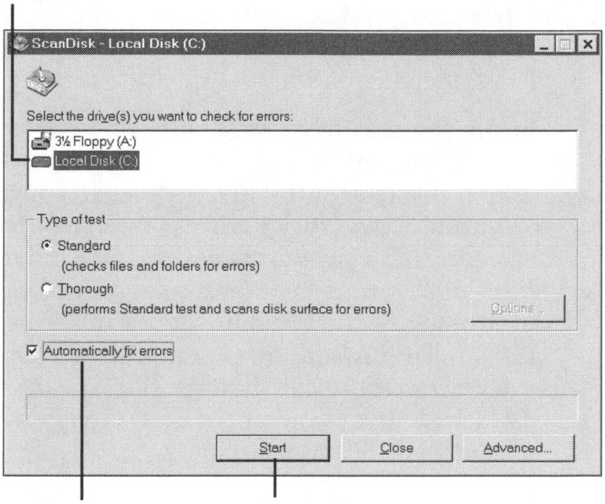

*ScanDisk can repair most
disk problems.*

ScanDisk can
automatically fix
disk errors.

Click Start to begin.

2. Click the letter of the drive you want ScanDisk to check.

3. To check for and repair only file and folder errors, click the **Standard** option; to check the disk for defects (in addition to file and folder errors), click **Thorough.** (Thorough can take hours; select it only if you're on your way to bed.)

4. If you want ScanDisk to fix any errors without asking for your confirmation, make sure that **Automatically fix errors** is checked. (I always choose this option, and I have never encountered problems with ScanDisk's doing something it was not supposed to do.)

5. Click the **Start** button.

Defragmenting Files on Your Hard Disk

Whenever you delete a file from your hard disk, you leave a space where another file can be stored. When you save a file, your computer stores as much of the file as possible in that empty space and stores the rest of the file in other empty spaces. The file is then said to be *fragmented,* because its parts are stored in different locations on the disk. This slows down your disk drive and makes it more likely that your computer will lose track of a portion of the file or the entire file.

383

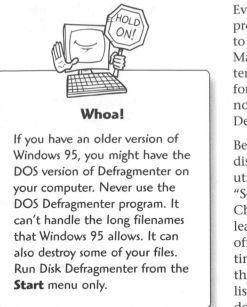

Whoa!

If you have an older version of Windows 95, you might have the DOS version of Defragmenter on your computer. Never use the DOS Defragmenter program. It can't handle the long filenames that Windows 95 allows. It can also destroy some of your files. Run Disk Defragmenter from the **Start** menu only.

Every month or so, you should run a defragmentation program to determine the fragmentation percent and to defragment your files if necessary. If you ran the Maintenance Wizard as explained earlier in this chapter, Windows Disk Defragmenter automatically performs the operation at the scheduled time. If you did not run the Maintenance Wizard, you can run Disk Defragmenter yourself.

Before you start Disk Defragmenter, it's a good idea to disable your screen saver and any power management utilities that might interfere with Defragmenter. See "Securing Some Privacy with a Screen Saver" in Chapter 5, "Using a Cool Desktop Background," to learn how to turn the Windows screen savers on and off. To disable the Windows power management settings, open the Windows Control Panel, double-click the **Power Options** icon, open the **Power Schemes** list, select **Always on**, and click **OK**. Save any open documents, and close any programs that are currently running.

Now you're ready to have Disk Defragmenter defragment your files. Follow these steps:

1. Open the **Start** menu, point to **Programs, Accessories, System Tools,** and click **Disk Defragmenter.** A dialog box appears, asking which disk drive you want to defragment, as shown in the following figure.

Defragmenter prompts you to select the drive(s) you want to defragment.

Select Drive	? X
Which drive do you want to defragment?	
💾 Drive C Physical drive ▼	
💾 Drive A Removable drive	
💾 Drive C Physical drive	
Copyright © 1988-1992 Symantec Corporation	
Intel Application Launch Accelerator	
intel Optimizers	
OK Exit Settings...	

Click the disk you want to defragment.

2. Open the **Which drive do you want to defragment?** drop-down list, and click the desired disk. If your computer has two or more hard drives, you can defragment all your disks by clicking **All hard drives.** (You don't need to defragment floppy disks.)

3. Click **OK.** Another dialog box might appear, indicating both the percentage of file fragmentation on the disk and whether you need to defragment the disk. Otherwise, Defragmenter starts defragmenting the disk, and you can skip to step 5.

4. If necessary, click the **Start** button. Defragmenter starts defragmenting the files on the disk.

5. Wait until the defragmentation is complete. It's best to leave your computer alone during the process. Otherwise, you might change a file and cause Defragmenter to start over. Don't run any programs or play any computer games.

Inside Tip

The **Advanced** or **Settings** button in the opening Disk Defragmenter dialog box lets you specify how you want Defragmenter to proceed.

Making Windows Start Faster

Windows is a slow starter, even on a quick machine. If you have some power-saving features on your computer, you can make Windows start a lot faster. Instead of turning your PC off and on, use the **Power** or **Power Management** icon in the Control Panel to have Windows put your PC in sleep mode when you're not using it. Then, you can quickly restart by pressing the **Shift** key or rolling the mouse around.

If your computer has advanced power-saving features, you might also be able to shut it down by placing it in Standby mode. When you're done for the day, click the **Start** button and click **Shut Down.** In the Shut Down dialog box, click **Stand by** and then click **OK.** To restart your computer, press the **Shift** key.

In addition to Standby mode, some systems support Hibernation mode. After a specified period of inactivity, or when you choose to place the computer in Hibernation mode, Windows saves all open files, makes a record of which programs were open, and then completely shuts down the computer. When you press the power button to restart your system, Windows automatically runs the programs that were running when the computer entered Hibernation mode and opens any documents that were open so that you can immediately pick up where you left off.

If you need to turn your computer completely off, try the following to reduce the startup time:

➤ To prevent Windows from running programs that are on the **StartUp** menu, hold down the **Shift** key right after you log on to Windows. If you don't log on to Windows, press and hold down **Shift** when you see the Windows splash screen (the screen that appears before you get to the desktop).

➤ To remove programs from the **StartUp** menu, right-click the taskbar, click **Properties,** click the **Advanced** or **Start Menu Programs** tab, click the **Remove** button, and click the plus sign next to **StartUp.** Click the program you want to remove, and then click the **Remove** button. (Be careful. If you have an antivirus program that runs on startup, you might want to keep it on the **StartUp** menu.)

➤ To quickly restart Windows without restarting your computer, click **Start, Shut Down, Restart.** Hold down the **Shift** key while clicking **Yes** or **OK.**

If you have Internet Explorer on your computer, and you have your Windows desktop displayed as a Web page, the active desktop components can add a lot of time to the Windows startup. If you don't use the desktop components, turn them off. Right-click a blank area of the desktop, point to **Active Desktop**, and choose **Customize My Desktop.** Remove the check mark next to every desktop component, and then click **OK.** Also consider turning off **View as Web page.** Right-click the desktop, point to **Active Desktop**, and, if **View as Web page** or **Show Web content** is checked, click the option to remove the check mark.

Inside Tip

Every computer comes with a set of startup instructions called the BIOS (Basic Input/ Output System). These instructions include boot settings that can make your computer start faster. For instance, you can enter a setting to have your computer start directly from drive C (instead of checking drive A first). Check the startup screen or your computer's manual for instructions on accessing the BIOS settings, but don't change any settings you are unsure of.

Boosting Performance with Shareware Utilities

Does your 56Kbps modem seem slow? Does Windows frequently lock up or display the "insufficient memory" message, even though your computer has more than 64MB of RAM and plenty of free disk space? Has your computer's performance become so degraded that you just can't stand using your computer for another day? Then it's time to bring out the big guns—utility programs designed to optimize your computer automatically.

The following is a list of shareware programs, along with information on where to find out more about them and where to go to download the latest version:

➤ **MemTurbo,** shown in the following figure, is a memory (RAM) optimizer. When you exit some programs, they fail to free up the memory they were using, reducing the amount of free memory available to other programs. MemTurbo reclaims this memory to make programs run faster and prevent Windows from locking up. You can find out more about MemTurbo and download a trial version at www.memturbo.com.

➤ **WinOptimizer** is designed to pick up where the Windows Maintenance Wizard leaves off. It clears redundant, duplicate files from your system and streamlines the Windows Registry to boost overall system performance. You can learn more about WinOptimizer and pick up a shareware version of it at www.ashampoo.com.

➤ **TweakDUN** is an Internet connection optimizer for Windows. It automatically adjusts the Windows Dial-Up Networking settings to make Windows transfer data more efficiently over a modem connection. If you're using a 56Kbps modem and you aren't ready to move up to an ISDN, DSL, or cable connection, TweakDUN can improve your current connection speed. Check it out at www.pattersondesigns.com/tweakdun. (You should also check out Download Accelerator at www.speedbit.com.)

➤ **SiSoft Sandra** is a system information utility that provides a complete inventory of your system's resources. Sandra shows you the processor's type and speed, the amount of memory, the amount of free storage space, the monitor make and model, and descriptions of all installed peripherals. When you want to know more about your computer, check out Sandra at www.sisoftware.demon.co.uk/sandra/.

Computer Cheat

If you don't have a utility for re-claiming memory, shut down Windows and restart your computer. You might need to do this every day or two to keep your computer running smoothly.

MemTurbo reclaims memory from selfish programs.

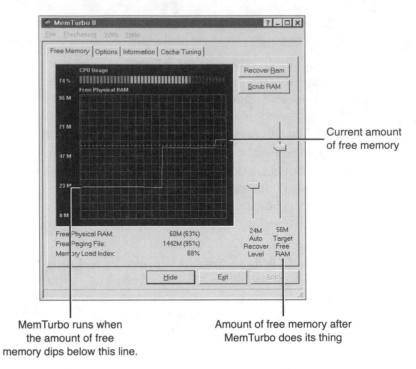

Current amount
of free memory

MemTurbo runs when
the amount of free
memory dips below this line.

Amount of free memory after
MemTurbo does its thing

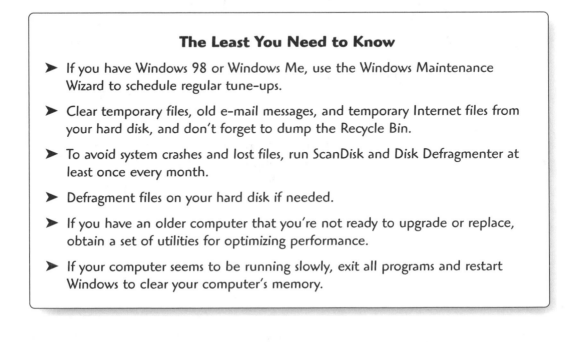

The Least You Need to Know

➤ If you have Windows 98 or Windows Me, use the Windows Maintenance
Wizard to schedule regular tune-ups.

➤ Clear temporary files, old e-mail messages, and temporary Internet files from
your hard disk, and don't forget to dump the Recycle Bin.

➤ To avoid system crashes and lost files, run ScanDisk and Disk Defragmenter at
least once every month.

➤ Defragment files on your hard disk if needed.

➤ If you have an older computer that you're not ready to upgrade or replace,
obtain a set of utilities for optimizing performance.

➤ If your computer seems to be running slowly, exit all programs and restart
Windows to clear your computer's memory.

Glossary: Speak Like a Geek

When you flip through computer documentation, books, and magazines, you might begin to feel as though you just stepped into the tomb of King Tut. How do you interpret the hieroglyphics stamped on your computer? How do you make sense of all the cryptic terms? Where can you get translations for the most common acronyms?

Well, you've come to the right place. Although this limited glossary can't possibly cover all the gobbledygook you'll encounter in the world of computers and the Internet, it does define enough basic terms to get you through your next job interview.

ADSL (asynchronous digital subscriber line)   A communications technology that allows fast data transfers over standard copper phone lines. "Asynchronous" indicates that the system uses different data transfer rates for upstream and downstream communications—typically 32Mbps for downstream traffic and 32Kbps to 1Mbps for upstream traffic. ADSL is the most common type of DSL used in North America. See also *DSL* and *SDSL*.

application   Also known as a *program*. A set of instructions that causes a computer to perform a specific task, such as word processing or data management. An application can also be a collection of programs, called a *suite*.

ASCII file   A file containing characters that any program on any computer can use. Sometimes called a text file or an ASCII text file. ASCII is pronounced *ASK-key*.

attachment   A file that's tacked on to an e-mail message. Attachments let users exchange files without having to use disks.

BIOS (basic input/output system)   The built-in set of instructions that tells the computer how to control the disk drives, keyboard, printer port, and other components that make up your computer. Pronounced *BUY-ose*.

bit   The basic unit of data in a computer. A computer's alphabet consists of two characters—1 and 0. 1 stands for on, and 0 stands for off. Bits are combined in sets of eight to form real characters, such as A, B, C, and D. See also *byte*.

bits per second   A unit for measuring the speed of data transmission. Remember that it takes 8 bits to make a byte (the equivalent of a single character). Modems have common bps ratings of 28,800 to 56,600.

boot   To start a computer and load its operating system software (usually Windows).

bps   See *bits per second*.

browser   See *Web browser*.

burner   See *CD burner*.

bus   A superhighway that carries information electronically from one part of the computer to another. The wider and faster the bus (speed is measured in MHz), the faster your computer. The old ISA bus could carry 16 bits of data at a time; the newer PCI bus can carry 32 bits or 64 bits.

byte   A group of 8 bits that usually represents a character or a digit. For example, the byte 01000001 represents the letter A.

cable modem   A modem that supports high-speed connections to the Internet via a TV cable connection. (In order to use a cable modem, you must have a cable company that offers Internet service.) See also *modem*.

cache   A temporary storage area in memory or on disk that computer components and various programs use to quickly access data. Pronounced *cash*.

CD burner   A disc drive that lets you copy CDs and record tracks from audio CDs to blank CDs.

CD-R (compact disc recordable)   A storage technology in which a CD drive not only reads data from compact discs but also writes data to compact discs (special CD-R discs). A standard CD-ROM drive can only read data from a disc. See also *CD-ROM* and *CD-RW*.

CD ripper   A program that reads tracks from an audio CD and converts them into a digital file format that your computer can play. Using a CD ripper, you can create your own music mixes on your computer, transfer them to a portable MP3 player, and (with a CD burner) record your mixes to blank CDs. See also *MP3* and *CD burner*.

CD-ROM (compact disk read-only memory)   A storage technology that uses the same kind of discs you play in an audio CD player for mass storage of computer data. A single disk can store more than 600MB of information. Pronounced *see-dee-rahm*. See also *CD-R* and *CD-RW*.

CD-RW (compact disk rewritable)   A storage technology in which a CD drive reads data from a compact disc, writes data to a disk, and erases data from discs (CD-RW discs) to make them reusable. See also *CD-R* and *CD-ROM*.

cell   The box formed by the intersection of a row (1,2,3 ...) and column (A,B,C ...) in a spreadsheet. Each cell has an *address* (such as B12) that defines its column and row. A cell might contain text, a numeric value, or a formula.

chat   To talk to another person by typing at your computer. What you type appears on the other person's screen, and what the other person types appears on your screen. You can chat on the Internet or on an online service, such as America Online.

check box   A square next to an option that indicates whether the option is on (checked) or off (unchecked). You can select more than one option in a group of check box options. See also *option button*.

390

click   To move the mouse pointer over an object or icon and press and release the mouse button once without moving the mouse.

client   Of two computers, the computer that's being served. On the Internet or on a network, your computer is the client, and the computer to which you're connected is the *server*.

Clipboard   A temporary storage area in Windows that holds text and graphics. The **Cut** and **Copy** commands put text or graphics on the Clipboard, replacing the Clipboard's previous contents. The **Paste** command copies Clipboard data to a document. Some programs, such as Microsoft Office, have their own clipboards that can store multiple cut and copied selections. The Office 2000 clipboard, for instance, can store 12 cut or copied selections, and the Office XP clipboard can store 24.

COM port   Short for communications port. A receptacle, usually at the back of the computer, into which you can plug a serial device such as a modem, mouse, or serial printer.

command   An order that tells the computer what to do. In command-driven programs, you have to press a specific key or type the command to execute it. With menu-driven programs, you select the command from a menu.

command button   A control in a dialog box that typically confirms or cancels the dialog box. The three most common command buttons are **OK, Cancel**, and **Help.**

computer   Any machine that accepts input (from a user), processes the input, and produces output in some form.

context menu   A list of commands or options that pops up on the screen when you right-click a selected object or highlighted text. Context menus contain only commands that pertain to the selected object or text.

cookie   An electronic identification "badge" that many Web sites store on your computer to help identify you when you return to the site or to record items you buy as you shop online.

CPU (central processing unit)   The computer's brain. See also *microprocessor.*

crash   The failure of a system or program. Usually, you realize that your system has crashed when you can't move the mouse pointer or type anything. The term *crash* is also used to refer to a disk crash (or head crash). A disk crash occurs when the read/write head in the disk drive falls on the disk possibly destroying data.

cursor   A horizontal line that appears below characters. A cursor acts like the tip of your pencil; anything you type appears at the cursor. See also *insertion point.*

data   The facts and figures that you enter into the computer and that are stored and used by the computer.

database   A type of computer program used to store, organize, and retrieve information. Popular database programs include Access, Approach, and Paradox.

default The initial state of a setting or option. Most word processing programs, for example, are set up to print documents in portrait mode rather than in landscape mode. Portrait mode is said to be the default setting.

density A measure of the amount of data that can be stored per square inch of storage area on a disk.

desktop The main work area in Windows. The desktop displays several icons for running programs and accessing common Windows tools.

desktop publishing (DTP) A program that lets you combine text and graphics on the same page and manipulate the text and graphics onscreen. Desktop publishing programs are commonly used to create newsletters, brochures, flyers, resumés, and business cards.

desktop theme An ensemble consisting of a desktop background, animated screen saver, and interesting audio and visual effects that give Windows a unique look and feel.

desktop utility A computer-based version of a tool commonly found in an office, such as a calculator or notepad.

dialog box An onscreen box that lets you enter your preferences or supply additional information. You use a dialog box to carry on a "conversation" with the program.

digital camera A device for taking photographs and storing them as files rather than on film.

directory A division of a disk or CD that contains a group of related files. Think of your disk as a filing cabinet, and think of each directory as a drawer in the cabinet. Directories are more commonly called *folders*.

disk A round, flat, magnetic storage medium. A disk works like a cassette tape, storing files permanently so that you can play them back later. The disk itself is typically sealed inside a plastic case, so you rarely see the disk itself. See *floppy disk* and *hard disk*.

disk drive A device that writes data to a magnetic disk and reads data from the disk. Think of a disk drive as a cassette recorder/player for a computer.

DOS (disk operating system) DOS, which rhymes with "boss," is an old program that used to provide the necessary instructions for the computer's parts (keyboard, disk drive, central processing unit, display screen, printer, and so on) to function as a unit. Although Windows makes DOS nearly obsolete, you still see its name floating around in Windows.

DOS prompt An onscreen prompt that indicates that DOS is ready to accept a command. It provides no clue as to what command you should type. It looks something like C> or C:\.

download To copy files from another computer to your computer, usually through a modem. See also *upload*.

drag   To hold down the mouse button while moving the mouse. You commonly drag an object to move it or drag over text to select it.

drop-down list   A box that opens to reveal a selection of options when you click the arrow to the right of the box. Drop-down lists are commonly used in dialog boxes and toolbars to conserve space. Think of them as small menus.

DSL (digital subscriber line)   Uses standard phone lines to achieve data transfer rates of up to 1.5Mbps (9Mbps if you're within two miles of an ADSL connection center). Phone companies hope that advances in DSL technology and availability will help them compete with cable companies for Internet access and entertainment. See also *ADSL* and *SDSL*.

DVD (digital versatile disc or digital video disc)   Discs that can store more than seven times as much data as a CD, making them useful for storing full-length movies and complete multimedia encyclopedias. DVD drives are designed to handle the discs of the future and are also designed to play discs of the past (CDs).

e-mail   Short for electronic mail. E-mail is a system that lets people send messages to and receive messages from other computers. E-mail is available on networks, online information services, and the Internet.

emoticon   A text-only symbol commonly used in e-mail messages and chat rooms to quickly express an emotion or physical gesture. :), for instance, represents a smile.

Ethernet   A common local area network (LAN) protocol developed by Xerox Corporation that allows computers to communicate over network connections. Ethernet supports connection speeds of up to 10Mbps. 100BASE-T Ethernet supports speeds of up to 100Mbps, and Gigabit Ethernet supports speeds of up to 1 gigabit per second. See also *LAN, Mbps,* and *Ethernet adapter*.

Ethernet adapter   An expansion card that allows a computer to be connected to an Ethernet local area network. See also *Ethernet, LAN,* and *expansion board*.

executable file   A program file that can run the program. Executable files end in .BAT, .COM, or .EXE.

expansion board   A printed circuit board that plugs into a computer's motherboard and is designed to add a specific capability to a computer. Common expansion boards include modems, sound cards, and video accelerators. See also *expansion slot* and *motherboard*.

expansion card   See *expansion board*.

expansion slot   An opening on the motherboard (inside the system unit) that lets you add devices to the system unit, such as an internal modem, sound card, video accelerator, or other enhancement. See also *expansion board*.

extension   The portion of a filename that comes after the period. Every filename consists of two parts—the base name (before the period) and the extension (after the period). The filename can have up to eight characters in DOS and Windows 3.x and can have up to 255 characters in Windows 95 and later. The extension (which is optional) almost always consists of three characters.

family tree program   See *genealogy program*.

field   A blank in a database record into which you can enter a piece of information (such as a telephone number, a ZIP code, or a person's last name).

file   A collection of information stored as a single unit on a floppy or hard disk. Files always have a filename to identify them.

file format   An organizational scheme for the data that makes up a file. The simplest file format is text-only, which stores data as typed characters. Program files, graphics, audio-video files, and other file types are more complex and are stored as *binary* files in various formats. You can determine a file's format by looking at its filename extension. A graphics file, for instance, might be stored as a PCX, GIF, or JPG file.

File Transfer Protocol (FTP)   A set of rules that governs the exchange of files between two computers on the Internet.

fixed disk drive   A disk drive that has an unremovable disk, as opposed to floppy drives, in which you insert and remove disks.

flame war   A war of words between two or more people, typically waged in newsgroups or via e-mail.

floppy disk   A wafer encased in plastic that stores magnetic data (the facts and figures you enter and save). You insert floppy disks into your computer's floppy disk drive (located on the front of the computer).

folder   The Windows name for a directory, a division of a hard disk or CD that stores a group of related files. See also *directory*.

font   Any set of characters of the same *typeface* (design) and *type size* (measured in points). For example, Times New Roman 12-point is a font, Times New Roman is the typeface, and 12-point is the size. (There are 72 points in an inch.)

footer   Text that appears at the bottom of every page of a document. Footers are commonly used to insert the title of the document, the date on which it was composed, and page numbers. See also *header*.

format (disk)   To prepare a disk for storing data. Formatting creates a map on the disk that tells the operating system how the disk is structured. The operating system uses this map to keep track of where files are stored.

format (document)   To establish a document's physical layout, including page size, margins, headers and footers, line spacing, text alignment, graphics placement, and so on.

format (file)   See *file format*.

FTP   See *File Transfer Protocol*.

function keys   The 10 or 12 F keys on the left side of the keyboard, or the 12 F keys at the top of the keyboard (some keyboards have both). F keys are numbered F1, F2, F3, and so on, and you can use them to enter specified commands in a program.

GB   See *gigabyte*.

geek   1. An overly obsessive computer user who sacrifices food, sleep, and other necessities of life to spend more time in front of the computer. 2. A carnival performer whose act usually includes biting off the head of a live snake or chicken.

genealogy program   Software that helps you lay out and print a family tree. Most commercial genealogy programs provide additional tools for researching your lineage.

gigabyte   A thousand megabytes. Often abbreviated as GB. See also *megabyte*.

GPS (global positioning system)   A satellite technology that lets a receiver pinpoint its location anywhere in the world. GPS systems are commonly used in cars to direct the driver to his or her destination.

handheld computer   An electronic organizer, complete with a calendar, calculator, address book, and notepad, that fits in the palm of your hand.

handle   A square, circle, or other shape that appears on the border of a picture, text box, or other object when the object is selected. You drag a handle to resize an object.

hard disk   A disk drive that has an unremovable disk. It acts as a giant floppy disk drive and usually sits inside your computer.

Hayes-compatible   A modem that uses the Hayes command set to communicate with other modems over the phone lines. Hayes-compatible modems usually are preferred over other modems because most modems and telecommunications software are designed to be Hayes-compatible.

header   Text that appears at the top of every page of a document. Headers are commonly used to insert the title of the document, the date on which it was composed, and page numbers. See also *footer*.

highlight   To select text in order to cut, copy, delete, move, or format it. When you highlight text, it typically appears white on a black background.

history list   A list of the names and addresses of Web sites and pages you've accessed with your Web browser. Your Web browser keeps a history list so that you can quickly return to sites even if you've forgotten a site's address.

hot swappable   A feature of some computer devices that allows you to connect them to a computer safely without turning off the computer's power. In most cases, you should shut down your computer before connecting a device, such as a printer or monitor, to keep from damaging the device or your computer. With other devices, such as USB scanners and USB joysticks, you can safely connect the device while the computer is running and then immediately start using the device. See also *USB (Universal Serial Bus)*.

HTML (Hypertext Markup Language)   The code used to create documents for the World Wide Web. These codes tell the Web browser how to display the text (titles, headings, lists, and so on), insert anchors that link this document to other documents, and control character formatting (by making it bold or italic).

hyperlink   Icons, pictures, or highlighted text commonly used on Web pages and in help systems that point to other resources. On Web pages, text hyperlinks typically appear blue and underlined.

icon   A graphic image onscreen (a tiny picture) that represents another object, such as a file on a disk. Icons can be found almost everywhere in Windows: on the desktop, on toolbars, on menus, and in dialog boxes. Icons commonly represent applications, utilities, disks, folders, and files.

IM (instant message)   A private message that reaches the recipient almost immediately after the user sends it. IMs are commonly used in America Online to communicate privately with other users.

insertion point   A blinking vertical line used in most Windows word processors to indicate the place where any characters you type are inserted. An insertion point is equivalent to a cursor.

instant message   See *IM (instant message)*.

integrated program   A program that combines the features of several programs, such as a word processor, spreadsheet, database, and communications program.

Intellimouse   A type of mouse designed by Microsoft that has a wheel between the left and right mouse button. The wheel lets you scroll without using a scrollbar and perform other special tasks.

interface   A link between two objects, such as a computer and a modem. The link between a computer and a person is called a *user interface* and refers to the way a person communicates with the computer or a program.

Internet   A group of computers all over the world that are connected to each other. Using your computer and a modem, you can connect to these other computers and tap their resources. You can view pictures, listen to sounds, watch video clips, play games, chat with other people, and even shop.

Internet service provider (ISP)   The company that you pay in order to connect to their computer and get on the Internet.

IRC (Internet Relay Chat)   The most popular way to chat with others on the Internet. With an IRC client (chat program), you connect to an IRC server, where you are presented with a list of available chat rooms. You can enter a room and then start exchanging messages with others in the room.

ISDN (Integrated Services Digital Network)   A system that allows your computer, using a special ISDN modem, to perform digital data transfers over special phone lines. Non-ISDN modems use analog signals, which are designed to carry voices not data. ISDN connections can transfer data at a rate of up to 128Kbps, compared to about 56Kbps for the fastest analog modems.

ISP See *Internet service provider*.

Kbps (kilobits per second) A unit used to express data transfer rates, typically for modems. A kilobit is equivalent to 1,000 bits. See also *bits per second*.

keyboard The main input device for most computers. You use the keyboard to type and to enter commands.

kilobyte A unit for measuring the amount of data. A kilobyte is equivalent to 1,024 bytes (each byte is a character). Kilobyte is commonly abbreviated as K, KB, or Kbyte.

LAN (local area network) A system of interconnected computers designed to let users share hardware, software, and data and to communicate with each other via e-mail. A LAN is typically confined to a limited area, such as an office, building, or small group of buildings. See also *WAN*.

laptop A small computer that's light enough to carry. Notebook computers and subnotebooks are even lighter.

link See *hyperlink*.

load To read data or program instructions from disk and place them in the computer's memory, where the computer can use the data or instructions.

log off To disconnect from a network or from the Internet.

log on To enter your user name and password in order to establish a connection to a network or the Internet. See also *user name*.

mail merge A feature of most word processing programs that allows you to link an address book with a form letter or mailing label document to generate a set of personalized form letters and/or mailing labels.

mail server A computer on a network whose job it is to receive and store incoming mail and route outgoing mail to the proper e-mail boxes on other mail servers. See also *e-mail*.

Mbps (megabits per second) A unit used to express data transfer rates for high-speed communications. A megabit is equivalent to 1,000,000 bits. See also *bits per second*.

megabyte A standard unit used to measure the storage capacity of a disk and the amount of computer memory. A megabyte is 1,048,576 bytes (1,000 kilobytes). This is roughly equivalent to 500 pages of double-spaced text. Megabyte is commonly abbreviated as M, MB, or Mbyte.

memory An electronic storage area inside the computer used to temporarily store data or program instructions when the computer is using them. Also referred to as RAM.

menu   A vertical listing of commands or instructions displayed onscreen. Menus organize commands and make a program easier to use. Most applications's menus appear on a *menu bar,* a band near the top of the application's window. To open a menu, you click its name on the menu bar. See also *context menu.*

microprocessor   Sometimes called the central processing unit (CPU) or processor, this chip is the computer's brain; it does all the calculations for the computer.

modem   An acronym for modulator/demodulator. A modem is a piece of hardware that converts incoming signals (from a phone line, cable service, or other source) into signals that a PC can understand and converts outgoing signals from the PC into a form that can be transmitted.

monitor   A television-like screen on which the computer displays information.

morph   To gradually transform one image into another or to distort an original image in a creative manner.

motherboard   The main printed circuit board inside a computer through which all other devices communicate. The printed circuit board contains the microprocessor and memory chips, expansion slots for plugging in accessories, and connections for the disk drives and other devices. See also *microprocessor, memory, expansion slot,* and *expansion board.*

mouse   A handheld device that you move across the desktop to move an arrow, called the mouse pointer, across the screen. You can use the mouse to move the insertion point (or cursor), select and move items (such as text and graphics), open menus, execute commands, and perform other tasks.

mouse pointer   An onscreen arrow that scurries across the screen as you move the mouse. You move the tip of the mouse pointer over an item to *point* to it. See also *mouse.*

MP3   Short for *MPEG audio layer 3.* A digital audio format that compresses audio files to one-twelfth their original size with an imperceptible loss of quality.

MPEG   Short for *Moving Pictures Experts Group.* An assembly that sets standards for digital video recording and file formats.

MS-DOS (Microsoft Disk Operating System)   See *DOS.*

multitasking   The process of performing two or more computer tasks at the same time. For example, you might be printing a document from your word processor while checking your e-mail in Prodigy.

network   A system of interconnected computers designed to allow users to share hardware, software, and data. See also *LAN* and *WAN.*

network protocol   See *protocol.*

newsgroup   An Internet bulletin board for users who share common interests. There are thousands of newsgroups, ranging from body art to pets (to body art with pets). Newsgroups let you post messages and read messages from other users.

notebook   A portable computer that weighs between 4 and 8 pounds.

online   Connected, turned on, and ready to accept information. Used most often in reference to a printer or modem.

online service   A network that allows members to obtain information, communicate, and get files via a modem connection. Common online services include America Online, Prodigy, and CompuServe.

option button   A circle next to a setting that indicates whether the setting is on or off. You can select only one option in a group of options. If you select an option other than the option that is currently selected, the option you select is turned on, and the other option is turned off. See also *check box*.

pane   A portion of a window. Most programs display panes, so you can view two different parts of a document at the same time.

parallel port   A connector used to plug a device, usually a printer, into the computer.

partition   A section of a disk drive that's assigned a letter. A hard disk drive can be divided (partitioned) into one or more drives, which your computer refers to as drive C, drive D, drive E, and so on. The actual hard disk drive is called the *physical drive,* and each partition is called a *logical drive;* however, these terms don't matter much— the drives still look like letters to you.

patch   A set of program instructions designed to fix a programming bug or add capabilities to a program. On the Internet, you can often download patches for programs to update the program.

path   The route that the computer travels from the root directory to any subdirectories when locating a file.

PC (personal computer)   A computer designed to help a user perform practical tasks, such as typing documents and performing calculations. PCs are much smaller and less powerful than mainframe computers. The term *PC* is commonly used to refer to computers that run Windows or Linux, as opposed to Apple computers, which run MacOS.

PC card   An expansion card that's about the size of a credit card but thicker. It slides into a slot on the side of a notebook computer. PC cards let you quickly install RAM or a hard disk drive, modem, CD-ROM drive, network card, or game port without having to open the notebook computer. See also *PCMCIA*.

PCMCIA (Personal Computer Memory Card International Association)   An organization that sets standards for notebook computer expansion cards. These credit-card-sized expansion boards originally were designed to add memory to laptop computers but are now used to add modems, network connections, digital video cameras, USB ports, and other devices. See also *PC card*.

peripheral   A device that's attached to the computer but is not essential for the computer's basic operation. The system unit is the central part of the computer. Any devices attached to the system unit are considered *peripheral,* including a printer, modem, or joystick. Some manufacturers consider the monitor and keyboard to be peripheral, too.

personal finance program   Software that helps you write checks, reconcile your accounts, track investments, calculate loan payments, budget, and perform other money-management tasks.

PIM (personal information manager)   Software that helps you manage your schedule, contacts, e-mail, and other business-related and personal aspects of your life. A PIM typically contains an address book, a calendar, a list of things to do, and an e-mail program.

pixel   A dot of light that appears on the computer screen. A collection of pixels forms characters and images on the screen.

PnP (plug-and-play)   PnP lets you install expansion cards in your computer without having to set special switches. You plug it in, and it works.

pointer   See *mouse pointer*.

port   A receptacle at the back of the computer. It gets its name from the ports where ships pick up and deliver cargo. In this case, a port allows information to enter and leave the system unit.

PPP (Point-to-Point Protocol)   A language that computers use to talk to one another. What's important is that when you choose an Internet service provider, you get the right connection—SLIP or PPP.

processor   See *microprocessor*.

program   A group of instructions that tells the computer what to do. Typical programs are word processors, spreadsheets, databases, and games.

prompt   A computer's way of asking for more information. The computer basically looks at you and says, "Tell me something." In other words, the computer is *prompting* you or prodding you for information or a command.

protocol   A group of communications settings that controls the transfer of data between two computers.

pull-down menu   A menu that appears near the top of the screen, on the menu bar, listing various options. A menu's contents are not visible until you click the menu. The menu then drops down, covering a small part of the screen.

Quick Launch Toolbar   A toolbar that's nested in the Windows taskbar and that provides convenient access to the programs you use most often. Microsoft introduced the Quick Launch toolbar in later versions of Windows 95 and kept it as a standard feature in Windows 98. See also *toolbar*.

random access memory (RAM)   A collection of chips your computer uses to store data and programs temporarily. RAM is measured in kilobytes and megabytes. In general, more RAM means that you can run more powerful programs and more programs at once. Also called *memory*.

record   Used by databases to denote a unit of related information contained in one or more fields, such as an individual's name, address, and phone number.

Recycle Bin   A virtual trash can into which Windows places files and folders when you choose to delete them. The Recycle Bin is a temporary storage area that acts as a safety net for deleted files. If you delete a file or folder by mistake, you can usually retrieve it from the Recycle Bin.

RF-return   Short for Radio Frequency-return, a method by which a cable company establishes two-way communication between your computer and the network over a single cable. Cable systems were originally designed to carry data only one way: from the cable company into homes. In older cable systems, you must use a modem to send e-mail and requests to the network over the phone lines. See also *telephone-return*.

ripper   See *CD ripper*.

ROM BIOS   See *BIOS*.

scanner   A device that converts images, such as photographs or printed text, into an electronic format that a computer can use. Many stores use a special type of scanner to read bar code labels into the cash register.

screen saver   A program that displays a moving picture on your computer screen when the computer is inactive. Screen savers are typically used as decorative novelties and to prevent passersby from snooping.

Screen Tip   See *tooltip*.

scroll   To move text up and down or right and left on a computer screen.

scrollbar   A band, typically displayed along the bottom and right edge of a window, used to bring the contents of the window into view.

SDSL (synchronous digital subscriber line)   A communications technology that allows fast data transfers over standard copper phone lines. "Synchronous" indicates that the system uses the same data transfer rates for both upstream and downstream traffic. In Europe, SDSL (Symmetric DSL) is most common. SDSL lines use the same data transfer rates for both upstream and downstream traffic. See also *DSL* and *ADSL*.

server   Of two computers, the computer that's serving the other computer. On the Internet or on a network, your computer is the *client,* and the computer to which you're connected is the *server*.

shareware   Computer programs you can use for free and then pay for if you decide to continue using them. Many programmers start out by marketing their programs as shareware, relying on the honesty and goodwill of computer users for their income. That's why most of these programmers have day jobs.

401

shortcut   A cloned version of an icon that points to a document or program on your computer. Shortcuts let you place programs and documents in more than one convenient location on your computer.

software   Any instructions that tell your computer (the hardware) what to do. There are two types of software: operating system software and application software. *Operating system software* (such as Windows) gets your computer up and running. *Application software* lets you do something useful, such as type a letter or manage your finances. Other types of software include *games* and *utilities* (programs for maintaining and optimizing your computer).

speech recognition   A technology that allows your computer to "understand" spoken commands and take dictation.

spin box   A control in a dialog box that displays an up and down arrow for changing a setting incrementally. In most cases, you can type a specific setting in the spin box or click the arrows to increase or decrease the setting. For example, you might use a spin box to adjust a document's margin settings by tenths of an inch.

spreadsheet   A program used for keeping schedules and calculating numeric results. Common spreadsheets include Lotus 1-2-3, Microsoft Excel, and Quattro Pro.

Start button   The button in the lower-left corner of the opening Windows screen that provides access to all the programs on your computer.

status bar   The area at the bottom of a program window that shows you what's going on as you work. A status bar might show the page and line number where the insertion point is positioned and indicate whether you are typing in overstrike or insert mode.

style   A collection of specifications for formatting text. A style might include information on the font, size, style, margins, and spacing. Applying a style to text automatically formats the text according to the style's specifications.

surge suppressor   A device that prevents power spikes and dips from damaging a computer and its peripheral devices.

system tray   The area on the right end of the taskbar that displays the current time, as well as icons for programs that are running in the background.

tab stop   A setting commonly used in a word processor that specifies where the insertion point will land when you press the **Tab** key. Tab stops are typically set at a half-inch, unless you change them.

table   A feature in most word processing programs that helps you align text in rows and columns.

taskbar   A fancy name for the button bar at the bottom of the Windows desktop. The taskbar includes the **Start** button (on the left) and the system tray (on the right).

TCP/IP (Transmission Control Protocol/Internet Protocol)   A set of rules that governs the transfer of data over the Internet.

telephone-return   A method used by some cable systems to allow a computer to send signals and data upstream to the network via a standard modem connection. With some cable systems, you can only receive data from the network over the cable connection. To send e-mail, upload files, or even request Web pages (by typing addresses and clicking links), you communicate via the phone line using a standard modem. See also *RF-return*.

text box   1. A rectangular area commonly found in dialog boxes and on forms into which you type specific entries. When you choose to save a file, for instance, you type a name for the file in the **File name** text box. 2. A box that can be drawn on a document to hold text that's separate from the document. In desktop publishing programs, you can enter text into various text boxes and then arrange the text boxes on a page.

toolbar   A strip of buttons typically displayed near the top of a program window, below the menu bar. The toolbar contains buttons that you can click to enter common commands, allowing you to bypass the menu system.

tooltip   A small text box that displays the name of a button when you rest the mouse pointer on the button. Tooltips help you figure out what a button does when you can't figure it out from the picture. Also known as a *Screen Tip*.

TV tuner card   An expansion board that lets your computer receive and display TV programs via cable, satellite, or amplified antenna. See also *expansion board*.

undo   A feature in most programs that lets you reverse one or more actions. For example, if you delete a paragraph by mistake, you can choose the **Undo** command to get it back.

uninterruptible power supply (UPS)   A battery-powered device that protects against power spikes and power outages. If the power goes out, the UPS continues supplying power to the computer so that you can continue working or safely turn off your computer without losing data.

upload   To send data to another computer, usually through a modem and a telephone line or over a network connection.

URL (Uniform Resource Locator)   An address for an Internet site.

USB (Universal Serial Bus)   The ultimate in plug-and-play technology, USB lets you install devices without turning off your computer or using a screwdriver. USB lets you connect up to 127 devices to a single port. See also *hot swappable*.

user name   A unique name you choose or have assigned to you by a network administrator, commercial online service, or Internet provider. Your user name gives you access to the network or system and provides you with an identity that other people can use to contact you.

utility   A program designed to optimize, protect, or maintain a computer rather than perform a task for the user. Utilities include backup programs, antivirus software, and memory optimizers.

video capture   The process of transferring video clips to your computer (using a camcorder or VCR) and storing the video as a file on a hard disk or CD.

virtual   Not real. Virtual worlds on the Internet are three-dimensional computer-generated areas that you can navigate but never physically enter—unless, of course, you're Keanu Reeves or Sandra Bullock.

virtual memory   Disk storage used as RAM (memory).

virus   A program that attaches itself to files on a floppy or hard disk, duplicates itself without the user's knowledge, and might cause the computer to do strange and sometimes destructive things, such as reformatting your hard drive.

wallpaper   A graphic design that appears as the background for the Windows desktop.

WAN (wide area network)   A system of interconnected LANs (local area networks) typically set up to let users exchange e-mail and share data over greater distances. See also *LAN*.

Web   See *World Wide Web*.

Web browser   A program that lets you navigate the World Wide Web (the most popular feature of the Internet). See also *World Wide Web*.

Web server   A computer on a network whose job it is to make Web pages available upon request. When you use a Web browser to open Web pages, you connect to a Web server.

windows   A way of displaying information on different parts of the screen. When spelled with an uppercase "W," used as a shortened form of "Microsoft Windows."

wizard   A series of dialog boxes that lead you step by step through the process of performing a task.

word processor   A program that lets you enter, edit, format, and print text.

word wrap   A feature that automatically moves a word to the next line if the word won't fit at the end of the current line.

worksheet   Another common name for a spreadsheet. See *spreadsheet*.

World Wide Web   A part of the Internet that consists of multimedia documents that are interconnected by links. To move from one document to another, you click a link, which might appear as highlighted text or an icon. The Web contains text, sound and video clips, pictures, catalogs, and much more. See also *Web browser*.

More Computer Resources for the Computer Enthusiast

Though I would like to claim that this book has everything you need to become an expert computer user, that would be quite a stretch ... even for me. Learning to use a computer is a lifelong adventure. Every day, I encounter a new problem or discover that I can do something on the computer I never knew was possible. To help you further explore and bond with your computer, I've put together this list of killer resources. Here, you'll find a list of the books, magazines, and online resources that I have found most helpful.

Books

Joe Kraynak, *Easy Internet,* Que, 2000. Hey, I need to plug my own books, too! This heavily illustrated guide takes you on a tour of Internet, showing you how to do everything from basic browsing to publishing your own Web pages. You also learn how to send and receive email, chat, post messages in newsgroups, and place free long-distance phone calls over the Internet.

Paul McFedries, *The Complete Idiot's Guide to Microsoft Windows Millenium,* Que, 2000. No personal computer user should be without a solid book on how to use Windows. Written in an entertaining and engaging style, this book takes you from the basics to more advanced Windows features, with plenty of pictures and step-by-step instructions. I highly recommend any books penned by Paul McFedries.

Stepen Sagman, *Troubleshooting Microsoft Windows,* Microsoft Press, 2000. Most of the time a computer acts up, novice users assume that the computer is at fault. In most cases, however, software is causing the problem. Every beginning user should have a good troubleshooting guide in his or her computer library, and this is the best I have found.

Mark Thompson and Mark Speaker, *The Complete Idiot's Guide to Networking Your Home,* Que, 1999. If you have two or more computers in your home or small business and you want to network them to share equipment and resources, check out this book. Presented in a clear, easy-going style, the authors show you how to set up a network to share an Internet connection, play multiplayer games, and share files, folders and printers amongst all your home computers. The authors show you how to set up a network using standard network cables, phone lines, and even wireless devices.

Ron White, *How Computers Work,* Que, 1999. If you're interested in learning more about what's going on inside your computer, *How Computers Work* is the best illustrated guide on the market. Ron White leads the tour, providing plain-English descriptions of computers and peripheral devices.

Magazines

Smart Computing one of the few computer magazines that still offers hands-on, step-by-step instructions on how to troubleshoot common computer problems and get the most out of your computing experience. This magazine also features hardware and software reviews and tips for using Windows and the most popular Windows applications. If you have an Internet connection, you can subscribe online at www. smartcomputing.com. Otherwise, call 1-800-733-3809.

Family PC is a great magazine for learning how to put your computer to work for you in your home and help your children get up to speed on the computer … assuming, of course, that you have children. The articles in *Family PC* focus on using the computer to perform specific tasks, such as planning a garden, designing your own home, and managing your finances. You'll also find tips for making the computing experience safe and rewarding for your children. If you have an Internet connection, you can subscribe online at www.familypc.com.

PC Magazine is the computer magazine of choice for business people and those who like to keep up on the latest technology. If you're a rank beginner, this magazine may not appeal to you, but if you're learning computers in a corporate setting and need to be well-informed, *PC Magazine* is a good choice. If you have an Internet connection, you can subscribe online at www.zdmcirc.com.

Computer Gaming World is an excellent magazine for computer game enthusiast. This magazine is packed with reviews of the latest games along with tips and tricks from master gamers. If you have an Internet connection, you can subscribe online at www.zdmcirc.com.

Resources on the Web

ZDnet at www.zdnet.com is the place you go for help when you don't know where to go for help. Ziff Davis, the site's host, publishes most of the magazines listed in the previous section and features many of its articles online. In addition, you can find help for troubleshooting problems and assistance in finding the best hardware and software for your needs.

clnet at www.cnet.com is like having a free computer library right on your computer. Here, you find links to hardware and software reviews, technology news, freeware and shareware versions of popular programs, instructions and tools for building your own Web site, and even a searchable database for troubleshooting computer problems.

Webopedia at www.webopedia.com features a searchable database of computer terms and definitions. Whenever you come across a computer term whose definition eludes you, go to Webopedia and look it up.

The PC Guide, by Charles M. Kozierok at www.pcguide.com provides a comprehensive explanation of how each component in a computer functions. If you want to learn more about computers, don't skip past this site. And, while you're there, check out the System BIOS section to find out how to tweak your computer's startup settings to enhance its performance.

Microsoft Knowledge Base at search.support.microsoft.com is a search engine designed to help users troubleshoot problems with Windows and other Microsoft software. Whenever an error message pops up on your screen, this is the first place to go for help. This site has solved dozens of problems that have had me stumped.

McAfee Anti-Virus Page at www.mcafee.com/anti-virus is an excellent site to visit to learn more about computer viruses and how to prevent them from infecting your system. This site also contains a link that displays a list of know virus hoaxes (phony warnings), so when someone sends you an email message warning of a virus, you can determine if the threat is real or fake.

DSLReports at www.dslreports.com provides tools and information about high-speed Internet connections. Click the **Tools** link and click **Speed Tests** to access a page for testing your Internet connection speed. I've used this site many times to gather information about my cable connection before calling my cable service's technical support number. Having details about my connection speed helped me convince technical support that my connection wasn't up to snuff.

Macmillan USA at www.mcp.com is the place to go when you're looking for a book on a specific computer application or topic. Click the desired imprint (*Idiot's Guides*, Que, Sams, BradyGames, or Macmillan Software) and start exploring.

Videos and Interactive Training CDs

Video Professor provides interactive training CDs for Windows and the most popular Windows applications. You pop the CD into your computer's CD-ROM drive, and then follow the onscreen instructions to proceed through the course. Video Professor isn't the greatest for learning specifics, but each course provides a great overview of how to use the most common features of a program. To learn more about Video Professor or to order a course, call 1-800-525-7763 or go to www.videoprofessor.com.

Keystone Learning Systems offers a wide selection of courses on video, CD-ROM, and DVD. These courses are a bit pricey, but they're very comprehensive. Also, if you're having trouble finding a video on a particular program, chances are that Keystone Learning Systems has the course you need.

LearnKey is the self-proclaimed leader in video and CD-based computer education and has a wide selection of products ranging from beginner-level courses to certification programs. Like Keystone Learning Systems' products, these courses can be a bit pricey, ranging from about $60 to over $3,000. To check out what LearnKey has to offer, go to www.learnkey.com or call 1-800-865-0165.

Index

Symbols

3COM Web site, 227
3D audio game hardware, 262
401(k) accounts, 243

A

ABC News Web site, 216
accessing chat rooms
    Chatting.com, 199
    Flirt.com, 199
    Yahoo!, 197-199
Accessories command
    (Programs menu), 37
Accessories menu (Games),
    35-43
    FreeCell, 38-39
    Hearts, 40-41
    Minesweeper, 41-42
    Pinball, 42-43
    Solitaire, 37-38
    Spider Solitaire, 42-43
accounts
    online banking
        cash transfers, 255
        records downloads, 255
    personal finances
        transactions, 243
        types, 242-243
    Quicken
        creating, 243-244
        reconciling, 247
        transaction recordings,
            244
AccuWeather Web site, 218
Acer Web site, 226
action/fighting games, 260
activating/deactivating
    screen savers, 57
    Web style desktops, 14-15

active desktops. See also
    desktops
    appearance settings, 53-54
    channel bars, 53
    components, 53-54
    gallery, 54
    Quick Launch toolbars, 53
    Web Styles, 53
Add New Hardware Wizard,
    installing device drivers,
    9-10
add-on programs, handheld
    devices, installing, 340-341
Add/Remove Programs panel
    programs, installation/
        uninstallation, 35, 37
    Windows Setup tab
        indicators, 36
Add/Remove Programs utility
    programs, deleting, 86-87
adding. See also inserting
    borders (documents), 109
    buttons (Quick Launch
        toolbar), 31
    pictures
        captions, 297
        Kodak Picture CD,
            295-296
        tables, 134
    tables
        borders, 133
        shading, 133
address books, 126
    creating (Microsoft
        Outlook), 127
    tables, creating (Microsoft
        Word), 126-127, 130-131
Address toolbars, 69
Address.com, free ISP, 167
addresses
    envelopes
        printing, 100-101
        mail merges, 145

mailing labels, 144-145
outgoing e-mail messages,
    180
Web pages
    deciphering, 208
    typing in browsers, 207
Adler Planetarium Web site,
    290
ADSL (Asynchronous DSL),
    153
adventure games, 260
advertising materials,
    Microsoft Publisher, 123
albums, digital photography,
    304
aligning text in documents,
    96-97
AltaVista Web site, 208
Amazon.com Web site, 328
America Online. See AOL
American Heritage Dictionary,
    271
Ameritrade Web site, 221
analog videos
    conversion to digital, 352
    PC connections, 353
Ancestry.com Web site, 312
antistatic wipes (monitor
    cleaning), 375
antivirus programs, 186
AOL (America Online)
    chat rooms
        entering, 194-195
        maximum persons, 195
        member profiles, 195
        privacy warnings, 196
        private messages, 196
        public, 196-197
    Instant Messenger, 200-202
    memberships
        cancellations, 166
        information, 162
    parental controls, 282-284
    payment plans, 162

applications, installation requirements. *See also* programs
CPU, 80
disk space, 80
DVD drives, 81
monitors, 80
mouse, 80
operating systems, 80
RAM, 81
software, 80
sound cards, 81
arcade games, 260
Arrange menu commands, 121
arranging images, frame layers (Microsoft Publisher), 121
arrow indicators, menus, 19
Art Dabbler, 277
art skill software programs
Art Dabbler, 277
Crayola Creativity Packs, 277
Flying Colors, 277
ImaginAction, 277
JumpStart Artist, 277
You Can Draw!, 277
ArtToday Web site, 235
asset accounts, 243
Associated Press Web site, 217
ATI All-in-Wonder card (TV), 345-346
attachments
documents, 185-186
e-mail viruses, 186
audio. *See also* sound
digital cameras, 301
CD burners, 331-332
clips, 225
data
CD Red Book format, 321
CD rippers, 322
CD-R, 322
CD-RW, 322
MP3 format, 321-328
equipment
assigning specific sounds to events, 63
playing CDs, 64
recording audio clips, 65-66

selecting sound schemes, 63
testing, 60
troubleshooting problems, 62
volume controls, 60
streaming
Liquid Audio, 323
RealAudio, 323
Audiofind Web site, 328
AudioGalaxy Web site, 328
autoformatting tables, 133
autoinstalling programs, 84
autolaunching programs
document openings, 32
startup, 30
Task Scheduler, 71-72

B

B-City, associated costs, 235
background music, digital video clips (Windows Movie Maker), 357-358
backgrounds (desktop themes)
color schemes, 49
icons and visual effects, 51-52
installing, 48
screen savers
activating/deactivating, 57
passwords, 57-58
selecting, 56-57
selecting, 48-49
wallpapers
applying, 51
copying from Web pages, 51
image types, 51
banners
creating (Microsoft Publisher), 121-122
printer settings, 121-122
beaming (handheld devices)
data, 341
files, 337, 341
Beyond.com Web site, 266-267
BigFoot, 209

BIOS (Basic Input/Output System), 386
BitMorph, 305
bits per seconds (bps), 150
Blockbuster Video Web site, 223
board games, 260
bookmarking Web pages, 211-212
books as resources, 405-406
borders, adding
documents, 109
letterheads, 112
tables, 133
Borders and Shading command (Format menu), 133
Borland Web site, 226
brochures (Microsoft Publisher), 123
Broderbund Web site, 227, 308
Brother Web site, 227
budgets (Quicken)
categories, 249
creating, 248-249
entries
creating, 249
modifying, 249
reports, 250
building Web pages, 231-234
burners (audio CD burners), 331
business-related hosting services
B-City, 235
Netscape Virtual Office, 234
selection criteria, 235
Yahoo! Small Business, 235
Buy.com Web site, 266-267

C

cable connections (computer placement), 4
cable modems
availability, 154
connecting, 156
connection speeds, 154
costs, 154

Ethernet adapters, 156
indicator lights, 156
RF-returns, 154
upload problems, 154
calculators (Quicken)
College, 250
Loan, 250
Refinance, 250
Retirement, 250
Savings, 250
camcorders (digital video)
clips
audio backgrounds,
357-358
editing, 354
recording, 354-355
saving, 354
splicing, 356-357
equipment setups, 353
IEEE-1394 (FireWire),
351-352
USB connectors, 351-352
cameras. *See* digital cameras
cancellation of online service
memberships
AOL, 166
CompuServe, 166
MSN, 166
Prodigy Internet, 166
Canon Web site, 227
captions (Kodak Picture CD),
297
card games, 260
cascading windows, 22
cash accounts, 242
CBS News Web site, 216
CBS Sportsline Web site, 219
CD rippers, function of, 322
CD-R
CD-Recordable, 322
CD-Rewritable, 322
CDs
custom mix creations,
333
duplicating, 332
data storage, 322
versus CD-RW, 322
CD-RW
CDs
custom mix creations,
333
duplicating, 332

data storage, 322
versus CD-R, 322
CDNOW Web site, 225
CDs (compact discs), 321
burners, 331-332
commercial audio clips,
copyright restrictions,
329
custom mixes (Easy CD
Creator), 333
data storage, 322
duplicating (Easy CD
Creator), 332
jukebox players
RealJukebox, 324
Windows Media Player,
324-326
playing music, 64-65
Red Book format, 321
versus MP3 clips, 328
cells (spreadsheets)
addresses, 127-128
formulas, 127-128
censoring software
Cyber Patrol, 285
Cyber Snoop, 286
CYBERsitter, 285
Net Nanny, 286
censorship (internet)
AOL parental controls,
282-284
censor programs, 285
history lists, 281-282
Internet Explorer censor
controls, 284
CFSB Direct Web site, 221
changing windows, 22
channel bars (active
desktop), 53
channels, WebTV, 346
Charles Schwab Web site, 221
chat rooms
AOL
entering, 194-195
maximum persons, 195
member profiles, 195
privacy warning, 196
private messages, 196
public, 196-197
Chatting.com, 199
Flirt.com, 199

instant messaging options,
200-202
locating Web sites, 197-199
Yahoo!, 197-199
Chatting.com Web site, 199
Cheater's Guild Web site, 267
CheatStation Web site, 267
check boxes (dialog boxes), 20
checking accounts, 242
checks
ordering, 246
printing, 245-246
child safety (Internet)
AOL parental controls,
282-284
censor software
Cyber Patrol, 285
Cyber Snoop, 286
CYBERsitter, 285
Net Nanny, 286
censorships, 281-282
guidelines, 280-281
history lists, 281-282
importance of parental
supervision, 281
Internet Explorer censor
controls, 284
children's activities
Adler Planetarium Web
site, 290
Library of Congress Web
site, 290
Louvre Art Museum Web
site, 289
Museum Network Web site,
289
Museum of Science and
Industry Web site, 290
New York Museum of
Modern Art Web site, 289
pen pals
epals.com, 290
KeyPals, 290
Penpal Box, 291
Smithsonian Institution
Web site, 289
White House for Kids Web
site, 288
Yahoo! Gameroom,
286-287

Children's Software Review
Web site, 277
cleaning procedures
disk drives, 378
keyboards, 376
monitors, 375
mouse, 376-377
PCs
equipment, 373-374
rubbing alcohol, 377
vacuuming procedures,
374-375
printers, 377-378
spills, 376
clearing
files from hard disk
performance tuning,
381-382
ScanDisk, 382-383
history lists, 211
clicking (mouse), 15
clip-art, inserting on
letterheads, 111-112
CLIPART.COM Web site, 235
Clipboard, data storage, 104
close-talk microphones
noise reduction guidelines,
368
speech recognition
requirements, 364
testing, 364-365
closing windows, 22
CNN Web site, 216
CNN/SI Web site, 219
Cognitive Technologies Web
site, 277
College Calculator (Quicken),
250
colors
desktop settings, 74-75
modifying schemes, 49-50
Columbia Book of Quotations,
271
columns (tables)
deleting, 131
setting, 130
width modifications, 131
command buttons (dialog
boxes), 21
commands
Arrange menu, 121
Edit menu, 105

File menu
Page Setup, 98, 107
Print, 110
Format menu
Borders and Shading,
133
Paragraphs, 97
Insert menu
Date and Time, 94-95
Picture, 134
New menu folder, 30
Programs menu
(Accessories), 37
speech recognition soft-
ware, 369
Start menu programs,
27-28
Table menu
Formula, 132
Sort, 132
Table AutoFormat, 133
Tools menu
Envelopes and Labels,
100
Letters and Mailings,
139
Spelling and Grammar,
105, 107
View menu
Folder Options, 15
Header and Footer, 108
Compaq Web site, 227
*Complete Idiot's Guide to
Microsoft Windows Millenium,
The*, 405
*Complete Idiot's Guide to
Networking Your Home, The*,
405
*Complete Idiot's Guide to
Quicken 2000, The*, 242
composing form letters, 139
CompuServe
memberships
cancellations, 166
information, 162
payment plans, 162
computer games. *See* games
Computer Gaming World, 406
computer manufacturers
software patches, down-
loading, 225
Web sites, 226-227

computers
connection guidelines, 6-7
parental supervision, 281
placement considerations,
3-4
cable connections, 4
electrical requirements, 4
environment concerns, 4
magnetic fields, 4
phone jack connec-
tions, 4
startup procedures, 7-8
surge supressors, 5
turning off, 10-11
unpacking guidelines, 5-6
configuring
Internet connections,
169-172
online banking (Quicken
settings), 252-253
connections
analog camcorders to PCs,
353
hardware guidelines, 6-7
Internet
settings, 169-172
testing procedures, 172
troubleshooting tips,
173-174
modems
cable types, 156
DSL types, 155
external, 154-155
internal, 154-155
ISDN types, 155
standard types, 155
Palm IIIc to desktop
computers, 337-339
VCRs to PCs, 353
Content Advisor (Internet
Explorer), 284
Content tab (Help system), 25
context menus, 19
Control Panel
Add/Remove Programs
icon, 86-87
desktop themes
installing, 48
selecting, 48-49
Sounds icon, 60
Scheme list, 62-63

conversions
  analog video to digital video, 352
  voice dictations, 367-368
Cookie Central.com, 213
cookies
  Cookie Central.com, 213
  deleting, 213
  disabling, 213
  function of, 212
copying
  CDs (Easy CD Creator), 332
  digital camera pictures, 301
  MP3 clips to portable MP3 players, 330-331
  Web images to wallpapers, 51
copyright laws, commercial audio clips, 329
Corel Web site, 227
costs of online services
  AOL, 162
  Compuserve, 162
  MSN, 162
  Prodigy Internet, 163
CPU, program installation requirements, 80
cradles, handheld devices, 336
Crayola Creativity Packs, 277
creating
  accounts (Quicken), 243-244
  address books
    from tables (Microsoft Word), 126-131
    Microsoft Outlook, 127
  banners (Microsoft Publisher), 121-122
  budgets (Quicken), 248-249
  CD custom mixes (Easy CD Creator), 333
  desktop folders, 30
  greeting cards (Microsoft Publisher), 116-117
  letterheads, 111-112
  public chat rooms (AOL), 196-197
  text boxes (Microsoft Publisher), 120

Creative Labs Web site, 227
credit card accounts, 242
cropping images (Microsoft Publisher), 119
cursor-movement keys (keyboard), 17
CUSeeMe videoconferencing, 202
custom installations (programs), 85
cutting text in documents, 104-105
Cyber Patrol (censoring software), 285
Cyber Snoop (censoring software), 286
CYBERsitter (censoring software), 285
clnet Web site, 227, 407

D

damaged files, removing with ScanDisk, 382-383
data, beaming, 341
databases
  family trees, searching (Family Tree Maker), 309-310
  records
    filtering, 129
    management of, 129
  relationals, 126
  tools, 129
Date and Time command (Insert menu), 94-95
dates, inserting
  documents, 94-95
  letterheads, 111
defragmenting files (Disk Fragmenter), 383-385
deleting. *See also* removing
  columns, 131
  desktop icons, 76
  files (Recycle Bin), 24
  programs (Add/Remove Programs utility), 86-87
  rows, 131
  text, 92
Dell Web site, 227

desktops. *See also* active desktop
  colors
    schemes, 49-50
    settings, 74-75
  display areas, 73-75
  folders, creating, 30
  fonts, 49-50
  icons, 13
    deleting, 76
    organizing in folders, 77
    rearranging, 75-76
    underlined appearances, 14-15
    visual effects, 51-52
  multiple users, 55
  My Computer, 23
  Recycle Bin, 24
  screen savers, 56-58
    activating/deactivating, 57
    passwords, 57-58
    selecting, 56
  settings, locking, 55
  shortcut icons
    creating, 28-29
    documents, creating, 32
    launching programs, 28-29
    taskbars, 13
  themes, 47-50
    color schemes, 49-50
    disk space consumptions, 48
    installing, 48
    selecting, 48-49
  utilities, 13
  wallpapers
    applying, 51
    copying from Web pages, 51
    image types, 51
  windows
    cascading, 22
    changing, 22
    closing, 22
    maximize size, 22
    minimum size, 22
    moving, 22
    resizing, 22
    tiling, 22
  Windows Explorer, 23-24

Desktop toolbars, 69
device driver hardware, installing (Add New Hardware Wizard), 9-10
devices
    connection guidelines, 6-7
    information, System Properties dialog box, 81
dialing out (modems), troubleshooting tips, 156-158
dialog boxes
    check boxes, 20
    command buttons, 21
    Display Properties, 49-50
    drop-down list boxes, 20
    list boxes, 20
    option buttons, 20
    question mark buttons, 21
    radio buttons, 20
    sliders, 21
    Sounds and Multimedia Properties, 60
    spin boxes, 21
    System Properties, 81
    tabs, 20
    text boxes, 20
digital cameras
    pictures
        copying to computer, 301
        ordering high-quality prints, 302
    popularity of, 300-301
    price ranges, 301
    settings
        audio, 301
        flash, 301
        resolutions, 301
    uses, 300-301
digital photography
    creating albums, 304
    Kodak Picture CD
        adding, 295-296
        captions, 297
        e-mailing, 298-299
        editing, 296
        printing, 297-299
        viewing, 294

morphing programs
    BitMorph, 305
    Elastic Reality, 305
    Morph Man, 305
    Paint Shop Pro, editing features, 303
digital signatures, e-mail encryptions, 190-191
digital video
    analog conversions, 352
    camcorders
        IEEE-1394 (FireWire), 351-352
        shopping guidelines, 351-352
        USB connectors, 351-352
    clips
        editing, 354
        saving, 354
        Windows Movie Maker, 356-361
    equipment setups, 353
DirecPC (satellite connection service), 154
directories, purpose of, 23
Disk Defragmenter, launching, 383-385
disk drives, cleaning, 378
disk space
    availability
        checking, 82-84
        freeing, 83
    program installation requirements, 80
    versus memory, 81
Display Properties dialog box, 49-50
documents
    borders, 109
    dating, 94-95
    e-mail attachments, 185-186
    file extension associations, 32
    footers, 108
    formatting changes, undoing, 105
    headers, 108
    insertion points, 92-94

letterheads, 111-112
line numbers, 109
line spacing, 97
margins
    mirror, 108
    settings, 98, 107-108
naming, 98-100
paragraphs
    indenting, 96-97
    new, 92
    spacing options, 98
print options
    collating, 110
    landscapes, 108
    number of copies, 110
    paper sources, 109
    previews, 109
    portraits, 108
    quality, 110
    troubleshooting tips, 110-111
programs, launching from, 32
red/green line error indicators, 94
saving, 98-100
shortcut icons, 32
spell check (Word), 94
text
    alignment options, 96-97
    cutting, 104-105
    deleting, 92
    pasting, 104-105
    resizing, 95
    selection options, 104
    spell check, 105-107
    typing, 92-94
    zooming, 92
vertical alignment, 109
views
    Normal, 93
    Outline, 94
    Print Layout, 93
    Web Layout, 93
domain name server (DNS), ISPs, 169
DOS games, running under Windows, 262-264

downloading
  games
    compressed types,
      265-266
    Free Games Net, 265
    GameGenie.com, 265
    Gamer's Inn, 265
    The Games Network,
      264
    HotGames.com, 264
    self-extracting types,
      265-266
    ZDNet GameSpot, 264
  MP3 clips, 327-328
  RealJukebox, 324
  shareware programs, 340
  Windows Media Player,
    323
dragging (mouse function), 16
driving/simulation games,
  260
drop-down list boxes (dialog
  boxes), 20
DSL modems (digital
  subscriber lines)
  ADSL (Asynchronous DSL),
    153
  connecting, 155
  issues for consideration,
    153
  SDSL (Symmetric DSL), 153
  transmission speeds, 153
DSLReports Web site, 407
duplicating CDs (Easy CD
  Creator), 332
DVD drives, program installation requirements, 81
DVD videos
  additional menu opotions,
    348
  display resolutions, 347
  playing, 348

E

E*TRADE Web site, 221
e-mails
  abbreviations, 188-189
  addresses, ISPs, 169
  attachments, 185-186

digital video movies
  (Windows Movie Maker),
  359
emoticons, 187
encryption
  digital signatures,
    190-191
  PGP (Pretty Good
    Privacy), 191
  S/MIME, 190-191
etiquette, 189-190
flaming, 189
folders, 183
formatting enhancements,
  183-184
free services, 186-187
  Excite, 187
  Hotmail, 187
  Yahoo!, 187
  ZDNet onebox, 187
incoming messages,
  182-183
ISP information
  accounts, 178
  e-mail address, 178
  incoming mail (POP3),
    178
  outgoing mail (SMTP),
    178
links, 184
mail servers, 178
messages
  forwarding, 183
  replying, 182-183
Netscape Messenger,
  179-180
outgoing messages,
  180-181
Outlook Express, 178-179
pictures
  inserting, 184
  Kodak Picture CD,
    298-299
EarthWatch Web site, 218
Easter Eggs, 267
Easy CD Creator
  copying CDs, 332
  custom mix creations, 333
Easy Internet, 405
eCircles
  online communities, 199
  voice support, 202

Edit menu commands
  (Undo), 105
editing
  digital video clips, 354
  pictures (Kodak Picture
    CD), 296
educational software
  *American Heritage
    Dictionary,* 271
  art skills
    Art Dabbler, 277
    Crayola Creativity
      Packs, 277
    Flying Colors, 277
    ImaginAction, 277
    JumpStart Artist, 277
    You Can Draw!, 277
  Children's Software Review
    Web site, 277
  *Columbia Book of
    Quotations,* 271
  Encarta Desk Encyclopedia,
    271
  Encarta Desk World Atlas,
    271
  *Encarta Manual of Style and
    Usage,* 271
  *Encarta New World
    Almanac,* 272
  *Encarta New World
    Timeline,* 272
  Knowledge Adventure, 273
  language skills
    JumpStart Spanish, 276
    Microsoft Creative
      Writer, 274-275
  Math Blaster, 273
  Microsoft Kids, 274
  multimedia encyclopedias
    Encyclopedia Britannica,
      269
    Microsoft Encarta,
      270-271
  Reader Rabbit, 272
  Roget's Electronic Thesaurus,
    271
  Teach Me Piano, 275
  The Learning Company,
    272
  Web sites
    Fun School, 272
    SmarterKids.com, 272
    SuperKids, 272

Elastic Reality (image morphing program), 305
electronic bill payments, online banking (Quicken settings), 253-255
electronic day planners, PIMs (Microsoft Outlook), 127
ellipsis (…), 19
emoticons, e-mail symbols, 187
Encarta Desk Encyclopedia, 271
Encarta Desk World Atlas, 271
Encarta Manual of Style and Usage, 271
Encarta New World Almanac, 272
Encarta New World Timeline, 272
encryptions
    e-mails
        digital signatures, 190-191
        PGP (Pretty Good Privacy), 191
        S/MIME, 190-191
        VeriSign, 190-191
encyclopedias (multimedia)
    Encyclopedia Britannica, 269
    Microsoft Encarta, 270-271
enlarging taskbars, 77
envelopes
    printing, 100-101
    mail merges, 145
Envelopes and Labels command (Tools menu), 100
Epals.com Web site, 290
Epson Web site, 227
ESPN Web site, 219
Ethernet adapters, 156
etiquette (e-mail), 189-190
Excite Web site, 208
expansion slots, 152
external modems
    connecting, 154-155
    indicator lights, 151

F

families
    instant messaging, 200-202
    online communities, eCircles, 199

Family PC, 406
Family Tree Maker
    databases, 309-310
    entries
        adding, 315-316
        appending, 316
        printing, 316-317
    online resources, 311
family trees
    lost relative searches, 314
    newsgroup resources, 313-314
    online research, 311
    programs
        Family Tree Maker, 308-310
        Generations Family Tree, 308
        shareware samples, 308
        Ultimate Family Tree, 308
    Web sites
        Ancestry.com, 312
        FamilySearch, 313
        GENDEX, 313
        Genealogy Home Page, 313
        Genealogy.com, 312
        GenExchange, 313
        Gensource.com, 312
FamilySearch Web site, 313
favorites, bookmarking Web pages, 211-212
faxes, modem support, 151
field codes, inserting form letters, 139-143
file associations, MP3 players, 329
File menu commands
    Page Setup, 98, 107
    Print, 110
filename extensions, 32
files
    beaming, 341
    compressing/decompressing (WinZip), 265-266
    defragmenting (Disk Defragmenter), 383-385
    deleting (Recycle Bin), 24
    e-mail attachments, 185-186

folders, purpose of, 23
    locating
        My Computer, 23
        Windows Explorer, 23
    moving (Windows Explorer), 24
    removing
        performance tuning, 381-382
        ScanDisk, 382-383
    restoring (Recycle Bin), 24
fill patterns, tables, 133
filtering records, 129
financial programs. *See* personal finance programs
Find People Fast Web site, 314
flaming e-mail messages, 189
flatbed scanners, 303-304
Flirt.com Web site, 199
floppy disks
    programs, installing from, 86
    write protections, 86
Flying Colors software, 277
Folder command (New menu), 30
Folder Options command (View menu), 15
folders
    creating, 30
    desktop icons, organizing, 77
    purpose of, 23
    startup programs, 30
    transforming into toolbars, 69-71
fonts
    desktops, 49-50
    point size, 95
    sources, 95
footers, 108
foreign language software, JumpStart Spanish, 276
form letters
    composing, 139
    field codes, 139-143
    Letter Wizard (Microsoft Wizard), 139
    mail merge
        executing, 143-144
        process, 137-138
        query preferences, settings, 143-144

Format menu commands
    Borders and Shading, 133
    Paragraph, 97
formatting e-mails, enhance-
    ment options, 183-184
Formula command (Table
    menu), 132
formulas, inserting tables, 132
forwarding e-mail messages,
    183
frames
    grouping, 121
    layering, 121
    pages, 119
free e-mail services, 186-187
    Excite, 187
    Hotmail, 187
    Yahoo!, 187
    ZDNet onebox, 187
Free Games Net Web site, 265
Free-Backgrounds.com Web
    site, 236
FreeCell, 38-39
freeing disk space, 83
friends
    instant messaging, 200-202
    online communities,
        eCircles, 199
FrontPage Express, 230
Fujitsu Web site, 227
Fun School Web site, 272
function keys (keyboard), 17
Future Games Network Web
    site, 267

G

GameGenie.com Web site,
    265
Gamer's Inn Web site, 265
games
    categories
        action/fighting, 260
        adventure, 260
        arcade, 260
        board, 260
        card, 260
        driving/simulation, 260
        role playing, 260
        sports, 260
        strategy, 261

components, installed
    status, 36-37
DOS running under
    Windows, 262-264
downloading
    compressed types,
        265-266
    self-extracting types,
        265-266
Easter Eggs, 267
FreeCell, 38-39
Hearts, 40-41
hint/cheat sites
    Cheater's Guild, 267
    CheatStation, 267
    Future Games Network,
        267
    GameStats, 268
    IGN Guides, 268
    Super Games, 268
installing, 35-37
Minesweeper, 41-42
online purchase sites
    Beyond.com, 266-267
    Buy.com, 266-267
    Gamestop.com, 266-267
    Outpost.com, 266-267
Pinball, 42-43
required hardware
    3D audio, 262
    controller/joysticks, 262
    SVGA video, 261
Solitaire, 37-38
Spider Solitaire, 42-43
Web sites
    Free Games Net, 265
    GameGenie.com, 265
    Gamer's Inn, 265
    The Games Network,
        264
    HotGames.com, 264
    Yahoo! Gameroom,
        286-287
    ZDNet GameSpot, 264
GameStats Web site, 268
Gamestop.com Web site,
    266-267
Gateway Web site, 227
GENDEX Web site, 313
genealogy
    entries, 309
    lost relative searches, 314

newsgroup resources,
    313-314
online research, 311
programs
    Family Tree Maker,
        308-310
    Generations Family
        Tree, 308
    shareware samples, 308
    Ultimate Family Tree,
        308
sites
    Ancestry.com, 312
    FamilySearch, 313
    GENDEX, 313
    Genealogy Home Page,
        313
    Genealogy.com, 312
    GenExchange, 313
    Gensource.com, 312
Genealogy Home Page Web
    site, 313
Genealogy.com Web site, 312
Generations Family Tree, 308
GenExchange Web site, 313
Gensource.com Web site, 312
Gigabeat Web site, 328
Go.com Web site, 208
Google Web site, 208
grayed out menu
    commands, 19
green/red line indicators
    (Microsoft Word), 94
greeting cards
    creating (Microsoft
        Publisher), 116-117
    Web sites, 200
grounded outlets, computer
    placement, 4
grouping frames, 121

H

handheld devices. *See also*
    Palm IIIc
    accessories, 341-342
    add-on programs, 340-341
    cradles, 336
    data
        beaming, 341
        styluses, 336

desktop software, 337-339
handwriting recognition
    software, 337
infrared ports, 337
scanners, 302
shareware programs, 340
synchronizing with desk-
    top computers, 336
text entry, 337
typical features, 335
handwriting recognition
    software, 337
hard disk, disk space
    checking availability, 82,
    84
    freeing, 83
hardware
    connection guidelines, 6-7
    device drivers, installing
        (Add New Hardware
        Wizard), 9-10
    games
        3D audio, 262
        joysticks, 262
        SVGA video, 261
    information, System
        Properties dialog box, 81
    unpacking requirements,
        5-6
Hayes Web site, 227
Header and Footer command
    (View menu), 108
headers, 108
headings, table entries,
    130-131
headphones, 64-65
Hearts
    network connections,
        40-41
    playing, 40-41
help systems, navigation of
    online services, 165
Help window (Contents
    tab), 25
Hewlett-Packard Web site, 227
Hibernation mode (power
    saving feature), 385-386
hiding taskbars, 76-77
hint/cheat Web sites (games)
    Cheater's Guild, 267
    CheatStation, 267
    Future Games Network,
        267

GameStats, 268
IGN Guides, 268
Super Games, 268
history lists
    children's surfing habits,
        viewing, 281-282
    Web browsers
        clearing, 211
        viewing, 210-211
Hitachi Web site, 227
home pages, changing Web
    browsers, 212
home computers, placement
    considerations, 3-4
hosting services (business-
    related)
    B-City, 235
    Netscape Virtual Office,
        234
    selection criteria, 235
    Yahoo! Small Business, 235
HotDog, 230
HotGames.com Web site, 264
Hotmail (free e-mail service),
    187
How Computers Work, 406
HTML (Hypertext Markup
Language)
    tags, 230
    tools
        FrontPage Express, 230
        HotDog, 230
        Netscape Composer, 230
        Web Studio, 230

I

IBM ViaVoice (speech recogni-
    tion software), 365
IBM Web site, 227, 277
icons, 13
    desktops
        deleting, 76
        organizing in folders, 77
        rearranging, 75-76
    toolbar commands, 21
    underlined appearances
        (Web style), 14-15
    visual effects, 51-52

IEEE-1394 (FireWire) (digital
    camcorder), 351-352
IGN Guides Web site, 268
images
    frames
        arranging, 121
        grouping, 121
        handles (Microsoft
            Publisher), 119
    pages
        cropping, 119
        inserting, 119
    tables, adding, 134
ImaginAction software, 277
Inbox, viewing e-mail
    messages, 182-183
incoming e-mail
    checking, 182-183
    POP3, ISP information, 178
indenting paragraphs, 96-97
InfoSpace (people locator
    service), 209
infrared ports (handheld
    devices), beaming functions,
    337
Insert menu commands
    Date and Time, 94-95
    Picture, 134
inserting. *See also* adding
    borders, 112
    clip-art, 11-112
    date codes, 111
    dates in documents, 94-95
    e-mail links, 184
    field codes, 139-143
    formulas (tables), 132
    images (Microsoft
        Publisher), 119
    lines, 112
    photographs in e-mails,
        184
insertion points, 92-94
installing
    add-on programs, (hand-
        held devices), 340-341
    desktop themes, 48
    device driver hardware
        (Add New Hardware
        Wizard), 9-10
    games, 35-37

online services, 163-164
programs
  automated
    components, 84
  custom options, 85
  from floppy disks, 86
  lack of disk space
    messages, 83
  manually, 84-85
  minimal options, 85
  minimum hardware
    requirements, 80-81
  typical options, 85
speech recognition
  software, 365
TV tuner cards, 345-346
WebTV, 346
Windows Media Player,
  323
instant messages
  AOL Instant Messenger,
    200-202
  MSN Messenger, 200-202
  Yahoo! Messenger, 200-202
Intel Web site, 227
IntelliMouse, wheel
  scrolling action, 16
  zooming action, 16
interactive gaming, WebTV,
  347
internal modems
  connecting, 154-155
  expansion slot require-
    ments, 151
Internet
  child safety
    AOL parental controls,
      282-284
    censorship, 281-282
    Cyber Patrol, 285
    Cyber Snoop, 286
    CYBERsitter, 285
    guidelines, 280-281
    Internet Explorer censor
      controls, 284
    Net Nanny, 286
  connections
    configuring, 169-172
    testing, 172
    troubleshooting tips,
      173-174
  phone calls, Net2Phone,
    201-202

Internet Connection Wizard,
  169-172
Internet Explorer
  Content Advisor, 284
  cookies
    deleting, 213
    disabling, 213
  history lists
    children's surfing habits,
      281-282
    clearing, 211
    viewing, 210
  home pages, changing, 212
  launching, 206
  Quick Launch toolbar, 22
  Search bar, 209
  Web pages, bookmarking
    favorites, 211-212
Internet keyboards versus
  standard keyboards, 18
Internet Movie Database Web
  site, 223
Internet service providers.
  See ISPs
Internet Underground Music
  Archive Web site, 224
investing (online)
  Ameritrade, 221
  Charles Schwab, 221
  CSFB Direct, 221
  E*TRADE, 221
investment accounts, 243
Iomega Web site, 227
ISDN modems
  channels, 152
  connecting, 155
  costs, 153
  speeds, 152
ISPs (Internet service
  providers)
  Address.com, 167
  connection types
    PPP, 168
    SLIP, 168
  domain name servers
    (DNS), 169
  e-mail information
    accounts, 178
    addresses, 169, 178
    incoming mail (POP3),
      178

Netscape Messenger
  settings, 179-180
outgoing mail (SMTP),
  178
Outlook Express
  settings, 178-179
Juno, 167
locating, 167-168
mail servers, 169, 178
NetZero, 167
news servers, 169
password selections, 168
phone number
  connections, 168
selection criteria, 167-168
username selections, 168
versus online services, 161
Web browsers, customized,
  206
ITU standard, modem
  connections, 151
IUMA (Internet Underground
  Music Archive) Web site, 328

J

Jasc Software Web site, 303
joysticks, 262
jukebox CD players
  RealJukebox, 324
  Windows Media Player
    changing skins, 326
    playlists, creating,
      324-326
JumpStart Artist software, 277
JumpStart Spanish, 276
Juno, 167

K

keyboards
  cleaning guidelines, 376
  cursor-movement keys, 17
  Esc keys, 17
  function keys, 17
  Internet styles, 18
  numeric keys, 17
  Pause/Break keys, 17
  Print Screen/SysReq
    keys, 17

419

Scroll Lock keys, 17
shortcut keys, 18
KeyPals Web site, 290
Keystone Learning Systems, 408
kilobits per second (kps), 150
Knowledge Adventure (educational software program), 273
Kodak Picture CD options
adding pictures, 295-296
captions, 297
e-mailing, 298-299
editing, 296
printing, 297-299
viewing, 294

L

landscape orientation, printing, 108
language software programs
JumpStart Spanish, 276
Microsoft Creative Writer, 274-275
launching. *See also* opening; startups
Disk Defragmenter, 383-385
games, 35, 37
Internet Explorer, 206
programs
desktop shortcuts, 28-29
document openings, 32
keyboard shortcuts, 29
Quick Launch toolbars, 31
Start menu, 27-28
startup, 30
taskbars, 22
Web browsers, 206
WebTV, 346
WordPad, 92
layering frames (Microsoft Publisher), 121
Learning Company, The, 272
LearnKey, 408
Letter Wizard (Microsoft Word), 139

letterheads
creating, 111-112
inserting
borders, 112
clip-art, 111-112
date codes, 111
lines, 112
letters (form letters)
composing, 139
field codes, 139, 143
mail merges, 137-138, 143-144
Letters and Mailings command (Tools menu), 139
liability accounts, 243
Library of Congress Web site, 290
lightning protection, surge suppressors, 5
lines
inserting, 112
numbering, 109
spacing, 97
links, inserting in e-mails, 184
Links toolbar, 69
Liquid Audio, streaming audio, 323
list boxes (dialog boxes), 20
Loan Calculator (Quicken), 250
locating
chat room Web sites, 197-199
files
My Computer, 23
Windows Explorer, 23
ISPs, 167-168
locking desktop settings, passwords, 55
Look4MP3 Web site, 328
Lotus Web site, 227
Louvre Art Museum Web site, 289
Lycos Web site, 208

M

magazines
as resources, 406
Web sites
clnet, 227
Windows Magazine, 228
ZDNet, 227
Magic Mouse Web site, 277
magnetic fields (computer placement), 4
mail merges
form letters
executing, 143-144
field code insertion, 139-143
process, 137-138
query preferences, settings, 143-144
printing addresses
envelopes, 145
mailing labels, 144-145
mail servers, ISPs, 169, 178
mailing labels, printing addresses (mail merge), 144-145
maintenance. *See* performance tuning
manual installations, 84-85
margins
settings, 98, 107-108
mirror, 108
Math Blaster software program, 273
maximizing windows, 22
McAfee Anti-Virus Page Web site, 407
Media Player, 64-65
megabits per second (Mbps), 150
memberships (online services)
cancellations, 166
signing up, 163-164
memory
speech recognition requirements, 364
versus disk space, 81
MemTurbo (shareware performance utility), 387

menus
  arrow indicators, 19
  bypassing toolbars, 21
  content styles, 19
  ellipsis (...), 19
  light gray appearances, 19
  location of, 19
  opening, 19
  smart, 20
messages (e-mail)
  abbreviations, 188-189
  emoticons, 187
  encryptions, 190-191
  etiquette, 189-190
  flaming, 189
  forwarding, 183
  replying, 182-183
Micron Web site, 227
Microsoft Creative Writer, 274-275
Microsoft Encarta, 270-271
Microsoft Hearts Network, 40-41
Microsoft Kids (educational software program), 274
Microsoft Money (personal finance program), 242
Microsoft NetMeeting (videoconferencing), 202
Microsoft Outlook
  creating address books, 127
  features, 127
Microsoft Publisher, 116
  banners, creating, 121-122
  brochure examples, 123
  frames
      grouping, 121
      layering, 121
  greeting cards, creating, 116-117
  images
      cropping, 119
      handles, 119
      inserting, 119
  pages
      dotted lines, 119
      frames, 119
      zooming, 117-118
  save publication options, 118
  text boxes
      creating, 120
      filling, 121

  moving, 120
  normal, 118
  WordArt, 118
Microsoft Web site, 227
Microsoft Word
  creating address books, 126-127, 130-131
  documents
      naming, 98-100
      red/green line error indicators, 94
      saving, 98-100
      spell check, 105-107
      views, 93
  envelopes, printing addresses, 100-101
  Letter Wizard, 139
  margins, setting, 107-108
  paragraph spacing options, 98
  text
      alignment options, 96-97
      reformatting, 95
      resizing, 95
      typing, 92-94
MIDI (Musical Instrument Digital Interface), 276
Minesweeper, 41-42
minimal installations (programs), 85
minimizing windows, 22
mirror margins, 108
MLB Web site, 219
modems (MODulators/DEModulators)
  cables
      availability, 154
      connecting, 156
      connection speeds, 154
      costs, 154
      Ethernet adapters, 156
      indicator lights, 156
      RF-returns, 154
      upload problems, 154
  connections
      externally, 154-155
      internally, 154-155
      troubleshooting tips, 157-158

data transmission process, 150
dialing out, 156
DSL
  ADSL (Asynchronous DSL), 153
  connecting, 155
  issues for consideration, 153
  SDSL (Symmetric DSL), 153
  transmission speeds, 153
ISDN
  channels, 152
  connecting, 155
  costs, 153
  speeds, 152
speeds
  bits per second (bps), 150
  common rates, 150
  limits, 152
standard modems
  benefits, 152
  connecting, 155
  fax support, 151
  internal versus external, 151
  ITU standards, 151
  serial port connections, 151
  speed options, 151
  USB connections, 151
  V.90 standards, 151
  videoconferencing support, 152
  voice support, 152
uses, 149-150
modifying
  budgets (Quicken), 249
  column widths (tables), 131
  desktops
      color schemes, 49-50
      screen size, 73-75
  icon appearances, 51-52
  pictures (Kodak Picture CD), 296
  row heights (tables), 131
  text appearances, 95

money market accounts, 243
monitors
cleaning guidelines, 375
desktop color settings, 74-75
resolutions, DVD videos, 347
screen savers
activating/deactivating, 57
passwords, 57-58
selecting, 56
unpacking guidelines, 5-6
Morph Man (image morphing program), 305
morphing tools
BitMorph, 305
Elastic Reality, 305
Morph Man, 305
motherboards (expansion slots), 152
Motorola Web site, 227
mouse
cleaning, 376-377
clicking, 15
dragging, 16
IntelliMouse
scrolling action, 16
zooming action, 16
pointing, 15
program installation requirements, 80
Screen Tips, 21
movies sites
Blockbuster Video, 223
Internet Movie Database, 223
Paramount, 223
trailers, viewing, 224
moving
files (Windows Explorer), 24
icons into folders, 77
insertion points, 92
mouse
click action, 15
dragging, 16
pointing action, 15
text boxes (Microsoft Publisher) 120
windows, 22

MP3s
audio clips
copying to portable MP3 players, 330-331
file associations, 329
audio data compressions, 323
commercial audio clips, copyright restrictions, 329
distribution sites
Amazon.com, 328
IUMA, 328
MP3.com, 328
RollingStone.com, 329
TUCOWS, 329
file compression standards, 225
functions, 322
music clips, downloading, 327-328
Napster controversy, 327
portable units
copying MP3 clips, 330-331
RAM capacities, 330-331
search sites
Audiofind, 328
AudioGalaxy, 328
Gigabeat, 328
Look4MP3, 328
MP3Board, 328
MP3Search, 328
MusicMatch, 328
Palavista, 328
versus CD clips, 328
MPEGs (Motion Picture Experts Group), 225
MSN (Microsoft Network)
memberships
cancellations, 166
information, 162
payment plans, 162
MSN Messenger, 200-202
MSNBC News Web site, 216
multimedia resources
ArtToday, 235
CLIPART.COM, 235
cInet, 236
Free-Backgrounds.com, 236

multiple users, protecting desktop settings, 55
multiple windows, opening Web browsers, 210
Museum Network Web site, 289
Museum of Science and Industry Web site, 290
museums
Adler Planetarium, 290
Library of Congress, 290
Louvre, 289
Museum Network, 289
Museum of Science and Industry, 290
New York Museum of Modern Art, 289
Smithsonian Institution, 289
music sites
audio clips, playing, 225
CDNOW, 225
Internet Underground Music Archives, 224
RollingStone.com, 225
SONICNET, 225
music software, Teach Me Piano, 275
MusicMatch Web site, 328
My Computer, locating files, 23
MyGreetingCard.com Web site, 200

N

naming documents, 98-100
Nando Sports Times Web site, 219
Napster controversy, 327
National Weather Service Web site, 218
NaturallySpeaking (speech recognition software), 365
command entries, 369
voice-to-text conversions
misinterpretations, 368
punctuation additions, 367

navigating
    online help systems, 165
    Web pages, 206
NBA Web site, 219
NEC Web site, 227
Net Nanny (censoring software), 286
Net2Phne, 202
NetGreeting.com Web site, 200
Netscape Composer (HTML tool), 230
Netscape Messenger, settings, 179-180
Netscape Navigator
    cookies
        deleting, 213
        disabling, 213
    history lists, viewing, 210-211
    home pages, changing, 212
    Web pages, bookmarks, 211-212
Netscape Virtual Office, associated costs, 234
NetZero, 167
New menu commands (Folder), 30
New York Museum of Modern Art Web site, 289
news servers, ISPs, 169
news sites
    ABC News, 216
    Associated Press, 217
    CBS News, 216
    CNN, 216
    MSNBC News, 216
    USA Today, 217
    Yahoo! Daily News, 217
newsgroups as a genealogy resource, 313-314
NFL Web site, 219
NHL Web site, 219
Normal view, 93
numeric keys (keyboard), 17

O

old photographs, scanning, 303-304
online banking
    cash transfers, 255
    electronic bill payments, 253-255
    Internet connection configurations, 252-253
    monthly costs, 251
    transaction records, downloading, 255
online communities (eCircles), 199
online games, Yahoo! Gameroom, 286-287
online help, Contents tab, 25
online investments, tracking (Quicken), 256
online services
    alternatives, 167
    AOL
        chat rooms, 194-197
        memberships, 162, 166
        payment plans, 162
    CompuServe
        memberships, 162, 166
        payment plans, 162
    drawbacks, 167
    free trial offers, 162
    help systems, navigating, 165
    installing, 163-164
    mail servers, 178
    MSN
        membership 162, 166
        payment plans, 162
    phone charges, local versus long-distance, 163
    Prodigy Internet
        memberships, 163, 166
        payment plans, 163
    signing up, 163-164
    versus ISPs, 161
opening. *See also* launching; startups
    menus, 19
    multiple browser windows, 210

operating systems, program installation requirements, 80
option buttons (dialog boxes), 20
Order command (Arrange menu), 121
ordering checks (Quicken), 246
outgoing e-mails, addressing, 180-181
outgoing mail (SMTP), ISP information, 178
outlet testers, grounded outlets, 4
Outline view, 94
Outlook Express, settings, 178-179
Outpost.com Web site, 266-267

P

Packard Bell Web site, 227
Page Setup command (File menu), 98, 107
pages
    dotted lines, 119
    frames
        grouping, 121
        layering, 121
    images
        cropping, 119
        handles, 119
        inserting, 119
    saving, 118
    text boxes
        creating, 120
        filling, 121
        moving, 120
    zooming, 117-118
Paint Shop Pro, 303
Palavista Web site, 328
Palm IIIc
    accessories, 341-342
    add-on programs, installing, 340-341
    desktop software, 337, 339
    shareware programs, downloading, 340
Panasonic Web site, 227
Paragraph command (Format menu), 97

paragraphs
  indenting, 96-97
  new entries, 92
  spacing options, 98
Paramount Studios Web site, 223
parents
  AOL parental controls, 282-284
  Internet Explorer censor controls, 284
  monitoring of child's computer usage, 281
passwords
  locking desktop settings, 55
  screen saver settings, 57-58
pasting text, 104-105
Pause/Break key (keyboard), 17
PC Guide Web site, 407
PC Magazine, 406
PCGreetings.com Web site, 200
PCs
  analog camcorder connections, 353
  cleaning equipment, 373-374
  connecting to Palm IIIc, 337-339
  DVD videos
    display resolutions, 347
    playing, 348
  handheld devices
    add-on program installations, 340-341
    synchronization process, 336
  vacuuming, 374-375
  VCR connections, 353
  WebTV
    channel changers, 346
    installing, 346
    interactive gaming, 347
    launching, 346
pen pal Web sites
  epals.com, 290
  KeyPals, 290
  Penpal Box, 291
Penpal Box Web site, 291

people locators
  Find People Fast, 314
  search engines
    BigFoot, 209
    InfoSpace, 209
    WhoWhere, 209
  USSearch.com, 314
  Yahoo!, 314
performance tuning
  BIOS settings, 386
  files
    defragmenting (Windows Disk Defragmenter), 383-385
    removing (ScanDisk), 381-383
  shareware utilities
    MemTurbo, 387
    SiSoft Sandra, 387
    TweakDUN, 387
    WinOptimizer, 387
  startup time reductions, 385-386
  Windows Maintenance Wizard
    launching, 380
    time settings, 380
personal finance programs
  accounts
    401(k), 243
    assets, 243
    cash, 242
    checking, 242
    creating, 243-244
    credit cards, 242
    investments, 243
    liability, 243
    money markets, 243
    reconciling, 247
    saving, 242
    transaction records, 244
  budgets
    categories, 249
    creating, 248-249
    entries, 249
    modifications, 249
    reports, 250
  checks
    ordering, 246
    printing, 245-246

financial calculators, 250
online banking
  cash transfers, 255
  electronic bill payments, 253-255
  Internet connection configurations, 252-253
  monthly costs, 251
  transaction record downloads, 255
Quicken. *See* Quicken
selection process, 242
personal information managers (PIMs), Microsoft Outlook features, 127
PGP (Pretty Good Privacy), e-mail encryption program, 191
phone calls, Internet services, 201-202
phone jacks (computer placement), 4
photograghs, 303. *See also* pictures
PhotoRecall (digital photography albums), 304
Picture command (Insert menu), 134
pictures
  digital cameras
    audio settings, 301
    copying to computers, 301
    flash settings, 301
    high-quality prints, 302
    resolution settings, 301
  digital photo albums, creating, 304
  inserting
    e-mails, 184
    tables, 134
  Kodak Picture CD
    adding, 295-296
    captions, 297
    e-mailing, 298-299
    editing, 296
    printing, 297-299
    viewing, 294

morphing programs
  BitMorph, 305
  Elastic Reality, 305
  Morph Man, 305
  Paint Shop Pro, editing
    features, 303
  scanning, 303-304
PIMS. *See* personal
  information managers
Pinball, 42-43
placement considerations
  (computers), 3-5
  electrical requirements, 4
  magnetic fields, 4
  phone jack connections, 4
  surge suppressors, 5
playing
  CDs, 64-65
  DVD videos, 348
  games
    FreeCell, 38-39
    Hearts, 40-41
    Minesweeper, 41-42
    Pinball, 42-43
    Solitaire, 37-38
    Spider Solitaire, 42-43
playlists, creating (Windows
  Media Player), 324-326
pointers (mouse functions), 15
POP3 (Post Office Protocol),
  incoming e-mails, 178
portable MP3 players
  copying MP3 clips,
    330-331
  RAM capacities, 330-331
portrait orientations, printing,
  108
power-saving modes
  Hibernation mode,
    385-386
  monitor appearances,
    10-11
  Standby mode, 385-386
  waking up from, 10-11
PPP (Point-to-Point Protocol),
  ISP connections, 168
prefab greeting cards, creating
  (Microsoft Publisher),
  116-117
previewing printed
  documents, 109
Print command (File menu),
  110

Print Layout view, 93
Print Screen/SysReq keys
  (keyboard), 17
Print Shop Deluxe, 116
printers
  cleaning guidelines,
    377-378
  paper thickness, 123
printing
  banners (Microsoft
    Publisher), 121-122
  checks (Quicken), 245-246
  documents
    collation options, 110
    landscapes, 108
    number of copies, 110
    paper sources, 109
    portraits, 108
    preview options, 109
    quality settings, 110
    troubleshooting tips,
      110-111
  envelopes
    addresses, 100-101
    mail merges, 145
  family trees, view options
    (Family Tree Maker),
    316-317
  mailing labels, mail
    merges, 144-145
  pictures (Kodak Picture
    CD), 297, 299
private messages, sending
  (AOL), 196
processors, speech recognition
  requirements, 364
Prodigy Internet
  memberships
    cancellations, 166
    information, 163
    payment plans, 163
profiles (AOL chat rooms)
  editing, 195
  privacy warnings, 196
programs. *See also*
  applications
    automating (Task
      Scheduler), 71-72
    deleting (Add/Remove
      Programs utility), 86-87
    desktop shortcuts, creating,
      28-29

floppy disks, installing
  from, 86
installation requirements
  Add/Remove Programs
    panels, 35-37
  automated compo-
    nents, 84
  CPU, 80
  custom options, 85
  disk space, 80
  DVD drive, 81
  lack of disk space
    messages, 83
  manually, 84-85
  minimal options, 85
  monitors, 80
  mouse, 80
  operating system, 80
  RAM, 81
  sound cards, 81
  typical options, 85
launching options
  document openings, 32
  keyboard shortcuts, 29
  Quick Launch
    toolbar, 31
  shortcut icons, 28-29
  Start menu, 27-28
  startup, 30
  taskbars, 22
locating
  My Computer, 23
  Windows Explorer, 23
software, 80
Start menu, rearranging,
  30-31, 68
toolbars, command
  icons, 21
Programs menu commands
  Accessories, 37
  Start menu, 27-28
public chat rooms, creating
  (AOL), 196-197
publishing Web pages, Yahoo!
  GeoCities, 231-234
punctuation, voice dictation
  (speech recognition
  software), 367
purchasing games online
  Beyond.com, 266-267
  Buy.com, 266-267
  Gamestop.com, 266-267
  Outpost.com, 266-267

Q

question mark button (dialog boxes), 21
Quick Launch toolbar
    active desktops, 53
    buttons
        adding, 31
        defaults, 31
    Internet Explorer, 22
    launching programs, 31
Quicken (personal finance program)
    accounts
        401(k), 243
        assets, 243
        cash, 242
        checking, 242
        creating, 243-244
        credit cards, 242
        investments, 243
        liabilities, 243
        money markets, 243
        reconciling, 247
        savings, 242
        transaction records, 243-244
    budgets
        categories, 249
        creating, 248-249
        entries, 249
        modifications, 249
        reports, creating, 250
    calculators, 250
    checks
        ordering, 246
        printing, 245-246
    online banking
        cash transfers, 255
        electronic bill payments, 253-255
        Internet connection configurations, 252-253
        monthly costs, 251
        transaction record downloads, 255
        tracking online investments, 256
QuickTime Player, viewing movie trailers, 224

R

radio buttons (dialog boxes), 20
RAM (random access memory), program installation requirements, 81
Reader Rabbit, 272
RealAudio
    downloading RealJukebox, 324
    streaming audios, 323
    Web site, 225
RealJukebox, CD juke box functions, 324
RealPlayer, playing audio clips, 225
rearranging
    desktop icons, 75-76
    Start menus, 30-31, 68
reconciling accounts (Quicken), 247
recording
    audio clips (Sound Recorder), 65-66
    digital video clips (Windows Movie Maker), 354-355
    transactions (Quicken), 244
records (databases)
    fields, 129
    filtering, 129
recurring payments (online banking), 254-255
Recycle Bin
    deleting
        desktop icons, 76
        files, 24
    property settings, 25
    restoring from files, 24
Red Book format (CDs), 321
red/green line indicators (Microsoft Word), 94
reducing startup times, 385-386
Refinance Calculator (Quicken), 250
relational databases, 126
removing
    columns, 131
    desktop icons, 76

files
    performance tuning (ScanDisk), 381-383
    Recycle Bin, 24
    programs (Add/Remove Programs utility), 86-87
    rows, 131
    text, 92
replying to e-mail messages, 182-183
reports, budgets (Quicken), 250
researching family trees
    Family Tree Maker, 309-310
    online resources, 311
resizing
    desktop display areas, 73-75
    text in documents, 95
    windows, 22
resolution (digital cameras), 301
resources
    books, 405-406
    magazines, 406
    videos and training CDs, 407
    Web sites, 406-407
restoring files (Recycle Bin), 24
Retirement Calculator (Quicken), 250
RF-return cable modems, 154
right-clicking program icons, shortcut creations, 29
Roget's Electronic Thesaurus, 271
role-playing games, 260
RollingStone.com Web site, 225
Rose Studios Web site, 277
rows (tables)
    deleting, 131
    height modifications, 131
    settings, 130
Roxio.com Web site, 332
rubbing alcohol as a cleaning agent, 377

S

S/MIME (Secure/Multipurpose Internet Message Extension), 190-191
Sagman, Stepen, 405
satellite connections, DirecPC, 154
saving
　digital video clips, 354
　digital video movies, 359
　documents, 98-100
　pages (Microsoft Publisher), 118
savings accounts, 242
Savings Calculator (Quicken), 250
ScanDisk, removing damaged files, 382-383
scanning
　e-mail attachments, antivirus programs, 186
　old photographs, 303-304
　types of scanners
　　flatbeds, 303
　　handhelds, 302
schedules
　programs, autoruns (Task Scheduler), 71-72
　recurring payments, online banking (Quicken), 254-255
　transactions, 244
schemes
　color, 49-50
　sounds 62-63
screen areas, resizing desktops, 73-75
screen savers
　activating/deactivating, 57
　passwords, 57-58
　Scrolling Marquees, 56
　selecting, 56
Screen Tips, 21
Scroll Lock key (keyboard), 17
scrollbars, window contents, 23
scrolling (IntelliMouse), 16
Scrolling Marquee screen saver, 56
SDSL (Symmetric DSL), 153

search engines
　AltaVista, 208
　Excite, 208
　Go.com, 208
　Google, 208
　Lycos, 208
　people locators
　　BigFoot, 209
　　InfoSpace, 209
　　WhoWhere, 209
　Yahoo!, 208
security
　e-mail encryptions, 190-191
　screen saver passwords, 57-58
selecting
　desktop themes, 48-49
　ISPs, 167-168
　screen savers, 56
　sound schemes, 62-63
　text options
　　entire documents, 104
　　large blocks, 104
　　line of text, 104
　　multiple paragraphs, 104
　　paragraphs104
　　sentences, 104
　　single words, 104
self-extracting game files, 265-266
sending
　e-mail messages, 180-181
　private messages, chat rooms (AOL), 196
serial ports, modem connections, 151
set top boxes. *See* WebTV
settings
　active desktops, 53-54
　mail merge query preferences, 143-144
　margins, 98, 107-108
　tab stops, 96-97
shading tables, 133
shareware utilities (performance tuning)
　MemTurbo, 387
　SiSoft Sandra, 387
　TwaekDUN, 387
　WinOptimizer, 387

shopping sites, safety guidelines, 219-220
shortcut icons
　creating, 28-29
　documents, creating, 32
　launching programs, 28-29
　Windows Explorer, 24
shortcuts keys, Windows key combinations, 18
Shutterfly Web site, 302
Sierra Web site, 308
signing up for online services, 163-164
SiSoft Sandra (shareware performance utility), 387
sizing desktop display areas, 73-75
skins (Windows Media Player), changing, 326
sliders (dialog boxes), 21
SLIP (Serial Line Internet Protocol), ISP connections, 168
Smart Computing, 406
smart menus, 20
SmarterKids.com Web site, 272
Smithsonian Institution Web site, 289
SMTP (Simple Mail Transfer Protocol), outgoing e-mails, 178
Snapfish Web site, 302
SoftImage Web site, 305
software, installation requirements. *See also* applications; programs
　CPU, 80
　disk space, 80
　DVD drives, 81
　monitors, 80
　mouse, 80
　operating systems, 80
　RAM, 81
　sound cards, 81
Solitaire, 37-38
SONICNET Web site, 225
Sony Web site, 227
Sort command (Table menu), 132
sorting table entries, 132

sounds
  assigning to events, 63
  clips
    recording (Sound
      Recorder), 65-66
    .WAV file extension, 66
  selecting schemes, 62-63
  testing close-talk
    microphones, 364-365
  volume control
    adjustments, 60-62
sound cards
  playing CDs, 64-65
  program installation
    requirements, 81
  speech recognition
    requirements, 364
  testing, 60
  troubleshooting
    problems, 62
Sound Recorder, 65-66
Sounds and Multimedia
  Properties dialog box, 60
Sounds icon (Control
  Panel), 60
spacing paragraphs, 98
Speaker, Mark, 405
speakers
  listening to CDs, 64-65
  testing, 60
  troubleshooting
    problems, 62
  volume control
    adjustments, 60-62
speech recognition softwares
  close-talk microphones
    noise reduction
      guidelines, 368
    testing, 364-365
  command entries, 369
  IBM ViaVoice, 365
  installing, 365
  NaturallySpeaking, 365
  requirements
    close-talk microphones,
      364
    memory, 364
    processor speeds, 364
    sound cards, 364

voice dictations
    misinterpretations, 368
    punctuation additions,
      367
    text conversions,
      367-368
  voice training utilities,
    365-366
spell check
  text, 105-107
  Word documents, 94
Spelling and Grammar com-
  mand (Tools menu), 105-107
Spider Solitaire, 42-43
spills, cleaning guidelines,
  376
spin boxes (dialog boxes), 21
splicing digital video clips
  (Windows Movie Maker),
  356
sports games, 260
sports sites
  CBS Sportsline, 219
  CNN/SI, 219
  ESPN, 219
  MLB, 219
  Nando Sports Times, 219
  NBA, 219
  NFL, 219
  NHL, 219
spreadsheets, 126-128
  addresses
    cells, 127-128
    sorting, 127-128
  displays, 127-128
  types of data, 127-128
standard modems
  benefits, 152
  connections, 155
  fax supports, 151
  internal versus external,
    151
  ITU standards, 151
  serial port connections,
    151
  speed options, 151
  USB connections, 151
  V.90 standards, 151
  videoconferencing
    supports, 152
  voice supports, 152

Standby mode (power saving
  features), 385-386
Start button, 13
Start menu
  programs
    launching, 27-28
    rearranging, 30-31
  rearranging items
    (Windows Explorer), 68
startups. *See also* launching;
  opening
  automatic launches, 30
  procedures, 7-8
stock brokerage sites
  Ameritrade, 221
  Charles Schwab, 221
  CSFB Direct, 221
  E*TRADE, 221
STOIK Software Web site, 305
strategy games, 261
streaming audio
  Liquid Audio, 323
  RealAudio, 323
styluses, handheld devices,
  336-337
Super Games Web site, 268
SuperKids Web site, 272
surge suppressors, UL
  ratings, 5
SVGA video, game hardwares,
  261
synchronizing handheld
  devices with desktop
  computers, 336-339
System Information tool, 82
System Properties dialog
  box, 81
system trays, 62

T

tab stops, setting (Word),
  96-97
Table AutoFormat command
  (Table menu), 133
Table menu commands
  Formula, 132
  Sort, 132
  Table AutoFormat, 133

tables
  address books, creating
    (Microsoft Word),
    126-127, 130-131
  autoformatting, 133
  borders, 133
  columns
    deleting, 131
    width modifications,
      131
  entries, 132
  formulas, 132
  headings, 130-131
  pictures, 134
  rows
    deleting, 131
    height modifications,
      131
  settings
    columns, 130
    rows, 130-131
  shading, 133
tabs (dialog boxes), 20
tags (HTML), function of, 230
Task Scheduler (automating
  programs), 71-72
taskbars, 13
  enlarging, 77
  hiding, 76-77
  program buttons,
    clicking, 22
TCP/IP (Transmission Control
  Protocol/Internet Protocol),
  174
Teach Me Piano, 275
technical support
  computer manufacturers,
    225-227
  online magazines, 227-228
television
  TV tuner cards, 344-346
    ATI All-in-Wonder card,
      345-346
    installing, 345-346
  WebTV
    call waiting
      requirements, 344
    changing channels, 346
    connecting, 344
    features, 344
    interactive gaming, 347
    launching on PCs, 346

  opening menus, 344
  PC installations, 346
  software, 344
temporary files, removing,
  381-382
testing
  Internet connections, 172
  sound cards, 60
  speakers, 60
text
  boxes
    creating, 120
    dialog boxes, 20
    filling, 121
    linked frames, 121
    moving, 120
    normals, 118
    WordArt, 118
  documents
    alignment options
      (Word), 96-97
    cutting, 104-105
    deleting, 92
    line spacings, 97
    pasting, 104-105
    resizing, 95
    spell checks, 105-107
    typing, 92-94
    zooming, 92
  e-mails, formatting
    enhancements, 183-184
  entries (handheld devices),
    337
  selection options
    entire documents, 104
    large blocks, 104
    line of text, 104
    multiple paragraphs,
      104
    paragraphs, 104
    sentences, 104
    single words, 104
  voice dictations
    converting, 367-368
    misinterpretations, 368
    punctuation additions,
      367
Thompson, Mark, 405
tiling windows, 22
titles, digital video clips
  (Windows Movie Maker),
  357

toolbars
  Address, 69
  as substitute for menus, 21
  command icons, 21
  Desktop, 69
  Links, 69
  transforming folders, 69-71
Tools menu commands
  Envelopes and Labels, 100
  Letters and Mailings, 139
  Spelling and Grammar,
    105-107
Toshiba Web site, 227
tracking online investments
  (Quicken), 256
trailers (movies), viewing, 224
training CDs as resources, 407
transactions
  recording accounts,
    243-244
  recurring, 244
  scheduled, 244
transforming folders into
  toolbars, 69-71
transitions, digital video clips
  (Windows Movie Maker),
  358-359
Transmission Control
  Protocol/Internet Protocol.
  See TCP/IP
Travelocity Web site, 222
troubleshooting tips
  disk space, 83
  DOS games, 263-264
  Internet connections,
    173-174
  modem connections,
    157-158
  printers, 110-111
  sound outputs, 62
*Troubleshooting Microsoft
  Windows*, 405
TUCOWS Web site, 329
tune-ups. *See* performance
  tuning
turning off computers, 10-11
turning on computers, 7-8
TV tuner cards, 344-346
  ATI All-in-Wonder card,
    345-346
  installing, 345-346

TweakDUN, shareware performance utility, 387
typing text in documents, 92-94

U

UFTree Web site, 308
Ultimate Family Tree, 308
underlined icons, Web style, 14-15
Undo command (Edit menu), 105
undoing changes, 105
unpacking computer equipment guidelines, 5-6
URLs
deciphering, 208
typing in Web browsers, 207
USA Today Web site, 217
USB connectors (digital camcorders), 351-352
USB ports (modem connections), 151
USSearch.com Web site, 314

V

V.90 standard modem connections, 151
vacation planning sites
Travelocity, 222
Yahoo!, 222
vacuuming PCs, 374-375
VCRs
digital video movies, outputting to VCRs (Windows Movie Maker), 360-361
PC connections, 353
VeriSign (e-mail encryption service), 190-191
vertical alignment options, 109
video capture cards, analog camcorder connections, 353
Video Professor, 407

videoconferencing
CUSeeMe, 202
Microsoft NetMeeting, 202
modems, 152
videos as resources, 407
View menu commands
Folder Options, 15
Header and Footer, 108
viewing
device information, System Properties dialog box, 81
documents
Normal view, 93
Outline view, 94
Print Layout view, 93
Web Layout view, 93
e-mail messages, 182-183
history lists, 210-211
pictures (Kodak Picture CD), 294
virtual games. *See also* games
Hearts, 40-41
Zone.com Web site, 43
viruses, 186
voice
recording (Sound Recorder), 65-66
support, 152
volume controls
adjusting, 60-62
setting options, 60-62

W

waking up from power-saving mode, 10-11
wallpapers
applying, 51
copying Web pages, 51
image types, 51
Web sources, 51
warranties, necessity of registrations, 6
.WAV files (Sound Recorder), 66
Weather by Email Web site, 218
Weather Channel Web site, 217

weather sites
AccuWeather, 218
EarthWatch, 218
National Weather Service, 218
Weather by Email, 218
Weather Channel, 217
Web browsers
bookmarking Web pages, 211-212
cookies
deleting, 213
disabling, 213
function of, 212
function of, 206
history lists
clearing, 211
viewing, 210-211
home pages, changing, 212
HTML tag interpretations, 230
ISP customized versions, 206
launching, 206
multiple windows, opening, 210
navigation functions, 206
page error messages, 206
search tools, 209
URLs
deciphering, 208
typing, 207
Web host, 231
Web Layout view, 93
Web pages
active desktop settings, 53-54
addresses, 207-208
bookmarking, 211-212
business-related hosting services
B-City, 235
Netscape Virtual Office, 234
selection criteria, 235
Yahoo! Small Business, 235
display error messages, 206
history lists
clearing, 211
viewing, 210-211

HTML
  tags, 230
  tools, 230
multimedia resources
  ArtToday, 235
  CLIPART.COM, 235
  clnet, 236
  Free-Backgrounds.com,
    236
navigating, 206
publishing, Yahoo!
  GeoCities, 231-234
startups, changing, 212
wallpaper sources, 51
Web sites
  Address.com, 167
  Adler Planetarium, 290
  Beyond.com, 266-267
  Broderbund, 308
  Buy.com, 266-267
  chat rooms, locating,
    197-199
  Chatting.com, 199
  child safety guidelines,
    280-281
  Children's Software Review,
    277
  Cognitive Technologies,
    You Can Draw! software,
    277
  computer manufacturers,
    225-227
    3COM, 227
    Acer, 226
    Borland, 226
    Broderbund, 227
    Brother, 227
    Canon, 227
    Compaq, 227
    Corel, 227
    Creative Labs, 227
    Dell, 227
    Epson, 227
    Fujitsu, 227
    Gateway, 227
    Hayes, 227
    Hewlett-Packard, 227
    Hitachi, 227
    IBM, 227
    Intel, 227
    Iomega, 227
    Lotus, 227

  Micron, 227
  Microsoft, 227
  Motorola, 227
  NEC, 227
  Packard Bell, 227
  Panasonic, 227
  Sony, 227
  Toshiba, 227
Cookie Central.com, 213
Corel (Art Dabbler
  software), 277
Cyber Patrol, 285
Cyber Snoop, 286
CYBERsitter, 285
clnet, 407
DSLReports, 407
eCircles, 199
educational software
  Knowledge Adventure,
    273
  The Learning Company,
    272
  Microsoft Kids, 274
Excite, 187
Flirt.com, 199
Fun School, 272
game sites
  Free Games Net, 265
  GameGenie.com, 265
  Gamer's Inn, 265
  Gamestop.com, 266-267
  The Games Network,
    264
  HotGames.com, 264
  hint/cheat sites, 267-268
  ZDNet GameSpot, 264
genealogy
  Ancestry.com, 312
  FamilySearch, 313
  GENDEX, 313
  Genealogy Home Page,
    313
  Genealogy.com, 312
  GenExchange, 313
  Gensource.com, 312
Hotmail, 187
IBM Crayola Creativity
  Packs, 277
Jasc Software, 303
Juno, 167
Library of Congress, 290
Louvre Art Museum, 289

Magic Mouse Flying Colors
  software, 277
McAfee Anti-Virus Page,
  407
movies
  Blockbuster Video, 223
  Internet Movie
    Database, 223
  Paramount, 223
  trailers, viewing, 224
MP3
  Amazon.com, 328
  Audiofind, 328
  AudioGalaxy, 328
  Gigabeat, 328
  IUMA, 328
  Look4MP3, 328
  MP3.com, 328
  MP3Board, 328
  MP3Search, 328
  MusicMatch, 328
  Palavista, 328
  RollingStone.com, 329
  TUCOWS, 329
Museum Network, 289
Museum of Science and
  Industry, 290
music
  CDNOW, 225
  Internet Underground
    Music Archive, 224
  RollingStone.com, 225
  SONICNET, 225
MyGreetingCard.com, 200
Net Nanny, 286
Net2Phone, 202
NetGreeting.com, 200
NetZero, 167
New York Museum of
  Modern Art, 289
news
  ABC News, 216
  Associated Press, 217
  CBS Newsw, 216
  CNN, 216
  MSBNC News, 216
  USA Today, 217
  Yahoo! Daily News, 217
online magazines
  clnet, 227
  Windows Magazine, 228
  ZDNet, 227

Outpost.com, 266-267
Palm.com, 341-342
PC Guide, 407
PCGreetings.com, 200
pen pals
   epals.com, 290
   KeyPals, 290
   Penpal Box, 291
people locators
   Find People Fast, 314
   USSearch.com, 314
   Yahoo!, 314
PhotoRecall, 304
Rose Studios ImaginAction
   software, 277
Roxio.com, 332
search engines
   AltaVista, 208
   Excite, 208
   Go.com, 208
   Google, 208
   Lycos, 208
   Yahoo!, 208
shopping safety guidelines,
   219-220
Shutterfly, 302
Sierra, 308
SmarterKids.com, 272
Smithsonian Institution,
   289
Snapfish, 302
SoftImage, 305
sports
   CBS Sportsline, 219
   CNN/SI, 219
   ESPN, 219
   MLB, 219
   Nando Times Sports,
   219
   NBA, 219
   NFL, 219
   NHL, 219
stock brokerages
   Ameritrade, 221
   Charles Schwab, 221
   CSFB Direct, 221
   E*TRADE, 221
STOIK Software, 305
SuperKids, 272
UFTree, 308
vacation planning
   Travelocity, 222
   Yahoo!, 222

VeriSign, 190-191
weather
   AccuWeather, 218
   EarthWatch, 218
   National Weather
   Service, 218
   Weather by Email, 218
   Weather Channel, 217
Webopedia, 407
White House for Kids, 288
Yahoo!, 187
Yahoo! GeoCities, 231-234
ZDNet, 340, 406
ZDNet onebox, 187
Zone.com, 43
Web Studio, HTML tool, 230
Web Styles
   activating/deactivating,
   14-15
   active desktops, 53
Webopedia Web site, 407
WebTV
   connecting, 344
   features, 344
   opening menus, 344
   PCs
      channel changers, 346
      installing, 346
      interactive gaming, 347
      launching, 346
   phone connections, call
   waiting requirements,
   344
   software, 344
White House for Kids Web
   site, 288
White, Ron, 406
WhoWhere (people locator
   service), 209
windows
   cascading, 22
   changing, 22
   closing, 22
   maximize size, 22
   minimize size, 22
   moving, 22
   resizing, 22
   scrollbars, 23
   tiling, 22

Windows
   determining versions, 14
   games
      Freecell, 38-39
      Hearts, 40-41
      installing and running,
      35, 37
      Minesweeper, 41-42
      Solitaire, 37-38
Windows 95, Help screen
   (Sound troubleshooter), 62
Windows 98
   Help screen (Sound
   troubleshooter), 62
   WebTV component, 346
Windows Explorer
   files
      locating, 23
      moving, 24
   shortcut icon, creating, 24
   Start menu items,
   rearranging, 68
Windows Help screen (Sound
   troubleshooter), 62
Windows Magazine Web site,
   228
Windows Maintenance
   Wizard
   launching, 380
   time settings, 380
Windows Me
   games
      Pinball, 42-43
      Spider Solitaire, 42-43
   Help screen (Sound
   troubleshooter), 62
   WebTV component, 346
Windows Media Player
   audio clips, 225
   changing skins, 326
   downloading, 323
   installing, 323
   movie trailers, viewing,
   224
   MP3 clips, copying to
   portable MP3 players, 331
   playlists, 324-326
Windows Movie Maker
   (digital video clips)
   background music,
   357-358
   e-mailing, 359

outputting to VCRs,
  360-361
recordings, 354-355
saving, 359
splicing, 356
title additions, 357
transitions, 358-359
WinOptimizer, shareware
  performance utility, 387
WinZip, compressing/
  decompressing files, 265-266
wizards, Yahoo! Personal Page
  Wizard, 233
WordPad, launching, 92
write-protected floppy
  disks, 86

X–Y

Yahoo! Web site
  chat rooms, 197-199
  free e-mail service, 187
  Gameroom, 286-287
  vacation categories, 222
Yahoo! Daily News Web site,
  217
Yahoo! GeoCities, publishing
  Web pages, 231-234
Yahoo! Messenger, 200-202
Yahoo! Personal Page Wizard,
  233
Yahoo! Small Business, 235
You Can Draw! software, 277

Z

ZDNet GameSpot Web site,
  264
ZDNet onebox (free e-mail
  service), 187
ZDNet Web site, 227, 340
Zone.com Web site, 43
zooming
  IntelliMouse, 16
  pages (Microsoft
    Publisher), 117-118
  text in documents, 92